KU-149-792

Working with Bernstein

Don't smoke! David Ben-Gurion to Leonard Bernstein, Tel Aviv, December 1963.

Working with Bernstein

A MEMOIR

Jack Gottlieb

Amadeus Press
An Imprint of Hal Leonard Corporation | New York

Also by Jack Gottlieb

Funny, It Doesn't Sound Jewish: How Yiddish Songs and Synagogue Melodies Influenced Tin Pan Alley, Broadway and Hollywood

Published in 2010 by Amadeus Press
An Imprint of Hal Leonard Corporation
7777 West Bluemound Road
Milwaukee, WI 53213

Trade Book Division Editorial Offices
19 West 21st Street, New York, NY 10010

Printed in the United States of America
Book design by Kristina Rolander

Library of Congress Cataloging-in-Publication Data

Gottlieb, Jack.
Working with Bernstein / Jack Gottlieb.
p. cm.
Includes bibliographical references and index.
ISBN 978-1-57467-186-5 (alk. paper)
1. Bernstein, Leonard, 1918-1990. 2. Musicians--United States--Biography. 3. Composers--United States--Biography. 4. Conductors (Music)--United States--Biography. I. Title.
ML410.B566G67 2010
780.92--dc22
[B]

2010010764

www.amadeuspress.com

For Daryl B., John W., Charlie H., and Craig U., who also experienced the same labor of love

Among quotations ascribed to Leonard Bernstein, the following is cited:

> *"To achieve great things, two things are needed:*
> *a plan, and not quite enough time."*

I have not been able to verify the source, but if he did say it, I would add:

> *"And maybe a little help."*

CONTENTS

PREFACE

Bernstein at "That Table" in his Dakota apartment.

In December 1997, Leonard Bernstein's household effects were sold at auction by Sotheby's in New York City. Part of the following memory piece about his studio in the Dakota apartment building was included in the catalog. When the family first moved into the residence—ideal for viewing the annual Macy's Thanksgiving parade—the studio was his wife's bedroom, and the studio was located on the ninth floor, former general servant quarters for the whole building. Unlike their living arrangements in previous city residences, the Bernsteins now kept separate bedrooms due to the exhaustive all-night working sessions Leonard Bernstein (LB) increasingly kept. After his wife died, LB moved the studio into her bedroom. Since then, every time I go by the building, I look up to the second floor, and I am filled with a Proustian longing for a lost time as I recall . . .

. . . that table in the inner sanctum, the "war room," the staging area for superhuman achievement. Where the Maestro marked up his performing scores in crystal-clear, intricate detail, like a fine jeweler polishing precious stones. Piled high with messages, the latest books, CDs, leather-bound music manuscript paper, schedules, scores from importunate composers, résumés from hopeful artists, all manner of folders including one labeled "Pansies" (from the French *pensées*, for "ideas"), in- and out-boxes overflowing with correspondence from all points of the globe. The scene of the sometime executed executive shift: move one piece of paper from the top of the heap to the bottom in the hope it will be forgotten by both sender and sendee. And it usually is. The shift often accompanied by a Maestronic maxim: "Leave alone, will fall off by self!"

The telephone at hand with numerous intercom and outreach buttons, always blinking, blinking. The smelly brass cigarette disposal bowl, the snuffers, the marble-stand lighter and the box of cigarettes. Smoke gets in your eyes—and nose and throat, not helped by the thick dust-catching window drapes. You leave the room in the vain hope the air will clear, and return to That Table choked with tchotchkes: a hotel bell, music toys, gadgets, kaleidoscopes. Photos of family in silver frames. Address books, one marked "Private." The appointment diary from which one could reconstruct the working life for that year. Cups for the Alpheus Music Writer and the "reddy-bluey" pencils. The Japanese gong bowl for worn-out pencil stubs, a kind of veterans home for "soldiers" (his word) of great music making. In ready reach, floor-to-ceiling shelves of study scores from Abe (Japanese) to Zwilich (American), every dictionary known to man, LPs, tapes, CDs, the latest audio equipment with a plethora of remotes. And always some part of that equipment breaking down in what came to be known infamously as the "Amberson Curse." (*Amber* in German is *Bernstein.*)

It's the scene where I learned to my mortification the true meaning of the "pH factor." Responsible for shepherding LB scores into print, two separate ones appeared with (1) AdolPH Green's name spelled as AdolF (on the dedication of *Fancy Free*; and LB rightly exclaims, "like Hitler!"), and (2) StePHen Sondheim's as SteVen (in the volume *Bernstein on Broadway*). Ah, the wounding mortification of it all! That "pH" could have as well stood for "Purple Heart."

Make an appointment for two p.m. to review proofs or do concert planning or go over scripts, program notes, or write out orchestrations on That Table. Rarely ever to begin at the agreed upon hour. Someone is usually ahead of you, broaching no interlopers. Often they are one of the "aitches," a Helen or a Harry. They make it clear in no uncertain terms that their agenda is more urgent, more *pressing*, more *important* than yours. You wait and wait. But once the meeting begins, do we get to the matter on hand? No way. There is always resistance. First come the news and jokes of the day, the plaintive blues about the state of the world, the gossip, the sharing of intimacies. The kids drop in to say hi. Sister Shirley gets comfy with a British *Listener* crossword puzzle, competing with Maestro to see who gets the right answer first. Long telephone interruptions, and before you know it, it's drink time. Not unadulterated Ballantine Scotch, mind you, but, as requested: "Colored water, please!" (Don't count the number of refills.) Julia—pronounced Spanish style—Vega, the ever faithful and beloved housekeeper, brings in a tray of cheeses and crackers to place on That Table. By now, work has begun, but soon it's time for dinner. "Want to stay?" Why not, it's irresistible. Great food, witty badinage, serious reflections.

Then back to That Table. By now the head is sloshing in wine and drowsiness has set in. But not for Maestro. His engine is just getting revved up. And so on and on, often past midnight. Trudge home body-weary, but brain teeming. That Table with the cabriole legs. Now that I think of it, *cabriole* (related to "caper," from the legs' resemblance to the forelegs of a capering animal) is the perfect word for that table since it did leap and take wing. I wouldn't have missed it for the world.

P.S. That Table sold for $2,300.

Introduction

A JEWISH AMERICAN OR AN AMERICAN JEW?

A 1947 black-and-white film called *Carnegie Hall* uses a thin clothesline of a story as an excuse on which to hang vignette appearances by musical greats of the day. Among these giants are conductors Fritz Reiner, Bruno Walter and Artur Rodzinski, each leading the New York Philharmonic (NYP). Reiner uses his baton vertically as if it were a dipstick, Walter is an old-world sober-sides, while Rodzinski is the liveliest. It is spellbinding to witness these capsule images of three men who were so crucial to the flowering of Leonard Bernstein's musicianship and celebrity. Originally, Serge Koussevitzky, Bernstein's supreme teacher, was scheduled to be part of the mix. If he had been, only Dimitri Mitropoulos would have been missing, to complete the roster of Bernstein conducting mentors. Conductor Leopold Stokowski also appears in the film, lit in a penumbra aura and undulating his hands as if giving a priestly benediction. Although not part of Bernstein's musical upbringing, Stokowski certainly was a harbinger—in Disney's *Fantasia*—of LB's championship of the arts in mass media.

The banal storyline is a variant of the old *Jazz Singer* plot. This time, however, instead of its being a Jewish cantor in conflict with his pop-singing secularized son, an Irish immigrant cleaning woman—devoted to the world of classical music—comes to a parting of the ways with her piano-playing son who craves the commercial world (oh horrors!) of Tin Pan Alley. All ends well when sonny boy appears on the stage of Carnegie Hall in a composition of his own called *57th Street Rhapsody*, a Gershwin-like potboiler featuring trumpeter Harry James, and actually written by the brothers Mischa and

Wesley Portnoff. (I never heard of them, either). Although earlier on in the film, big-band leader Vaughn Monroe shows up singing "Beware My Heart," a trite Sam Coslow song—you should see him winking acceptance of the aforementioned piano-player into his ensemble—this final scene is the only time when American music is given a nod in the movie.

It is fascinating to see how the story parallels the struggle between Bernstein and his father, less as a test of religious devotion (as in the plot of *The Jazz Singer*) or of art music as *heilige Kunst* (as in *Carnegie Hall*) than the practicality of music as a way to make a living, Samuel Bernstein's main headache about his son.

Shirley Gabis Perle, LB's old friend from Philadelphia, tells the following story: In 1983, when LB was recording *Tristan und Isolde* with Peter Hoffmann and Hildegard Behrens in Munich, he was joined at the Vier Jahreszeiten Hotel by Shirley, who was there with her composer husband, George. (The Perles were in Germany for a performance of George's *A Short Symphony*.) LB invited the Perles to join him and others for a swim in the hotel's pool, adjacent to his suite. Shirley protested, "No, I'll have a problem with my hair." LB said, "Don't worry, I'll dry it for you." George demurred, but the others went skinny-dipping. Afterward, LB served them hors d'oeuvres in an open robe. (Well, they were old friends and they had just been swimming naked, right?) LB then took Shirley into the bedroom and proceeded to blow-dry her hair. Shirley said: "Oh, Lenny, if only your father could see you now!" And thus it was, in one small way, that Samuel Joseph Bernstein's wish for his eldest son to go into the family hair beauty supply business had come true.

Nevertheless, Leonard did gain his father's blessing after LB's famed Carnegie Hall debut with the NYP, substituting for Bruno Walter in 1943. This historic event happened four years before the movie's opening, when Bernstein's renown was already in full bloom. So why wasn't Bernstein, himself, included in the film? After all, "American boy makes good" as a composer was the climax of the movie, and Bernstein by now had established his bona fides in the concert hall (Symphony No. 1, "Jeremiah"), in ballet (*Fancy Free*) and on Broadway (*On the Town*). Perhaps it was too soon for an American composer-conductor to be part of the pantheon. European maestros were still the sine qua non in classical music circles. Or perhaps something more sinister was going on, having to do with Bernstein's budding political activism. It so happens that one of the producers of the *Carnegie Hall* movie, the musically savvy Boris Morros, was, of all things, an FBI double agent.

Flash-forward to 1951, when Morros told Bernstein that he regarded him as a "Red" and would not hire him to score an upcoming movie.[1]

In a 1955 deposition he was required to submit to the State Department because renewal of his passport had been refused, Bernstein stated,

> I have been most active in the cause of Jewish philanthropy and the promotion of Israel as an independent state free from Soviet domination. I have been honored to accept invitations to preach the sermon in Jewish temples in Boston, Chicago and Houston. My religious training and belief would necessarily make me a foe of communism.

It is indisputable that "fellow travelers" and Jews were often linked together in the public mind, sometimes labeled as Judeo-Bolshevism. Unlike Reiner, Walter (born Schlesinger), Rodzinski and Koussevitzky, Bernstein was passionate and wide open about his political sympathies and his Jewish heritage.

Bernstein meeting Marc Chagall, Tel Aviv, 1963.

It was this Jewish legacy that helped shape and solidify the bond between Bernstein and myself. One treasured memento of that attachment took place in 1968 when LB gave me an *aliyah* at his son Alexander's bar mitzvah ceremony. (The honor consisted of being called up to the reading desk to chant the Hebrew blessings before and after the Torah reading.) Our Jewish attachment deepened over the years. It was inevitable when he wrote me a birthday song in 1983 that his lyric would be in Yiddish. Also, in the 1980s, Lenny was so excited when he first came across the Yiddish poem "Oif Mayn Khas'ne" ("At My Wedding") by Yankev-Yitskhok Segal that he felt compelled to share it with me on the phone. His enthusiasm for the poem was palpable, and his setting of it became one of the most intense pieces of his composing life, spiky music suggesting the fantastical paintings of shtetl weddings by Marc Chagall. During the days leading up to the 1963 premiere of his Symphony No. 3, "Kaddish" in Israel, we met Chagall by chance at a Tel Aviv outdoor café.

Then there was a letter to the editor that I wrote:

> *Music with Bowwow Beat*
> I was much amused by a listing in your Guide to the arts (June 11–17). For a concert of "Remembering Lenny," you state that "the New York Philharmonic will perform some of Bernstein's music with Jewish themes, including 'Fanfare for Bima.'"
>
> Bima in this instance is not the platform in the synagogue on which the Ark of the Torah stands, but the name of the cocker spaniel of Bernstein's mentor, conductor Serge Koussevitzky. The Fanfare is based on the theme that was whistled in the Koussevitzky household to call the dog.[2]

On manuscripts, LB would occasionally sprinkle sly Jewish tempo markings, such as "alleghetto" (a piano anniversary for Goddard Lieberson) and "moderato hassidicamente" (the Old Lady's Tango in *Candide)* or the wicked anagram inscription of "sekki" on *Bridal Suite* for piano in which a dance section is marked "Fast and Jewish." In response to the famous couplet "How odd of God to choose the Jews," for which there have been many rhyming responses—e.g., "Not so odd/The Jews choose God"—on the manuscript of *Arias and Barcarolles* he jots down the riposte, "But odder still are those who choose/A Jewish God the Jews refuse." With Mike Nichols, he concocts a wily parody of the Richard Rodgers song "The Sweetest Sounds":

The sweetest Jew I ever knew
'S a Jew named Jule Styne.
No words can praise his turn of phrase
And grand melodic line.
My heart just quakes the way he makes
The words and notes combine!
Be still my heart, his every fart
Is part of God's design.
That's why every day is a holiday
When I'm on my way
To work with Jule Styne!

On the other hand, in 1948 when he was studying with Yona Shamir in Tel Aviv, he wrote Hebrew poetry. Here is a translation of one of them:

A Poem for Yom Kippur
From left and right I hear the words
"We have sinned" (*ashamnu*);
We have dealt treacherously (*bagadnu*);
We have slandered (*dibarnu dofi*)."
But in my heart I hear another song.
I believe in the truth of art,
In energy, in emotion, in vitality,
This day I believe in wonder.
I believe in the person who comes
And will water the barren places,
But first and foremost, I believe in love.

And lest I be impatient,
I live as in a dream—
Waiting for a day of love,
Of understanding, this day.

Stephen Sondheim has said, "The first serious Jew I came into contact with was Lenny Bernstein. So many of the people that I admire in the arts are Jewish. And art is as close to a religion that I have."[3]

* * *

At the 1969 funeral of his father—which took place at Temple Mishkan Tefila in Chestnut Hill, Massachusetts—Rabbi Israel Kazis eulogized Samuel Bernstein as one who was completely involved in worship by always having "his mind in contemplation, his heart in love, his voice in song and his limbs in dance." Like father, like son. Early on, critics often were distracted by the Maestro's dancelike style as a conductor. But was this deliberate? He said no. When he would first review a video of himself conducting, there were times when he would grimace and groan at his podium manner. But he always protested that he was not aware of it during the performance. His podium manner had to be a burning need to communicate the composer's thought processes to both orchestra and audience, whatever the physicality it took to make it manifest. At times it was as if he were—in the title of one of his songs from *On the Town*—"Carried Away." One is reminded of words from Psalm 35:

> *Kol atsmotai tagilna badonai!* (All my bones shall exult in the Eternal One!)

This was an article of faith by which LB lived his life and created his works.

But it is one thing to be carried away as a performer and quite another matter as a composer. A conductor displays his art with a finished product; a composer is concerned with the yet-to-be, the making of that product. There are, of course, musicians like a red-hot jazz improviser, or a cantor possessed by spiritual fervor, who can achieve the best of both worlds simultaneously, as creator and re-creator. Above all else in his own compositions, Bernstein worked mightily to realize that paradoxical state of controlled spontaneity.

His earliest memory of music took place about 1926 at Mishkan Tefila (then located in Roxbury, Massachusetts) where, to quote him from an 1989 interview, "I felt something stir within me, as though I were becoming subconsciously aware of music as my raison d'être."

In fact, his first surviving completed piece was a setting of Psalm 148, which he recalled as having been written between 1932 and 1935. During the following decades he was to write some twenty works on Jewish themes that have had broad appeal for Jews and Gentiles everywhere.

The greater part of Bernstein's output was sparked by the interaction of his American conditioning and his Jewish inheritance, as in Symphony No. 3, "Kaddish" and *Chichester Psalms*, Hebrew-Aramaic words touched with a glint of the *West Side Story* sound. Other Jewish works of his are electric with American kinetic energy even though they are concerned with events that took place "over there." Among them, "Jeremiah," his 1942 symphony written in response to early reports of Nazi anti-Semitism, and *Halil*, his 1981 flute rhapsody about young lives laid waste in the Israeli Yom Kippur War of 1973.

More fascinating is how some of the non-Jewish works are flavored with Hebraicisms, including songs from his musical comedy *On the Town*. Two numbers from that show, "Ya Got Me" and "Some Other Time," are redolent of a cantorial mode known as Adonai Malakh (The Lord is King). The Finale of his Symphony No. 2, "The Age of Anxiety" and *Mass*, his theater piece based on the Roman rite, are both imbued with hidden and overt Jewish symbolism.

Many were those who pleaded with Bernstein to write a complete Jewish service. (His setting of the Hashkiveinu prayer was the only attempt.) I came across an undated jotting on a work he was contemplating, but never followed through on:

> *A Cantata on Hebrew-Yiddish Materials That Move Me*
> What are the Jewish roots I long for? Nostalgia for youth? Guilt towards my father? First real cultural exposure? First real music I heard (Braslavsky)! Seeking a larger identity—with a race or creed?—with a supernatural force? (But the latter word doesn't account for so many "Yiddish" responses). Seeking *any* identity? Common roots with siblings? Speaker (English), the singer (Heb. & Yiddish).

He concluded with titles of prayer, Bible and Haggadah passages:

> Yigdal, Sholem aleichem, Judith, Psalms (proud humility), Song of Songs, And it came to pass at midnight (*Vay'hi b'chatsi halaila* or *Dayeinu*).

Too bad he never wrote this cantata, although fragments of the above do appear in various works of his.

Bernstein was an unabashed eclectic, an ecumenical lover of the world, and it loved him in return. This, too, was part of his Jewish nature, for Judaism is based on commonality. (Jewish prayer, for example, calls on *klal Yisrael* [all of Israel]. There are many fewer Hebrew prayers for the individual.) LB was fiercely true to lifelong friendships that often came before his work.

On the other hand, he was unhappiest when not working; idleness made him melancholy. Music was his fix, and he experienced it as few of us ever will. I recall how drained he was after a performance of Tchaikovsky's Symphony No. 6 in B Minor ("Pathétique") in the late 1980s. He said he was "on the brink," meaning he was transported to a place that had no beginning or end. At such enviable moments, Bernstein was suspended between two worlds. In that timeless void he must have achieved the Hassidic ideal of fusion known as *d'veikut*, a kind of cosmic glue that leads one toward a sphere where mystical powers dwell, where joy is its own reward.

Arguably the most versatile musician of the twentieth century, Bernstein possessed an eclecticism that was a kind of migration through various lands of musical endeavor in pursuit of an artistic homeland. Such preoccupations were not unknown to other Jewish composers who crossed over from the rigors of concert-hall music to populist expressions in the theater and movies, among them Kurt Weill, Morton Gould, Marc Blitzstein, Erich Korngold, Aaron Copland, and, in the other direction, George Gershwin. Arnold Schoenberg, in his search for a new musical language that became dodecaphonism, was yet another breed of Jewish explorer.

The most potent musical demonstration of Bernstein's all-embracing talents is to be found in the multifarious national styles of his operetta *Candide*. Among its witticisms, there is the aforementioned Jewish tango and a parody of shofar calls. In fact, the opening of the Overture to *Candide* and indeed that of the *Symphonic Dances from "West Side Story"* (1961) can also be likened to shofar calls. His *Mass* (1971) manifested a pandemic religious sensibility, richly interwoven by strands of Catholic ritual with Jewish exegesis.

In his 1974 ballet *Dybbuk*, the composer utilized Kabbalah manipulations by assigning numerical values to musical intervals. (J. S. Bach had done much the same with musical pitches.) The result was an astringent but apt musical counterpart to the famous drama by Ansky. Other of his Jewish-based works include songs, choral and piano works.

* * *

Upon the death of my mother in 1966, I acquired a modest inheritance that allowed me to purchase a small property in lower Dutchess County, New York. I was still working part-time for LB and regularly drove down to Manhattan. One day I spotted on the Saw Mill River Parkway, two hitchhikers: Hassidic teenage boys, side-curls, black garb and all. It was such an unexpected sight that I felt compelled to pick them up. They weren't going very far, so quickly, to establish my credentials, I spoke a smattering of Yiddish to them. They asked me the usual what-do-you-do? When I told them I was in music, and knowing now I was a Jew, one of them blurted out, "Are you Leonard Bernstein?"

This is such a revealing account. The logical implication was that they had never seen LB on TV, and of course not in person, because their restricted upbringing did not allow them to view television, go to movies or attend such "amusements" as concerts. But by this time Bernstein was such an iconic name in the Jewish world that even the ultraorthodox contingent took pride in him. He had become one of the us-niks.

However, it had gotten to a point that within ten years of his storied debut, he was overwhelmed by the unending requests he received day after day to give this or do that for Jewish groups. It never stopped; and they were insulted when he had to refuse, and often gave him the impression that he was obligated as a Jew to fulfill their demands, as if he was their personal possession. On 19 April 1951 he wrote to Helen Coates, his secretary, from Cuernavaca, Mexico, "I want a little rest from being a professional Jew; I would love to be, for a while at least, just a human being."

But this was unthinkable, for the architecture of Bernstein's life rests on Jewish pillars. Unlike most other accomplished American-Jewish composers of the mid-twentieth century, he cultivated his Jewish consciousness as much as, if not more than, anything else. Among his papers, he asks himself a series of questions about (his) Judaism:

> Enough? Hanukah candles? Seder? Hi-Ho seats? 2, 3, 4 generations? What makes it want to continue? What is "it"? Is the Talmud even relevant? Why is it worth a Holocaust? Is anything worth a holocaust? NO.
>
> Trying to assimilate. To be balanced, at rest, stable in a goy society without relying too much on "Judaistic" principles. What are they? Abraham? Moses? Ghetto-traditional? Is Grossinger's enough? UJA?

Bernstein may not have been traditionally observant, but he was deeply Jewish in every other way. In fact, he once described himself as a "chip," not off the old block, but "off the old Tanach," the Hebrew acronym for the complete Bible. As a teenager he even flirted briefly with the idea of becoming a rabbi. As it turned out, he did become a kind of rabbi, albeit one without portfolio; and in fact, Hebrew Union College, the seminary of Reform Judaism, awarded him an honorary degree. Indeed, he was a thoroughly imbued, inbred, and—as he labeled his "Diaspora Dances" from *Jubilee Games*—a "socio-cultural, geo-Judaic" Jew by being:

- a practitioner of *tzedaka*, a believer in the efficacy of charitable giving;
- a benefactor for a host of students, endowing scholarships, providing instruments, and sponsoring talented youngsters;
- a fierce devotee of book learning, central to Jewish culture, and a master of wordplay, as well;
- a champion of the State of Israel from its inception, as performer and artistic ambassador; a musician-soldier who performed in the field during wartime conditions, under threat of military attack;
- an eloquent sermonizer on nuclear disarmament from synagogue and church pulpits;
- a defender of causes for the oppressed and disenfranchised in his benefit concerts for Amnesty International, and for victims of AIDS in "Music for Life" concerts;
- an inspiring teacher in the Talmudic style for a generation of music lovers, many of whom were first introduced to the delights of music by his televised concerts;
- a counselor to the troubled and a source of Solomonic wisdom, which he freely dispensed to anyone in earshot (sometimes, truth to tell, not always welcome);
- and one of the few celebrated twentieth-century composers whose catalog consists in large proportion of works on Jewish themes; about one-quarter of his orchestral music; half of his choral compositions; songs and other pieces.

He would faithfully call his mother every Friday (Shabbat) night wherever he was in the world, obeying the commandment to honor one's parents. His need to be in synagogue on Yom Kippur was seldom skipped. His Passover seders were jovial, raucous family affairs. In other words, like many American Jews, he practiced Judaism lite, but inhabited it as though it were body armor.

At the same time he was always tweaking the norms of Jewish conduct as if those boundaries could not contain him. Inside that enclosure he often pushed against the pillars, and at times, like the Biblical Samson, parts of the structure would come crashing down.

- He became a prominent conductor of the Vienna Philharmonic, despite protests from fellow Jews, and knowing full well that the Viennese populace was streaked with anti-Semitism.
- Although he wrote large works on nonreligious Jewish themes, he also wrote *Mass* and a *Missa Brevis*, but not a Jewish service, mystifying his Jewish devotees.
- He felt the same double-identity conflicts as Mahler, most prominently the conductor vs. composer struggle, but also Jewish vs. Christian demands, especially in the business world of orchestras. (Keep in mind that Koussevitzky wanted him to change his name to Leonard S. Burns.)
- He was dedicated to the Israel Philharmonic, but he endorsed playing the music of Jew-hater Richard Wagner in Israel.
- He was a married man with children, sanctioned by Jewish values, but also lived as a gay man, not acceptable.
- The infamous Black Panther fund-raiser and the "Radical Chic" ad hominem stink it raised concerning Jews, and which was to haunt him the rest of his life—and beyond.

* * *

The 1970 Tom Wolfe howl of "Radical Chic" (a term coined by Seymour Krim of the *New York Times* years earlier) still can be heard down throughout the years and throughout the land. During the 2008 three-month Bernstein Festival in New York City, the issue was inevitably raised. Here it was, almost thirty years later, and a newspaper reader barfed, "With friends like Lenny, who needs enemies?"[4] When I gave a lecture on LB in the early '90s, a dyspeptic question from the floor, "What about Radical Chic?" threw me for a loop. I couldn't answer mainly because I wasn't around from 1969 to 1972; but still it rankled. Trying to put the RC stigma into perspective would not do much good because Bernstein has been indelibly branded.

In 1959, he recorded the glorious *Gloria* of Francis Poulenc, which was released with his own *Chichester Psalms* (and with my jacket notes). On the basis of this success, in 1963, the New York Philharmonic commissioned Poulenc, among other composers, to celebrate the opening of the new hall at Lincoln Center. The result was a work called *Sept répons de ténèbres*, with Thomas Schippers at the helm. After the premiere, LB as music director received scathing letters from subscribers about the anti-Jewish sentiments, such as "perfidious Jews," expressed in the traditional liturgy for Holy Week. However, when he gave a performance with the NYP of Ernest Bloch's *Avodath Hakodesh* in 1960, I wonder if these same citizens wrote grateful letters of recognition.

On the Internet there is a long discussion of cuts Bernstein made in his NYP performances of Bach's *St. Matthew Passion,* supposedly based on his Jewish partialities. However, no mention is made that this was shaped for concert purposes and for a New York City audience. There are also questions on the Internet from a non-Jewish perspective on how he treated Handel's *Messiah.* At a rehearsal of "For unto us a child is born," he asked the women to perform the roulades of sixteenth-note groupings "as if you were a bunch of gossipy women at the back fence." They musically responded clean as a whistle. When rehearsing Bach's cantata *Christ lag in Todesbanden*, he told the chorus, "Your German sounds like Yiddish." Think of the various layers of meaning in that onion.

Since Bernstein's death, it has become fashionable for commentators to divide his career and compositions into two halves. They both begin with large Jewish works. The first period starts with his New York Philharmonic debut and "Jeremiah" (1942) and finishes with *West Side Story* (1957), mainstays for a life in music filled with impetuosity, New York City brashness and restlessness. The second half begins with his becoming music director of the NYP (1958), which inhibits his composing yield until "Kaddish" (1963), and goes through his last piece, the *Dance Suite* (1989). This latter time frame is when many of the projects and works are regarded as being increasingly laden with a sense of self-indulgence, and where his raring-to-go spirit takes on a gradual world-weariness. There are exceptions; the modest masterwork *Chichester Psalms* emerged only after a sabbatical year during which he labored to write on a grand scale. However, the battle with his Jacobean angel was not altogether unknown to his earlier days. He spoke of how the short work *Prelude, Fugue and Riffs* was more difficult to complete than the longer work, "Jeremiah." But when his ongoing zeal to take on societal challenges and to write something "of importance" was announced by those close to him, the news was met with skepticism and groans.

In the mid-1960s I had stated in a biographical piece that if he had given in to his critics by concentrating on only one activity, he would have ceased being Leonard Bernstein (see appendix 2, "Bernstein: A Brief Overview"). I believe that same criterion of letting him be himself has to be applied to these burdensome late years. Like others—particularly Jews—who went through the 1930s' (big *D*) Depression, his unabashed liberalism weighed him down with heavy issues and episodes of (small *d*) depression. Various theater projects were abandoned, among them a musical version of Thornton Wilder's *The Skin of Our Teeth* and *The Race to Urga* (by Bertolt Brecht). Three more plans that fell through were to be "frank" film collaborations, two with Franco Zeffirelli, a movie about Saint Francis that ultimately became *Brother Sun, Sister Moon*; another was to shoot *Aida* on location in Egypt; and the third was a motion picture musical attempt with Francis Ford Coppola that eventually became Coppola's *Tucker*. Some of the music LB wrote for *Brother Sun* went into *Mass* and material written for *Tucker* went into *Arias and Barcarolles*. He also wanted to write an opera based on Nabokov's *Lolita*. Perhaps if he had gotten Dietrich Fischer-Dieskau to play the role of Humbert Humbert, he might have undertaken it. I was present when he placed an overseas call to Fischer-Dieskau in Europe, trying to persuade him, to no avail.

Although Bernstein's output in later years would ease up with works such as *Divertimento, Arias and Barcarolles* and *Dance Suite*, the theatrical works written after *Mass*—*1600 Pennsylvania Avenue* and *A Quiet Place*—collapsed under their own weightiness. Toward the end of his life he was hoping to write a multilingual opera about the Holocaust; but this never got beyond convoluted plans with potential collaborators.

Many of the other large works that were fulfilled, did pertain to "important" social issues that few other composers of his time dealt with, and certainly not as consistently. These themes are manifested in both early and late works: "Jeremiah" (Holocaust); "The Age of Anxiety" (search for faith); *On the Waterfront* (McCarthyism, in part, and labor corruption); *Candide* (also McCarthyism, organized religion, and so on); *West Side Story* (racism and class struggle); "Kaddish" (fear of nuclear annihilation); *Mass* (loss of faith); *Songfest* (oppression of various minorities); and *Halil* (futility of war).

Whether or not it had an inhibiting effect on his muse, and despite all his personal demons, LB had the need, the passion and the guts to function according to a self-imposed altruism. Some critics contend that none of the abovementioned works is a so-called masterpiece, that he himself was all too aware of it and did not want to be known only for *West Side Story*—we should all be so fortunate—that he was at best a composer of light music. Maybe so, and perhaps no work of his will ever be regarded on the same exalted level as a Beethoven or Stravinsky symphony. Of course, Bernstein wrote more than just music for entertainment; but I question the notion that such music is reflexively presumed to be inferior to an assumed loftier and more intellectually challenging opposite. Must music written for popular consumption automatically be condemned to the nether regions of music history; and what if that kind of music has lasting power? In the twenty years after his death, Bernstein's output remains among the most played American music on the planet, all of it stamped with the honest essence of a man filled with a raging regard for humanity and its troubles.

Most remarkable about the early period is how he wrote "on the run," how the race toward completion was accomplished everywhere from hospital beds to airport terminals. *Wonderful Town* was realized in little over a month. *West Side Story* and *Candide* were composed simultaneously. Ditto for the scores to *Serenade* and *On the Waterfront*. At the Watergate Hotel in Washington, I worked with him day and night to get both the *Slava!* Overture and Meditation No. 3 for Cello and Orchestra written in about ten days' time. But that was in 1977 and the adrenalin rush was not as potent for him as it had been earlier on. The body was no longer as able to keep up with the spirit. This, I submit, was LB's tragic flaw: for as much as he may have desired it, the prodigious facility of his wunderkind twenties could not continue to work its magic in his later years. As with most of us, he truly hated getting old. Part of being so famous meant that he became a captive of his prior output, and this had a suppressive effect on composing, often resulting in less spontaneity. Beyond the constraints of his inner editor, the effects of aging, of sluggish metabolism, physical changes and lessening energy, the overextension of work commitments on all fronts were contributing factors and must be taken into account. In any event, there is a great deal of very beautiful music within his latter-day output, if not in toto.

This is a book by a composer about a composer. I call him composer rather than musician—which is what he called himself and encompasses all his other abundant attributes—because that is what interests me the most. Ever since I heard the old Capitol LP of *Fancy Free* (recorded in 1952) with its cover of John Kriza and Norma Vance of Ballet Theatre and conducted by Joseph Levine, I was hooked.

While I was writing, I reread various accounts and reckonings on the life of LB. He is considered by some detractors—such as stage director Jonathan Miller—to be excessive, over the top. Recording producer Paul Myers notes that his life journey, which began as a Peter Pan, ended up as a kind of portrait of Dorian Gray. Critic Terry Teachout characterizes his subordinates as having been "sycophants." Good grief, was I, am I considered to be one of those fawning types? Certainly there were times when the Maestro's ego had to be massaged, when kowtowing was the better part of valor—especially when it got tangled up with one's source of livelihood. There may have been some whitewashing on my part, but, in all honesty, any so-called flattery from me usually was based on genuine admiration, even awe. There also were other times when he asked for my opinion and I gave it to him unvarnished. One of those instances was after the first rehearsal of *Opening Prayer* in Carnegie Hall, in 1986. I made it plain that I thought the piece was not any great shakes. He angrily retorted in front of others, "Don't you patronize me!" This was such a rare and unhappy moment that it might have jaundiced my lackluster feelings about the piece.

Is this book biased? You bet it is! However, I fervently hope it is not hagiographic. But writing it has also been a slippery slope. So much has already been written about LB that it is nigh impossible to find a fresh angle or material. The man certainly was not a saint, and I dearly want to be honest in my assessment, and testify to the fact that he sometimes lacked discipline and exhibited shameless behavior—*sin vergüenza*, in the words of Julia Vega. Nonetheless, I have been associated with him for such a long time—I was even named in his will—that any negative observations might be regarded as ungrateful or worse. It is a most fine line that I now tread.

Part One

A GRAB BAG OF MY LIFE WITH LB

An informal mix of reminiscences, anecdotes, observations, testimonies, little known facts and hitherto unpublished, unconstrained writings by the Maestro.

1 New York, New York

Remembering LB

I saw Leonard Bernstein in action for the first time at a Carnegie Hall concert, 17 February 1951. Unforgettable to this day, it was a judiciously balanced concert of masterpieces from the romantic era juxtaposed against the masterpiece of all pieces in the twentieth century. I was up there with the gods, in the top row of the top balcony. Years later, when I got down to the stage as his assistant (a word I detest), I would joke, at least for a few years, "I went from the heights of obscurity to the depths of [*pause for dramatic effect*] obscurity."

I was introduced to him in the summer of 1952 by Jack Urbont, my Queens College (NYC) composer-chum, on the Tanglewood grounds next to Hawthorne Cottage. Like most people, I did my level best to act casual in the presence of celebrity. He was warm, gracious, and immediately one could tell that when he spoke to you he gave you his full attention.

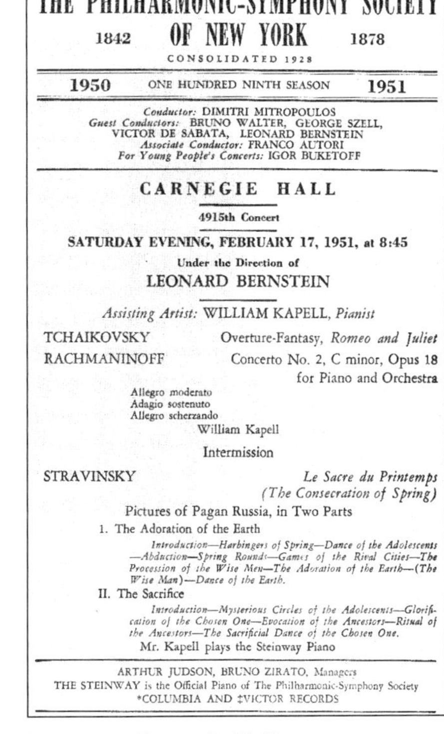

THE PHILHARMONIC-SYMPHONY SOCIETY
1842 OF NEW YORK 1878
CONSOLIDATED 1928

1950 ONE HUNDRED NINTH SEASON 1951

Conductor: DIMITRI MITROPOULOS
Guest Conductors: BRUNO WALTER, GEORGE SZELL, VICTOR DE SABATA, LEONARD BERNSTEIN
Associate Conductor: FRANCO AUTORI
For Young People's Concerts: IGOR BUKETOFF

CARNEGIE HALL

4915th Concert

SATURDAY EVENING, FEBRUARY 17, 1951, at 8:45

Under the Direction of
LEONARD BERNSTEIN

Assisting Artist: WILLIAM KAPELL, *Pianist*

TCHAIKOVSKY — Overture-Fantasy, *Romeo and Juliet*

RACHMANINOFF — Concerto No. 2, C minor, Opus 18 for Piano and Orchestra
Allegro moderato
Adagio sostenuto
Allegro scherzando
William Kapell

Intermission

STRAVINSKY — *Le Sacre du Printemps (The Consecration of Spring)*
Pictures of Pagan Russia, in Two Parts
1. The Adoration of the Earth
Introduction—Harbingers of Spring—Dance of the Adolescents—Abduction—Spring Rounds—Games of the Rival Cities—The Procession of the Wise Men—The Adoration of the Earth—(The Wise Man)—Dance of the Earth.
II. The Sacrifice
Introduction—Mysterious Circles of the Adolescents—Glorification of the Chosen One—Evocation of the Ancestors—Ritual of the Ancestors—The Sacrificial Dance of the Chosen One.
Mr. Kapell plays the Steinway Piano

ARTHUR JUDSON, BRUNO ZIRATO, Managers
THE STEINWAY is the Official Piano of The Philharmonic-Symphony Society
*COLUMBIA AND ‡VICTOR RECORDS

Program, Carnegie Hall concert, February 1951.

After Queens College, I entered the masters program at Brandeis University in 1954, where LB was guest professor and where he began to know me as a composer (see "Candide Goes to College"). Following Brandeis, I got my doctorate at the University of Illinois. My thesis was on Bernstein's music, the first of its kind. This gave him the opportunity to address me in a Groucho Marx voice as "Doctor Gottlieb," the name of the impresario played by Sig Ruman in the movie *A Night at the Opera*.

Bernstein at the Hollywood Bowl, 1955.

As a kind of test run, in August 1955 I helped him out at the Hollywood Bowl Festival of the Americas, where he presided over a panel on the subject of jazz. I got to meet the legendary Billie Holiday, one of the panelists. During a rehearsal break, I heard a young André Previn dash off the "Masque" section of LB's "The Age of Anxiety" as if it were child's play. There were movie stars: an informal lunch in a Beverly Hills home with Van Johnson, Shelley Winters and her then husband Tony Franciosa. I was in my midtwenties, and this was heady stuff for me. In the fall, when I returned to my graduate fellow teaching job at the University of Illinois, and mentioned meeting these celebs to my students, their response was a dismissive, "Yeah, sure."

Johnny (as he was then called, later John) Green with the Los Angeles Philharmonic orchestra gave the West Coast premiere of LB's *Symphonic*

Suite from "On the Waterfront." That night, after the performance, I recall how LB marveled at the wide array of variously colored toiletries in Green's dressing room. It sticks in my mind because in the late 1980s in LB's country house, I came across him examining my toiletries and commenting on how much he could tell about someone from such sundries.

In September 1958, after he had become music director of the New York Philharmonic (NYP), he hired me; but at the beginning the job was not precisely defined. Quickly it grew hydra-headed into long hours as gofer, go-between and go bananas! My main job at first was to

Leonard Bernstein Heads Philharmonic

By ROSS PARMENTER

Leonard Bernstein has been named the musical director of the New York Philharmonic for the next three years.

He will be the first American-born conductor and the second youngest to hold the post, which has been held by such men as Walter Damrosch, Willem Mengleberg, Arturo Toscanini, Artur Rodzinski and Dimitri Mitropoulos.

It was Mr. Mitropoulos who announced his successor yesterday. He said he was not resigning, but "abdicating with joy." He said that the 39-year-old Mr. Bernstein, who is his co-conductor this season, was his choice as the man to take over the full responsibility of the orchestra's musical direction.

The announcement was made

Mr. Keiser and Bruno Zirato managing director of the orchestra, were the other speakers. Among the things that were not said were that next season Mr. Bernstein will conduct a minimum of sixteen weeks and that Mr. Mitropoulos will be back as one of the guest conductors in the orchestra's other sixteen weeks. Also Mr. Bernstein's term has been set for three years to insure the orchestra of continuity of leadership during the period of transition as it moves into its new quarters in the Lincoln Center for the Performing Arts.

COMPOSERS AWARD NAMES FIRST WINNER

Jack Gottlieb, a Queens College graduate now studying for a doctorate in music at the University of Illinois, has been announced as the first winner of the National Federation of Music Clubs' Devora Nadworney memorial award of $600.

The award, in memory of the mezzo-soprano, was given to the Federation by Miss Nadworney's sister, Mrs. Robert Wakefield of Jersey City.

Mr. Gottlieb won the award with the first movement of a "Symphony of Operas." He also won a $125 prize in the 1957 Young Composers Contest of the Federation with his "Quodlibet," a group of children's songs with English text.

The other winner in the composers' contest was Robert Lombardo, a graduate of the Hartt School of Music in Hartford, who won $175 for his "Tre Laude," a sonata for flute, viola and contrabass.

"Leonard Bernstein Heads Philharmonic" by Ross Parmenter, followed by an article about JG. Is this merely serendipity or something else? *New York Times,* 20 November 1957.

In Studio 61 at CBS, recording an episode of *Lincoln Presents Leonard Bernstein and the New York Philharmonic*: "The Infinite Variety of Music"; 9 February 1959. *Front:* JG giving cues; *back, left to right:* Hal Warner (technical director), William A. Graham (director), and Bruce Minnix (assistant director).

examine scores submitted by postulant composers for possible performance. Since the deluge of scores became too much for him to handle, I took on the job somewhat on the order that a producer hires a play-reader. It was my business solely to separate the wheat from the chaff, to bring to his attention only those scores worthy of possible NYP performance. Like a Supreme Court nominee, I tried very hard never to make any decision on the basis of my own taste, but only in terms of the professional quality of a work, no matter what its stylistic content. The process of examining these scores followed a strict routine: acknowledgment, summation on file cards and action taken. It was not easy—composers are notoriously sensitive; however, I did my level best to remain impartial. At first, encouragement of raw talent was also involved, but that became less and less practical for lack of time.

The job soon expanded into other areas and grew like Topsy—and Turvy. I sometimes found myself on what seemed like a 24-hour call, especially demanding when it came time for television work, *Omnibus*, Young People's Concerts, the NYP on tour. This included script conferences—LB wrote every one of his scripts, edited and timed in these meetings—research on everything from the medieval zink to a Joplin piano rag, cue sheets so that the orchestra knew what was coming and how fast, camera plotting and, calling out shots while positioned behind the TV director, coaching performers, editing of tapes, general help to the production staff. Exhilarating but tough work.

I maintained LB's music and record library—also a file on scripts, articles, artists' brochures, score catalogs, and so on. Missing gaps, from the standard repertoire, were filled in. I kept an up-to-date list of every score owned, and filled many notebooks of concert programs, with timings of each work.

Acting as a catch-all liaison, I was in direct contact with publishers, artists, managers, orchestra personnel and administrative staffs. I worked with stagehands about any special setups. I made suggestions at recording sessions and even participated in a few. (On the Columbia LP recording *Humor in Music*, I am the one playing the top riffs on the piano in Milhaud's *Le boeuf sur le toit*. I was also among those who recited the Kaddish prayer in the recording of the Bloch *Sacred Service*.) The thought and time that LB put into the prime matter of program planning was almost enough to constitute a job in itself. There were even moments when an idea of mine was actually implemented.

Close to my heart were the editing jobs I did on three of Bernstein's popular books. First was *The Joy of Music*, on which I had the pleasure of working with the genial Henry Simon of Simon and Schuster.[1] The next two books, also S&S publications, were co-edited with gentlemen who have since become distinguished men of letters: Michael Korda on *Young People's Concerts for Reading and Listening* and Robert Gottlieb (no relation) on *The Infinite Variety of Music.* (I did not work on the other two books, *Findings* and *The Unanswered Question.*)

Final preparation of music scores, in varying stages of completion, also came within my province. Obviously I learned a great deal about the music publication business, not all of it pleasant. Take the following passage from a book, a dropping from the pen of Hans W. Heinsheimer, of G. Schirmer, Inc., LB's first major music publisher:

> Bernstein is a publisher's dream . . . best of all, he is almost never seen. His scores, proofs, musical directives and wishes are delivered through a musical assistant—and his wishes are wishes, never orders, and when they sound like orders we know it is the assistant speaking and pay no attention.[2]

What arrogance! Abe Friedman, LB's lawyer,[3] persuaded me not to raise a fuss, even though in a subsequent paragraph, Heinsheimer got him mixed up with Gordon Freeman, LB's CPA. I had a call from the rental library of Music Theater International, asking me what to do with the original oversize full Broadway score of *West Side Story*, as orchestrated by Sid Ramin and Irwin Kostal. (MTI's custom was to rent out piano-vocal scores with instrumental cues for performance.) I said I'll be right over to pick it up. Then, like a dutiful puppet, I passed along this precious artifact to Heinsheimer for safekeeping. Later on, when we asked for its return, he refused to give it up. I did

JG shlepping LB's clothes, Venice 1959.

have gratifying associations at G. Schirmer with, among others, Paul Wittke and, especially, with Neil Baudhuin, who became a close friend. When LB's music was turned over to Boosey & Hawkes, I was fortunate to interact with such cooperative professionals as W. Stuart Pope, Bob Holton, Bob Wharton, Sylvia Goldstein and Sue Klein.

With a few exceptions, my hand is to be found all over most of the Bernstein manuscripts from "Kaddish" onward. In some publications where a page of LB manuscript is reproduced, my handwriting has even sometimes been designated as LB's, a far more elegant penmanship than mine. The same observation applies to my emendations on Young People's Concerts scripts.

I tried to keep pace with musical trends and events through periodicals and concerts, informing LB of anything significant; and I was present at all rehearsals (the "brass is too loud" department) and auditions. More tedious were my chores as shlepper of his concert clothes and scores in New York and on tour.

The most glamorous dividend was the opportunity to meet many famous people—from the previously mentioned and other movie stars (Marlene Dietrich!) to most of the major mid-twentieth century composers and performers to political leaders—and to see much of the world on tour with the orchestra: Europe, some places more than once, Russia, Japan, and Israel. It never was a soft-cushioned vacation. Work on tour often was more wearing than in New York. Lenny was not Superman. There were occasions when he had to take an upper to keep going. He smoked incessantly. At concerts, in between numbers he had to take a drag offstage, and, during rehearsals, sometimes onstage, too—as well as on airplanes, in cathedrals and other forbidden areas—to the consternation of many officials.

After LB's tenure as music director of the New York Philharmonic (1958–66), when he became laureate conductor, I continued to do freelance work with him until 1970. Then, for four and a half years, I went in pursuit of other occupations, a period I later termed as "time off for good behavior." That meant I was not present during the creation of *Mass* and *1600 Pennsylvania Avenue*—nor, of course, any of the other earlier musicals—the Harvard lectures (*The Unanswered Question*) and the uproar over the Black Panthers fund-raiser. However, LB and I did stay in touch.

In 1977 I read a want ad in the *New York Times* that began, "International musician seeking. . . ." I called Harry Kraut (HJK), LB's manager, and asked if that could possibly be *The Man*. Harry said, "Yes; you interested?" Thus did I rejoin the Maestro's employ as his editor of print music, books, program and jacket notes and catalogs. Since Lenny's death I have continued to serve in lesser capacities, and currently have the distinction of being the senior member on staff.

* * *

Not stated in all of this were the more personal interactions, anecdotal reminiscences, and factoids about the hectic everyday goings-on of my job, matters dealt with in part 1 of this book. Felicia Bernstein was the calming factor in all of this turmoil. A gifted amateur painter and pianist, and a consummate actress, she collaborated with her husband as the *diseuse* in Debussy's *Le martyre de St. Sébastien*, in Honegger's *Jeanne d'Arc*, in the Lukas Foss *Parable of Death* and the "Kaddish" Symphony that LB wrote with her in mind.

Felicia Montealegre as Jeanne d'Arc.

Ballerina-actress Vera Zorina (Brigitta Lieberson), her friend, was engaged by LB to be the narrator for the Milhaud *Les Choéphores*. Seeing those two lovely dames chatting together was delighting in a pair of petite, elegant and cultured twins. Felicia also was the reader in my Friday evening service, *Love Songs for Sabbath*, presented in 1966 at the Jewish Community Center, White Plains, New York, with choreography by Anna Sokolow, a woman who figured in LB's introduction to Copland years before. When it came to the Kaddish part of the service, Felicia's gripping reading of a Rilke poem recited over organ music brought her to tears.

She referred to all mundane, daily activities as "the kitchen of life." When I ran errands, purchasing a toothbrush for the Maestro and the like, I was part of that "kitchen." But at the same time I was witness to great artistry in action as I watched and heard major and lesser works of the symphonic repertoire being shaped into thrilling concerts—at least once sprinkled at a rehearsal with the Maestro's direction to "take it from bar sixty-nine, pardon the expression." I even participated in a percussion rehearsal for the "Masque" in "The Age of Anxiety," where I played the celesta—unknown to the musician's union, ahem. Earlier, under LB's direction, I sang in the chorus for Beethoven's *Missa Solemnis* at Tanglewood, so uplifting that choral singing should be required of everyone. As time went on, the lively activity became a juggling act of not being able to distinguish what mutual roles LB and I were playing, sometimes separate, at other times all mixed up together: boss/employee, mentor/student, big brother/little brother or just plain friends.

LB on his seventieth birthday with the author, Stille House, Great Barrington, Massachusetts, 1988.

I preferred calling him Leonard simply because I did not enjoy being one of the crowd to address him as Lenny. However, I wrote a song for his seventieth birthday on 25 August 1988, which began:

Lenny by any other name
Remains a talented guy.
Still, many spell Lenny with "I-E,"
But Lenny is spelt with a "Y."
Then he has problem number nine,
About which he's none too keen.
Nine are the letters in Bern-STEIN,
But never, no never, Bern-STEEN!
(I mean, it's not Albert Ein-STEEN,
Or Gertrude STEEN or Franken-STEEN.)

Occasionally I would come into contact with his doctors. An early song called "Afterthought" was dedicated in memory of Hyman J. Rubinstein, a dentist who I think was the one to repair LB's deviated septum in 1944 (see essay on *On the Town*). After an appointment with Ron Odrich, a subsequent dentist who was also a clarinetist, LB wrote *Visione Fugitiva*, a clarinet solo based on musical pitches printed on an eye chart hanging on the office wall. Later on, Odrich expanded the solo into a piece called *Leonardo's Vision*. (I never found out why it was eye chart instead of a diagram of teeth.) *Chichester Psalms* was dedicated to Cyril ("Chuck") Solomon, his primary physician who had played a role in getting the Chichester commission. Chuck was a *heimishe* (friendly, welcoming) fellow who passed away much too soon. Dr. Kevin Cahill, who is also a writer of Irish history and world matters, was LB's doctor during his last decade.

LB's psychiatrists were another matter. He never dedicated a piece to any of them, but he did believe in the power of psychiatry with the fervor of a religionist. Given his superior gift of gab, he must have been a spellbinding case study. During a summer in the mid-'60s, when I was slogging through the Thomas Mann *Joseph Trilogy* on Cape Cod, LB stopped off to see me. He had been visiting Sándor Radó, his vacationing shrink, who was in the vicinity. LB confided to me that Radó had introduced him as one of his patients at a cocktail party and shown him off like a prize monkey. He soon left Radó and began treatment with Dr. Willard Gaylin.

This intense introspection and preoccupation with himself resulted in keen insights that, from time to time, had him acting as doctor as well as patient. Many were those who sought counsel with him, ranging from despairing university students to the marital problems of friends to a troubled orchestra player he saved from committing suicide. There also was a less attractive side to this particular talent of his. He pressured one of his family members, against their will, to see his doctor. Then there was the "toilet analysis," when he had me sit on the commode cover while he was taking a shower and proceeded to tell me everything that was wrong with me.

Several of us were also "handled" by Paul Zea, a chiropractor, whose bone-crunching technique actually was enjoyed by LB. Less conventional was the work of Rita Hartinger, the "hair-popping lady." To help prevent baldness, her method of "lifting the scalp from the bone structure" actually produced a popping sound. It may have helped, but I can certify that it hurt like hell.

There were times when LB could be downright disdainful. If the word *career* were applied to him, he would react, "I don't have a career" [sniff, sniff] as if to say, "I have a calling." He resented being compared to George

Gershwin. At dinner there was a greenish something on the table that I could not identify nor knew how to eat. I grew up in a household of Jewish East-European origin that had never seen this thing called an artichoke. I was made to feel like a bumpkin. On other occasions, a comment of mine would elicit a "Hello?-duh" kind of exasperated expression for its patent obviousness. When

Poster of LB and Sigmund Freud. The caption reads, "On 5 November 1985, Leonard Bernstein and the Vienna Philharmonic present a benefit concert for the Sigmund Freud Society at the Musikvereinssaal."

others would utter a similar self-evident remark, LB might point out, "You just pulled a Gottlieb." Not very charming. Or he would dream up a ditty that did not show off some employees, family and friends in the best light:

Who's Out There (Christmas 1981; third verse omitted)
Oh, HJK has got B.O., Ho ho,
And Daryl don't know where to go, Hi ho.
Shirley's got her annual crud,
And Epstein's got some shit in his blood.

Refrain:
So who's out there this very merry Christmas?
Who's out there, who's happy and healthy and relatively free?
I can think of three (Relatively.)
Alexander, Nina, Jamie and possibly, just possibly me!
Oh, Richard's stomach's in a whirl, Ho ho,
And Bart's got fired, lost his girl, Hi ho.
Oh, Joseph's at a total loss,
And poor Jack keeps crying, "Who is the boss?"
(Refrain)

On the other hand, I was able to get into the Columbia University swimming pool facility because of his honorary doctorate. Getting an honorary degree could work wonders for him also. He enjoyed playing squash at the Yale Club in New York City, but his squash partner, a Yalie, had to pay a visitor's fee for him each time. He pleaded, "Couldn't you speak to someone to let me become a member?" He even wrote a letter to the head of the club on NYP stationery. No luck; membership could be granted only to Yale graduates. Then, as related by Luis D'Almeida, LB was notified he was to be awarded a degree by the university. In great excitement he phoned his squash buddy and informed him that he did not care so much about receiving the honor as much as how he would be now be able to become a member. LB played squash with rigorous determination, although he usually lost. Losing any kind of game was anathema to him even if the winner was one of his children, who would occasionally triumph in a family game of cutthroat anagrams—cutthroat because everyone was on all the time to yell out new combinations.

He could be playful, but there were times when his inner child would erupt into a streak of naughty-boy behavior. A small dinner party I gave—

where he and Maestro James Levine were guests, along with Bob Kirkland and Paul McKibbins—deteriorated into a syllabub dessert–throwing contest, initiated by him. He delighted in burning cork from wine bottles to make up his face to look like a demented Rasputin. Or he would perform, to the tune of "I Love You, Truly," "A Porgy by Ethelbert Nevin":

> I loves you Porgy, truly dear,
> Don't let him take me, I'se a feared.
> Don't let him handle me wid his hot hand,
> I loves you, Porgy, you's my man.

According to John McClure, in 1983, LB and Herbert von Karajan were staying at the same hotel in Munich, with LB in the penthouse suite and HvK just below him. After midnight, LB and his guests started singing Gilbert and Sullivan songs in a loud party mode. The concierge called up and asked them to keep it down, that they were disturbing Maestro von Karajan's sleep. This only goaded the assembled to continue their shenanigans. The concierge called again to say that von Karajan had checked out.

Bruno Zirato pointing to Franco Passigli, a UN aide, at the United Nations, with JG in back. December 10, 1958.

He remembered birthdays and was lavish in gift-giving. Above all, he was devoted to a legion of people as they were to him. So much so that it could get out of hand when he was unable to fulfill the expectations and demands of the assorted mob. Bruno Zirato, manager of the New York Philharmonic when LB first became famous, said, "Lenny's like a whore; he can't say no." This echoes an observation of Sam Bernstein: "It was fortunate [my] son had not been born a woman because he was incapable of saying 'no.'"[4] He lived life to the hilt, could not tolerate boredom and needed to fill all his waking hours.

Tallulah Bankhead declared something that could apply equally to LB: "I have three phobias which, could I mute them, would make my life as slick as a sonnet, but as dull as dish water: I hate to go to bed, I hate to get up, and I hate to be alone."[5] During his conducting mode, LB stayed up long after others had folded their tents. And why not?—performing artists are on an endorphin high after a concert and it takes more than a while to come down. Getting him up and going in the morning could be a Sisyphean challenge. As for not being alone, to the best of my knowledge during the years I knew him, he never had dinner by himself.

Once, as we were entering the National Theater in Washington, he sniffed the air and declaimed the memorable phrase "*Ah, la vie de théâtre!*" He loved theater in all its forms, and he loved collaborating. It was no problem for him to do the initial heavy work on a project because he knew that his ideas would exfoliate once he shared them with others. He could study a score with lapidary precision, but better yet was the joy of working it out with orchestras. This was the same when he wrote television scripts that were then edited with a team, and obviously when he was working with a choreographer, a lyricist, a director, or an orchestrator in the theater.

But it was another matter when time came to undertake the solitary work of symphonic composition. He did not seem to mind if I were in a nearby room and could hear him struggling at the piano. Other composers would not have tolerated that for an instant. Complete isolation for him meant there was a monster in the room, his alter ego. Now he would use the night to get away from people and the phone. When he finally was "in the zone," he lost all sense of time elapsing; food and drink did not matter; other folks did not exist. He worked like a demon to achieve this state of transport, but it became more and more difficult, if not impossible, with the passing years. On such days a good time at dinner was not had by all.

Home and Office

On bus trips around Manhattan, there are days when I travel by all three former Bernstein family residences—crosstown for a doctor's appointment from my Upper West Side apartment building, through Central Park to the East Side, past the second residence at Seventy-ninth Street and the southeast corner of Park Avenue. Then, to do some errands, I transfer downtown Lexington Avenue, followed by the crosstown bus going west on Fifty-seventh Street, and at Seventh Avenue, past the Osborne, the first residence; and finally, back uptown on Central Park West, past the Dakota, at West Seventy-second, their last New York City home. Along the way I also can view all three buildings that housed Amberson, Inc., the Bernstein business offices: on West Fifty-seventh, around the corner at Fifty-sixth Street and Sixth Avenue (that's what New Yorkers still call it, not Avenue of the Americas), and the one that was located at Central Park and Sixty-third Street.

If I go back home on Broadway, at West Sixth-fifth Street the alternative sign below reads LEONARD BERNSTEIN PLACE. But Bernstein's place is hardly escapable on bus-less days. Concerts, radio, TV, reviews, festivals, the Internet, newspapers (such few as still exist), phone calls, e-mail, you name it—Lenny, Leonard, Leonardo "the one and every" everywhere, and seemingly as much as before.

* * *

On 25 August 1952 (on LB's thirty-fourth birthday), the Bernsteins began family life at 205 West Fifty-seventh Street. Situated diagonally across from Carnegie Hall, the Osborne is the second-oldest apartment building in the city. The ten-room family household was on the fourth floor right (4B). The prior occupant had been the Mindlin family. Mike Mindlin Jr. became a Bernstein family bosom buddy, and produced LB's 1967 documentary film, *Journey to Jerusalem*. In 2009, the same apartment was sold to Adam Guettel, the show composer, whose mother, Mary Rodgers, was intimately involved with LB's Young People's Concerts. There is something very comforting about these "bookend" associations.

Bernstein's dark studio with battleship gray–painted walls was on the second floor left (2DD). Dark was how he liked it, with no distractions from sunlight or outside noise. It probably was his first genuine "quiet place" (a phrase that originates in his one-act opera *Trouble in Tahiti* and later as the title of his three-act opera). The Osborne is where he wrote the music for *West Side Story.*

The photos seen here on the wall of the Osborne studio traveled with him to his last studio in Fairfield, Connecticut. They now dwell at the Library of Congress. My work area was in a backroom that resembled a dungeon. Helen Coates, his secretary, lived on the ninth floor. In 2007, an apartment was misleadingly advertised for sale as Bernstein's studio, when actually what went on the market was the Coates apartment seven floors above. (It was sold to Robert Osborne—same spelling as the building—the affable host of the Turner Classic Movie Channel.) After the family moved out of the Osborne, Miss Coates remained behind and the LB studio was turned into a kind of shrine-cum-archive.

Author in LB's Osborne studio, August 1960.

In 1961, the Bernsteins were "moving on up to the east side, to a deluxe apartment in the sky," a fifteen-room penthouse duplex at 895 Park Avenue. LB was now at the peak of his New York Philharmonic music directorship, and the Park Avenue address had the aura of being an official residence. However, his studio was confined to a single room on the bottom floor. (I inherited his couch, covered in firehouse red—his favorite color—where his composing flights of fancy took shape. In fact, I gradually came into possession of various furniture and fine arts pieces that originally were in the various Bernstein domiciles.) A summer retreat in Vineyard Haven, Massachusetts, and later a weekend home on Fox Run Road in West Redding, Connecticut, did not offer much space for private study, either. The growing need for such lebensraum was resolved in June 1962 when they acquired a country estate in Fairfield, Connecticut. A prefabricated building was imported to become LB's studio.

Known as the Casita (Little House), it was attached to a former horse stable, but unfortunately was subject to continuing drainage problems.

The Fairfield studio.

Another kind of plumbing problem was the vexing water tower above the dining room at the Park Avenue penthouse. Every time the tower motor turned on, dinner talk got louder and louder, without anyone being aware why. When the family moved to their last New York City address, Felicia first made sure to test the possible noise level, but this time from the subway not so far below.

This final move occurred in February 1974, when they returned to the west side of town into the famed Dakota co-op building, at 1 West Seventy-second Street, the oldest apartment house in the city. The second floor quarters (Apt. 23) were not as large as 895 Park Avenue. To make up the difference, two small studios on the top floor (originally servant quarters) were purchased, one as LB's workplace (Apt. 92, where I had a desk), the other (Apt. 126) for out-of-town family and guests. But before any of this could be accomplished, the Dakota's board of directors required that the Bernsteins get letters of recommendation! One of them was from Lauren (Betty) Bacall, their close friend who already lived there. Miss Bacall joked that if she and LB had been married, they would not have had to change the monogram on their bed linen. News anchor Peter Jennings took this one step further. He saw Bacall wearing a sweater initialed LB on the left shoulder. Jennings observed he once had a girlfriend who had a similar sweater marked LB and RB—for left breast and right breast.

Interior wall of the Fairfield studio.

The Household Staff

With Gail Jacobs, a decorator friend, Felicia selected fabrics and furniture for the last two Bernstein apartments. Felicia's taste in decor was eclectic: Russian, American, Italian and French antiques that gave off an air of informal elegance, warm and inviting. The Bernsteins had a Renoir painting in their possession for a few days, but returned it. Once, over tea, I asked Felicia why they did not own more paintings. She replied that they preferred spending money on servants. No doubt this was a carryover from her own upbringing in Chile with a household staff, which included a nanny who was known as "Mamita."

In the early days, I enjoyed taking the Bernstein children, Jamie and Alexander, to the circus and the like, privileged to have their care entrusted to me. It was Julia Vega, the nanny who mostly reared them, who eventually became the *ama de llave*, the housekeeper. Julia so steadfastly held onto her sense of position in the "upstairs-downstairs" class system that she became a kind of patrician in her own right. She waited on me and many others for more than fifty years, while retaining a dignity that would have put many a blue blood to shame. LB wrote a *cueca* (Chilean dance) in tribute to her, with part of his lyric reading, "*Viva la Julia, la Diva, oye, la buena Chilena!*"

Julia's opposite in personality was the family cook, the ever cheerful and outgoing Rosalia Guerrero, who died at a young age. Rosalia is the name of one of the Shark girlfriends in *West Side Story*, and the ship that goes down in “Bon Voyage” from *Candide* is named *Santa Rosalia*. Subsequent cooks included Guillermina Miranda and the aptly named Anita Salse (an Italian word for *sauces*).

Author with Jamie and Alexander Bernstein, Martha’s Vineyard, 1958.

Julia Vega, at LB’s Fairfield, Connecticut, estate, 1960s.

Felicia was the go-to person among her friends for finding cleaning women, always of Hispanic origin (she was born in Costa Rica and raised in Chile), and referred to herself as "the Spic and Span Employment Agency" with self-deprecating humor. Carol, a political refugee from Allende's Chile, was hired as a maid for a while. It was hard to keep a straight face when her pronunciation of *kitchen* came out as sounding like *chicken*. According to John Walker, Carol went on to become a taxicab driver—you are reading that correctly. Over the years, I always found the maids to be kind and helpful. Their names had a musical lilt: Gigi Cantera and Sireña Carranza. Others had first names that blended into a kind of song lyric: "Cristina, Aida, Marcellina and Tina."

On the other hand, the Bernsteins were not so fortunate with their male household staff. An agitated Felicia phoned me one evening to ask if I knew where their overdue chauffeur, Robert "Lucky" Beckwith, and the Lincoln Town Car might be. I had no idea; and suggested she call a mutual acquaintance. Big mistake. She protested, "Why would our chauffeur be with a friend of ours?" I weakly replied something about their being chummy. Alas, Beckwith was an AWOL marine, his employment a deception that could have come straight out of the *Catch Me If You Can* movie. He was eventually arrested in Florida for speeding in the Lincoln. (Beckwith gave me a Twelve Tribes of Israel medallion that I still keep on my key chain.)

More car trouble happened with Michael Winter, a Cockney fellow, who was a combination driver and valet. He was "imported" by the Bernsteins after he had driven them around in London. Alas, Winter turned out to be a drunkard who trashed the family station wagon on a New York expressway.

LB's concert tails, tuxedos and capes were tailored by Otto Perl, his shirts by Carlin Poster. But his taste in store-bought clothes often was not the height of fashion for any season. Felicia would keep him in check, but she was not always around when he was on tour.

Osvaldo Mellin, from Brazil, who had been Rock Hudson's valet, did not last long as LB's gentleman's gentleman. It was ludicrous to see him scrambling with the Maestro as to who was to put what leg into which pair of pants. When there was some misunderstanding, and Osvaldo was confronted by LB about it, he memorably replied, "You no shpeak me shpeak, I no shpeak nada"—translation: "If you don't specifically instruct me to tell you something, then I say nothing at all."

After Felicia died, Chan from China was another one of the cooks. But he seemed not to know any other cuisine than his native culinary art. Oh, and then there was the time, reported to me by Ann Dedman Neal, he went on a rampage with a cleaver in his hand in pursuit of LB.

Sparkly Ann Dedman would have never been hired as family cook in Felicia's lifetime. First off, she was not Chilean, but she also refused to wear a uniform, and enjoyed swimming in the country house outdoor pool along with the guests. This would have been deemed unseemly in the eyes of Felicia (as it certainly was for Julia) who believed that servants should not intermingle. To get the job, Ann had to audition three times. The first time was set for the delectation of LB and his associates, Harry Kraut and Margaret Carson. The latter two informed her that the Maestro did not care for fish, then said he was not coming to that audition, and so she ordered a striped bass. But then he did arrive and enjoyed the meal, fish and all.

Ms. Mary Thorne, a proper English lady who had managed Seranak, the Koussevitzky estate at Tanglewood, was employed to manage the household at the Dakota, but did so gingerly because Julia, who had seemingly retired as "forewoman," was always around with critical eyes and ears.

Patty Pulliam succeeded Ann Dedman. Patty and her husband, Sergei Boyce, are now caretakers of the country estate. They are among that special and small class of *menschen* I have been fortunate to know, fundamentally decent folks, filled with integrity and responsibility.

The Business Staff

In the beginning was Helen Grace Coates. His name for her was La Belle—as in the Offenbach operetta *La belle Hélène*—but never in her presence. It was not meant to be a compliment, for La Belle could also be La Bête. She was a formidable part of his life from the time he was fourteen, as his piano teacher, until her death when she was nominally still his secretary. While I was first finding my way in the job, she and I were friendly. Or to put it another way, I was meek in her company. We started off on the right foot because I had returned a fifty-dollar loan from LB; and, as she told me, I was the only one who had ever done that. (In 2009, while examining old business papers for appraisal purposes, I came across that canceled check from the early 1950s in her bookkeeping accounts. How extraordinary that it still is extant.) She would invite me to a casual dinner at her apartment, always preceded by "the sun-is-over-the-yardarm" cocktails.

Almost inevitably, we had an altercation. I don't recollect what it was about; but, as it had occurred with others, whatever the leveling off was after the dust had settled, that became the degree of one's not-so-friendly acquaintanceship with her from that time henceforth. Although, to be fair, she did write me several letters that were kind and helpful in the early 1970s when I was living in Saint Louis.

Helen Coates at Lewisohn Stadium, New York City, 1950s.

Soon after her death on 27 February 1989 at the age of eighty-nine, a private commemoration was held at LB's Dakota apartment, an occasion at which he unexpectedly put me on the spot and asked me to offer some words, presumably laudatory. But I had little to say because starting in the mid-'80s, our relationship had turned stone cold. Was I to inform the assembled group that when I visited her in the hospital she had sputtered: "What are *you* doing here?" Not long before then, when I was laid low with an illness, I wrote her a note asking forgiveness for whatever injury, imagined or otherwise, I may have caused her, to which she replied in a phone call that she did not know what I was talking about, and that I should seek psychiatric help. Grace may have been her middle name, but she was not always full of it.

In one of his letters to her, dated 2 September 1965, LB wrote, "I have decided to reengage Jack G. for the coming year, to everyone's surprise, including mine. It's for the best, I feel sure." I have no idea what triggered this reluctance; but I would like to believe he was mollifying Miss Coates. He remained steadfast to her through thick and thicker. She had few secretarial skills—no shorthand, no dictation, needed him to spell words out, although she could type out very long, dense single-spaced letters. He dedicated his first book to her for "selfless devotion," and indeed it was. He wrote two piano anniversaries for her. One of them misfired, however, because it gave the date of her birth. That was a *shrek* and a half, "How could you!" said she. Another anniversary became a Meditation in *Mass*.

She was born 19 July 1899 in Rockford, Illinois, to Marvin Amos Coates and Grace Lucille Hand, and had a younger married brother. Her mother was related to Justice Learned Hand of the Supreme Court. She had the burden of caring for her aged, infirm mother who lived with her for a long time at the Osborne. I never heard a word about her father. Most of Felicia's and Lenny's letters to her conclude with greetings to her mother.

By coincidence, she attended the Garrison Elementary School in Rockford, and LB went to Garrison Grammar School in Roxbury, Massachusetts. In 1943, when his conducting life took off, he asked her to move to New York City from Boston to manage all the demands on his professional life. He had a stiff-necked accountant, H. Gordon Freeman, and a good-hearted, avuncular lawyer, Abe Friedman, who also was Copland's attorney. (After Abe died, Ellis J. Freedman took over. When Ellis passed away, the chain of Freeman, Friedman and Freedman was broken by attorney Paul H. Epstein, currently the senior vice president of the Bernstein Office). But lawyers and a CPA are not hired to grapple with fan mail, press clippings and requests for appearances that pour in from all over the map. Miss Coates became known throughout the music world as the iron fist in the velvet glove. During his worldwide travels, LB wrote to her continuously and at length. These more than eight hundred letters, including responses from her, can be seen online as part of the Bernstein collection at the Library of Congress, an archive that is probably unrivaled in American music and would not have been come to pass in the age of e-mail.

There was some understandable standoffishness between Miss Coates and Felicia. How could there not be? A picture of Helen at the Bernstein wedding shows her with a look of displeasure. One dispute that I witnessed between the two of them was about the uniform of a Holocaust victim—who had been a flute player—given to LB when he performed at a displaced persons camp in 1948. Felicia wanted it thrown out because it still carried a smell. Under her breath, Helen har-rumphed at me, "How dare she?" Presumably the artifact was trashed.

In any event, Miss Coates truly was a consummate curator of the flame. But for all her dedication to LB, she continued to maintain the air of a New

England spinster—rumor was that she had received a marriage proposal—with the demeanor of a fussbudget biddy. One day the phone rang on my desk in the studio; it was Frank Sinatra asking for LB, who was not available. I took the message, hung up and passed it on to her. She blew a gasket. (There was an inside line between the studio and her upstairs lair; but it was not possible to forward an outside call to her.) All the same, *goodness gracious*, how could I, a mere underling, have the gall to take such a call! As years went by, things got worse. It did not matter that I was not the only one who endured her hen pecks.

Miss Coates and LB in the Osborne studio, known as the shrine, both of them in an almost reverential pose. The open door led to the back room, the author's work area.

More than once, LB also had enough of her officiousness, and actually dismissed her by mail, too nervous to do it person. She managed his daily finances, and I remember seeing a letter he wrote to the aforementioned Gordon Freeman, asking for advice on what to do about her (Freeman later also got the boot.) But LB, at least, before Amberson Enterprises was launched, really could not do without her. At the age of forty-four, she gave over the rest of her life to him and made herself indispensable. When she was due for a session with LB at the Dakota, he would say to his daughter Nina, "Helen is going to HAVE ME at four o'clock!" Complain as he did about her getting on his nerves, he had only himself to blame when she also got drawn into his private life. She had keys to his various apartments; and she would at times come upon him and an "overnight guest." In the 1940s, Bill Hewitt, a one-time lover of Marc Blitzstein, also had a fling with LB. When Helen came in the next morning, she asked him to leave his address and phone number in case the Maestro wanted to see him again.[6]

* * *

"Various apartments" is putting it mildly. In 1939, LB had lived for a while in Greenwich Village at 61 East Ninth Street, when he was an erstwhile pianist for the Revuers, Comden and Green, et al., at the Village Vanguard, a nearby nightclub. His permanent move from Boston to Manhattan was in 1942—actually not so permanent as he led a nomadic life, pitching his tent almost anywhere. There were no less than four different addresses in the 1942–43 season. The two in 1942 were 158 West Fifty-eighth Street, at the Park Savoy Hotel (where nearby, years later, the first Amberson office was located), and at 15 West Fifty-second Street—one biographer says it was the top floor; another says it was the basement. Whichever floor it was, West Fifty-second was known as the Jazz Street in those days, and LB's pad was cheek-to-jowl with such clubs as the Three Deuces and the Downbeat, featuring the likes of Billie Holiday and Charlie Parker.

The season of 1943–1944 was another frenetic year. In September 1943 he took up residence in Studio 803 at Carnegie Hall. (These days it is part of the administrative office complex at the hall.) Why there? Because it had been a library space for the New York Philharmonic, and that is how he found out about its availability—through Bruno Zirato, the NYP manager. It could be that the hilarious Madame Dilly, the dipsomaniac vocal teacher of *On the Town* was inspired by one or more characters Bernstein encountered at the Carnegie Hall studios (according to Jerry Robbins' biographer Amanda Vaill, Sono Osato's coach was the role model). Even so, he did not remain there very long. In fact, there were four more moves in 1944–45, three in 1944 alone!

There is correspondence from two other possible lodgings in 1943. One—from LB to Serge Koussevitzky—cited 40 Charlton Street as the return address. The other, from Aaron Copland to LB and from LB to Miss Coates, was the Chelsea Hotel on West Twenty-third Street, famous for many artist residencies, among them Dylan Thomas, Thomas Wolfe and Virgil Thomson. Since there is no plaque outside the hotel for Bernstein, as there are for those three "Thomases," one assumes that his time there was at someone else's indulgence or as a temporary stopgap.

All this peripatetic activity had to be due, at least in part, to the transient nature of New York City lives, loves and professions, especially during those pre– and post–World War II years. But his growing fame and better paycheck also was a contributing factor. For instance, the solitary move in 1945 was to a penthouse at 1239 Broadway, near West Thirtieth Street. Nevertheless, the grand total of a dozen different addresses that mark Bernstein's early, vagabond days in the city, 1942 to 1950, averages out to 1.5 places per year! Even for the prodigious Bernstein, we can only imagine how he ever got any work done.

In late 1944, for less than a year, 40 West Fifty-fifth Street was occupied by LB, which was then taken over by his sister Shirley,[7] where she remained until her death in 1998. A record stay—at least for him—was at 32 West Tenth Street, near Sixth Avenue, three years starting in 1946. With Jerry Robbins, Oliver Smith, Paul and Jane Bowles as nearby neighbors, one could leap from rooftop to rooftop, scramble down fire escapes and drop in on folks unannounced. No doubt this second experience of living in Greenwich Village contributed to the creation of *Wonderful Town* on Broadway.

Bernstein claimed that the West Tenth Street address was the model for the across-the-courtyard building in Alfred Hitchcock's 1954 movie thriller *Rear Window*. Jimmy Stewart—who plays a Peeping Tom—secretly observes one of the tenants, a frustrated songwriter who finally makes it big on Broadway. Before that happens, however, Grace Kelly comments on the wonderful piano music she hears wafting across the courtyard on a hot summer day as the writer struggles with his muse. What lends some credence to the assertion that the West Tenth Street building was the mise-en-scène for *Rear Window* is not the piano music (by composer Franz Waxman) but the fact that near the top of the film, the opening of *Fancy Free* is heard as source music for a female dancer in one of the apartments. Another clue to LB's claim is that Stewart tricks the villain in the movie to meet him at the Albert Hotel, a well-known watering hole located at Eleventh Street and University Place, a block or so away.

There is one other convoluted twist to all of this: Hitchcock was nominated for the Best Director Oscar in 1954, but lost out to Elia Kazan for *On the*

Waterfront, score by Bernstein—nominated for Best Score, but which lost out to *Seven Brides for Seven Brothers* by Adolph Deutsch and Saul Chaplin. Go figure.

Saul Chaplin was also the vocal arranger for the 1949 movie version of *On the Town.* No doubt Comden and Green protested the decision of Arthur Freed, head of his own unit at MGM, to jettison much of the Bernstein score as being too arty for movie audiences. "Contractually, he [i.e., Freed] was not obligated to use all of the Bernstein score . . ."[8] It took some persuading, but Comden and Green ultimately agreed to do a book rewrite and lyrics for seven new songs with Roger Edens and for very good money "in addition to their share of the 60 percent of the $250,000 the studio had paid for the motion-picture rights."[9] Not at all shabby. It is regrettable that they could not have persuaded the studio executives to include at least one or two other LB songs. I say this, if for no other reason than it was actually LB who wrote the words for the refrain of "New York, New York," and, for the stage version, the song "I Can Cook Too." However, Comden and Green are credited with writing all the lyrics. Betty was upset and protective when the 1997 full vocal score for the show came out, stating that LB had written "additional lyrics," and all the printed scores had to be covered over with a label drawing of a dancing sailor.

On the other hand, let us be grateful that LB's lachrymose lyric for what became the classic ballad "Lonely Town" in *On the Town* never saw the light of day. It began:

> Our love has bloomed so well,
> Don't let it die!
> Don't let our chance for happiness go by.
> We two were made for it.
> For how were we to tell
> That by and by
> Our love would swell like early morning sky.
> I'm so afraid for it.

Once again the issue of lyric authorship came up soon after the premiere of *West Side Story* in Washington. (Saul Chaplin was also the associate producer of the *WSS* movie.) The first printing of the vocal score stated, "Lyrics by Stephen Sondheim and Leonard Bernstein." We know that LB wrote the words for an early draft of "One Hand, One Heart" and for "Maria," and it is likely he co-wrote words for other numbers. He crossed out his name when he autographed the score for me on 1 March 1959, having given full credit to Sondheim. When he offered further to make a royalty adjustment, Sondheim said it was not necessary, a decision Steve came to regret.

The Amberson Office

The boundless, ongoing activity got to be too much for any one secretary, lawyer or CPA. Accordingly, in 1969, after LB's last concert as music director of the New York Philharmonic, Amberson Enterprises, Inc. was launched. At that concert the Maestro threw out his baton to the audience, which was caught by Charlie Roth, a notorious stalker of LB. Roth returned the baton to Miss Coates. From now on she was mostly relegated to deal with the avalanche of personal correspondence. Abe Friedman continued to be astute in negotiating contracts, and with the debonair Schuyler Chapin at the helm, Amberson film and video productions soon followed. Schuyler went on to manage the Metropolitan Opera in 1972, and that is when Harry J. Kraut came onto the scene. I met Harry shortly after the 8 September 1971 premiere of *Mass* at the opening of the Kennedy Center in Washington. The introduction took place at the nearby Watergate Hotel, where LB was

Helen G. Coates and Harry J. Kraut, Merkin Concert Hall, New York City, 1980.

staying. It was an uneasy encounter and in retrospect, that is how it remained throughout our subsequent relationship after he was named executive VP of Amberson. It was as if part of his training at the Harvard Business School was how to keep everyone tense and on their toes. Some of the uneasiness was due to Harry and Helen's having a really tough job; and from their point of view, I guess I got in the way.

They not only had to compete for time alone with LB, they were perforce the buffer zone between him and the gnawing public. From now on, if there were any unpleasant deed to be repaired or executed, it was Harry's responsibility to take care of it. He could not but help develop a fierce reputation. LB used him as a go-between to chew me out on several calls from overseas for some problem or other with orchestral parts. The worst one of these incidents was when the parts for the opera *A Quiet Place* had been left out on a loading dock at the Washington airport, where they got soaked in the rain because, they contended, I had not seen to it that they had been properly wrapped by the music librarian at La Scala opera house in Milan. (Who else could they blame?) It turned into a big brouhaha when the Library of Congress had to use their conservation experts to get the parts in working order for performance. I wanted to be buried alive.

The first address for the Amberson office and staff was at 1414 Avenue of the Americas, a penthouse that had once been the New York residence of Gloria Swanson, of *Sunset Boulevard* fame. Within the space a princely studio with access to the terrace was designed for LB's use. He may have been there once or twice, but soon retreated to his New York apartment. It simply was not his style "to get up, get dressed and go the office," and certainly not to such plush surroundings. Amberson subsequently moved around the corner to 24 West Fifty-seventh Street, one floor below Boosey & Hawkes, LB's new publisher. Next was a move close to the Lincoln Center locality, at 25 Central Park West. Today the company, now known as the Leonard Bernstein Office, is housed on West Twenty-seventh Street. At the height of its existence, Amberson was a whirlwind of full-time employees, part-timers and other revolving door types whose connections with the company I never could quite decipher, although I am sure their meter was always running. The personnel over the years could consist of video managers, marketing and artistic consultants, directors of business affairs, accountants and bookkeepers, lawyers, designers, press relations and promotion/publicity liaisons, agents, archivists, foreign coordinators, advisors, assistants, receptionists, and errand boys. Assorted others, to be sure;

and to list them all by name would use up a tree trunk. Four of them have been on staff for at least twenty-five years; others were let go rather quickly—a few under some rather dramatic circumstances.

My Successors

The more complicated the machinery became, the more LB felt trapped, caught in a vise from which he could not extricate himself. "Turka" (Kraut anagrammed) was LB's occasional nickname for Harry. At times of tension, he would taunt Harry as the "muffin man," from the children's rhyme—and much resented by HJK. Inevitable frustrations set in as can be discerned from a riff on a Mother Goose rhyme LB jotted down on the back flyleaf of his score to Mozart's Symphony, No. 35, the "Haffner" (housed at the NYP Archive):

> Ding dong bell, pussy's in the well,
> Who the fuckin' Mudder put her in?
> Little Mudder Fucker Tao-tse-pin.
> Who the fuck is gonna pull her out?
> Little mudder-fucker Harry Kraut.

So many people now depended on LB's ability to generate "product." We all tried to make it easier for him, obviously not always successful. By "we," I refer specifically to the gentlemen who replaced me, fellows who had to function well both with household and office staff. Harry would gather applicants for this position at a kind of cocktail party with LB. The gambit was to see who could best hold their liquor. Those who could manage well were deemed better candidates for the job.

The assistants who followed me included (not necessarily in order) were: Peter Clark, Greg Martindale, John Walker, Jonathan Brill, Paul DeHueck, Peter Lieberson, Daryl Bornstein, Richard Charlie Harmon (Charlito), Phillip Allen (Flip), Craig Richard Nelson (Crane) and, to flip the names, Richard Craig Urquhart (Cuqui). Some of the guys moved on to institutions like the Met Opera and the PBS network or they have become respected practitioners in artist management, a recording engineer, a Hollywood actor, and an orchestral librarian. No doubt their time with Bernstein helped them find such employment.

Lenny's kids. *Standing, left to right*: John Walker, Charlie Harmon, Daryl Bornstein and JG. *Seated*: Patty Pulliam and Jamie Bernstein. NYC, 20 July 2008.

There were still others who pitched in on one project or other.[10] But none of us were or are conductors, a whole other breed. Late in life LB referred to some of his conducting students as disciples, as if he were a Hassidic rebbe trailed by a troupe of acolytes. With all the laudations heaped upon him over the years, how could he not have been affected by it all? At the same time, he would gloss over it with self-imposed put-downs such as, "He was at the height of his decline" or "cut down in the prime of his old age." He relished being called the Maestro but didn't mind being referred to as the "Maest." Michael Barrett nicknamed him "the Mo." Lenny, in return, called him "Mino," minor maestro, and Barrett's wife, Leslie, was "Lezbo." (Or was this a reference to King Minos and the isle of Lesbos?) Both appellations are emblazoned on one of the dedications in *Arias and Barcarolles*, LB's last major work that, in turn, became "*As and Bs*." "A of A" was "The Age of Anxiety"; "TinT," *Trouble in Tahiti*; "JewGames," *Jubilee Games*, "Troon," the Norton lectures at Harvard, and so on.

"Crayfish" was Carlos Moseley, manager of the NYP; "Sky" was Schuyler Chapin, his manager; "Swoozy," Stephen Wadsworth Zinsser, his opera collaborator; Betty Comden was "Bedim"; "La Patita," Patty Pulliam, his devoted cook; "Humpy" was Humphrey Burton, his longtime concert film director and biographer; "BB," his brother; and "Spike," his yet unborn grandson who was born exactly one year to the day before LB's death!

Usually it was those he felt most relaxed with who received these sobriquets. A few others (very few) got bricks instead. The most prominent one was "Black Jerome" for Jerry Robbins, an identity not exclusive to LB. Arthur Laurents said that "there were only two things feared by Lenny, Jerry Robbins and God."

I was his "Jeckele," sometimes "Yankele," affectionate Yiddish diminutive labels. And as for my last name, I was tickled more than pink to come across his handwritten language constructs on an edition of the Köchel-Mozart catalog—rather nice company for my name to keep.

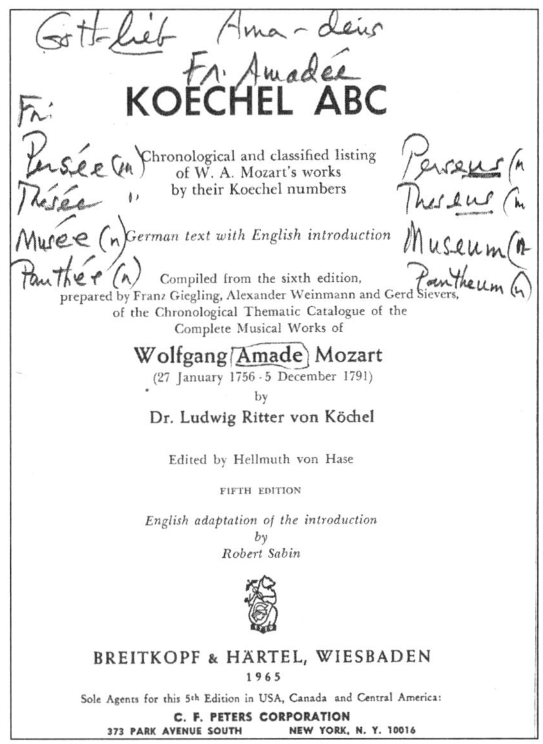

Gott-lieb Ama-deus

Fr. Amadée

Fr:

KOECHEL ABC

Pensée (n) Chronological and classified listing of W. A. Mozart's works by their Koechel numbers — Perseus (n

Thésée " — Theseus (n

Musée (n) German text with English introduction — Museum (n

Panthère (n) Compiled from the sixth edition, prepared by Franz Giegling, Alexander Weinmann and Gerd Sievers, of the Chronological Thematic Catalogue of the Complete Musical Works of — Pantheum (n)

Wolfgang Amade Mozart

(27 January 1756 - 5 December 1791)

by

Dr. Ludwig Ritter von Köchel

Edited by Hellmuth von Hase

FIFTH EDITION

English adaptation of the introduction

by

Robert Sabin

BREITKOPF & HÄRTEL, WIESBADEN

1965

Sole Agents for this 5th Edition in USA, Canada and Central America:

C. F. PETERS CORPORATION

373 PARK AVENUE SOUTH NEW YORK, N. Y. 10016

LB's conjugations.

Overheard

It was my job to wake the Maestro up and get him on time to whatever hall he was scheduled. Sometimes, especially for morning rehearsals, it could be a struggle, for LB could offer resistance with the best of them. The few times we were late—happily, never seriously so—one guess as to who got the blame. Various of my successors adopted different methods. Richard Nelson placed a warm damp washcloth on his forehead. Charlie Harmon, when they were in Vienna, ordered morning coffee that came with a bowl of whipped cream, and proceeded to dip Maestro's hand into the *Schlag*. Or Charlie would sit down at the piano and play something deliberately bad to rouse the man.[11] These tactics were especially pressing since Viennese concerts on Sundays began at 11 a.m. Craig Urquhart and Michael Barrett once had to drag him into a cold shower.

I never had to resort to such extreme measures, probably because he was younger and could get going more easily in those days. Once he was roused, it was my or his practice to turn on the radio to station WQXR, New York City's classical music radio station. Of course, most of the time he knew the pieces that were playing, but not always. On such exceptional occasions, we would play a guessing game. Here are three such occurrences.

Number one: Neither of us knew the work, but I picked a relatively obscure Russian composer, more as a gag than anything else, and asserted: "Oh, that's by Nikolai Medtner." The piece was over and Bingo! it was identified as Medtner's. LB turned to me, "How did you know that?" Secretly gloating at my supposed vast erudition, I calmly responded, "Well, of course I do, and I'm surprised that you, of all people, don't."

Number two: A modernist work was playing, and again, neither of us recognized it and could not even make a guess. Competition and composition over, we heard from the announcer: "You have just heard Elliott Carter's Concerto for Orchestra with the New York Philharmonic, conducted by Leonard Bernstein." Let that sink in and speak for itself. The work, inspired by Saint-John Perse verse, was premiered on 2 February 1970 and recorded a week later.

Number three was a more severe matter. In 1985 he heard a Scarlatti sonata, but the artist was not announced. He was frustrated, and wanted to know the name of the pianist, instructing me to find out. I called the station, and they said there was no such sonata playing at that hour, which I reported back. The Maestro was indignant: "Don't tell me that; I heard it, and I want to know who it is." More calls and more stonewalling. Finally, it was discovered that it had been played as a last-minute replacement for something else that had been scheduled, and not written down on the air-time log. The pianist was an unknown Polish artist, Marek Drewnowski.

When Drewnowski, in Rome at the time, got a phone call from Harry Kraut, and heard that LB was interested in him, the startled artist at first believed it to be a prank; but soon enough was convinced. He was asked to perform the Brahms Piano Concerto No. 1 at Tanglewood, a piece he had never played in public before, although he professed to know it. His performance was not exactly stellar, and I subsequently wondered why LB was so insistent that the BSO hire him. Could it have partly been due to our doubting his word when trying to find solve the mystery? There are two other minor errors connected to this affair. In an interview, Drewnowski claimed that Bernstein had heard him on a car radio, and John Rockwell, reviewing the concert in the *New York Times*, said the radio station was WNCN.

A curious corollary to all this: As related by Daryl Bornstein, one day in New York City, LB got into the passenger front seat of a car. The radio was playing a classical piece of music. The Maestro reached over and turned it off, saying, "There's too much music in the world."

Not That There's Anything Wrong with That

Two New York dowagers are walking past a Lincoln Center poster publicizing Leonard Bernstein. One says, "I hear that Bernstein is gay." The other, "Is there nothing that man cannot do?"

On 3 December 1976, the noted composer Benjamin Britten died. Britten was also well known for his lifelong partnership with tenor Peter Pears. That day, Bernstein led a concert with the NYP that featured the Shostakovich Symphony No. 14. The burden of the symphony (really a song cycle) was about death. That fact, coupled with Britten's demise, moved LB to address the audience, in part, with the following remarks:

> We seem to have been losing the giants of tonal composition with alarming rapidity in the last few decades. We lost Bartók and Hindemith in rapid succession, and that left the father of us all, Stravinsky, whom we lost five years ago and that left Aaron Copland who, though very much alive and kicking, has all but stopped composing for the last ten years. And that left us with two giants, Shostakovich, whose greatest masterpiece I believe we are about to hear tonight, and Benjamin Britten. And last year, we lost Shostakovich and this morning we lost Benjamin Britten. And that's that. There goes an era. It is the end, and we can count only on an inner surge of tonal vitality to bring music back to something like what it was in the days of those giants. There is a curious coincidence in this double death of Shostakovich and Britten, in that this fourteenth symphony that we are about to hear was dedicated to Britten and, in fact, it was Ben who gave the first performance of it, conducted it himself in Aldeburgh, in England, at his festival some years ago. And it meant a great deal to him, he

> considered it one of the great masterpieces of the twentieth century, and I agree with him . . .
>
> [Here he discussed the Shostakovich symphony with no more on Britten, until the very end.]
>
> . . . I would be personally very grateful if you would stand with me for a few seconds for Ben Britten.

Somewhere before that last sentence, LB supposedly tacked on comments that at the time were considered to be indefensible:

> Studying this work, I came to realize that as death approaches an artist must cast off everything that may be restraining him, and create in complete freedom. *I decided that I had to do this for myself, to live the rest of my life as I want.* [emphasis added]

It was an open secret that LB was a gay man, and if this foregoing statement was to be regarded as a public declaration of his sexuality, one would think it would have been a big news item. But only one periodical, *New York Magazine* (the same rag that had published the "Radical Chic" venom in 1970) quoted LB's putative resolution, and only some three weeks later, on 20 December,[12] Humphrey Burton reproduced the words in his biography as fact. But there is no written documentation of those words in LB's hand nor was the statement recorded. To complicate matters further, Schuyler Chapin stated that it was at a press conference when Bernstein declared, "There comes a time in life when a man must be what he really is."[13]

Everyone I know in the Bernstein circle believes there was a tacit, if not explicit, agreement between Felicia and her husband that as long as he kept his indiscretions to himself and never made them public or known to her, it was indeed his life to live as he saw fit. This meant that almost right from the start their relationship was not monogamous. (According to Ellen Adler, Aaron Copland, upon hearing that LB might get married, exclaimed to his cousin Harold Clurman: "No! He's not housebroken.") The understanding allowed for indiscretions, but not for the humiliation of exposure. Therefore, I find it difficult to believe that he would have so blatantly betrayed this accord in a public arena. It not only was foreign to his nature, it was also not in his best interest. But more to the point, commentators have not made mention of the most compelling argument for him not to go public: his mother was still alive. She must have heard enough gossip to arouse her misgivings, but LB's generation did not allow for such intimate disclosures to one's parents. Nevertheless, I take it on faith that he said something like this at a press conference or at a concert—with the caveat, I am convinced, that if Britten had not died that day, the ad-libbed conviction would not have spilled out of him.

The previous July, LB had embarked on a yearlong tryout of living with Tom Cothran, a younger man. In late October, the *New York Daily News* disclosed that the Bernsteins had separated; but there was no mention that this was due to a same-sex affair. It ultimately was a disaster for all concerned, especially for Felicia. I was not around in 1976; but I can attest to the fact that up until that time theirs had been a close, tender, and fun-loving marriage. Yes, it was complicated by their silent pact. Felicia once confided to me, "Why do we put up with him?" "Because," she answered her own question, "we love him." It was not a question of gay vs. straight or male/female. Rather, it was about two human beings who cared deeply for each other.

Felicia Bernstein at the West Redding, Connecticut, home in the 1950s.

Felicia could be delightfully loopy, but she relished playing the "first lady" role in a Pauline Trigère gown. The Bernsteins' sense of playfulness was irresistible. Evidence can be seen in home movies, one of them a parody of Puccini's *Tosca*. Felicia worked assiduously on miming the Maria Callas recording. She and Lenny burlesque the scene where Felicia, as Tosca, stabs Scarpia—Lenny in Groucho Marx makeup. After Tosca places a wooden saint on his chest and leaves the scene, this particular Scarpia reaches into his shirt and with a leer to the camera, replaces the cross with a Star of David. And then there's the movie where LB comes in on water skis as Pharaoh playing to Felicia as Pharaoh's wife.

Why would he betray the covenant he had made with his wife? Of course, Bernstein was far from being the only married man who has led such a double life, especially onerous in the era before the Stonewall rebellion in

The Bernsteins at the opening of the *West Side Story* movie, Rivoli Theater, New York City, 1961.

1969. However, by 1976, the gay rights movement was in full swing, and the big push to "come out" was pervasively in the air. (The scourge of AIDS was yet to emerge.) LB was a huge public figure and he enjoyed that status; but just as Felicia had endured varying degrees of mortification through their previous twenty-four years together, so—I am conjecturing—he had been building up a pressure cooker of "guilt-burgers" (a Lenny neologism) that ultimately broke open. I offer this not as a refutation or excuse, but only as an explanation of his behavior and of its timing. As he had done before and would again, he could have thrown caution to the winds by going public. More than once he got away with behavior that would have been unthinkable for others. The conspicuous outbursts—some delivered under the emboldening influence of drink—have been well documented:

- His toast at daughter Jamie's wedding, proclaiming her new husband's attributes, he ended by saying, "and he's straight!"
- The launching of the new *Grove's Dictionary*, at which British prime minister Harold Macmillan was present, when LB went off on a tangent scolding the audience and the *New York Times* for not having paid attention, two days prior, to the seventeenth anniversary of JFK's death in Dallas.
- The postpremiere banquet for *A Quiet Place*, where he dubbed the city of Houston a "cowtown."
- The Black Panther fund-raiser that he was not expected to attend, but did anyhow, and where he made condescending observations that were subsequently turned against him and Felicia.

In May 1981, Mayor Teddy Kollek delivered some remarks at the conclusion of a live television broadcast celebrating the liberation of

Jerusalem, after which Lenny planted, without warning, a kiss on the lips of the startled mayor, proclaiming to all the viewers that it was "a giant step for gay liberation." On several occasions I saw him exercise a kind of droit du seigneur authority in his attempts to seduce younger men, who managed to resist him. He did exude sexual vibes, and was attractive to both men and women—although at times he must have faced the dilemma of many famous people, namely, how much is the attraction toward the person *sui generis* and how much toward the person as celebrity? He told Tom Steele, a musician friend who also was a publisher of the New York City gay newspaper *The Native*, that Tom was the only one in LB's circle who did not expect any favors from him. And, yes, LB did have numerous affairs, more with males than females. (In the late 1950s, he was observed weeping at a wedding where both bride and groom had, separately, been lovers of his. We will never know if his tears were due to relief or regret.) There is no need to be more specific than this. But we should ask why is this tendency to dwell on an artist's sex life of interest? Does it reflect in their works?[14]

In LB's case, I would say it was consistent with his all-embracing eclecticism. Stephen Sondheim observed that for LB, "The idea of family was deeply rooted . . . It had nothing to do with pretending to be heterosexual . . ."[15] As one who had lived through the Holocaust era, Bernstein, the father of three children, was attached to the belief in Jewish continuity, just as Bernstein, the musician, was tireless in his efforts to win the respect and love of the Vienna Philharmonic Orchestra members who were conditioned by Nazi ideology.

A theory also has been floated about that he married to get ahead in the straitlaced world of orchestral conducting. But Dimitri Mitropoulos, a single gay conductor, managed very well. Another myth has it that LB outed Mitropoulos to be able to take over as music director of the NYP. Both of these are vindictive expressions of fertile fantasies.

Setting the Record "Straight"

Most readers will probably recognize "Not that there's anything wrong with that" as a quote from a *Seinfeld* episode. Apparently some authors do believe there is, indeed, something wrong with being homosexual. Of all the Bernstein biographies, Humphrey Burton's is the most thorough and dispassionate, with sharp insights into Bernstein's loves and family life. Unlike the muckraking job of Joan Peyser in 1987, Burton addresses Bernstein's sexuality without being sensationalist. However, even he sometimes uses an infelicitous phrasing. For example, he says that LB had, with the aforementioned resolution made at the concert, "come out in a flamboyant way." The choice of the word *flamboyant* with all its gay stereotypical connotations shows insensitivity, as does the following statement from this Brit's distinct point of view: "With Tom Cothran at his side he moved on to Paris, where he could fantasize about being Oscar Wilde to Cothran's Lord Alfred Douglas."[16]

Book reviewer Christopher Lehmann-Haupt applied the following censure to Peyser's notorious LB biography: "In recent decades we have been inundated with a '. . . proliferation of pathographies, those lurid voyeuristic works that relentlessly focus on the subject's foibles and failings.'"[17]

Among Peyser's many swipes at LB is that he has "never been kind to women"; that "always hungry to experience everything, [he] must have felt envy at his wife's having gone through childbirth." Good God! Another choice morsel from the Peyser stewpot, is this one about Felicia: "The only . . . piece [LB] dedicated to Felicia . . . was one of *Four Anniversaries.*"[18] But if Peyser had bothered to look at the piano-vocal score of a little item called *West Side Story*, she might have noticed the following dedication to LB's wife: "To Felicia, with love."

One late night LB told me of certain dicey incidents in his past with an outlook that I might become his memoirist. I informed him that the items were in the Peyser book. He had not read it and was deflated. Perhaps if I had said nothing, we would have continued. Peyser wined and dined me in an attempt to wheedle out gossip; I withstood her blandishments. But because of the Peyser exposé, when Meryle Secrest was writing her LB biography, we were instructed not to talk to Secrest. I doubt it would have done much good if we had been interviewed as one of the questionable secrets Secrest reveals is, "In years to come Bernstein would actively proselytize for the advantages of homosexuality,"[19] a maxim that might have come straight out of the gay basher playbook.

Or take the John Gruen memoir *Callas Kissed Me . . . Lenny Too!* Aside from the title's confusing syntax (did Callas kiss Lenny?), Gruen indulges in inexcusable exaggeration. Regarding LB's sex life, he says that Peyser's book revealed "every last gay encounter and relationship." Really? Including the one with Gruen? About personal matters, he claims, "It was agreed I would be discreet."[20] Hah! Gruen based his book on his previous volume, *The Private World of Leonard Bernstein,* and gave a set of the taped interviews to LB with the proviso that they would not be used without Gruen's permission. Nevertheless, it was acceptable for him to exploit the tape contents only as he saw fit, and to aver that Felicia was also smitten by him. Anything but!

This is only the tip of the innuendo iceberg. Overlooked in all of this and other breathless copy is Bernstein's pioneering efforts in the fight against AIDS:

- The Gay Men's Health Crisis benefit in 1983 in Madison Square Garden for a performance of the Ringling Bros. Circus, with LB conducting the circus orchestra.
- The American Foundation for AIDS Research dinner at the Public Theater in 1986 at which Bernadette Peters brought everyone to tears singing "My Buddy," and where all the performers sang "Somewhere" with LB at the piano.
- The Music for Life concert at Carnegie Hall in 1987, a benefit for that raised $1.7 million, at which LB and James Levine played the Andante from Mozart's two-piano Sonata in D Major.
- "Serenade: A Musical Tribute to Mathilde Krim" at Carnegie Hall in 1988, raising the first million dollars for amfAR's community-based clinical trials program, which went on to create a nationwide network of HIV/AIDS clinical research centers—"thanks," in the words Dr. Krim, "to the man who helped get it all started, Leonard Bernstein."

After a Central Park concert with the NYP, when Patty Pulliam introduced LB to her mother, Carolyn, LB embraced Mrs. Pulliam with: "Thank God, you didn't abort her!" This extraordinary utterance has to be viewed in context. Earlier that day a young protégé told LB that he had just gotten news that he was HIV positive, and his mother's response was, "I should have aborted you when I found I was pregnant." What a godforsaken woman.

On 12 July 1997, I wrote the following letter to the editor of the *New York Times*:

> Your July 11 news article on the poet Adrienne Rich's rejection of the 1997 National Medal of Arts reports that Alexander Crary, chief of

staff of the National Endowment for the Arts, said that he knew of no other artist who had declined the award.

In 1989 Leonard Bernstein refused the National Medal of Arts from President Bush. A grant from the N.E.A. to Artists Space, a nonprofit gallery in New York City, had been revoked because of its AIDS exhibition.

This was unacceptable to Bernstein, who wrote a song, "The N.E.A. Forever March," in observance of the happening. Its lyric began:

Everyone got a medal but Bernstein, . . .

(For the complete text, see my discussion of *Dance Suite.*)

2 On the Road

Travel Adventures

In the Car

When Bernstein heard that conductor Zubin Mehta had been given a vanity license plate of MAESTRO, LB requested the same from New York State. The best they could come up with was a plate that read MAESTRO I. This was affixed to his Mercedes convertible; but the 1 had been placed so close to the MAESTRO—by convicts?—that it looked like MAESTRO I, for which some onlookers read as OY, and found it hilarious. There were times, nonetheless, when such an accolade seemed to give him too much license.

Bernstein was a notoriously careless—at times even reckless—driver. Born under a lucky star, he acted behind the wheel as if he were invincible. As Michael Barrett relates, a passenger calls out, "Lenny, pick a lane, any lane!" Maestro wonders, "Why is that cop following me? I set the cruise control at eighty-five!" LB would discourse and get so carried away by the sound of his voice that, according to his children, he once found himself going into oncoming traffic. Ann Dedman recalls he once scraped a tollbooth and, Harry Kraut, that he did not realize he had come to a complete standstill in the middle of Route 7 traffic.

Notwithstanding: we were in downtown Manhattan. I was in the backseat of a car driven by composer Lukas Foss, with LB seated beside him. Caught in one of those confusing Greenwich Village grids, Foss accidentally went the wrong way down a one-way street. A cop pulled the car over and started to read Foss the riot act, when LB reached across and said something to the effect that Lukas was a foreigner not yet familiar with the city's traffic patterns. The cop reacted, "Oh, it's you, Mr. Bernstein. Well, make sure that this doesn't happen again." He tipped his hat and was gone.

Quite the opposite happened with another cop. A slow-moving line of cars was wending its way to a NYP tour concert in Red Rocks, Colorado, LB's limo among them. As the limo came into the stage door area, it was stopped by a trooper who insisted on a twenty-five-cent parking fee. "But I have the Maestro with me," said the driver. "Eh, eh," replied the unswayed guardian of the law, "you still have to pay the two bits." Those who were in the car with LB broke down into such gales of laughter—almost wetting their pants—that the "*Candide* Overture," which opened the concert, must have shot off like a rocket.[1]

On 19 April 1961, with Helen Coates as his passenger, LB drove from Richmond, Virginia, to Raleigh, South Carolina, as part of that spring's NYP eventual tour to Japan. He got caught speeding. It turned into a Southern cracker kind of travesty. A bond had to be posted to release them. One can only wonder what Miss Coates was feeling. Was *La Belle Dame sans merci*?

Then there was the evening when LB's car ground to a halt, stuck in the same traffic as concert-goers on their way to one of his programs. A patron of the arts in another lane recognized him and yelled out, "Well, now at least we won't be late for the start!"

During the writing of the 1965 musical *Do I Hear a Waltz?* lyricist Stephen Sondheim was subject to the dismissiveness of composer Richard Rodgers. Steve and I were passengers in a car, with LB at the wheel, as we drove past the Fairfield, Connecticut, home of Rodgers. Unforgettable to me was the spectacle of Steve giving the finger to that house along with a Bronx cheer, short of mooning himself to express his scorn for Rodgers.

Usually in New York City, LB used the Dav-El limousine service. As reported by Charlie Harmon, he once attended an event by himself (most unusual) at the Union Club in Manhattan's East Sixties. It was wintertime, snowing, and the Dav-El driver had the motor running to keep warm. It was LB's penchant to arrive late at events and leave them late. By the time he was ready to go home, the car had run out of gas! The streets were deserted and Bernstein had no other choice but to hitchhike, very hard to imagine. Few cars were on the road, but one finally pulled over. A couple inside was hunting for a hotel, and LB told them he would put them up for the night at the Alcott, near his building on West Seventy-second Street, in return for a ride. This worked out fine until some days later—not just after that one night—the couple called him up to say that they were checking out and expected him to pay the full bill.

The Great Buick Takeover

It is Friday, 11 February 1983, and we are getting ready to go back to the Big Apple from the country home in Connecticut. The radio has been broadcasting dire warnings of an impending snowstorm, but the Boss keeps on dawdling, even though he knows he has an important meeting at the Dakota at 6:00 p.m. Finally, at 2:00 p.m., we pile into the station wagon—we consisting of me at the wheel, LB in the front seat, and Julia Vega in the backseat with Tookie, the poodle, and two caged parakeets.

As we get onto the Merritt Parkway, the snow begins to fall. Gentle and pretty at first, it becomes so heavy that we have to come to a complete stop just beyond the intersection with the Cross Westchester Expressway (CWE). LB has been his usual extroversive self, blasting music on the tape deck, puffing cigarette smoke in my face. But as he becomes more and more irritable—even going so far as to call me a "neurotic creep"—a car in front of us suddenly veers to the left and crosses over the grass median, defying all lawful protocol, and heads in the other direction to get onto the CWE. "Look at that," say I, "can you believe anyone would have the nerve?" LB, responds in a deep grumble: "I would." How else am I to interpret the grunt other than to follow the same path? Julia and the animals are mute. So I take the dare and cross over the median. Now we are behind a slow line of cars on the CWE entrance ramp; but when we make it onto the main drag, we find it is just as bad up there. What to do? I decide to take the first exit on the right, and we go north, creeping along in the same direction from which we had just come, this time on an ancillary country road. More snow. Some twenty minutes later, we are back on the Merritt Parkway, gingerly

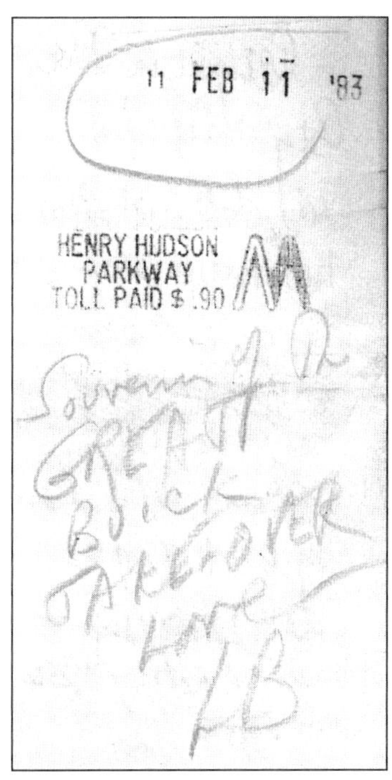

Toll receipt signed by LB, 1983.

proceeding south again, arriving at the same spot where I had first turned off, and then a slow crawl beyond. Now it has become a blizzard. (Shades of the Kennedy inaugural twenty years earlier.) Finally, we get to the Cross County Expressway with little visibility ahead. Julia, by this time, is surely praying. Blinded by the elements, I can move no further, at which point LB says, "Get out, I'm taking over." I am furious and anxious, not exactly in a friendly mood myself. But then the Maestro swerves into a snowbank, and it is all I can do to stifle laughter. Somehow, he manages to spin the wheels out of the slush, and we barely make it back to the Dakota in time for his meeting. A trip that normally takes an hour to an hour and a half took four hours.

I had the toll receipt, which I instructed him to autograph. Julia made a vow not to drive with him again if she could help it.

LB on motorcycle, at the airport in Lima, Peru, 1958.

Other Modes of Travel

He also could indulge in daredevil pursuits. Not generally known was his skill in snow and waterskiing, tennis and horseback riding. Because I joined the employ of LB and the NYP—a

LB in airplane cockpit somewhere over the Andes on the New York Philharmonic tour in May 1958.

joint arrangement—in September 1958, I was not on the South American tour in the spring of that year. In Lima, Peru, he was asked to pose for a picture outside an airport while sitting on a motorcycle. "I don't ride a motorcycle. It would be phony." But the photographer persuaded him to try it after someone showed him the basics. To the complete disbelief of his colleagues, LB jumped on, drove off at top speed across the airfield, slowed down briefly to

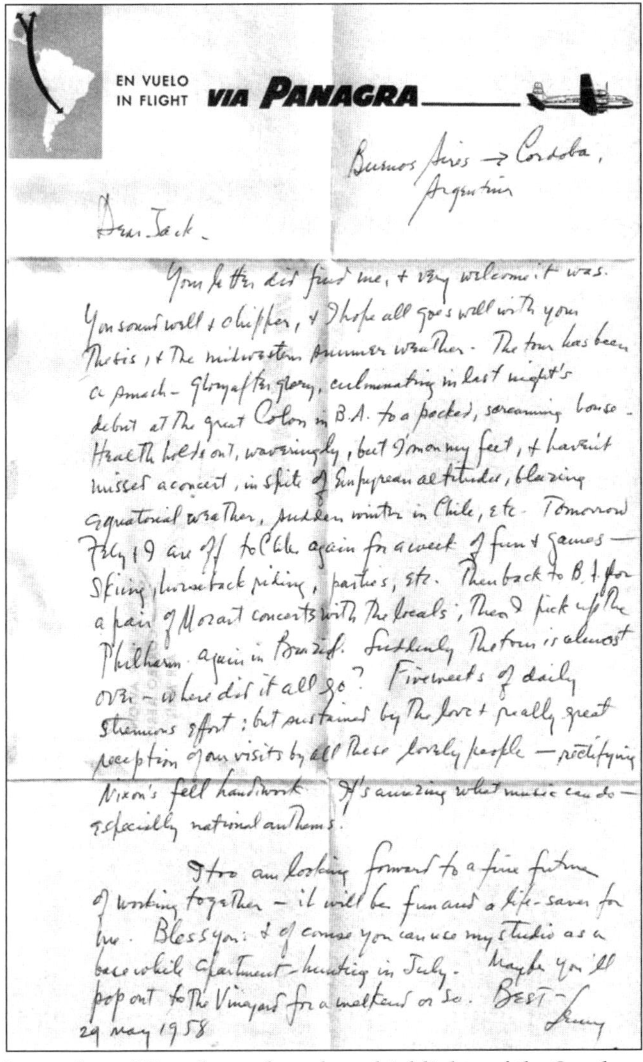

EN VUELO
IN FLIGHT **VIA PANAGRA**

Buenos Aires → Cordoba,
Argentina

Dear Jack –

Your letter did find me, + very welcome it was. You sound well + chipper, + I hope all goes well with your thesis, + the midwestern summer weather. The tour has been a smash – glory after glory, culminating in last night's debut at the great Colon in B.A. to a packed, screaming house. Health holds out, waveringly, but I'm on my feet, + haven't missed a concert, in spite of Empyrean altitudes, blazing equatorial weather, sudden winter in Chile, etc. Tomorrow Felicia + I are off to Chile again for a week of fun + games – skiing, horseback riding, parties, etc. Then back to B.A. for a pair of Mozart concerts with the locals; then I pick up the Philharm. again in Brazil. Suddenly the tour is almost over – where did it all go? Five weeks of daily strenuous effort; but sustained by the love + really great reception of our visits by all these lovely people – rectifying Nixon's fell handiwork. It's amazing what music can do – especially national anthems.

I too am looking forward to a fine future of working together – it will be fun and a life-saver for me. Bless you: + of course you can use my studio as a base while apartment-hunting in July. Maybe you'll pop out to the Vineyard for a weekend or so. Best –

Lenny

29 May 1958

Letter from LB to the author about highlights of the South American NYP tour.

demonstrate a few tricky maneuvers, and came to a stop. "Now," he declared, "you can take the picture."[2]

But that was not his only audacious venture on that trip. Somewhere over the Andes the pilot made the announcement, "Ladies and gentlemen of the orchestra, this is to inform you that Maestro Bernstein is at the controls flying the plane." A hush fell upon the cabin captives, knuckles clenched, some faces turning whiter than white.

Bette Davis Sat on My Lap

On Sunday, 22 January 1961, I wrote down the bulk of this crackling tale while it was still fresh in my mind. Over the years, the retelling of it became my occasional party piece, and although I never added any embellishments, there were gaps that I have now been able to flesh out thanks to the magical power of the Internet. Almost all the cast of characters who are mentioned are gone now, but that does not diminish their ongoing presence in the American collective consciousness nor does it lessen the vividness of the events.

The adventure and misadventures begin a week ago Sunday, on the fifteenth, when LB & Co. undertake the taping of a TV show on musical romanticism, a script in which he perplexingly says, "The romantics give us back our moon, which science has taken away from us and made into just another airport" (mystifying because this was 1961 and Neil Armstrong did not land on the moon until 1969). A ninety-minute special, "Ford Presents Leonard Bernstein and the New York Philharmonic," it is riddled with format and rehearsal problems, and takes over nineteen hours to complete, well into the next day. What with the traditional drink with crew and staff in the Irish bar across the street from the studio—at First Avenue and Seventy-third Street—I am not in bed until 4:00 a.m. Four or five hours later, L. informs me that I am to go with him to Washington that afternoon to help out in the JFK inaugural gala, for which he has written a fanfare that he is to conduct along with other pieces. So much for advance notice.

Misadventure No. 1 occurs when by chance, going out to the airport in a hired limo, we happen to travel down Central Park South, instead of through the park. Stuck in traffic—a harbinger of things to come—there is a knock on the car window: "Mr. Bernstein, I have your plane tickets here!" The man had just missed us at the Osborne—the nearby family residence on West Fifty-seventh Street and Seventh Avenue—and, again by chance, he has recognized LB in the car.

Misadventure No. 2: We get to the airport to find that we have the wrong flight number. No big deal; it gets straightened out. On the plane headed for the same destination are—and here begins the name dropping—William J. Vanden Heuvel, a notable figure in Democratic party circles; Richard (Ricky) Leacock, one of the filmmakers of *Primary*, the cinéma vérité documentary on Kennedy's 1960 campaign in Wisconsin, and also the director of the New York Philharmonic 1959 TV show in the USSR; and actor Fredric March with his actress-wife, Florence Eldridge, both magnificent in the previous year's movie version of *Inherit the Wind*, the play about the infamous Scopes monkey trial of 1925.

Misadventure the third concerns the hotel; but, as it turns out, this one is a most fortunate snafu. Landing in Washington, we're told we are booked at the Alban Towers, not the Woodner, as previously informed. (I must have notified Felicia of the change. Alban Towers, a hotel-apartment building located on Embassy Row, Massachusetts Avenue NW, was the campaign headquarters for the supporters of JFK.) We arrive at the hotel where I experience the ever-lasting frisson of meeting another hotel guest, the one and only Bette Davis. (Lenny had met her in Hollywood in 1945, and idolized her.) As one of the participants in the forthcoming celebration, she is here with her daughter Barbara (a.k.a. B.D., later notorious for writing a memoir that trashed her mother). Improbably, Mother Davis is located directly across from my room. I am properly awestruck; a star—or is it a meteor?—has descended to my terrestrial level.

That night Lenny and I go to the National Theater to see the Washington tryout of *Midgie Purvis*, a Mary Chase comedy, which proved to be the last Broadway appearance of Tallulah Bankhead. (It lasted only a month at the Martin Beck in New York City, the theater where *Candide* also had about the same short run, first time around.) Tedious fluff. After the performance, I am introduced to Robert Whitehead, who, with Roger Stevens, had produced *West Side Story*, Whitehead's wife, Virginia, and the great actor Burgess Meredith, the play's director. Then—trumpets, please—Miss Bankhead, in person! (In his early days at Tanglewood, it was rumored that L. had had more than a dalliance with her after she "had admired his back muscles" at a concert.)

Well, such carryings on, dahling! A real Lulu that Tallu, and as expected from a dame famous for not being a teetotaler, drinks abound in her dressing room. She pours it on and overflows—with Joycean chitchat, that is. But "no never mind"; to have met both Davis and Bankhead in one night is more than enough intoxication for the likes of me. Imagine meeting the two vixens of Lillian Hellman's *The Little Foxes* within hours of each other, and each in her unique way a superb and bitchy Regina Giddens, Bankhead on stage and Davis on screen. (Since Hellman was LB's collaborator on *Candide*, there are not even two degrees of separation.)

The next day, 18 January—the day before the inauguration, is the rehearsal for the gala bash, to take place that night. We drive to the Washington National Guard Armory in Davis's car, with, of course, the great lady, her daughter, LB and me. Upon arrival, I find myself hurtled into the vortex of Messrs. Frank Sinatra and Peter Lawford—who have put together this enormous shindig to help pay off the Democratic National Committee's campaign debt—Gene Kelly (who with Sinatra was one of the sailors in the movie adaptation of LB's musical *On the Town)*, Joey Bishop (born Gottlieb), Tony Curtis and Janet Leigh. In addition to Miss Davis and Mr. March, there are such other distinguished heavyweights as Sir Laurence Olivier, Sidney Poitier and Anthony Quinn. The singers run the gamut from the team of Louis Prima and Keely Smith to Harry Belafonte, from Nat King Cole and Ella Fitzgerald to Ethel Merman and Helen Traubel (there's a pair of warblers for you!). Comic legends are also on the roster: Jimmy Durante, Milton Berle and Alan King, along with other leading lights of American popular culture.

The delectable Kay Thompson (singer, actress, composer and author) is assisting producer Roger Edens in the preparations. (Edens was the journeyman MGM staff musician who had written new songs for the movie of *On the Town.*) It is an amazing array of luminaries among whom Lenny quite holds his own, for by now he had become a shining TV presence. He draws a lot of attention in terms of reaction from one celebrity to another, many of them who probably already knew each other. Or was it because he was perceived as being more of a highbrow? So many cross-currents are stirring. I notice that Johnny Carson, renowned host of NBC's *Tonight Show*, seems to be too shy to come over and introduce himself; and when I point this out to Lenny, suggesting that he go say hello, he reacts disdainfully, as if such a move would be beneath his dignity.

The rehearsal consists of long stretches of waiting around. Confusion prevails. Even at this stratospheric level of artistic accomplishment, the ass knoweth not the elbow. "Should we paint the stools white?" is one of the burning issues. Miss Davis puffs away at her inevitable cigarette, but LB is a close second in that regard. (Olivier is seen in the middle.)

Bette Davis, Laurence Olivier and LB, at rehearsal for JFK Inaugural Gala, 19 January 1961.

Finally, at 5:00 p.m. we leave to return—or so it was intended—to the hotel to change into fancy duds for the gala. On the way back, we are to drop off Carmen Matthews, the noted television actress. But we never make it. Now comes the heart of the tale. The town is in the midst of one of its biggest snow snarls ever. How would the celebs have known? They were indoors all day and no one had bothered to tell them. Washington is famous for shutting down government even at the hint of snow, and this storm eventually became at least a six-incher. At seven thirty or thereabouts, we are still quite a few long blocks from the Alban Towers, stuck in Dupont Circle. LB is getting very fidgety about his wife, who is driving down from New York City with their friends Adolph Green and Michael (Mendy) Wager and Arthur Judson, the head of Columbia Artists. Are they stranded somewhere on a highway? (Remember, cell phones have yet to be invented.)

Both he and Miss Davis (especially) are groaning aloud, "I have to pee!" She repeats it enough times for me for to spring into action. Isn't that what assistants are supposed to do? I leave the jammed-in car and knock randomly on a nearby door, which turns out to be the entrance to a private club—it could have been the Sulgrave or the Cosmos. I explain the situation, drop the names of the needy ones, and at last they scurry in to relieve themselves.

What to do next? While they wait at the club, I decide to trudge through the snow to State House, an apartment building in the vicinity where Miss Matthews is staying. I go up to the eighth floor, knock on the appointed door and get no reply. Her host is probably also caught in a traffic mess. In desperation, I knock on the apartment next door. Again, no answer. Utterly despondent, I go back toward the elevator when I hear that second door open. I yell out, "Anyone there?"

A middle-aged lady listens to my tale of woe, me looking like a madman, breathless and unkempt. After hearing the sorry narrative—mind you, the gala is scheduled to start at eight forty-five—she calmly replies, "You need a police escort," and picks up a phone to say, "This is Congresswoman Marguerite Church," and makes the arrangements. My jaw drops. Yes, the city is the national seat of administration, and its officials need to live somewhere, but this had to be greater than mere happenstance, more like a miracle.

LB, Davis, B.D. and Matthews having abandoned the club and car—whatever happened to the driver?—and slogged through the slush, have arrived, making a melodramatic entrance. I had called the hotel to inquire about Felicia and her passengers. Phone lines are down or busy, but I manage to get through. Felicia had left a message saying they were thirty miles outside of town. LB is immensely relieved, wiping away a tear. Carmen Matthews reaches Lawford at the Armory to relay the circumstances, but is suddenly cut off. Disarray reigns supreme again. Congresswoman Church makes some tea and hot chocolate. Another couple, also guests of Matthews' host show up, and both apartments become an open thoroughfare.

Finally, the police car arrives with two burly cops. Shoes are quickly put on, and we all pile in, the seven of us somehow squeezed together, sitting on laps—Miss Davis on mine—heads scrunched under the low roof. With one cop directing, we proceed to hop over curbs onto the sidewalks of Washington, around stalled cars, onto trolley tracks, weaving in and of storefronts. It's a scene out of a movie, but more a roller-coaster ride than a police chase. Thrilling and unforgettable. We reach the armory; the officers deposit us; I get their names and that of their unit.

For a while, during this precious time, I consider myself to be a chum of Bette—after all, as my lap sitter, we are now on a first-name basis. She, however, is a glum chum since she is going to be forced to appear in front of the president-elect in her day clothes (a blue jacket and skirt). No exit, no way to change into a glitzy gown at her Hollywood best. She is seething. At some point she turns to me to complain about LB: "He treats me like a Warner Brothers extra!"

The gala has been delayed for the sake of the tardy ones. (In an interview Bernstein later gave to the John F. Kennedy Library, he said we had arrived "unwashed, unchanged, un-blacktied, and everybody was in a kind of special blizzard festive mood . . . which made the occasion more exciting actually than even it might have been. It was amazing that everybody got there at all.") Harry Belafonte provides Lenny with a dress shirt, two sizes too big, and I supply the Maestro my cufflinks. Handsome Harry ties rubber bands into my cuffs, and subsequently inscribes his photo in the program book with the instruction, "Keep stretching, Jack." (A day or so later, gossip columnist Dorothy Kilgallen reports that she had offered Davis her dress or brocaded coat, which was politely refused.)

We manage to trundle LB over to the opposite side of the Armory where the musicians are, while on the loudspeaker it is announced that Nelson Riddle, not the composer, will conduct LB's new *Fanfare for JFK*, even though L. has by now managed to sneak onto the platform. He takes over for Riddle in the middle of the piece. Fanfare over, there is a pregnant pause while thousands wait. Was that a Bernstein or a Riddle? After a feeble, unmiked announcement, LB conducts "The Stars and Stripes Forever." It's beginning to look like a comic routine.

Nevertheless, the rest of the evening goes remarkably well. The stars make a grand march entrance to the jaunty tune of "Walkin' Down to Washington," the official 1960 Democratic Party song written by Dick Sanford and Sammy Mysels. They jubilantly wave banners and balloons. L. leads "Anchors Aweigh" for the presidential party entrance. (Keep in mind that "Hail to the Chief" is not yet operative.) Mahalia Jackson shakily sings "The Star-Spangled Banner." Sinatra, the emcee for this shindig, introduces Miss Davis who, along with March, Poitier, Olivier and Quinn, deliver a text by written by Norman Corwin called "Club Sandwich in Four Parts." Among other presentations in act 1, Traubel sings "A Mighty Fortress Is Our God" juxtaposed to Sinatra's rendition of another kind of fortress, "The House I Live In."

Act 2 opens with the new fanfare again; then LB conducts the "Hallelujah" Chorus (did I mention the chorus?); and then, for some inexplicable reason, he is the one who introduces Ethel Merman, which he does with her advance apologies for not having been able to make a costume change. (Throughout the evening, the Republicans of course are blamed for the weather.) LB does not, however, introduce Milton Rosenstock, veteran Broadway conductor, who leads the band for Merman's "Everything's Coming Up Roses." It is a safe bet that Rosenstock is there at Merman's insistence.

Other performers follow; and right before JFK speaks at the end of the program, Eleanor Roosevelt, Mr. March and Miss Traubel take part in a segment called "A Moment with Lincoln." During intermission, the band had played a favorite piece of Lincoln's called "The Silver Bell Waltz." (This many decades later, one wonders if such references to a Republican past might have been premonitions of the by now well-known eerie coincidences yet to occur between the two leaders: Lincoln elected in 1860, Kennedy in 1960; Lincoln's secretary a Kennedy and Kennedy's a Lincoln; both assassinated and both succeeded by VPs named Johnson.)

Mrs. Kennedy, in a stunning Oleg Cassini gown, leaves at 12:30 a.m., but her husband sticks it out. (It was said that she was still recovering from the birth of John Jr. Years later she autographed the evening's program booklet for me when she was an editor at Macmillan Publishers.) The gala finishes about 1:30 a.m.; and afterward, we go to a private party given by Ambassador Joseph Kennedy (at the Jefferson Hotel?), and this Jack gets to shake the hand of Big Smiling Jack himself! Bedazzled am I. He is taller than expected, and greets me with a warm, "Hello." The scene feels unreal because it all seems so easy. Just simple folk out for a good time, right? Where's the Secret Service? Had I been cleared by the FBI?

The entire Kennedy clan is there (minus Jackie) along with much of the Hollywood contingent. The president-elect is dancing nonchalantly ten hours or so before his rendezvous with "Ask not what you can do for you country." LB startles me when he cuts in on Kennedy's dancing with Afdera Fonda. [The fourth wife of actor Henry Fonda, 1957–61, she was alleged to have had an affair with Kennedy during the very first week he was in the White House. If true, could that consideration have contributed to Jackie's early departure?] Kennedy walks away with a shrug. Later I ask LB how he had the balls to exhibit such lack of etiquette, if not respect. He replied that he could then say ever after he had cut in on a president of the United States. (Technically only eight hours away from the Oval Office, but who's counting?)

(In his interview, LB put a different spin on it: "I made the inexcusable blunder of cutting in on him as he was dancing with a friend of mine . . . and since people were cutting in all over the floor, I thought nothing of doing otherwise, except that I had forgotten I was cutting in on the president [*sic*]. He did look pale for a moment . . . the girl was furious." One cannot help but recall that at another gala affair—this one at the opening concert of the then named Philharmonic Hall at Lincoln Center—during the intermission, LB had famously planted a sweaty kiss on Mrs. Kennedy's visage, seen on national TV and widely censured as impolitic.)

Lenny's pals, Adolph Green and Mendy Wager, suddenly appear. Depleted after their thirteen-hour drive down from New York City with Felicia at the wheel, they had found a telegram waiting at the hotel from Ambassador and Mrs. Joseph Kennedy inviting them (obviously at LB's instigation) to the party. Felicia begged off out of sheer exhaustion and went to bed; but Adolph and Mendy were not to be denied. (Where did Arthur Judson end up?) On top of their harrowing trip, they found that the only way to get to the party was to tramp by foot a considerable distance through the sloppy mess outside. The telegram is their open sesame to the guards at the door. Lenny introduces them to the prez-elect, who graciously sympathizes with what they have gone through. Miss Davis is also worn out and leaves. The rest of us return to the hotel at about 5:30 a.m. (LB always was a night owl, and I am not.)

The day of the nineteenth, we skip going to the actual inauguration ceremony, and watch the proceedings on television along with the rest of the country, feeling especially empathetic for poet Robert Frost's fumblings in the cold outdoors. (LB's guest tickets to the swearing-in were given to Adolph and Mendy.) In the afternoon, I manage to slip away and go out to Silver Spring, Maryland, for a quick visit with my sister Irene and her family.

At the Statler Hilton, where one of the formal balls takes place that night, the freshly minted president and first lady brush right past me. Another wow moment; but the ball otherwise strikes me as being rather like an overblown high school prom. Lenny and Felicia are invited to go to Sinatra's postball party, but cannot accept as we must drive that night to Philadelphia for a Pension Fund benefit concert he is to conduct on Saturday night with the Philadelphia Orchestra. We arrive in Philly at 5:30 a.m. Friday morning, making it two all-nighters in a row. It is one of the rare times I have an opportunity for an extended chat with Felicia.

One further mishap awaits us. For the 104th anniversary at the Academy of Music, William Smith conducts the first half of the program in Poulenc's Organ Concerto and selections from Verdi's *Otello*. LB takes over the all-American second half with his *Candide* Overture, Gershwin's *An American in Paris*, Copland's *Lincoln Portrait*, and, with the Singing City Choir, "The Battle Hymn of the Republic." The latter two works are performed in observance of the centennial of the Civil War, an anniversary that had been formally declared by President Eisenhower. But the ghost of Lincoln still haunts us. During Efrem Zimbalist Jr.'s narration of *Lincoln Portrait*, a bank of overhead cameras falls down inches away from the first row of the audience, narrowly missing the people. Since the narration could not be heard, the piece has to be repeated from the start.

For me, the bloom has come off the rose; but the postconcert ball at the Bellevue-Stratford Hotel is a pleasant surprise. We ride back to New York on Sunday in time to view the show on romanticism at the Osborne apartment, which by now feels like it was done ages ago.

Bette Davis autographed photo, 1962.

Postscript

So many mini-disasters, but oh, Lord, what fun! I invited Miss Davis to a Valentine's Day concert of all-Bernstein music with the NY Philharmonic at Carnegie Hall, scheduled for a few weeks later. She, however, called me the day before to say she had to have emergency dental work and could not make it after all. Just as well, because I would have been a miserable wreck as her escort. Her autographed photo arrived about a year later. With it was a handwritten letter in red ink on baby blue stationery embossed with "Bette" in red:

> Hi, How dreadful to have taken so long to give you a photograph. How are you? It was just a year ago! Have hated snow ever since! [She drew a smiley face.] B.D. is at the Grier School in Penn—and loving it—Robin [unclear] is in Florida—and I am slugging it out nightly here—but have no complaints.
>
> My best to you. Bette D. Jan. 16, 1962

—a bittersweet keepsake of my brief but intense encounter with one of the immortals.

Marguerite Stitt Church, the U.S. representative from the thirteenth district of the State of Illinois from 1951 to 1963, was named by Kennedy to be a United Nations delegate, even though she had been frankly negative about some of his policies. LB sent her thank-you flowers, and on 24 January 1961, she responded:

> The flowers are a happy reminder of circumstances which might—without them—today appear to be sheer fantasy. I do appreciate your thoughtfulness. Surely, this Republican was glad that she was able, at long last, to provide one police car for the good of her country—and for the rescue of people like yourself who were giving so much.

I also wrote to her, asking for the name of the person to be thanked for the police escort. Her reply on congressional stationery was dated 6 February 1961:

> Your letter brings reality again in the memory of a night which otherwise, I am inclined to believe, could never have happened.

She supplied the name of the commissioner, to whom she had also personally written, and concluded,

> With appreciation of your kindly comment on my activity on that fateful evening, and with best wishes, I am . . .

On 13 February, LB wrote the following letter to Robert J. McLaughlin, president of the Board of Commissioners in the District of Columbia:

> I can hardly find words to tell you how grateful I am for your providential intervention on the night of January 18 when Miss Bette Davis and I were marooned somewhere on Massachusetts Avenue. We should never, certainly, have arrived at the Armory Gala, even late as we did, without your kind help.
>
> I would like to add a special word of commendation for the two fine officer-gentlemen who rescued us. They were gallant, courteous, and sympathetic, and they helped to turn a grisly experience into a delightful and exciting one. They are Officers McCune and Keene, 31 Scout. My thanks to them and to you.
>
> Sincerely,
> Leonard Bernstein

Happy days—alas, not yet here again. LB felt uncommonly close to the Kennedys, and they, especially Jackie, reciprocated in kind. And why not? They were arbiters of good taste, and that included serious music. Has there ever been a president and first lady more supportive of and interested in the arts? As of this writing, we can only hope.

On Tour

1959 NYP Tour of Europe and the Soviet Union

On the good advice of Helen Coates, I kept a diary of the international tours I was fortunate to join. The most prominent was the first one, twenty-nine cities, seventeen countries, fifty concerts in seventy days! What made it truly special was the time spent in the Soviet Union—ten concerts in Moscow and eight in Leningrad (now Saint Petersburg)—where American music played by the NYP helped to begin the thawing out process of the cold war. Here are excerpts from the journal:

> *Athens, Aug. 4* Acropolis illuminated in sharp contrast to the neon city lights below. Ancient ruins versus World War II destruction. On the street we meet Adlai Stevenson who is here on some kind of oil reserve investigation. *Aug. 5* Concert in a stunning setting at the foot of the Acropolis in the Herod Atticus Theatre; reception at American Embassy given by Ambassador Ellis O. Briggs, chat with Blanche Thebom, opera singer who had performed LB's early song cycles. Then we explore waterfront dives, where we are serenaded by a girl singer. *Aug. 6* Shipping magnate Empiricos invites us to go yachting on the blue Aegean where one can see clear down to the bottom sand; sheer indolence. Meet Katina Paxinou, actress (*For Whom the Bell Tolls* movie).

> *Beirut, Aug. 7* LB cannot appear in Lebanon, too risky. Tommy Schippers takes over and I am to assist him. He and I go see an ugly belly dancer. Taxi driver asks us if we want girls. On return, we get frisked by soldiers. We run out of gas in front of American embassy.

> *Baalbek, Aug. 8* Reception luncheon at a garden paradise high in the mountains. Bible country: Bedouins, camels, cedars of Lebanon.

At a café in Athens, 8 May 1958. *Left to right:* JG, Nikiforos Naneris, LB, a local composer (name unknown) and Kostas Paniaras.

Concert in huge austere Roman ruins; no acoustics. Reception at Temple of Baachus. Wadada, our guide, is a frustrated piano teacher. *Aug. 9* Given guided tour of the Baalbek ruins. Drive back to Beirut. Take a small boat out for a midnight swim in the Mediterranean.

Istanbul, Aug. 10 Back with LB. Minarets, mosques, reception by the USIS, hotel overlooking Bosphorus Straits. We hear that Seymour Lipkin's concert was a smash. *Aug. 11* I go to Hagia Sofia by myself, breathtaking. Then the Blue Mosque, the labyrinthic covered bazaar, a maze of five thousand shops, which is like the Thief of Baghdad, Seventh Avenue and the Lower East Side all wrapped in one. The Piston Concerto for Orchestra has a cold reception. *Aug. 12* To Topkapi museum, exhibits ranging from harem contents to crown jewels. Alas, the Copland *Billy the Kid* lays an egg.

Salonkia, Aug. 13 Charming, unspoiled seaport; dumpy hotel. Concert for three thousand in YMCA outdoor basketball court. I turn pages for "Age of Anxiety." Poor sound, piano out of tune, lights go out; I try to get LB dressed in the dark. Reception is beer and lemonade. Orange moon over silhouetted ships. *Aug. 14* Day off. With Jack Frizzelle

Tommy Schippers and LB, Salonika, Greece, 1958.

[NYP staffer]. Beach trip over an hour away on an ithmus, shabby and smelly. LB dines with Menotti and Paxinou.

Salzburg, Aug. 15 Green Bavarian countryside in sharp distinction to the near-east dustiness. My room in the Bristol Hotel overlooks Mozart's Wohenhaus. Town a baroque jewel. Von Karajan attends concert Bus to Judensburg (!) for reception by Vienna Philharmonic. Mitropoulos makes entrance with LB to great applause. *Aug. 16* See Mozart sights, cathedral. Orchestra at rehearsal now sounds like its old beautiful self. Help Felicia get evening things; she gets cramps. Meet Mitropoulos, actress Lilly Darvas and Jerry Robbins.

Warsaw, Aug. 17 Monstrous Palace of Culture amidst ruins and rubble. For the first time, I'm on same floor as LB. The whole orchestra is given a communal meal. *Aug. 18* We meet Ralph Bunche, UN special undersecretary. Press interviews; they show interest in modernists like Stockhausen. Concert hall is like a catacomb, very live. LB does a spellbinding *La valse*. Food is more Russian than Polish. *Aug. 19* Three-hour a.m. rehearsal. Meet Robbins on the street. *Aug. 20* Tour the Old Quarter, rebuilt in seventeenth-century style, with old paintings used as reference. To ghetto quarter, skeleton of Gestapo headquarters building, sewer beneath was conduit for rescue supplies. Guide tells horror stories, but when asked about the ghetto prior to the war, he gets indignant and says, "We Poles were liberal minded."

Moscow, Aug. 21 Upon landing, there are three touching reunions with relatives of orchestra members. Hotel Ukraina built two years ago, but looks fifty. LB does not care for his suite; to be changed. Drab streets, beefy street cleaning women, outdoor vendors with one fruit load per stand. *Aug.22* Art Museum, well executed paintings, but not art. Walk to Red Square. LB's cousin, Michel Chajaboim from south Russia, appears. Concert well received, but not overboard. LB plays Mozart to a fair-thee-well. *Aug. 23* Tour of Kremlin, enchanting. Icons, fallen tower bell, crown jewels, carriages, thrones. Then Lenin's tomb, long lines. Go to American Fair at Sokolniki, big crowds. Rousing concert. Meet composers Dmitri Kabalevsky and Aram Khachaturian, and Osgood Caruthers and Max Frankel of the *New York Times*. Toilet in my room gurgles, then roars like the *1812* Overture. *Aug. 24 Le sacre* rehearsed with extra Russian musicians; a first for them. Waiting for Saudek team to arrive; they are bogged down with visa problems. Maids in LB's room think I am a thief.

Aug.25 LB's forty-first birthday. gifts pour in. Luncheon for the orchestra, caviar and vodka a gift from the David Kaisers. LB goes to see the minister of culture. Concert is a fantastic and historic event. LB talks to audience about Ives and Stravinsky. Meet playwright Paddy Chayevsky. *Aug. 26* Throughout the week, Pat Judd, Clara Simons and others (all NYP'ers) have fallen down on stairs in the hall. *Billy the Kid* leaves audience cold. Meet ballerina Maya Plisetskaya and violinist David Oistrakh. We learn that plainclothesmen in the hotel sidle up to groups of musicians and try to listen in.

LB in the midst of Russian populace at the American Fair in Moscow, 1959. Near the center top is JG and immediately below him is Carlos Moseley.

Aug.27 Back to American Fair, where LB gives interview on RCA color TV, to be seen every day at the fair, but he is irritated that it won't be heard in Russian translation. We now discover that we've been tailed all over town. Felicia in a hurry to meet up with Zorina. Two composers arrive to discuss possible exchange with U.S. counterparts. Reception at U.S. ambassador's. Meet Leonid Kogan, violinist, and Mstislav "Slava" Rostropovich, cellist. Leave on 11:30 p.m. train for Leningrad.

Leningrad, Aug. 28 Arrive 9:45 a.m., cold, wet, sleet (which remains throughout our stay here). To Europeiskaya Hotel. Then to Hermitage Museum. Mon Dieu! room after room of the most extraordinary treasures. Thank heaven, the chandeliered concert hall is across the street from the hotel. LB is pressured to take solo bow after the orchestra has left the stage. His uncle shows up from Siberia. The city is more sophisticated than Moscow, but still nothing frivolous can go on here; everything must count for something. *Aug. 29* About fifteen of us go to the Old Synagogue with prayer books, shawls and caps, which cynics claim will be sold. Only old people here, the Soviet system waiting for them to die out. Neon Star of David and candelabra; sweet-voiced crying cantor. I am given an *aliyah.* An old lady asks me to give her best to my Ma, who she does not know. No community to build on, so very sad. Stop by the Rimsky-Korsakov conservatory. Play a little

Greeting Tommy Schippers at Moscow train station. Carlos Moseley (assistant manager of NYP) in back of him, JG on the right.

piano; try to compose a bit. *Aug. 30*, Tour summer palace of Peter the Great, very grand, with view of the Gulf of Finland. Back at the Hermitage, we are taken into the Treasure Room, with gold dating back to eighth century BC. Stop at "anti-religion" museum, so named by Americans; then to music store.

Aug. 31 Meet Schippers at train station. Half his baggage has disappeared. Get him settled, then take bus tour to Alexander Nevsky cemetery with graves of Tchaikovsky, Glinka, Rimsky-Korsakov, Mussorgsky, Borodin, Stravinsky's father. The country is a curious paradox of preserving the past, but with no allegiance to that past. I have mysterious skin rash (bedbugs?). Tommy, who is not well, gives erratic performance. *Sept.1* Tommy's bags were sent to Stalingrad! Bernsteins go to Peterhof. Schippers concert this night is much better; but his clothes only arrive at 10:30 p.m. My itch is worse. *Sept. 2* After various duties, I go see movie of *The Idiot*, very old-fashioned. Sun finally comes out. Double-duty, pack some LB bags and help Schippers. LB goes to the home of two young jazz aficionados, very hush-hush.

Kiev, Sept. 3 On my first jet ride. Suffer intense sinus pain, head splitting apart. Southern landscape loveliness. The VIPs go shop for embroideries; I go to bed, but get up in time to see charming Durov Circus. We are with Torschenko, famous Russian comic actor; crowds stare at us because of him. *Sept. 4* I get locked in my room; have to piss in a window pot. Tommy calls for me and is able to open the door. With Natasha, our interpreter, we go to Lavra Monastery, overlooking the Dnieper River, down into the catacombs. Except for candles, eerie, pitch-black dark. Groups of old women singing a nasal kind of organum in thirds at each mummified saint. Petrified hands, straight out of Edgar Allan Poe. Monks talk to no one. At lunch Natasha, our interpreter, says she is convinced the U.S. press is full of lies, to which I respond that we can pick and choose what to read. Schippers' concert a big success. *Sept. 5* Off to Vladmirsky Cathedral, hear remarkable four-part harmony; then to Santa Sofia (a name that means "divine wisdom"). Lunch on a moored boat; get a haircut, powdered with a paint brush; buy ceramics. Felicia feeling sickish again and LB with a cold curses the fact the printed program on the sixth lists everything *not* being played. I get into a political argument with Natasha. *Sept. 6* LB concert at twelve noon is warmly received. Mary Ahern and Bettina Dilworth, of the Saudek group, suddenly appear. Telegram arrives saying Sam Bernstein will soon arrive. Terrific spreads in *Time* and *Life* magazines. With orchestra, we go see *Swan Lake* in Kiev Opera House; male dancers are awful. *Sept. 7* Walk around by myself, prices in stores are ridiculously high. Mary works with LB on Moscow script. I drink too much vodka and insult Tommy. Huge mob after LB concert, almost a riot and police are called in.

Moscow, Sept. 8 Doc gives me ephedrine, which relieves me of pressure pain on plane. Hotel room now directly across LB. With orchestra, we see *Prince Igor* at the Bolshoi theater. Opulent, but only so-so voices. Sam Bernstein has arrived. *Sept. 9* Dick Thomas of Saudek team calls a meeting with technicians at hall. It is George Judd's birthday [NYP mgr.]. Meet with Ricky Leacock, the TV director. Go see *Giselle* with Galina Ulanova and Federev, her partner, at Bolshoi, a superb event. Catch tail end of Schippers' concert. Reception by Soviet Musicians Guild: they play a first-rate *Peter and the Wolf, Flight of the Bumblebee,* kazatzka dancers, etc. Bernsteins have gone to visit Boris Pasternak, the author of *Doctor Zhivago* whose designation for the Nobel Prize in 1958 clashed with Soviet authorities and caused him to go into hibernation.

Moscow, Sept. 10 TV rehearsal at ten. Start making cue sheet for the orchestra. Meet with four Russian musicians who will help cue cameramen. Back at hotel, Tommy's sick with throat ailment. Type up cues. Pete Regan [NYP stagehand] tries to fix broken zipper on suitcase; no luck. With LB and Carlos Moseley, we go to Union of Soviet Composers. A fascinating and irritating two hour debate on ideologies. LB gets into a bout with Dmitri Kabalevsky and loses his temper. He is quite persuasive, but never the twain shall meet. In my partial transcription of their conversation, which follows, LB's refers to Tikhon Khrennikov, a composer-bureaucrat who was head of the union, but who was not present on that day:

LB: "At the meeting I had with Khrennikov, he left us with a puzzling state of affairs. Maybe it was due to bad translation. He said that it was this body of composers which makes decisions of which music is to be heard and thereby decides public opinion."

DM: "We *influence* public opinion."

LB: "How so?'

DM: "For example, if the Philharmonic in Kiev is not doing enough Soviet music, we inform the Ministry of Culture."

LB: "You know there is a difference between prejudice and conviction. Only the second is positive."

DM: "And what are your artistic principles?"

LB: "Divided. As a composer I do what I feel. As a conductor I do what I consider good, what I like."

DM: "Ah, so you decide."

LB: "Only as an individual, not as a collective unanimous group."

Back to hotel, get Tommy ready for concert he is to conduct (Beethoven No. 8, Barber *Medea,* Wagner *Lohengrin* and Menotti *Island God*). Afterward, he's become quite ill; rush him back to hotel. Three doctor specialists: one for nose to chin, second for chin to throat and third for throat to chest. Get final cues straightened out, give to Clara [Simons] to mimeograph for orchestra. Felicia gives me a hard time [don't remember why]. Big day ahead.

Sept. 11. Although it is otherwise etymologically derived, I am convinced that Russian bureaucracy is the true meaning of "red tape." Up early for rehearsal of TV show in Tchaikovsky Hall, *LB and the NYP in Moscow.* Do timings with Bettina Dilworth. Dry run under the most primitive conditions. Cameras have to be reloaded every ten minutes. Much time wasted with language barrier. LB has a cold and throat problem like Tommy's. Back to hotel for lunch; he gets into tails for show at 3:00 p.m. Russian translations fail to arrive. Delayed start while Anatole Heller [tour mgr.] explains what's going on to the audience. LB gives downbeat for national anthems as Leacock yells out: "The race is on!" From then on it seems like constant disaster. The audience is restless. The script is on the musical similarities between Russians (Shostakovich No. 7) and Americans (Copland *Billy the Kid*). LB understandably nettled by four interruptions in movement one of the Shosty work. Violinist Sam Fishzohn passes out and has to be taken off stage. Somehow the show finishes right under the wire by 6:00 p.m. Shostakovich, who has been in the audience, rushes like a squirrel to the stage and takes his bow. Overall, a messy event; but I have the feeling it is going to turn out well (to be shown in the U.S. on Oct. 25). Dinner quickly gulped down. One suitcase has to be abandoned, again a broken zipper. While LB is doing the evening concert, I pack his stuff, then go to the hall for Barber *Essay*, Beethoven No. 7, Shostakovich No. 5. Highly charged evening since Boris Pasternak is in attendance. He comes to Lenny's dressing room during intermission followed by a flock of cameras and a horde of Russian celebs. He has a beautiful face and speaks a broken but charming English about musical aesthetics, "getting down from heaven to earth after such music." I get his and Shosty's autographs.

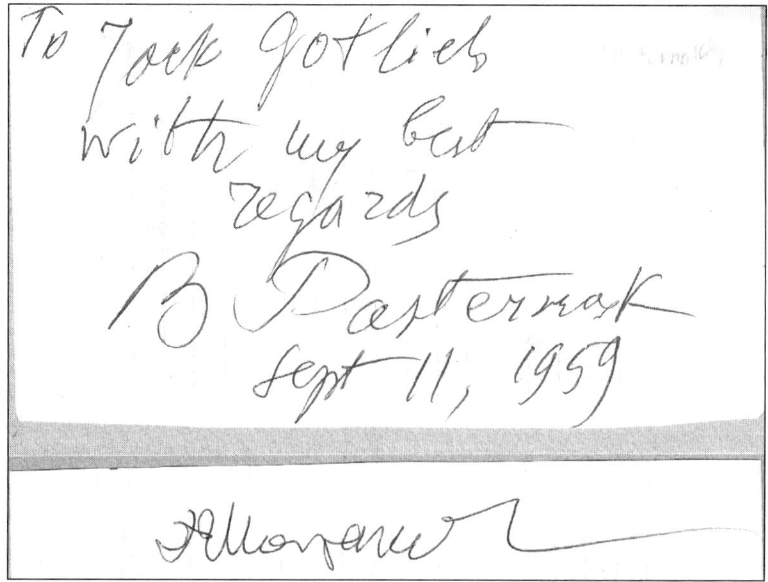

Autographs of Boris Pasternak and Dimitri Shostakovich, Moscow, 1959.

Young Russians leave a message: "We ask you to play The Question Is Left Without an Answer by the composer Ives. A group of musicians is asking you about it." Huge ovation at end of concert. Girls bring on flowers for all the men. More crowded in the dressing room with Kabalevsky, Shosty and his son Maxim, Pasternak, Kiril Kondrashin, et al. Finish packing, now the zipper is broken on L's suit bag! I am up until 3, and have to be back up again at 5:30. Farewell to Grossland.

Amsterdam, Sept. 12 Everyone relieved to leave the USSR. Shostakovich and son are at airport; they are off to Poland. LB allows me to stay in Amsterdam, while he goes to Scheveningen. Go antiquing with Tommy and the Kaisers. Buy a beauty of a nineteenth-century wooden jewel box. City so beautiful, open and free. Have lunch at exotic Balinese restaurant, at least twenty small sampling dishes. Later, Tommy, Jack F. and I go to another Balinese joint, get quite high and jolly. *Sept. 13* Take canal trip past rich folks homes into main harbor. Buy Delft cufflinks. Sylvia Kaiser buys an Egyptian scarab necklace, a bargain. Take train to Scheveningen, very much like Coney Island. LB has a cold. He is missing cigarettes (my fault), duffel gift bag is broken (my fault), unpacking and packing (my fault), and 'tis wrong of me to stay in Amsterdam (my fault). *Sept. 14* to Rijksmuseum for Rembrandts. Tommy and I go see flick *Woman in Question*. At night, we enjoy an English revue, *Going Dutch*.

Düsseldorf, Sept. 15 Schiphol airport is a free port and the orchestra buys like mad. Immediate press interviews on arrival. To Hotel Eden, Königsallee is called the Fifth Avenue of all Germany. Otherwise, a provincial town. Concert hall is circular, a reconverted observatory. Sit in hall for Tchaikovsky Fourth. LB is right, alas, Schippers is too goyish, uninvolved with both music and players. Reception at USIS house.

Essen, Sept. 16 Bus trip to Essen, seems like the Connecticut turnpike. Tommy gives me gift of beautiful Gucci green wallet and mother-of-pearl stickpin. I am very touched. I feel I never want to stop touring and at same time I am dying to get back home.

Wiesbaden, Sept. 17 Arrive Frankfurt by 11, take bus to Wiesbaden. Hotel Blum. Spa region, lovely resort for old folks. Concert in Kurhaus where there's a gambling casino. In nearby Bonn, we go to see Beethoven house.

Luxembourg, Sept. 18 Not much to do here except nap and eat great food. The Belgian royal highnesses appear at the concert, Tommy's last.

Paris, Sept. 19 Tommy in distress. I am at Hotel Élysée Palace; LB, who is at the George V, is wan and hoarse. Felicia is here with her mother, the kids and Julia. Cab to Heugel & Co., music store; persuade them to mail music to Venice for upcoming TV show. Go to Louvre; walk along the left bank. Tommy now is incapacitated. Concert at the Palais de Chaillot. At American Embassy reception, Abe Friedman shows up; how nice. Pianists Artur Rubinstein, Jean Casadesus, and Philippe Entremont; composer Georges Auric, American ambassador Amory Houghton. I adore the symmetry of this great city. *Sept. 20* Sightsee. Phone LB, he needs *La Marseillaise*. I take care of it, thence, doing all the tourist bits, to Arc de Triomphe, Eiffel Tower. Later, LB upsets me by saying I'm a disappointment, which I ascribe to his sinus upset, fatigue and my friendship with Tommy. Concert is at the Palais de Chaillot, much like Radio City Music Hall. Wander around Montmartre, strike up a conversation with a Frenchman; we discuss movie actors, such as "Um-Fray Bo-gar."

Basle, Sept. 21 On bus to airport, converse with Harold Gomberg about oboes. Introduce myself to Noël Coward at the Swiss hotel. No chance to see town. Concert at Casino Hall. Go back to hotel to get opium for LB's trots. Time Mozart movements for TV show. Besides Coward, Robert Oppenheimer and wife are at concert. Basle, between France and Germany is dichotomously torn with a hotel named both Drei Königen and Trois Rois.

Munich, Sept. 22 Get some LB laundry done. Vier Jahreszeiten Hotel [which LB enjoyed several times years later]. Have venison for the first time and get cramps. Much evidence of bombings. Felicia has a cold. Gigantic roar of approval at concert end.

Belgrade, Sept. 23 On plane, work with LB on Mozart cadence examples. Ladders used to descend from place. Hotel Metropole. Walk and shop. At hotel the men are maddened that they have to pay for water. Concert in the Trade Union Building is a comedy of errors. LB leaves stage wrong way, water glass is broken on the piano, everyone is edgy and knocked out. Little beaver me goes a-packing LB's stuff.

Zagreb, Sept. 24 Edgar Taft Benson, head of Mormon church and of U.S. Dept. of Agriculture, enters Belgrade hotel as we leave. Arrive Zagreb at noon, to Esplanade Hotel. Men distressed with their fleabag hotel. Charming eighteenth-century type town. Feeble reception at concert, but fabulous spread at reception by our embassy. Concert probably was loved by the audience, but we've been spoiled elsewhere by uproarious cheering. Town is regressive despite Tito's "advances."

Venice, Sept. 25 We pack the baggage truck ourselves; at airport discover that a big-shot customs man has removed all the bags from the truck. Then police have to check the plane for possible stowaways (no wonder!). At Treviso airport another delay for us to declare cigarettes. Finally arrive onto the enchanted waterways of Venice. Ah, Venezia, even in the rain. To Hotel Bauer Gruenwald, where, at lunch, Igor Stravinsky is sitting at a table (hooray!) and LB is at another table with David Diamond (boo!). At 4:30 to we go Teatro Fenice, where the concert will be held. A tiny baroque jewel [later destroyed in a fire]. Sightsee, buy Venetian glass. Molto bello.

JG and LB at Teatro La Fenice, Venice, 25 September 1959.

Sept. 26 TV rehearsal. LB needs Mozart sonata and I go hunting for it in town. Chat with Mary

Ahern about my frustrations with LB; she gives me sound advice. *The Ageless Mozart,* TV show goes well. Concert at night televised to seven countries by Euravision, but crazy, random shots, all wrong. Post concert, meet Luchino Visconti. *Sept. 27* Free day. Grand Canal tour.

Milan, Sept. 28 Now, when leaving Venice, it is, of course, sunny. LB relates his Stravinsky talk to me. Igor says Stockhausen is important; LB detests Robert Craft. Get on plane A, but find it cannot take off, so we get on plane B. In Milan, I am alone with LB in car and we clear the air with each other and discuss the future. At his suite at Hotel Grand Duomo we wait for delivery of the luggage, but there is a porter's strike in town. Eat at Galleria, go to rehearsal at Piccola Scala. Bags arrive at 7:15 p.m.; we carry them up to rooms. Concert in La Scala is a crazy mix; I meet Ricordi family. *Sept. 29* LB stays in bed all day. Have packages wrapped for shipping. See *Last Supper* by Leonardo (the other one) and go to top of the Duomo. Supper alone with LB, Felicia arrives.

Hamburg, Sept. 30 I listen to Felicia and LB discuss the Callas and Tebaldi "war." Four hundred and fifty empty seats at concert; first time there is such a large gap. Conservative seaport town; they need to be shown first, like Missourians. Felicia's piano teacher from Chile is here. Late at night, I visit whorehouse alley where the prostitutes sit in the windows on display like Macy's bargain basement. One wears Lillian Russell–type boots with lace stockings.

Berlin, Oct. 1 Felicia has left one bag behind, so I have to wait for B plane until bag is returned. Fifty-minute trip. Found out later that when plane A almost touched ground, it immediately went up again because it overshot the runway. Hilton Hotel, lunch with Stockhausen and wife; we discuss the problems with his *Gruppen* piece. Touring into East Berlin, tailed by Soviets. Banners declaring tenth year of *Demokratische Deutsche Republik.* Mr. Daly of State Dept. guides us back into western sector, where we visit destroyed Nazi sites. New hall, *Hochschule für Musik* is very live; much stomping cheering. My Tanglewood teacher Boris Blacher and his wife are here. LB is interviewed for the armed forces in Germany.

Oslo, Oct. 2 Three-and-half-hour trip over gorgeous fjords. Hotel Continental. Tour the fecund Vigeland Sculpture Park. Early concert since King Olaf V will be present. At end, cheers stop as king exits, then picks up again; it's like an old movie comedy scene. Anne Brown, the original Bess of *Porgy and Bess*, is at concert.

Helsinki, Oct. 3 At last night's royal dinner, LB apparently goofed by not speaking to lady on his left, Crown Princess Astrid. Town looks like Moscow, but they loathe the Russians here. Palace hotel had been built for the Olympics. See movie, *Devil's Disciple*. Want to take a sauna bath, but can't swing it. Town is too American influenced. *Oct. 4* It's Rosh Hashanah. Small hall with corkscrew stairway to get to stage.

Turku, Oct. 5 Uneventful. Some of the men go to Sibelius Museum. Immediately after concert, off to airport. There are two official languages; Turku is Finnish and Abo is Swedish. The Finns resent the Swedes. Gloomy north country, gloomy folks.

Stockholm, Oct. 6 Grand Hotel. One of Felicia's bags again missing. Tour city with Bernsteins and others. At lunch, LB plays salon piano music. Back at hotel, Felicia's bag has been found. I get a steam bath and massage. Tremendous audience response. Letter arrives for Bernsteins from Pasternak via his Swedish publisher. *Oct. 7* Free day. See old town. While packing, lights go out all over town for about fifteen minutes. I go to opera, Verdi's *Masked Ball*. Produced in its original intended Swedish setting; last scene depicts the opera house we are sitting in.

Göteborg, Oct. 8 Nudie magazines on display, even pencils with twirly girlies that undress. Meet conductor Dean Dixon and wife at concert. Afterward, get smashed on aquavit. Have relaxed time with the Bernsteins; rarely have felt so at home with them.

London, Oct. 9 Three-and-a-half-hour trip. Soon there will be no more of bassoonist Manny Zegler's shout of "Hey, zitdowndere!" Stratford Court Hotel, crummy. Off to Claridge's. Bernstein bags arrive with broken brandy and perfume bottles inside. Ruined clothes. Since it's a weekend, no laundry can go out. See poor production of *WSS*. At first blush, I don't like London as I did Paris. *Oct. 10* Sightsee. Taxi to Festival Hall concert gets caught in traffic jam; we are late; BBC Third Programme radio delay. Meet writers Stephen Spender and Vladimir Nabokov, Ambassador John Hay Whitney, British composers Richard Arnell, Arthur Benjamin, Peter Fricker, Edward Rubbra, and pianist Harriet Cohen. *Oct 11* More sightseeing. At hotel, a woman named Roberta greets me with "Weren't you at Brandeis?" Small world, after all.

[*Since the entries above were day by day, only selected days are cited from subsequent tours.*]

Berlin, 1960

Sept. 26 Burtie Bernstein's beguiling humdinger of an account about this trip says it all.[3] The concert culminated with LB at the piano playing Beethoven's first concerto. Earlier in the day, LB relates a dream he has had about me. He is to play a concerto, but the piano does not work. I am called in to fix it.[4]

Japan, April–May 1961

Baltimore, Apr. 17 A disheartening opening concert. Most memorable is the Hotel Lord Baltimore since LB initials are all over the joint, on doorknobs, linens, glasses, etc.—unavoidable. There are eleven bags to manage. I will be rooming from time to time with Elyakum Shapira or Seiji Ozawa, assistant conductors.

Vancouver, BC, Apr. 22 I get a box of buttons from the town's pops conductor who also owns a dress store. We mark the box, "Boss pills for Relief from Sluggish Personnel."

Tokyo, Apr. 26 Through Paul Jacobs, NYP pianist, meet three visiting avant-garde Italian composers: Luciano Berio, Bruno Maderna and Severino Gazzelloni, the dean of Italian flutists.

Shizuoka, Apr. 28 Arrive by car at Minaguchi-ya, the retreat made famous by Oliver Statler in his book *Japanese Inn*. How does one begin

Sorting the laundry at Minaguchi-Ya. Haru-yo is behind JG.

to describe the girls, the service, the tatami, the bamboo, flower shrines and scrolls, the quiet, formal, dignified gardens, the view of Mount Fuji in all its glory? Breathtaking green hills and ocean bay. Concert in an unusual diamond-shaped hall. Back to the Inn for wonderful public bath; then the girls get us undressed and redressed in kimonos for an elaborate dinner. Escorted back and forth to rooms. Peace, heaven, paradise. Based on this and other emotive experiences in Japan, LB wrote five haiku poems, duplicating in English the Japanese prescribed form of seventeen syllables for each haiku, which I set to music.

I. Loveliest at Minaguchi-ya
Was Haru-yo.
And saddest, too. (Okitsu)

II. Waterfall of Seiken-ji
Has taught me to hear
The sound of silence.
(Seiken-ji is a historic Buddhist Temple in Okitsu.)

III. The beggar is asleep
Over his coinpot
In the wild neon night.
(Re: Shinju-ku, the approximate Tokyo
equivalent of east Greenwich Village in the 1960s.)

IV. If I were Buddha
And could reverse at will,
I'd make
To-kyo Kyo-to.

V. Haiku is a magic art.
Each time I make one,
The tulips open.

Tokyo, May 6 A half-hour before the afternoon concert at 2:00 p.m., I realize that I did not bring LB's daytime conducting clothes because I was preoccupied with his last-minute dictation about the Ives piece to be delivered in Japanese by someone else. With Teddy, from the Tourist Bureau, I make a mad dash back to hotel via car, subway and taxi. Heart palpitations, pulse fluttering like hummingbird wings. Arrive at hotel at 2 and get back to hall at 2:30. LB has gone on stage with Elyakum's clothes. My lapse was inexcusable. [But I was not the only one to make such gaffs. In 1982, an assistant had inadvertently left behind the conducting score of *Le sacre du printemps* in a Mexican hotel room. The ninety-mile-an-hour race back to retrieve it turned out to be unnecessary because the Maestro went ahead and conducted it by heart.] Concert followed by a reception at American ambassador Edwin Reischauer's residence, followed by an enormous feast at a restaurant given by composer Toshiro Mayuzumi.

August 1977 Tour with Israel Philharmonic in Austria and Germany

On this trip LB is erratic and moody. His struggle is bound up with the need to be with his wife who is seriously ill, and with the demands of the elaborately made plans for this, the first All-Bernstein Festival in Europe. Mine is a delicate retelling not only because of his dilemma, but also because I am made privy to three seesaw romances—two straight, one gay—in our immediate crowd. To make matters worse, Harry Kraut feels he must act as majordomo and supervise all our interactions with LB, to ease Maestro's distress.

Aug. 10 On the plane alone with LB, he speaks of his children, former assistants, how certain musicians should have been further ahead than they were, about the sometime deviousness of HJK. He tells me about the session the family had had the day before with a cancer shrink expert—what if Felicia dies? Once settled at the Orly Hilton in Paris, he reflects on the previous year's turmoil regarding Tom Cothran, Felicia and her illness, the meaning—if there is any—of it all, the frustration, the guilt, the confusion. How all his gay friends had been against the liaison, how his kids were now better able to cope with it all, and Felicia's radiation machine in the hospital, on which she was positioned like a work of art. [Decades later, Dr. Steven Horowitz, my cardiologist, informed me that he was one of Felicia's doctors. Pure happenstance.] His life, from now on, is totally centered on her. He calls her in New York; Harry Kraut calls from Vienna. We watch Ava Gardner and James Mason in *Pandora and the Flying Dutchman* on the hotel TV. LB tells me how much Sinatra adored Gardner, his house plastered with her photos; but Ava threw him over in favor of bullfighters.

Paris, Aug. 11 Suave Rolf Zitzlsperger is here to start on the TV interview surrounding the August 25 birthday concert in Mainz. We request something from the hotel to tack up LB posters in the room. Bellboy: "*Voulez-vous scotch*?" (meaning Scotch tape). LB overhears him and says, "We have scotch here" (meaning Ballantine's liquid gold).

Paris to Vienna, same day I ask him, "Do you still get nervous conducting?" Reply: "Always, my heartbeat goes up, I get sweaty." Met in Vienna by Harry Kraut and Jeff Voorhees, who will act as LB's valet. It's Jeff's birthday come midnight; LB keeps asking him, "Have you gotten laid?" Hotel Sacher is very grand with brocaded walls, crystal sconces, heavy drapes, light feather down wrappers on bed, huge tub. LB "volunteers" Susanne Baumgërtl to Jeff as his birthday present! I don't remember this kind of gaucheness from him in the past.

Vienna, Aug. 12 Rehearsal of "Kaddish" and *Chichester*. Lunch in a restaurant, formerly Göring's hangout, now run by an Israeli. Meet Princess Lili Schönburg. Mendy Wager arrives with Bob Osborne. L., suddenly very long-faced, gets up and leaves. We are momentarily stunned. At the door, one of the personnel points to the direction he went. I follow, catch up and plead, "Please, come back." "Leave me alone," says he. I trail him back to the hotel on the other side of the street.

Aug. 13 We take a five-hour drive through *Sound of Music* countryside to where we will be housed, at a Castle (Schloss) Tentschach in the Carinthian mountains, southern Austria. Bear rugs, antlers, turrets, music room, chapel. L. calls it a "farm with cancer."

Aug. 14 Rehearsal at Congresshalle, Villach (or Osiach). Off to the left at some distance is the Wörthersee where Mahler wrote several symphonies. Have to change my room since L. can hear me coughing and I can hear him snoring next door.

Aug. 15 Harry asks me to drive the Peugeot to Villach, beginning an unhappy affair with this car and its unfamiliar right-sided steering wheel. Back at the Schloss, I work on transferring corrections into LB's new score of *Songfest.* I put on a recording of Mahler No. 9 (Giulini and the Chicago Symphony). Lovely mood and the just the right place to hear it.

Aug. 16 On drive to concert, I get stopped by *polizei.* They will not allow me into concert hall. Lots of dignitaries, Israeli ambassador, governor of province, head of all Austrian theaters, and so on. Finally I say, "*Ich bin der Assistent des Dirigenten. Es wird schlecht, wenn ich bin spät*"—or in so many words. Cop snorts, "Aah, go in"—or in so many words.

Aug. 18 After lunch, most of us line up by fence next to pool for informal snapshots. Suddenly the fence itself snaps and we all fall down. Lukas hurts his hand, gets a headache, lies down. Postconcert that night, I am assigned to drive the Peugeot back to the castle on a dark, rainy, slick Hitlerian autobahn with cars honking at me with their lights on high all the way. Can't see a thing, foreign car, foreign country. Oy vey.

At the fence near the schloss. *Left to right:* JG, Harry Kraut, Claire Burton, Jeff Voorhees, Michael Wager, Lukas Foss and Karen Davidson.

All fall down.

Aug. 19 Bad news: Felicia is deteriorating. Go back? Stay, delay, cancel, suffer loss of income from recordings and TV? Alert airlines and all legions concerned. Make contingency plans. L. smokes some pot to ease his anxiety, and we skip going to the concert of his chamber music. L. recites dirty limericks in front of young Claire Burton. He and Mendy do a Gallagher and Sheen vaudeville routine. After dinner, at which we recite Kiddush over wine and say a Motsi over bread, five of us get hysterical in a game of round robin Ping-Pong. This leads to other castle games: (1) try to identify a mostly hidden person who reveals only a piece a skin, and (2) Sardines: hide and when someone is found, remain silent with that person or persons.

Aug. 20 Postconcert it is decided that "Kaddish" revision must be severely cut. At reception, L. proceeds to publicly humiliate entrepreneur Marcel Prawy, calling it a Prawy Festival, shoving in his knife. Then he gets on the case of Abe Cohen (IPO manager). He challenges HJK to speak, and when he does not, L. says, "You're fired!" He's a wild man.

Aug. 23 Deutsche Grammophon sit-down reception in "Winter Palace" of hotel with Steven Paul, DG's USA representative. Frau Rauchhaupt (literally, "Smoke Captain"), his boss, is a former nun, very much a Helen Coates type. LB, the 'soul of discretion,' praises everyone, including Marcel Prawy, making up for his diatribe of August 20.

Aug. 24 Press interview. I comment on LB's music that no matter how literary or theatrical it might be, it is never program music. Allusions are abstracted, as they are in Mahler. There is never an exact correspondence of note to idea.

Aug. 25 Mainz L.'s fifty-ninth birthday. I give him an inscribed Havdalah cup. Gifts pour in all day. Montserrat Caballé appears for rehearsal; she does not know the piece ("Kaddish" solo). She hedges, is insecure, but LB coddles her. After concert, birthday bash on Koblenz ship. Big spread for whole orchestra and invitees. As the boat makes its *Fahrt*, I booze it up with wine. Speeches, photographers; LB confides he is bored. Gabriella Fuchs is lined up in case Caballé cannot cut the recording.

Aug. 26 Recording "Kaddish" all day. Caballé does scads of takes. The VIPs all leave for Salzburg on a private plane. I have to stay behind because Mendy has lost his passport. He eventually finds it in the concert hall. Oh, frabjous joy!

* * *

Felicia died on 16 June the following year. This was particularly rough on LB's youngest daughter, Nina, who was sixteen years old and, unlike her two elder siblings, still living at home with her father. Now she had to suffer through various kinds of awkwardness brought on by him. I witnessed him trying to persuade Nina to have dinner with him and Tom Cothran or wheedling her to be his "date" on a visit to Jimmy Carter. But even more difficult for her was that she had to put up with the tyranny of Julia Vega as duenna. As long as Felicia was alive, Jamie and Alexander did not have to bear the full brunt of Julia as governess or even as a substitute mother. Luckily Aunt Shirley was of great comfort to Nina, and during the summers, Nina found escape under the protective wings of the Susan and Yehudi Wyner family.

Tommy Schippers died in December of the same year, and also of lung cancer.

In High Places

As part of the 1960s "in" crowd, LB found himself next to Adlai Stevenson at a gathering. Truman Capote was nearby, and after hearing Capote speak—in a notably strange and querulous voice—Stevenson turned to LB and asked, "What planet are we on?" LB of course supported Stevenson in his presidential bids. Even more so did he get on the bandwagon for Eugene McCarthy, and in fact wrote the "A Shout for McCarthy" rally song for him in August 1968. He was friendly with Eleanor Roosevelt, Arthur Schlesinger and other leading lights of the Democratic Party.

He met Eisenhower on several occasions (see "*Arias and Barcarolles*" about one fateful meeting). He exchanged greetings with Nixon in South America, where LB, on tour with the NYP, was cheered and Nixon was not. The lingering effects of this account must have affected Nixon's negative view of LB, when the question came up whether Nixon should attend the premiere of LB's *Mass* at the opening of the new Kennedy Center. On the Nixon tapes between 9 August and 29 September 1971, Nixon and Haldeman discuss LB's "absolutely sickening" behavior onstage of kissing men on the mouth, and Nixon's ultimate accolade is to call LB a "son of a bitch." I'm sure the feeling was mutual.

But in the words of Stephen Sondheim, it was the Kennedys' "bringing back style to the White House . . ." and "making it a cultural lighthouse . . ." where "Bernstein will play on the Bechstein piano"[5]—although the closest I know of him playing that make of piano was in Paris and London, as seen on the dust-jacket cover of this book.[6]

Schuyler Chapin witnessed LB's embracing Edward Heath at 10 Downing Street, where LB inquired of the prime minister, "How is your tottering government tonight?"[7] I saw him cut in on Kennedy dancing the night before JFK's inauguration (viz. "Bette Sat on My Lap"). On one of his several visits to the White House during that administration, Bernstein sat in JFK's rocking chair in the family upstairs quarters and casually asked the president, "Who's taking care of the candy store?"

The summer after JFK was assassinated, Jackie and her children visited the Bernsteins at their country home. John Jr., who was not yet three years old, slipped away from his nanny, and somehow was able to open the door of the Secret Service station wagon in the driveway, although it was built like a tank. Once inside, he managed to release the brake. The car went slowly down a small incline to be stopped by a large tree on the property. There was marginal damage to tree and car; but John Jr. appeared to have a jolly old time, a harbinger of his later swashbuckling days.

LB also took part in the inauguration of Jimmy Carter and was especially charmed by Rosalynn. In 1980, when he received the Kennedy Center honors, LB, his children, his mother and her sisters, were guests of the Carters at the White House. It happened to be the first night of Hanukkah. Julia Vega had packed a small menorah and candles for the Washington trip. While the family was alone in the Lincoln Bedroom, they lit the first Hanukkah candle and sang the Hebrew blessing. Before they left, Alexander made sure that the still-burning candles were carefully placed in the bathroom sink. (Lord knows what the cleaning staff made of it the following morning.) Although this incident has been reported in other books, they do not convey the end of the story. The family showed up late to the Kennedy Center—*after* the president had arrived; but because the event was being taped for national TV, the president had to be the last one to appear. So Carter was obliged to make a second entrance!

In Mexico, on 15 February 1979, at a lavish state dinner following a concert, LB persuaded Carter and President López Portillo to sit down together.[8] This coup probably emboldened LB to tell Carter that when he, Carter, sounded artificial and therefore "bad," it was in the voice of Ham

Jordan, Gerald Rafshoon and other advisers in Carter's circle; but when he sounded "good," he was trusting his own basic sound instincts. Carter said that no one had ever dared say that to him before. On his personal card he wrote an invitation to LB: "In April, when convient [*sic*] for you, let me know when you can come to supper. J. Carter."

Later on, in Washington after a National Symphony Orchestra concert, Barbara and then VP George H. W. Bush, Secretary of State George Schultz and his wife, Helena, were in the Green Room, and overheard by Charlie Harmon. LB shunted them off onto his mother who was there with her two sisters, Dorothy and Bertha. Bush observed that the concert was "like a football game, with four quarters and a half-time." Barbara shot him back a dirty look.

In Israel, LB was on a first-name basis with Golda Meir, Moshe Dayan, Teddy Kollek and David Ben-Gurion. Postconcert, he dined in Austria and Germany with chancellors Bruno Kreisky, Franz Vranitzky, Willy Brandt, Helmut Schmidt and Helmut Kohl. He enjoyed the company of Lord Snowdon and Princess Margaret of England. (Ah, but did he address them as Tony and Maggie? After all, in rehearsals with the London Symphony Orchestra, he referred to Sir Edward Elgar as Eddie.) Other leading politicos he socialized with were President Václav Havel of the Czech Republic, Prime Minister Lech Wałesa (Poland), American ambassadors Shirley Temple Black (Czechoslovakia) and Henry A. Grunwald (Italy), and so on. He hobnobbed with numerous mayors and governors, a long list.

As also reported by Charlie Harmon, in June 1985, after he conducted a Mahler No. 9 performance with the Vienna Philharmonic at the Concertgebouw in Amsterdam, Queen Beatrice greeted LB in the dressing room. Queen B. asked, "Do you mind if I smoke?" Bernstein blurted out, "Thank God!"

Sam Bernstein told Mary Ahern, who told it to me, that "I tried to give him *eytse* [counsel] not to lose his way in high places." (I am supplying the Yiddish word she could not recall.) At the Vatican, he was indeed in a high place up on a scaffold during the restoration of Michelangelo's Sistine Chapel ceiling, where he and Craig Urquhart were nose to the outstretched hands of Adam and you-know-WHO. Afterward, with Quincy Jones—in town for a Michael Jackson concert—they were given a personal tour of Pope John Paul II's private quarters. (In 1973, Bernstein led a performance at the Vatican of his *Chichester Psalms* in the presence of Pope Paul VI; and in 1981 he presented his "Kaddish" Symphony at the Vatican before John Paul II. Not bad work for a "nice Jewish boy" from Lawrence, Massachusetts.)

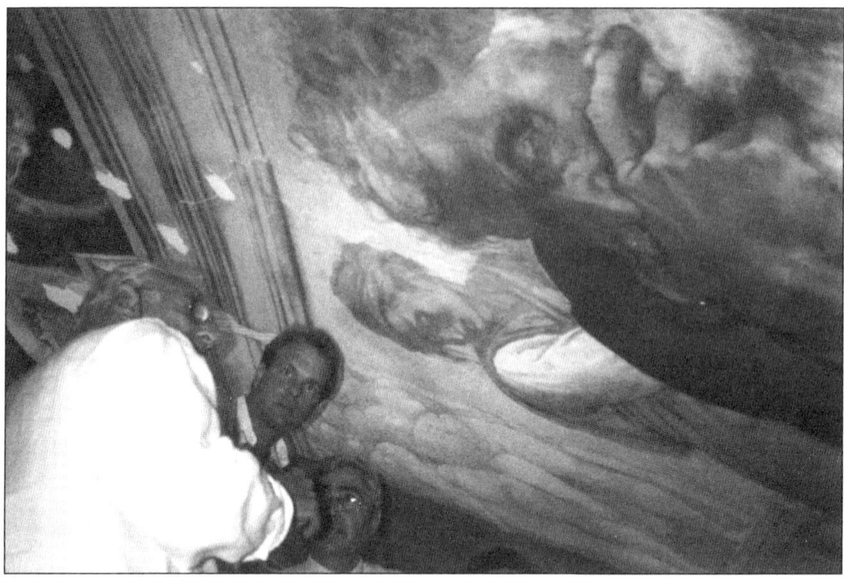

LB and Craig Urquhart at the Sistine Chapel ceiling next to the prophet Jeremiah.

LB, Pope John Paul II and Alessandro Siciliani, manager of the Santa Cecilia Orchestra. The pope is holding LB's score of the "Jeremiah" Symphony. The Hebrew inscription is "Hanukkah."

3 In the Workroom

The Art of Recycling

Six years after the premiere of "Kaddish," I received a letter from LB, dated 30 April 1969, from the Dan Hotel in Tel Aviv:

> Back in the same Kaddish-suite, with that view of the sea, that furniture, that bedroom—the nostalgia is almost too much. You, Ofra, Rovina [i.e., Bikel, Hannah]—you all people the suite. But this time the music is easier (Psalms) and the chorus good and no ghastly crises—yet.

Ah, but his search to find the right notes for the Psalm settings was another matter. Bernstein was never one to let a good tune go to waste. Collaborating with Jerry Robbins, Comden and Green, an adaptation of Thornton Wilder's *The Skin of Our Teeth* was one of various abandoned stage projects on which he had spent almost a year. (The Wilder play was later musicalized by Kander and Ebb, but never made it to New York.)

On 29 November 1964, LB mailed a bitter letter:

> Skin is stalled. Life, this agonizing November, is a tooth with its skin stripped off. I don't know what I'm writing. I don't even know what I'm *not* writing. . . . I can't get over Kennedy or Marc. Life is a tooth without skin. [Both Kennedy and Blitzstein, the victims of senseless murders.]

But all was far from lost. All three movements of *Chichester Psalms* have material originally drafted for the stage show. The music for Psalm 108 had been a number called "Chorale: Save the World Today" in *Skin*, while the song "Here Comes the Sun" (apparently it had alternative title of "Rolling On") triggered Psalm 100. The movement 3 tune for Psalm 133 was a "War Duet" in *Skin,* a tune which could not escape our mischievous name for it as "The Hawaiian Palms," the latter word an anagram, of course.

Movement 2 begins with what has been the song "Spring Will Come Again," becoming Psalm 23; and in response to the request of the dean of Chichester Cathedral for a touch of *West Side Story*, LB obliged with a truncated version of an act 1, scene 1 song cut from *WSS* called "Mix." This was to have been sung by the Jets, and became the basis for the diatribe of Psalm 2. Both the "Spring" song and "Mix" were performed one after the other for the first time at a concert I produced at New York City's Jewish Museum in October 2008. A reviewer said, "It was like watching one of the great magic tricks in history explained."[1]

When Anita sings "We'll have our private little mix tonight" in the brilliant Quintet from *WSS*, she gives a new twist to the cut number. In the movie version, a revealing detail, which pinpoints the battle lines between the gangs, may have been missed by viewers. As the gangs get ready to mix it up in the Rumble, there is a building in the background with the word WAR painted on it in large letters. As the camera moves closer to us, the background exposes the full word to be WAREHOUSE. The Psalmist may ask, "Why do the nations rage?" So as to the question, "What are the Jets and Sharks doing in an English cathedral?" the reply, alas, is that the warfare between teenage gangs is a microcosm of warring nations. That the composer was able to blend both of these wildly contrasting theater numbers—the sweet, lyrical spring song and the sour, nervous combative number—into a fused setting with Hebrew words is a wonder to behold. In a nutshell, then:

from *Skin of Our Teeth*	to *Chichester Psalms*
1. "Save the World Today" & "Here Comes the Sun"	Mvt. 1
2. "Spring Will Come Again" and "Mix" (from WSS)	Mvt. 2
3. "War Duet"	Mvt. 3

Changing from English to Biblical Hebrew is not all that difficult because accents in Hebrew are much more consistent than the irregularities of English.

Nevertheless, to have found the suitable Psalm text to fit the given tune had to be something like looking for a needle in a haystack. In *Chichester Psalms* Lenny the alchemist takes common metal (metal of the commoners?) from the transient show-business world, and transmutes it into gold, into what may well endure as one of the more lasting pieces of choral literature. He need not have despaired.

* * *

Bernstein's recycling practice has been described as raiding the "bottom drawer," a pejorative term that suggests "bottom feeding." It implies the creative artist is somehow cheating by not beginning with a clean slate. But the recycling of music and language is not at all an uncommon process of composers. About half of the two dozen numbers in the Bach B-Minor Mass (1733) are revisions of movements from his earlier cantatas, with the German texts changed to Latin ones. Handel was notorious for recycling his earlier stuff—and also for simply swiping movements from other composers. One of the best known examples is by Beethoven: the finale of the *Prometheus* ballet (1801) provides the material for one of the twelve orchestral contredanses (1802) and for the Op. 35 piano variations (1802), and eventually becomes the finale of the "Eroica" Symphony (1809), all four in the key of E-flat major.

Bernstein did a heap of recycling, turning out "top-drawer" works. Often the earlier pieces were smaller brainchildren incorporated and transformed into works of maturity, specially notable in his sets of piano "anniversaries," the nuclei for some orchestral works.

Seven Anniversaries

Originally written as a Partita in 1942, it was at first a set of five pieces consisting of a Prelude, Gavotte, Sarabande (In Memory of N.K.), Passacaglia and Gigue. Then it became a set of *Six Pieces* and finally *Seven Anniversaries*. Perhaps the dedication in memory of Nathalie Koussevitzky, the first wife of Serge Koussevitzky, triggered the idea to convert the subsequent all the other pieces into *Anniversaries*, making it more marketable than a dry-bones Partita. The Koussevitzky "In Memoriam" became the peroration at the end of "Jeremiah."

Five Anniversaries

The first four went into *Serenade*; the last one into music for *Peter Pan*.[2]

Thirteen Anniversaries
The first two had originally been the piano work *Moby Diptych*, a one-for-one exchange with no alterations. "For Stephen Sondheim" was used in the first version of *A Quiet Place*. No. 7, "For Helen Coates," became "Meditation No. l" in *Mass*. No. 9, "For Jessica Fleischmann," was transformed into "Leah's Dance" from *Dybbuk*. "For Claudio Arrau," No. 11, had originally celebrated the date LB met Felicia for the first time at a reception given for Arrau after a recital he had given. No. 12, "For Aaron Stern," was used in *Opening Prayer,* and No. 13, "For Ellen Goetz" became the conclusion of *Arias and Barcarolles*.

Other Recyclings

1. "Afterthought," a song, "The Intermission's Great," a number written for *On the Town*, and part of the 1940 Violin Sonata went into the ballet *Facsimile.* The Scherzo from the 1937 Piano Trio became "High School Girls" in *On the Town*.
2. "Ain't Got No Tears Left," a song originally written for *On the Town*, became the virtuoso "Masque" section of "The Age of Anxiety," and a variation from the early Violin Sonata went into "The Seven Ages" section. The opening clarinet duet in "Anxiety" was originally written as a separate piece for Koussevitzky.
3. "Big Stuff," a song, grew into a full-blown pas de deux in *Fancy Free*.
4. *Candide*: Humphrey Burton says that the music originally intended for the "Venice Scene" became "Gee, Officer Krupke" in *WSS*, with lyrics by John Latouche that concluded, "Where does it get you in the end?" "Sheep Song" in *Candide* had been the choral piece *The Lonely Men of Harvard*, and a "Love Duet" from *Candide* (no words) was transformed into "One Hand, One Heart" in *WSS.* On the other hand, the music for "Oh Happy We" in *Candide* was originally intended to be a duet between Tony and Maria in *WSS*, a tea party scene that was dropped. "Conch Town," a piano solo, became, in part, "America" in *WSS.* "Make Our Garden Grow" was at first "A Valentine for Jamie and Alex."
4. "Turkey Trot" in *Divertimento* was, to begin with, a birthday present for Harry Kraut.

5. Remnants of *Prelude, Fugue and Riffs* went into "Conquering the City" and "Conversation Piece" in *Wonderful Town*. The music of this lullaby, written upon the birth of his first daughter, went into *Wonderful Town* as "A Quiet Girl":

   Sleep long, my innocent,
   Grow strong, my heaven-sent.
   Dream where you come from:
   This world is hard.
   This song I sing you,
   This love I bring you,
   Rest while you can now:
   This world is hard.

"Greeting," a lullaby written upon the birth of his son, found a home in *Arias and Barcarolles*.

6. "For Helen Coates" was the basis for "Sanctus" in *Mass*. "Shivaree" and "Warm-Up" went directly into *Mass*.
7. The Latin Choruses from *The Lark* grew into the *Missa Brevis*.
8. From *1600 Pennsylvania Avenue*: "Grand Ol Party" and "Rehearse," songs, were incorporated into *Slava!* "American Dreaming" and "This Time," ensemble pieces, were the sources, respectively, for "Sam's Aria" and "Dede's Aria" in *A Quiet Place*; "Middle C" was transmuted into "To What You Said" in *Songfest*.
9. *Opening Prayer*, an independent piece written for the refurbishment of Carnegie Hall, became "Benediction" in Concerto for Orchestra. At the top of the first page of the manuscript for *Opening Prayer* there is the marking "For Carnegie Hall, 15 Dec. '86. Remembering Dimitri M., Harold G., Alma M., Bruno W. . . ," some of the ghosts from LB's past who had inhabited Carnegie Hall. The final page is dated "Laus Deo, 3:05 a.m., 4 Dec. '86."

* * *

One of the more intriguing recyclings involves three late Bernstein works that have a symbiotic relationship: *Dybbuk* (1974), *CBS Music* (1977) and

Halil (1981). The first is a mother lode that feeds into the other two. Least known is the middle work, written at the behest of William Paley, head of the CBS broadcasting company. Paley, on the board of the NYP and the one who supported the Young People's Concerts, asked LB to write theme music for the fiftieth anniversary of the network in 1978. The resulting "Fanfare and Titles" was heard on air as written, but four other short pieces; "Quiet Music," "Blues," "Waltz," and "Chorale" were to be exploited in a mix-and-match mode. Paley then commissioned writer Norman Corwin to pen an ode, *To Network at Fifty*. For this tribute, LB had me arrange the underscoring, using his material, orchestrated by Sid Ramin, and conducted by Elliot Lawrence. Recited on air by Walter Cronkite, it was broadcast on 1 April 1978, and began:

> First a panel lit up, reading ON THE AIR. A shingle hung out in the sky, denoting open for broadcast, then words and music.

The head motif consists of three notes: C, B-flat (B in German) and E-flat (Es in German) to stand for the CBS call letters. This profile of a descending major second and a rising interval of the fourth happens to be indigenous to parts of the *Dybbuk* ballet, particularly in a pas de deux section titled "LC" (for the doomed bride and groom, Leah and Chanon), dated "4 Feb. '73." It was a section that was eventually cut from the ballet, but subsequently thirteen bars from it were incorporated into the flute concerto, *Halil* (at *con moto, ardente*). This is done so smoothly that the lift would not be apparent even to discerning ears. But more front and center, LB organically merges the complete "Fanfare and Titles" of the *CBS Music* into *Halil* (*Allegro con brio*). No seams show. It is a feat of legerdemain accomplished by a musical magician at the top of his game.

Lenny and Aaron

In 1949, Aaron Copland praised LB's early works—emphasis on early—at its best as "music of vibrant rhythmic invention, of irresistible élan, often carrying with it a terrific dramatic punch." But he also said at its worst it was "conductor's music, eclectic in style and facile in inspiration" (in the book *Copland on Music*). This could have only meant that Copland heard the strains of other composers' music seeping into Bernstein pieces.

It is a common game for musicians to detect prior sources—and sometimes gloat over them—in listening to later works. The pop song "I'll Be Seeing You" seems to have an antecedent in the last movement of Mahler's Symphony No. 3, although I doubt that Sammy Fain, the songwriter, was familiar with the symphony (not the same thing as consciously adapting a tune from classical repertoire and popularizing it, a practice refined into a big-time hits by song writer Ted Mossman in the 1940s). Or take the opening (starting at bar 14) of Copland's *Billy the Kid* as a possible source for an interlude in the last movement of LB's "Jeremiah" Symphony (at rehearsal. no. 6).

A big tune in LB's "Kaddish" Symphony (at letter *V* in the third movement) has also been criticized as sounding Coplandish, specifically like *Appalachian Spring* (after rehearsal bar 14). However, as I have demonstrated, the "Kaddish" lyrical line grew out of preceding nonlyrical material in the symphony, not from Copland.[3]

The song "I Have a Love" from *West Side Story*, according to John Mauceri, is "a direct quotation of the 'Redemption through Love' motif from Wagner's *Götterdämmerung*."[4] I do not question that they these melodic lines are virtually identical, but I disagree that Bernstein made a "direct quotation." Like the affinity between the "Kaddish" and *Appalachian Spring* melodies, "I Have a Love" is an inventive outgrowth of previous phrases in the song, developed from Maria's "It isn't true, not for me." Bernstein did not musically allude to Wagner, as Mauceri more than implies, because Sondheim's words are about love's salvation.

The chords from another *WSS* song, "Somewhere," again claims Mauceri, "are taken from *Rite of Spring*." Well, yes, Stravinsky (in part 2 at rehearsal bar 102) has the last bars of "Somehow, some day, somewhere" sound off in the trumpets; but they are hardly the chords that accompany the song in *WSS*. Burton Bernstein, the composer's brother, hears a reminiscence of the Adagio movement from Beethoven's Piano Concerto No. 5 for the beginning of "Somewhere;"[5] and I have written about how the song's "Hold my hand and I'll take you there" bears a resemblance to a secondary phrase in Tchaikovsky's *Swan Lake*.[6]

Is there anything noteworthy (pun intended) about this detective work on "Somewhere"? If one were to put together Beethoven at the beginning, Tchaikovsky in the middle and Stravinsky at the end, would it all add up to "Somewhere"? Of course not.

Does Copland's critique of "conductor's music" still hold true for LB melodies written after Copland's 1949 statement? Bernstein always said that composers stand on the shoulders of their forebears. That may have been a rationalization on his part, nor I do not rise to his defense—so to speak—in all instances. It is difficult to explain away the uncanny likeness between "Maria," again from *WSS*, as not (subliminally?) originating from Blitzstein's opera *Regina* (act 1, scene 1).

A more curious influence came in the form of custom-made manuscript paper that had been given to LB by Darius Milhaud. The layout of the stave groupings on the paper dictated how he came to orchestrate a section of a large work. Maybe it was *Mass;* I do not remember.

* * *

Bernstein and Copland! The names alone encapsulate American twentieth-century music in all its vertiginous variety. Born eighteen years apart, they died within two months of each other. Not only were they lifelong colleagues and comrades, they also were teachers for and of each other. While it has been noted that Bernstein's music was sometimes influenced by his older friend, it also can be said that the clattering start of Copland's *Music for a Great City,* evocative of a subway ride, is inspired by *West Side Story*. It was Bernstein who wrote the ricky-tick barroom piano sequence in Copland's *Rodeo.*[7] Copland was a major player in Hollywood, Bernstein a giant on Broadway. Both, however, met on common ground in the field of ballet, contributing equally to our rich dance heritage. Indeed, it is the rhythmic force of their music: jagged syncopations, asymmetric meters, jazzy ostinatos that is so distinctly theirs and so very American.

But there were also notable differences between the two. Copland was the "plainer" one, Bernstein the flashier showman. The Lincoln-esque Copland always saw both sides of an issue, practicing moderation in all things; Lenny was the passionate profligate, overextending himself, taxing his associates. Apollonian versus Dionysian. A- versus B-type personalities.

Despite these dissimilarities, they saw eye to eye when it came to rejecting artificial barriers between so-called high art and popular entertainment. Their melodic language both reflected and generated vernacular trends. Copland once wrote to his early biographer Arthur Berger, "You overdo the dichotomy between my 'severe' and 'simple' styles. The inference is that only the severe style is really serious. I don't believe that."

All America was grist for their mills—from Copland's score for *Of Mice and Men* with bucolic scenes of barley wagons and threshing machines or Bernstein's take on the harsh realities of dockhands loading those sacks of grain into the ship holds in *On the Waterfront.*

Aaron Copland, JG and Robert Cornell, Essex House, New York City, 1980.

Late-Night Thoughts

(From the Prelude, Fugue and Riffs *newsletter of June 1999)*

On Books

Bernstein regarded the flyleaves of the books he read as blank canvases for poetry, musings and other annotations. Appraising V. S. Pritchett's tales *On the Edge of the Cliff,* he wrote, "I do admire people who have the patience to be in a Pritchett story. . . ." Or, on an edition of *King Lear*: "L's 'mid-life crisis' occurs at age 80. Hence, paranoia, need to be loved (bottomless well) and to have love constantly proven visibly and orally. . . ." [Almost sounds like a self-confession.]

But often the flyleaf comments are not related to the book at hand. They are, instead, aperçus that range from the philosophical (the aesthetics of a pet dog's lifted paw) to the practical (which assistant conductor to choose for Israel?); from tongue-in-cheek verse ("O Dryden is dry/Auden is odd . . .") to flowery poetry ("Bough-armed in the dark we lie/Craving the down-rush, in-spring, out-cry, . . ."). There also are anagrammatic word games ("Some Distasteful Composers: Suitable for butchers! (8)/A nemesis, literally! (8) . . . ," etc.), lists (e.g., earnings on tour), gestating ideas about works-in-progress (*A Quiet Place* and *Songfest*), political statements ("I want everyone to live, and live undeformed, well-fed, unpoisoned . . ."), epigrams ("I am thinking: 'I am thinking'"), and autobiographical irony ("Whaddya get from a cigarette . . . What's the answer? Cancer.").

Wit and wisdom overflow on these pages. From the back flyleaf of *Sextet* by John Malcolm Brinnin, here is Bernstein the humorist:

Double Dactyl
Biggity Wiggity Yosele Szigeti
Was a true klezmer, never played Ligeti.
Bach, Sarasate,
Oh yes, such legati!
But Ligeti? Szigeti
Cared not a figgity.

Another flyleaf poem, from *The Philosophy of Literary Form* by Kenneth Burke, is of particular interest for it virtually spells out the working method of Bernstein the conductor:

Life-lines
The phrase to be parsed:
Passive, interrogative,
Relative, negative.
The line to be scanned:
Spondee, ponderous,
One-footed, double-stressed.
Scan the life: parse the life:
Vice the versa, voice the verse:
Ponder the past: presént the future:
Double distress.

On Scores

If books were the target of his jottings, it was inconceivable that Bernstein could resist the flyleaves, as well as the interior pages, of his conducting scores. Now stored in the archives of the New York Philharmonic, these offer a cornucopia of insights for laypersons and scholars alike. As with the books, they reveal Bernstein's comedic and erudite gifts. "Does anyone read Byron anymore?" he asks on the first page of the score to Robert Schumann's *Manfred* Overture.

What a hoot to come across—in the last movement of Rachmaninoff's Piano Concerto No. 3— his observation of, "Four loathsome bars" (4 bars before rehearsal no. 59). Or his detective work listing of all the quotes of borrowed tunes in the score of Ives' Second Symphony or to marvel at his elegant harmonic analysis of the plagal cadences in Hindemith's *Mathis der Maler*. "The torment of Peter Tchaikovsky," he jots down on the last movement of Symphony No. 6, "No breaths (get a friend to help)."

The meticulously inscribed scores, mostly in red and blue pencil, provide a vivid window into the working mind of the conductor. Red markings were directives to librarians to copy into parts; blue ones were aides-mémoire for the music director, some of which also went into parts. If there were a change of mind or subsequent additions, Bernstein brought attention to them by putting a red x in the margin; once incorporated into the parts, these would be circled in blue.

But there is much more: two-bar phrases are indicated by a pyramid-shaped mark, three-bar phrases by a curve—a practice learned from Koussevitzky—six-bar phrases are indicated by a "5" in the penultimate bar linked with a flourish to a "6" in the last (groupings essential to grasping the formal structure); long and short slashes show subdivisions of the beat; Germanic-style abbreviations are used for entrances; for example, *K* for clarinets (*Klarinetten*), *P* for Trombones (*Posaunen*) so as not to confuse a *C* with contrabassoon or a *T* for trumpets; plus various other symbols (wavy lines, arrows) for new entrances, changes in articulations, dynamics, divisis, bowings (!)—in other words, the full arsenal of tools fashioned by a master maestro.

The precision of his markings reveals Bernstein's keen eye for details, which inevitably were transformed into intense listening experiences. He labored endless hours in preparation. In light of this, it was galling for him to read the one negative review he received for his first performances with the Philharmonic of Mahler's Symphony No. 5:

> I am among those who rejoice over the current vogue for Mahler's noble symphonic epics, and I have noted with great satisfaction Mr.

> Bernstein's increasing mastery of the subtleties of some of them. This mastery, I am afraid, does not as yet extend to the Fifth. Or perhaps the trouble is simply that Mr. Bernstein's phenomenal schedule as a public figure has not permitted him the time to gauge, adjust, and rehearse all its fine points. Specifically, I don't see why the opening triplets in the trumpet call that begins the work should be taken at a clip the renders clear articulation impossible. (They are not written that way.)"[8]

Bernstein's justifiably irritated reaction:

> I give up! Can't he even read what the composer asks for right on page one? If he can't read German, why is he a critic?

Mahler's footnote instructs:

> The upbeat triplets of this theme must always be performed somewhat hurriedly [i.e. *flüchtig*], quasi accelerando, in the manner of a military fanfare.

On Mahler

The Bernstein-Mahler *Partituren* are a godsend. Both were composer-conductors of the NYP, both were faith-seekers who sought and thought on a large scale. The following *selected* ruminations by Bernstein on the Mahler scores must be regarded as spur-of-the moment thoughts. He certainly would have scrupulously edited such spontaneity for publication. The only changes made herein are to spell out abbreviations, provide translations and to make minor adjustments for the sake of clarity.

Symphony No. 2, page 185:

Mahler's title for the Finale: *Der grosse Appell* ("The Roll-Call" or "The Call to Judgment") is irresistible fodder for Bernstein, who writes below it, "Big Apple." (Incidentally, the often irreverent puns that musicians sometimes write into their parts about each other, the music, and the conductor could, at the least, qualify for a series of Internet joke lists.) A visual kind of pun is established when Bernstein signals for the chorus to stand on Mahler's verse: *Was vergangen, auferstehen!* ("All that perished, rise again!"). Although this move cannot be seen on the Bernstein video of the Second Symphony with the London Symphony

Orchestra, the camera is panning down form the dome of Ely Cathedral you can actually hear the singers standing up on their wooden risers.

Symphony No. 4, flyleaf:

On 30 June 1987, Bernstein scribbled a yodeling tune with underlaid words: "We didn't sell out in Oslo/We didn't sell out the hall . . . Etc."

It was not wise to inform the Maestro before a performance on those exceptional occasions when there was not a full house. Sometimes, as in the Oslo program, on tour with the Concertgebouw in Europe, he could joke about it, but with a tinge of bitterness.

(Researchers will be fascinated by the green and red ink revisions in orchestration made by Mahler on one of the Bernstein [nonconducting] copies of the Fourth Symphony (Universal Edition). Another intriguing set of revisions may be observed on the score of the First Symphony, a copyist's paste-ups, with carefully drawn-in staves and notes.)

Symphony No. 5, flyleaf:

Rage-hostility. Sublimation by Mahler and hearer.

I. Angry bitter sorrow mixed with sad comforting lullabies—rocking a corpse.

II. Outburst of rage—more "public" version of private feelings in I. Ends with teeth still clenched, despite occasional hints of ultimate glory and salvation (choral, marches).

III. To hell with it—let's get drunk—A ball.

Symphony No. 6:

Taped across the first two pages of the score, in bold colors, we find a bumper sticker: MAHLER GROOVES. Since exclusively brass fanfares are playing lower down on the first page, only empty bars are covered up. A light touch, to be sure; but there on the flyleaf, LB's more profound and private observations can now can be shared with us:

Mahler: opera symphonica. #6 most operatic of all, perhaps because purely instrumental; yet finale resembles # [Symphony] 2 (recitative, hammer . . .). Basic elements (including clichés) of German music (Mozart-Schubert, Beethoven-Brahms, Liszt-Wagner, also Italian opera, etc.?) driven to their furious ultimate power. Result: neurotic intensity, irony, extreme sentimentalism, despair (that it can't go even further), apocalyptic radiance, shuddering silence, volcanic *Auftaken* [*sic*; *Auftakt*, "upbeat"], gasping *luftpausen* ["breathing spots"], titanic accents achieved by every means (sonic and tonic), ritards stretched to near motionlessness, dynamics over-refined and exaggerated to a point of neurasthenia, marches like a heart attack, old-fashioned 4-bar phrases punctuated in brass and fire, cadences that bless like the moment when an excruciating pain suddenly ceases.

The operatic Mahler: obviously so. Lieder origins, dramatic structure. Curtain-raising preludes, interludes, magnitude, intensity, vocality, climaxes, etc. Theatre: Pagliacci, Traviata (#6), Aida (#2), Tristan *überall*. Alas, Das Lied not here: the commentary on all 9 symphonies.

[page 12] From here on: major-minor alteration becomes harmonically thematic, integrated into the fabric of the harmony as common usage, like tonic, subdominant, etc.

Mvt. II: Tempos more or less like movement I; a reexamination of what can happen over marching A's in the bass.

Symphony No. 9, flyleaf:

The refined beauties of ambiguity, the obsessiveness of artistic creation. (How many Ländler, Wagnerian adagios, self-quotes, funeral "Konducts"" [i.e., cortèges] can one man produce?). Obsessiveness caused by urge to produce the perfect form of his "Vision." If he had lived, he might have tried 9 more times.

I. Death of tenderness and tonality.
II. Death of simplicity (innocence).
III. Death of society.
IV. Letting go (death of resistance, clinging to life).

[page 109] to lengthen the rests, the phrases themselves should be "spastic."

On page 115 of the First Symphony, LB states, "The pauses get longer, the music *bleibt* ['stays'] in tempo."

Page 172: He points out a self-quotation by Mahler from his 8th Symphony: "Mutter! Jungfrau! [the Virgin Mary]."

On the rear flyleaf the conductor writes out in longhand all the Mahlerian printed tempo instructions: *Adagissimo, langsam, zogernd, aüsserst langsam, ritard.* These outer extremes of slowness are seriously taken-to-heart by Bernstein, who writes on the last page, "Have the courage to remain in 8!"

Das Lied von der Erde, page 1:

> Sets theme of all 6 [poems]—Chinese torture (fortune?), bittersweet, fleetingness of life. The only permanence (hence, reality) is spring renewal, the earth itself.

Lieder eines fahrenden Gesellen, page 39:

LB contemplates the "Divine ambiguity" of Mahler's own lyric, "Nun fängt auch mein Glück wohl an?" ["Now my happiness begins?" which continues, "No, I never will be."].

"Ambiguity" is one of Bernstein's favorite motifs, integral to his Norton Lectures. On the flyleaf of the book *Noam Chomsky* by John Lyons, he writes:

> Ambiguity—keynote of interest in music and speech—opening of Beethoven #5: is it in E [flat]? B? No, C minor, which we learn only after 2nd fermata.

And on the 5/4 metered second movement of the score to Tchaikovsky's Sixth Symphony, he comments:

> Simultaneously {2/3} = ambiguity = charm . . .
> {3/2}

Fortunately, there is nothing ambiguous about the treasure trove of remarkably glossed conducting scores Bernstein has left behind for generations to dip into, to benefit therefrom and to be healed by the sheer beauty of his calligraphy.

Four Wedding Gifts

When lyricist-bookwriter Adolph Green married actress Phyllis Newman in 1960, LB wrote a new piano work for them, cleverly titled *Bridal Suite*—with the double meaning of both the hotel and musical kinds of suite. The Greens were supposed to play it side by side, his two hands on the bottom and Phyllis on top with only one hand. At least that was the intention. But, as Phyllis said, "We never were able to achieve that three-handed feat to our complete satisfaction—or anyone else's." (The suite also calls for two-handed and four-handed work.) With Phyllis as narrator, I produced a first-time recording of this charming work in 2009. Filled with affection and humor, the layout is:

Part I
Prelude (on familiar tunes)[9]
Three Variations on the Names Adolph Phyllis Green: Love Song, Chaplinesque and Chaplinade

Part II
Interlude: Bell, Book and Rabbi
Three Wedding Dances: The First Waltz, Cha-Cha-Cha and Hora

Three Encores, Obligatory
Modern Music, An Argument, Old Music, A Reconciliation and Magyar Lullaby

Prior to his daughter Jamie's 1984 wedding to David Thomas, LB composed *Meditations Before a Wedding,* a brooding and rather bizarre piano work with some song content. Part of this improvisatory piece became the foundation for the Prelude to *Arias and Barcarolles* of 1988. It is a strange commentary for a father to create for his offspring since it foretells a stormy romance despite the iterations of "I love you" in the singing part. It could well be that LB was projecting his own unhappiness about broken love affairs and other relationships.

Quite unlike this disturbing meditation was another one titled *A Meditation Before a Wedding*, a gift in May 1975 to Rosamond Bernier and John Russell upon their marriage. Russell was an art critic for the *New York Times*, and Bernier, who founded the art review *L'Oeil*, was not only well acquainted with great French artists of mid-twentieth century, but also with composers, probably because of her friendship with Copland and Boulanger. This lovely contemplative piece went through several transformations. At first it was known as "Middle C" in *1600 Pennsylvania Avenue.* Ultimately it became the setting for "To What You Said" in *Songfest.*

For the 1985 marriage of Felipe Wermus and Alexandra Wager, daughter of his longtime pal Mendy Wager, LB wrote a *Marche à la Chuppah* (wedding canopy) with a left-hand bass based on F and A, for the initials of the groom and bride. The composer was away in Japan, and I was enlisted to play it on a dinky, small organ rented for the ceremony which took place in Mendy's splendid apartment. It was obvious that the piece was written in haste for it was an embarrassment, not at all charming nor mitigated by the composer writing on the manuscript, "with love, knowing you will understand if it sounds just a soupçon Japanese."

Tsuris in Honduras

(Written for "Concordia Celebrates Leonard Bernstein," 7 June 1991)

Among the many regrets that lie in the wake of Bernstein's death is that he did not write his memoirs. What we do have in his voice are scattered reminiscences on film, in an unpublished commentary on photographs and in books by other authors. These are mostly about his career. There are letters, new interviews, after-dinner speeches, tributes to colleagues, and the like, from which a kind of memoir about the growing-up years could be constructed. We also have some clues in his music, especially in the short opera *Trouble in Tahiti* (or, in Bernstein lingo, *TinT*), words by the composer.

The original synopsis of the pencil libretto had seven characters: two singers, simply called Husband and Wife, and six speaking subsidiary characters: a male hairdresser, the Husband's secretary, the Wife's psychiatrist (whose only words were, "Good morning," when she entered and, "Time is up; see you Friday," when she left) and three fellow members of the Husband's gym. By the time this was typed up, some of them had acquired names: the Secretary became Miss Brown, one of the fellow-jocks was Bill and, most significantly, Husband and Wife were named Sam and Jennie—the names of Bernstein's parents. One must therefore assume there is some biographical intent (if not content) in *TinT*; and if the parents' relationship in the opera is troubled, it follows that the Bernstein home environment was not exactly a haven of tranquility. Actually, in the libretto's first draft, the breakfast exchanges between husband and wife were much angrier than the final version. All this is corroborated in the biographical book *Family Matters* (passim) by Burton Bernstein, the composer's brother. After the opera was premiered on 12 June 1952 at Brandeis University (which I attended), it was dubbed *Tsuris in Honduras*.[10]

The name Jennie, in the next draft, was replaced by Dinah, the name of Bernstein's paternal grandmother. One character who disappeared altogether was the hairdresser, a choice of occupation certainly derived from Samuel Bernstein's hair beauty supply business. Both of these decisions were part of the distancing process necessary to make the opera work, for while an annotator could yield to the temptation of spouting psychobabble in analyzing an artist's output, the works must still be able to generate universality out of its particulars—especially true in the musical theater, where words weigh as heavily as music. By substituting invisible presences (Miss Brown, Junior—ten years old, according to the first draft—Mr. Partridge, Bill and Psychiatrist) for actual subsidiary characters in *TinT*, the listener is enabled to bring his or her own life experiences to the situation, as one does in listening to an old-fashioned radio play; and by introducing the device of a Greek Chorus (the Dance-Band Trio), American universality, at least in terms of geography, is spelled out in suburbs from Scarsdale, New York, to Beverly Hills, California.

Among other suburbs ironically crooned about in the opening Trio, there is Wellesley Hills, a "closed" fashionable Boston suburb, and Brookline, one of the two upscale Boston suburbs then "available" to Jewish residents. (The other was Newton, where the Bernstein family did reside after many changes of address.) At the time *TinT* was written, however, the Bernstein elders lived in Brookline. In the final Trio, after the movie aria, Wellesley Hills is reiterated by the threesome, as if this particular suburb were closer to the Tahitian paradise unattainable to Dinah in the movie. Perhaps here we see a kind of memoir process at work. After all, the composer could have cited only one Boston suburb and found another place away from that area.

Even the Trio girl's scat sounds artfully include a memoir of sorts: "Abarbanel buys a visa" refers to Lina Abarbanell, the Viennese operetta soprano[11] and mother-in-law of Marc Blitzstein, to whom the opera is dedicated. This hidden homage is to a colleague whose style of musical theater very much influenced Bernstein's own approach.[12]

Left to right: Pianist Ivan Davis, LB, Marc Blitzstein and the author, at a Florida beach.

The same scat section touches on the American dream, as much valid in the 1990s as in the 1950s: suburban images of "Automobee. Ought to be Moby." for which read, "car for the road and books at home"; and "Sofa so far so . . ." or, "creature comfort, but watch out." The repetition of "little white house" by the Trio could be a corollary of the big one in Washington.

While one cannot picture Sam Bernstein pounding a punching bag or joining any kind of exercise program, he certainly was (paraphrasing words of the gym aria) one of the men who "made it," at least in the business world. Jennie Bernstein's love of the movies is affectionately recalled in the movie aria. She named her daughter Shirley Anne after Anne Shirley, a favorite movie star.

Incidentally, the first draft of the movie aria, sung by Dinah, had a jealous older sister of the native princess, who throws herself into the flaming pyre intended for the hero. There's general rejoicing and appeasement for at least *someone* has been sacrificed to the moon goddess. The hero, however, can no longer marry the Princess, and "is furious because he's lost a very good lay." In Dinah's words, "What a terrible awful movie!"

TinT is subtitled "An opera in Seven Scenes."

Prologue: mimed early morning franticness
Scene 1: Breakfast
Scene 2-A: OfficeSc. 2-B: Psychiatrist
Scene 3: Lunch
Scene 4-A: GymSc.4-B: Movie
Scene 5: Dinner

The final plan elaborates on the above symmetry:

Prelude: Trio
Scene 1: Breakfast Duet
Transition: orchestral
Scene 2: Sam's Office
(in compound meter, associated with Sam, who "pounds")
Scene 3: Dinah's Doctor's Office
(in duple meter, associated with Dinah, who feels "duped")
Scene 4: Street Duet
(in waltz time, Tempo di "Gymnopédie")
Interlude: Trio
Scene 5: Gym
(compound meter)
Scene 6: Movie
(duple meter)
Scene 6A: Sam comes home
(still "compounded")
Scene 7: Trio
Final Duet

The listener may not be aware of this balanced structure, but perhaps, because of it, *Trouble in Tahiti* is one of the most frequently played of American short operas. It allows us to identify with a "hot" situation in our own lives through the vehicle of a "cool" form imposed upon it by a master theater composer, distilled out of his personal life story.

About *Trouble in Tahiti* and *A Quiet Place*

Trouble in Tahiti, Bernstein's one-act opera, was first heard at Brandeis University's Festival of the Creative Arts in 12 June 1952 at an outdoor amphitheatre. Indeed, it was airy and fun, despite its ironic look at the institution of marriage. The first performance of its sequel, *A Quiet Place* (*AQP*) took place almost to the day thirty years later, on 17 June 1983, indoors at the Houston Grand Opera. And, yes, it was heavy and funereal. The title of *AQP* comes from "There Is a Garden" in *TinT*, an aria in which Dinah dreams of an elusive marital serenity. As *AQP* opens, we learn that she has died in a car accident (a suicide?), leaving her damaged family to sort itself out without her. The quiet she never found in life has beckoned in death.

Written between 1980 and 1983, *AQP* was a triple commission by Houston Grand Opera, Milan's La Scala and the John F. Kennedy Center for the Performing Arts. In Houston, *AQP* was performed after *TinT*.

For the revised version in Milan, July 1983, *AQP* became a three-act opera that enfolded *TinT* within its second act as two separate flashbacks.

Clockwise from top: JG with Melanie Helton, Timothy Nolen and Sheri Greenawald, cast members of *A Quiet Place*, Houston, June 1963.

The authorship of *AQP* is by Bernstein and librettist Stephen Wadsworth Zinsser, while Bernstein wrote both music and libretto for *TinT*. There are obvious autobiographical references to Bernstein's history in *TinT*. At the time of writing *TinT* in 1951, Bernstein had ample cause to reflect on the practice of marriage, as he himself had just gotten married. The quarreling couple in the opera reflect Bernstein's (read Junior?) memories of his parents' discordant relationship; perhaps he feared that he would repeat their mistakes. After Felicia's death in 1978, Bernstein updated Sam and Dinah's story to the tragic present of *AQP*. Wadsworth Zinsser's sister, Nina Zinsser, also had recently died in a car crash. (The opera is dedicated "To the Memory of F.M.B. and N.S.Z.")

Whereas *TinT* is one of the most played one-act operas, *AQP* has had a more troubled (pun intended) history. Perhaps one reason is simply the passing of time. *AQP*'s piano-vocal score describes *TinT*'s time frame as the early 1950s and *AQP*'s as early 1980s. That differential is significant since the scores reflect the state of music in their respective eras. *TinT* satirizes the popular sounds of the '50s, especially those of television commercials and clichéd movie songs ("Island Magic," for example, has a precedent in Warren and Gordon's "Tropical Magic" from the fluffy '40s flick *Week-End In Havana*). But by the 1980s, movie musicals were dinosaurs, and commercials were driven by the kinetic world of MTV. The music of *AQP* was no longer ironic commentary (i.e., on pop conventions), but sui generis, tortured, even atonal at times.

Bernstein was quite deliberate in juxtaposing one style against the other. The five pitches of the last chord of *TinT* are an A major 7 chord with the added tritone of D-sharp (a *West Side Story* harmonic trademark). It is the same chord that opens *AQP*. But in bar two of *AQP*, the remaining seven notes of the twelve-note scale are sounded together in a cluster. Watch out! We are plunged into an altogether different world, hexachordal, sort of dodecaphonic. Curiously, when *AQP* proved to be not as popular as *TinT*, Bernstein sincerely believed it would eventually find its niche on Broadway!

Only five characters inhabit the cast of *TinT*, while *AQP* has ten, along with a chorus. The orchestra for *TinT* is modest with a small percussion battery; but that of *AQP* is huge, including electric instruments unknown to the 1950s, with a battery that packs a wallop. Critics have pointed out that the inflated quality of *AQP* is its major stumbling block since it essentially is a stage piece about four characters. Indeed, when the quartet is interacting, the music of *AQP* truly soars. Listen to the consoling reconciliations of "Dear Daddy" in act 1 or the end of the opera. Divorced from its mise-en-scène, at moments like these, the music of *AQP* is a heartbreaker.

4 Keeping Faith

"Kaddish" Glories and Tribulations

The Bernstein score with which I was most intimately involved was his Symphony No. 3, subtitled "Kaddish." As in Mahler's life, summers—in this case, those of 1961, '62 and '63— were composing time for this busy musician. In June '62, LB worked on the symphony at the MacDowell Colony in New Hampshire. I also was in residence as a composer. We drove up together from New York City with him at the wheel in an open Lincoln convertible. On a country road, not far from the colony, the car broke down. A kind driver had a tow truck come get us. Soon a young mechanic arrived and it was decided that we would remain in the front seat of the convertible as he towed us onto the colony grounds. I had been there a few times before, but never had I arrived in, shall we say, such elevated circumstances.

LB at the Veltin Studio, MacDowell Colony, 1962.

A few days later, the car having been fixed, the grease monkey returned to pick up the boss. Back at the station, the mechanic asked LB if he would like to have a pair of recently born puppies. That was irresistible for him, and without thinking that it might be against colony policy, he agreed to take them. He then gave the guy his New York address if he should ever happen to be in town—an invitation evidently soon forgotten.

With Franny and Zooey.

All colony "fellows" had breakfast and dinner together. LB fast became the center of attention and popular with all the artists. His penchant for postprandial anagrams and Scrabble had few challengers, but those who took him on sometimes defeated him. In a send-off for a writer from the South who had completed her stay, LB invited some of us out for drinks in the town of Peterborough. He ordered screwdrivers all around, but the tavern only had prune juice. Not to be deterred, he had a pitcher concocted of vodka and prune juice, and named it the "Daphne," in honor of the departing author. It tasted not half bad. Even the administration was dazzled and could not deny him the dogs, which he named Franny and Zooey after the then best seller by J. D. Salinger. Ever dutiful, he fed and picked up after the pups. When he returned to his country home with the announcement of, "Look what I have!" Felicia said, "No way!" but only because little Franny and Zooey would have grown up to be big German shepherd animals. They had to be given away.

At a reception hosted by George Kendall, the colony director, and held at Edward MacDowell's home, LB surprised everyone by handing out a copy of a round he had written using every colonist's name and teaching it to them on the spot. This became the basis for the round sung by the boys' choir in the Scherzo of the symphony.

Oh yes, about the mechanic. One day, in the fall, he showed up at the Bernsteins' Park Avenue address—I don't think he phoned ahead—with his new bride, and Felicia, without having prior knowledge, invited them in until

Maestro came home. A rather awkward situation.

Working on "Kaddish" at the MacDowell Colony.

In the summer of 1963, when LB announced, "I finished!" (i.e., composing "Kaddish"), Felicia got up from her chair by the pool and with a joyous whoop jumped in fully clothed. In November, I helped out during a hectic three-week orchestration period at the country home. The first forty or so pages of the scoring for the Scherzo is in my hand, taken from a "road map" of directions LB provided. He permitted me to orchestrate the last two pages of this front batch on my own, which of course had to meet his approval. We accomplished all this in a cozy outcropping of the house known because of its stove as the Franklin room, redolent of the MacDowell Colony experience.

Later that month, on November 22, we were back in the city for a Young People's Concert staff meeting at Bernstein's study at Philharmonic Hall, then located next to the orchestra's library. During the freewheeling discussion about an upcoming Young People's script, Joe Zizza, the assistant orchestra librarian, interrupted us to relay the news that Kennedy had just been shot in Dallas. We were stunned, but somehow trudged on with our now considerably muted give-and-take when Joe returned to say that JFK was dead. Without much of a word, we closed shop. As LB and I were driving back uptown to the Park Avenue apartment, I turned to him and said, "Well, now I guess we know to whom the symphony is dedicated." He nodded in silence. That day the Bernsteins sent their children to see *Lawrence of Arabia*, the movie, while the parents mourned in private.

* * *

On 16 December 1964, LB presented the fair copy of what musicians call the "short" score to the John F. Kennedy Memorial Library. This manuscript was first passed along to Arnold Arnstein, the professional copyist for many Bernstein works. Arnie was a droll and acerbic fellow who always reminded me of actor Everett Sloane (known as Mr. Bernstein in the classic movie *Citizen Kane*), both in speech and looks. On the Scherzo LB wrote:

> Arnie, when copying this movement, leave a blank staff for the Speaker from the beginning up through S[taff]-3, bar 4, since all that music will be repeated *with* spoken words over it, on S-7 ff [staff 7 & following], and I'd hate to see you copy it all over again! Love, Lenny.

For years I had assumed the JFK Library also had the original full score, but they did not. Neither did the Library of Congress—in possession of every other original Bernstein manuscript. Big mystery, where is the handwritten full score?

In an extraordinary gesture of thanks, LB had the initial penciled draft of the work given to me. This was the manuscript he worked on at MacDowell. One hundred pages long, it was bound in black with gold lettering: "For Jack Gottlieb, in gratitude, L.B." Usually LB's conducting scores were bound in green, but the choice of black was most appropriate for the message conveyed by the work, a plea for sanity in a world gone amok. On the first inside cover page, he had jotted down various possible titles:

> *Kaddish for Us All:*
> 1. *To Avert the Evil Day*
> 2. *To Comfort God*
> 3. *To Affirm Life*
>
> *3 Reasons (ways) to say (for saying) Kaddish*
> *A Symphonic Play* [crossed out]
> *A Three-fold Kaddish*
>
> > Symphony No. 3 for mixed chorus, alto or soprano solo and large orchestra
>
> *Marches* [not clear], *Kaddish I, March, Kaddish II, Kaddish III*

The page also has a typical Bernstein doodling on the side—which I always took to be a sign of preoccupation with something else—and two jots of melody. On a following page he listed some of the liturgical functions of the prayer as other title possibilities: *Reader's Kaddish (short) Reader's Kaddish (long), Rabbi's Kaddish,* and *Mourner's Kaddish.*

Scattered throughout are small groups of Xed-out bars, certainly of interest to researchers. In the Scherzo movement, Biblical miracles are interpreted as:

> Rainbow, for the desperate; Pillar of fire, for the lost [and] Manna, for the hungry.

Other items in the draft include timings and tempo markings (*deliberate swing* that became *grotesque* in the printed score). Most curious is the subtitle for movement 2 (which became movement 3), *Pietà*, not exactly a word of Jewish content, originally considered as a solo for soprano with female chorus or boys' choir. Within these pages he wrote down immediate performance concerns:

1. call Leontyne?

I do not know if he ever did contact Leontyne Price; it would have been a wonder to hear her do the solo.

2. Israel speaker (Rovina?)

JG and Ofra Bikel greeting LB at Tel Aviv airport, December 1963.

The symphony was designed as a vehicle for Felicia. But the text, translated by Dan Miron, was to be given in Hebrew at the world premiere in Israel on 10 December 1963 in Tel Aviv where, with Ofra Bikel, I functioned as a go-between. Ofra and I arrived in Israel some days ahead of LB.

I was overjoyed to spend a few hours at the Tel Aviv residence of Prime Minister David Ben-Gurion and his wife, Paula (see the frontispiece), and during that time period I had the pleasure to be in the company of author-archaeologist Moshe Pearlman and artist Yossi Stern.

Hannah Rovina of the Habimah Theater was the Speaker in "Kaddish." (She was the one who had created the role of Leah in the classic Yiddish play *The Dybbuk.*) Earlier, on 10 August, LB had written his sister Shirley:

> I'm trying to get Rovina to do it in Israel and a good Izzy poet to translate it.
>
> It's terribly long! She never shuts up. But I think you'll be surprised by its power.

At the first reading rehearsal Rovina uttered the opening words *Avi* ("my father") in a deep resonant voice. LB fell to one knee, exclaiming she sounded as he had dreamed it. Alas, the honeymoon was short-lived because Rovina subsequently had great difficulty with cues.

Post-premiere toast in Tel Aviv, Israel, 1963. *Seated, left to right:* Abe Kaplan, Hannah Rovina, Jennie Tourel, JG, LB, Felicia Bernstein and Moshe Pearlman. Others unknown.

3. Schirmer [the publisher]: photostat originals, ink copy on tissues, subito!, print to Abe Kaplan [the chorus director], Israel Orch. (2), Tod P.

The latter stands for Todd Perry, manager of the Boston Symphony Orchestra. Part of the reason the commission was a long time aborning had to do with LB's search for a collaborator to write the Speaker's text. He had tried to use verse written—separately—by the eminent poets Robert Lowell and Frederick Seidel. In the letter to his sister, Bernstein said:

> I finally decided it had to be by me. Collaboration with a poet is impossible on so personal a work, so I've found after a distressful year with Lowell and Seidel . . .

Distressful it may have been, but Bernstein in his text was not averse to borrowing a central theme from Lowell:

> Our hands have turned creation on its head.
> Oh Father, do not bite your lip and frown;
> it hardly matters now if we made God,
> or God made us. Both suffer and exist.[1]

Compare that to the final speech in the symphony, wherein Bernstein asks God to "unfurrow your brow" and then:

> O my Father . . .
> We are one, after all, You and I:
> Together we suffer, together exist.
> And forever will recreate each other . . .

I wrote the program note for the premiere, which was reprinted for the first American performance on 31 January 1964. In another letter to his sister, dated 25 January and mostly about mourning the murder of his composer-chum Marc Blitzstein, LB spoke of his nervousness:

> Munch is in love with the piece, but scared witless and can't beat it (7/8 etc.). The chorus, Jennie T., oy . . ." [Note the T., as opposed to B., for Jennie, his mother.]

The American premiere in Boston was not critically acclaimed. LB spoke of the condescension he felt from fellow-composers Arthur Berger, Leon Kirchner and Harold Shapero, who had attended rehearsals. However, I am of the opinion that was how he imagined it in retrospect. Shapero was a boyhood buddy, and may have had the nerve to say, on the spot, that after the first two movements there was a "let-down." But if he did, it is hard to believe that Berger and Kirchner would have chimed in with the same doubts. It is almost as if LB had persuaded himself that because "Kaddish" was not a success, the reaction of Kirchner and Co. was one way to cope with the disappointment.

Later Revisions

The texts by poets Lowell and Seidel were eloquent attempts, but their words were more for reading than for speaking. In fact, Lowell described his attempts as "a bilge of declamation."[2] Bernstein's text, on the other hand, was certainly theatrical, and, for many critics, excessive. Accordingly, LB revised the text and also made it possible for the narration to be spoken by a man, changes that necessitated some minor adjustments in the music. This version premiered on 25 August 1978, LB's sixtieth birthday. Then in 2001, Jamie Bernstein wrote an entirely new text that she later characterized as: "My father's angry with God; I'm angry with my father."[3] That confession is particularly poignant because, according to Michael Wager, who first recited the 1977 revision, LB's original text was more about his relationship with *his* father, and less so with God. Furthermore, Wager says that LB "had hated his father" but had resolved such issues with the writing of "Kaddish."[4]

In 2003, Samuel Pisar, a friend of Bernstein's, wrote yet another version that reflected Pisar's experience as a Holocaust survivor. The main problem with this rendering is that in certain places it stretches the music with long-held chords or makes repeats to accommodate the text. This is particularly egregious when the big tune in movement 3, the Scherzo, that had been generated from a twelve-tone row in the first movement, is delayed for speechifying and thereby voids its evolution for the listener.[5]

LB was always tinkering with his works; but it would have been best if he had left this one alone, waited out his critics, and stayed with the concept as originally written for his wife. Or, as he once penned:

Sorrowful Song (Conundrum)
Last night I sat down
and wrote a poem.
This morning I looked at it
and didn't like it much,
So I started all over again,
Making minor, but significant changes.
This evening I looked at it
and didn't like it much better.
So I changed it back
to the original version
Which I wrote last night
And this is it.

Hilton Hotel, De Gaulle Airport, Paris, France. LB and the author, 1977.

Jennie Tourel

Jennie Tourel, what a wonder was she! Born Bella Davidovich[6] in Vitebsk, Russia (1900, the same year as Aaron Copland, who wrote the piano trio *Vitebsk* in 1929), she changed her name to Tourel after her voice teacher's name, Anna El-Tour. Among her many triumphs was her creation of Baba the Turk in Stravinsky's *The Rake's Progress*, in 1951.

Only a few twentieth-century singers have become linked in the public mind with composers of art songs: Peter Pears with Benjamin Britten, Pierre Bernac with Francis Poulenc, and Jennie Tourel with Leonard Bernstein. LB's song cycles *I Hate Music* and *La Bonne Cuisine*, his two Rilke songs and the song "Silhouette" were either premiered by or dedicated to Tourel. The "Jeremiah" and "Kaddish" symphonies were given their first performances with Tourel as soloist. The Jennie-Lenny team (Bernstein at the piano) also were heard in memorable recitals, including songs of Poulenc, as well as with the New York Philharmonic and other orchestras (Bernstein conducting) in works by Bach, Foss, Ravel, Berlioz and Mahler.

LB and JG with Jennie Tourel at the 30th Street Studio, Columbia Records, recording "I Hate Music," 18 November 1960. "To Jack and with 'I don't hate music.' With love, Jennie, 1961."

A word about the "Kaddish" connection. As previously discussed, on the first draft of his manuscript, LB had written down immediate performance concerns, among them "call Leontyne?"—that is, to do the soprano solo. He never got around to contacting Leontyne Price because once Tourel got wind of its solo, she would not let LB alone. Finally she convinced him to engage her by actually auditioning the whole piece for him in his country house. I sat there transfixed by the yearning Bellini-like bel canto line made golden in the mezzo voice of a song written for a silvery soprano. His hesitancy about her in this instance had been based on her ability to hit the high notes securely.

Two days after JFK's assassination, at the request of William S. Paley, head of the CBS network, LB led a memorial performance of Mahler's Symphony No. 2 in C Minor, "Resurrection," with the New York Philharmonic in a TV studio, a former movie theater on the east side of Manhattan. The Philharmonic had performed it in concert a short while before with Tourel as one of the soloists. Of course, like everyone else, Jennie was bewildered and grief stricken. Ordinarily, she was a first-class, solid musician, but this time she made a wrong pitch entrance in the "Urlicht" movement, her solo. Almost immediately she got back on track. However, this was never seen by the viewing public because at that moment the network had turned away from the Mahler performance to show Jack Ruby mowing down Lee Harvey Oswald.

She premiered one of my *Songs of Loneliness,* a cycle on poems of Constantine Cavafy, at Philharmonic Hall, Lincoln Center. When I became music director of Temple Israel in Saint Louis (the first part of my leave of absence from LB's employ) she gave a recital that included LB's "Lamentation"—with me at the organ—at the Temple, which was the talk of the town.

Her apartment was West Fifty-sixth Street around the corner from LB, buildings that almost abutted each other. Her postconcert soirees were convivial and cozy, with Joan Sutherland and husband Richard Bonynge among the many musical guests. They stayed well into the early morning hours enjoying Jennie's caviar, blini and her servings of gossip. Dear Jennie, such a delicious mix of glamour and yenta-hood.

Mass

In 1970, while I was living and working in Saint Louis, LB and I corresponded. I questioned how he, a self-conscious Jew—not the same thing as conscientious—could be writing a setting of the Catholic mass, especially the Credo text. He responded on 2 February:

> Dear Yankele: . . . This is a hasty farewell as I depart for a long European haul of three wintry months. Brr. And ugh. It couldn't be more badly timed: The Mass is not in shape to be left for 3 months on a shelf. It's been panic time. A lot written, but the final shape, the conception still eludes me. And collaboration trouble for a change. . . . Yes, I have set The Credo, but you'll understand why when you hear it. It culminates

> in a rock-song that begins: 'I believe in God, But does God believe in me?' Not your average Credo, you see . . . "[7]

From another letter later that year, on 5 November, he first congratulated me on my coinage of "Hi-Hos" for the Jewish high holidays, to which he subsequently dubbed Hanukkah one of the "Lo-Hos."

> I am going through that famous transition period of metamorphology from exhausted conductor to try-again composer. Pure agony. I am still contemplating that notion of a staged Mass for The Kennedy Center opening. As yet the concept is hazy. I try. Me, an official Washington composer?" [There was a P.S.: "I have a present for you—a pipe from Bruckner's very own organ! When will you come and collect it?" Alas, I never did.]

We had both been at the MacDowell Colony in early summer 1963. Now, on 12 December 1970, he unexpectedly wrote to me from there:

> Look where I am!! And in Watson [a studio], yet. And writing a mass. And really getting somewhere at last. And filled with memories that only you could share. . . .
>
> And I wrote a round for the Colonists, for Xmas (which I shall use in The Mass, natch), and using all their names, and even in F major! [He had done the same thing in '63, a round then used in the Scherzo movement of "Kaddish." The words for the round in *Mass* became "dubing, dubang" in the Alleluia.]
>
> *And* you don't know the Macdowell Colony unless you've been here in winter [I had been]—it's of an indescribable beauty—all green and white and pure—snow & pines and birches and wild moonlight.
>
> It's Kaddish time all over again, only now a lot of Latin. (I've just set the Confiteor with tone rows!), and it's good. Lord, [I don't think he means the Deity] could I use your advice and help on some of these ecumenical points. Like, for instance—what's the Hebrew equivalent of *Osanna in excelsis*? (The rest of The Sanctus is obvious in Hebrew, with some minor discrepancies). Could it be [he writes in Hebrew lettering]: *Hoshanah bimromim* or something similar? It doesn't seem right somehow and there's a complete change of meaning." [*Hoshanah*

actually means "save us." The equivalent of "Hosanna in excelsis" would be *Hallelu bimromim*, "Praise God in the highest places."]

On the side of the page he wrote, "This is the only letter I've written from here!"

Up to the last minute, in the as yet unfinished Kennedy Center, Bernstein had to endure jackhammers during rehearsals. After the premiere, he said of the blasting he got from the *New York Times*, "Plenty hammers." Critic Harold Schonberg (I regret that his name appears more than once in this book) had deemed it "a show-biz Mass, the work of a musician who desperately wants to be with it." When *Mass* was given a concert performance in Carnegie Hall by the Collegiate Chorale in 2002, Anthony Tommasini concluded *his Times* review, "In many ways, *Mass* is an earnest mess." But, he continued, "it got to this baby boomer [meaning himself]. Here is Uncle Lenny trying to make sense of it all. You have to love the guy." Vindication of a sort, I guess, even if the tone is still condescending.

Daryl Bornstein reports that during a later performance of *Mass* at the Kennedy Center, LB was standing at the back railing, vociferously making comments. A little old lady came up the aisle, shook her finger at him and said: "I know who you are. Shut up!"

A Jewish Mass or a Catholic Mitzvah?

(Originally written for the St. Louis Post Dispatch, *26 September 1971)*

The verdict is in. Even though there are voices yet to he heard from, it is safe to say that the critical reception to Leonard Bernstein's new *Mass*, written for the opening of the Kennedy Center in Washington, has resulted in a hung jury. The New York press has damned it, while the Washington contingent shouted hosanna! (Provincialism?) *Time* magazine says that the music "reflects a basic confusion," but *Newsweek* calls it "inspired on all counts." The first-nighters were determinably more cool than the less uptight preview audiences.

But in all the uproar about this great split decision of 1971, only passing mention has been made of a remarkable fact: that a distinctive Jewishness pervades this Catholic work. This is not because it is historically the first mass ever to he written by a Jew, but that it could have never been conceived by a "dyed-in-the-Agnus-Dei" Catholic in the first place. Those who would dismiss it, however, as a "show-biz" Mass have a fundamental misconception, since it is not a mass that incidentally uses theatrical devices, but as the composer subtitles it: "A Theater Piece for Singers, Players and Dancers" that uses the mass structure as its point of departure.

It is Bernstein's first theatrical effort since *West Side Story* (1957), although there have been two abandoned attempts since then, one based on Thornton Wilder's *The Skin of Our Teeth* and the other on Bertolt Brecht's *The Exception and the Rule*, parts from both having found a nesting place in *Mass*. Not only is the massive *Mass* more musically sophisticated than the 1957 landmark musical, but it also dims the lustre of the more recent *Jesus Christ Superstar*. At the same time it certainly is lower than the angels when compared to Beethoven's exalted *Missa Solemnis* or the austere *Mass* by Stravinsky, composers whose presences are felt in the Bernstein work. Nothing like it has ever been witnessed and experienced in a church or, for that matter, on a Broadway stage.

The reasons why a Roman Catholic composer could not or would not have given birth to this mass go beyond its nonliturgical aspects, since, most intriguingly, Bernstein has imposed upon it a decidedly Jewish weltanschauung. In order to accept this, the listener first had to decide for himself if a musician, in the fullest sense of that word, is qualified also to be a theologian. Or is this man a victim of a kind of megalomania?

In any case, the roots for the philosophic theme date from his "Kaddish" Symphony of 1963, which has a spoken text written by the composer. The Speaker, representing humanity, says of the Divine, "Together we suffer, together exist and forever will recreate each other." This Jewish view of life, of an ongoing interaction between God and Man, is like Martin Buber would have put it: the "I" is part of the "Thou" and vice versa. God thus is seen as a never-ending creative force, overcoming chaos in cooperation with man; and the composer's text for *Mass* vividly dramatizes this ongoing process.

If one regards classical Judaism as a religion of law and traditional Catholicism (that is, prior to Vatican II) as a religion of dogma, it might then be said that the one tells us what to do, while the other tells us what to believe. Blind faith is not as acceptable to the Jew as it has been to the Catholic. The Latin missal ironically, then, is a more commodious vehicle for Bernstein than the Hebrew siddur since it affords him the doctrinal targets for doubts, questions and even ridicule. But it must also be made clear that parts of the worship format, as used by him, are already passé since the house cleaning of Vatican II. Catholics in 1971, therefore, would he less likely to take offense at the so-called blasphemies than they would have before that innovative council took place in 1962–63.

Sections of church prayer do, of course, originate in synagogue prayer. Psalm fragments liberally dot the landscape in *Mass*. For example, in the prefatory sequence; and the De Profundis (part of the Offertory in *Mass*) is Psalm 130 in its entirety. The Lord's Prayer is derived from the Kaddish prayer, the Te Deum from the Aleinu, and the Sanctus grows directly out of the Kedushah. Bernstein explicitly stresses this latter kinship in a magical transformation from Latin to Hebrew —a particularly poignant moment that is both stunning for its theatricality and religiously moving for its unexpectedness.

During the Offertory scene, some golden ritual artifacts are brought to the front of the stage, and just as mice will play when cat's away, a bacchanalian dance develops around them, stopped dead in its tracks by the arrival of Big Daddy, the central character of the Celebrant. Could it be the dance around the Golden Calf and the sudden appearance of Moses? This Celebrant, who has been characterized as everything from a Christ-figure to a symbol of the Establishment, and who dissolves from innocence of belief (in blue jeans) to madness, as he loses grip on that belief (now richly clad in his props of burdensome robes) later on reinforces the Moses idea by smashing these same artifacts (not a crucifix as some viewers have reported) at the height of his disintegration. The tablets of the Ten Commandments hurled down from Mount Sinai?

But there is more subtle Jewish content than this. Leading up to that hair-raising moment of destruction, the climax of *Mass*, there is a chilling metamorphosis that seemingly twists the slogan of "war is hell" into "peace is hell." The stage writhes in a Dante-esque kind of infernal nightmare as the entire company goes hysterical with the plea, *dona nobis pacem* (give us peace).

One group screams, "We're fed up with your heavenly silence, and we only get action with violence," a couplet that might have come right out of the Book of Job (19:7): "Behold, I cry out: 'Violence!' but I am not heard I cry aloud, but there is no justice." Another group proclaims: "We're not down on our knees, . . . We're not asking you please; We're just saying: 'give us peace now!'"

Such a demand, not a request, is in the Judaic tradition of the Biblical Prophets and the series of personal confrontations with their Maker.

Furthermore, there is the famous Judgment Against God by Rabbi Levi Isaac of Berditchev (in eighteenth-century Ukraine) who declares to God: "I will not stir from this spot until there be an end to our persecution."

The Credo is set in mechanistic formula writing, using twelve-tone procedures and sung in Latin by a stuffed-shirt type of choir in robes, while juxtaposed to it is a rock style Non-Credo, sung in English by Street People in mod clothing, which has the chutzpah to say, "You, God, choose to become a man, To pay the earth a small social call; I tell you, Sir, you never were a man at all. Why? You had the choice when to live, when to die, and then become a God again."

This kind of Talmudic disputation is further substantiated by male choral responses of "possibly yes, probably no." One is strikingly reminded of Hassidic disciples at the feet of their beloved rebbe wrangling over details of Biblical law and interpretation.

This Jewish penchant for playing with words is exploited, through the form of acrostics and puns, by Bernstein and his collaborator, Stephen Schwartz (who, along with the conductor Maurice Peress, form a Trinity of Jews in the hierarchy of *Mass*). Thus the musical syllables of "mi" and "sol" become "me" and "soul" (surely a more meaningful punning than Oscar Hammerstein's saccharine "Do, a female deer," etc.). In the hauntingly beautiful mad scene (oddly reminiscent of the mad scene in Britten's *Peter Grimes*), "Amen" is transformed into "I'm in" ("a hurry") "If it all ends today" (read as "De") "Profundis" and the Hebrew word for Lord, "Adonai" (read as "I") "don't know, I don't no"—(that is, "know")—"bis, misere nobis."

There are musical puns also. The composer quotes a phrase from his "Kaddish" Symphony in one of the opening Kyries. He takes a Chilean folk song (Mrs. Bernstein was raised in Chile) called "Verso por la Sagrada Escritura" ("Verse for the Sacred Scripture") as a setting for the Epistle reading, proclaiming loud and clear: "You cannot imprison the word of the Lord." This also gives him the opportunity to quote actual letters from a conscientious objector and a member of the Catholic left, Daniel Berrigan. (The director of *Mass*, Gordon Davidson, had also directed *The Trial of the Catonsville Nine*, a play about the travails of the Berrigans). An orchestral meditation, later incorporated into the mad scene, is a passacaglia on the prophetic eleven-tone sequence from the last movement of Beethoven's Ninth Symphony, with reference, naturally, to the idea that "all men are brothers."

The music obviously, then, is highly eclectic. But this is nothing new with Bernstein; his output has always been thus. Nor is eclecticism in art a dirty word anymore these days. So-called quote-pieces abound. Lukas Foss's *Phorion* is based on Bach's E Minor Partita. Luciano Berio interweaves a movement from Mahler's Second Symphony in his symphony. Wesley Bolk's opera *Faust Counter Faust* is filled with previous Faustian musicalizations. In *Mass* there also are unintentional evocations of Kurt Weill (in "World Without End," an ecological plea), Gershwin's *Porgy and Bess* (in the taunting "Half of the People" and a Sporting Life kind of song called "Easy"), Mahler (the motive for "Kadosh, Kadosh"), Marc Blitzstein (in the song "Thank You") and others.

But the more interesting thing is that Bernstein quotes much from himself. The opening psalm "A New Song" uses a tune not unlike one found in the first movement of his violin concerto *Serenade*. The clarinets that accompany the song "I Go On" remind us of the opening of "The Age of Anxiety" (although the sung melody unfortunately comes out sounding like the pop song "I Remember You"). One of the dances suggests the "Profanation" movement of the "Jeremiah" Symphony; another breaks into a phrase straight out of the *Candide* Overture. The Gospel-Sermon "God Said" has an echo in "Gee, Officer Krupke" from *West Side Story*. Part of the Mad Scene, "Things Get Broken"—which the authors referred to as "Beserko"—could trace its ancestry to the aria "There Are Men" from *Trouble in Tahiti*. The Sanctus sounds like harmonic sequences used in his incidental music to *Peter Pan*.

Bernstein has somewhat justified all this mélange by stating that everything that he has composed up to the time of the *Mass* was, in some way, a preparation. His accomplishment is truly a spectacular triumph of mind over matter (chatter?). For despite its incredible diversity (which no other composer could have technically handled so well) and even in spite of its moments of questionable taste, he has succeeded gloriously in his intention "to communicate as directly and universally as I can, a reaffirmation of faith," and, one might add, of tonality.

Because of my professional relationship with Bernstein over the years, I have had to restrain myself to be as coolly objective as possible in this report. But if the reader will allow me to throw caution to the winds, I cannot help but say that *Mass* is the most significant breakthrough in the musical theater of our time. Amen, brother, Amen.

Three Meditations from *Mass* for Violoncello and Orchestra

Getting this work and the *Slava!* Overture into shape was the result of working with LB for ten straight days, including several all-night sessions, at the Watergate Hotel in Washington, D.C. The copyists were ensconced in the Howard Johnson hotel across the street (shades of the Nixon-era plumbers) ready to pounce on whatever sections I could deliver to them. The suite that LB occupied always had a mess of dishes left behind by room service; but the hotel menu is how I came to savor the gustatory sensation of steak tartare.

The pieces were cobbled together from previously written works, Meditation No. 3 from *Mass* and *Slava!* from *1600 Pennsylvania Avenue*. Five years earlier (1972), the Israel Philharmonic had premiered a third Meditation for Orchestra (not with cello solo) that was also fashioned from various sections of *Mass*. But LB was dissatisfied with that version and withdrew it.

For the layout of the cello adaptation, LB penciled in a sketchy road map for me to flush out. His blueprint included directions such as "ork. only to sc. p. 20, b. 10," "Fast & primitive (Acolytes in P-V, p. 58, b. 2)," and "with drum interps." These might seem cryptic to the casual reader, but they were perfectly clear to me.

The manuscript is dedicated "For Mstislav Rostropovich," with the added note, "For my dear Slava, as a token of more to come." I treasure a gift from Rostropovich, an autographed page of the solo part in Slava's hand.

(*From the full score, 1978, unsigned*)
Bernstein's *Mass: A Theatre Piece for Singers, Players and Dancers* was composed at the request of Jacqueline Kennedy for the inauguration of the John F. Kennedy Center for the Performing Arts in Washington, D. C., on 8 September 1971. The two orchestral meditations are used as instrumental interludes: No. 1 (*Lento assai, molto sostenuto*) between the "Confession" and the "Gloria;" No. 2 (*Andante sostenuto*) between the "Gloria" and "Epistle." Meditation No. 1 was originally written as a piano anniversary "For Helen Coates," Bernstein's longtime secretary. Meditation No. 2 is a set of four variations with a coda based on the eleven-note sequence from the Finale of Beethoven's Ninth Symphony that leads to the great choral outburst of "Brueder!" ("Brothers!"). The "Epistle" that follows is based on the more ancient outburst of Saint Paul to his Christian brothers.

Both meditations were arranged in 1971 by the composer for violoncello and piano, first performed by the composer with cellist Stephen Kates on 28 March 1972. Then in 1977 Bernstein transcribed the same pieces for cello and orchestra, to which he added a third meditation. This version was premiered by and is dedicated to Rostropovich and the National Symphony Orchestra on 11 October 1977, also at the Kennedy Center.

Meditation No. 3, also arranged for cello and piano, was stitched together from various parts of *Mass*: the "Epiphany," a kind of solo fantasia; "In Nomine Patris," a trancelike dance; and the Chorale "Almighty Father." Although some of these sections are widely separated in *Mass*, there is an underlying thematic unity, particularly between the Dance and the Chorale.

The composer provided the following commentary:

> Since *Mass* is primarily a dramatic stage production, these excerpts can convey at best only a certain limited aspect of its scope and intention. Essentially it is concerned with a celebration of the Roman ritual using the Latin text of the Catholic liturgy; but simultaneously there is a subtext in English reflecting the reactions, doubts, protests and questionings—positive and negative—of all who are attending and perceiving this ritual. By "all of us" I mean to include all who are assembled on stage and, by extension, the audience itself.
>
> The ritual is conducted by a young man of mysterious simplicity (called the Celebrant) who throughout the drama is invested by his acolytes with increasingly ornate robes and symbols which connote both an increase in the superficial formalism of his obligation and of the burden that he bears. There is a parallel increase in the resistance of the Congregants—in the sharpness and bitterness of their reactions—and in deterioration of his own faith. At the climax of Communion, all ceremony breaks down and the Mass is shattered. It then remains for each individual on the stage to find a new seed of faith within himself through painful meditation, enabling each individual to pass on the embrace of peace (Pax) to his neighbor. This chain of embrace grows and spreads through the entire stage, ultimately into the audience and hopefully into the world outside. The disposition of forces at the original production was in the pit: an orchestra of strings only, plus two organs and a percussion section. All other instrumentalists are on stage in costume and function as members of the cast. These include,

> wind, brass and percussion players, as well as Rock instrumentalists. There are three choruses: a formal choir seated in pews, a Boys' Choir and a so-called Street Chorus, many of whom function as vocal or dancing soloists and groups. All these forces perform with, against, or around the Celebrant. At certain moments of extreme tension, the Celebrant tires to control the situation by saying "Let us pray," and it is at these moments that the Meditations are played by the pit orchestra, while the entire company remains motionless in attitudes of prayer.

The composer had great difficulty persuading his collaborators to allow these interludes, especially No. 2, to take place because it was felt the action was stopped cold. Bernstein insisted on having both performed since, if for no other reason, by the time Meditation No. 2 began, the audience would have already experienced the interruption of No. 1, and would, perhaps, ruminate on what had just happened on stage. The jury is still out. In concert, of course, the listener is not distracted by such trappings.

The Little Motive That Could

(From Prelude, Fugue and Riffs *newsletter, 11 September 2005)*

The 2005 CD repackaging by the DG label of Bernstein's 1953 Decca LP recordings of five classic symphonies with spoken analysis was long overdue. More than fifty years later, I am entranced all over again by the Maestro's verbal agility and inimitable insights, particularly his treatment of the first movement from Brahms' Symphony No. 4 (reprinted in the book *The Infinite Variety of Music*). This is where Bernstein describes the main theme as blossoming from motivic intervals of the third, and where the rhythmic seed in a transition passage hatches a "huge, mad German tango."

Listening to Bernstein's discussion of how Brahms creates a magnificence (a full movement) out of a seeming insignificance (a tiny motive) reminded me of something I had long suspected was present in Bernstein's *Mass*, but had never before carefully considered. Although it has often been criticized as sprawling and de trop, I always felt that there is something musical going on in *Mass* that unifies its disparate songs, choruses, dances and instrumental interludes.

Much to my surprise, I have found out that little something also to be based on an interval of the third; but unlike Brahms, it is not primarily used

Transformations of the *Mass* motive.

as a source for development. Bernstein's work, after all, is not a symphony subject to the rigors of sonata form and the like. Instead, consistent with *Mass* as a theater piece and with Bernstein as a theater composer, the germinal motive is put to use as a dramatic character. In fact, it becomes a kind of cast member alongside the main persona of the Celebrant.

The full motive consists of three notes made up of an intervallic third (notes 1 and 2) that settles on the note that lies between (note 3). Its rhythm is a rapid anapest of two short notes followed by a longer stress. You can pronounce it aloud, say, in the articulation of "Jac-que-*line* Ken-ne-*dy*" (who had invited Bernstein to write the work). The composer referred to this kernel as the "Holy Spirit" motive (let's call it HSM); and, indeed, it is an animating force that not only sparks the beginnings of individual numbers, but also demarcates the formal design of part 1.

The opening, heard via tape on the glockenspiel, begins with the HSM, which reappears in the exact center ("First Introit") and at the end of part 1 ("Epiphany"). These markers—an ascending interval of the third followed by a downward second—are left intact. But the HSM is put into a different guise in the two numbers that precede and follow each of the subdivisions.

"A Simple Song," the first and best known song from *Mass*, begins its refrain with a repetition of the minor third (pitches E and G) on the words "I will sing the"; but on "Lord," the next word, instead of going down a step to F—the in-between note—Bernstein leaps to the F, a seventh above. It is the same resolution, but transferred heavenly upward. Near the end of the song, a cadence on the words "and walks in His ways" is shaped by a reordering of the pitches from 1-2-3 to 3-1-2. This permutation infiltrates the "Alleluia" that follows, where the same 3-1-2 cadence as "Simple Song" is prominently articulated.

The First Introit, the centerpiece of part 1, is a rondo divided into two subsections: "Prefatory Prayers," initiated by the HSM blaring forth in a kind of fanfare, and "Dominum vobiscum," which begins with a new pitch grouping of the motive, now as 2-1-3. The Second Introit ("In nomine patris"), a taped dance interlude, begins with the intervallic third, but the next note is the half-step above, not the in-between note. Immediately thereafter, however, notes 4, 5 and 6 are constructed by the now familiar HSM.

Perhaps the most magical moment in *Mass* is how this Near Eastern belly dance (labeled "Fast and primitive") evolves into the sublime Western-sounding chorale of the "Prayer for the Congregation" (Adagio). We are provided with the same melodic contour of the dance, now slowed down, and where the words "[Almigh]-ty Father" rest upon the HSM to assure us that all is right with the world. This feat comes close to Bernstein's description of Brahms' symphonic technique as, "wheels within wheels, all part of one great machine."

Part 1 concludes with "Epiphany," an oboe solo, triggered by the HSM, which nervously darts about somewhat dodecaphonically, creating a sense of foreboding that tells us all is *not* really well. Until the last number of *Mass*, the HSM nugget will appear twice: first, in its kosher state as a guitar lick to introduce and provide barbed commentary on the "Non Credo" (with its Talmudic debate of "possibly yes, probably no"); and, more innocently, in the mouths of the boys' choir singing "Sanctus, san-[ctus]." A claim could be made that it also opens "The Word of the Lord." Otherwise, the HSM no longer is an indicator of formal structure in the troubled environment of part 2. However, it does *act* in varying melodic anagrams: in the orchestral Meditation No. 1 as 3-1-2 (immediately after the first sounding note); in "God Said" as 3-2-1, on the words ["Let] there be light;" and in "I Believe in God" as 1-2, with note 3 going up a step.

Mass ends with "Secret Songs." After the Celebrant's breakdown in the Mad Scene ("Things Get Broken"), the HSM quietly returns to remind us that we unruly beings still can be guided by our inherent humanity. In a sermon he once delivered at All Souls Church in New York City, the composer described the soul as a "pilot light," always burning inside and available to provide us with compassionate outreach to others. At times Bernstein could be difficult and contrary (who isn't?), but no one can deny his enormous outreach. This is the message of *Mass*. Like Brahms', Bernstein's music is based on little locomotives that propel the work forward and us along with it on a journey of self-discovery. Sometimes it's a joyride; often it is not.

5 In Concert

Tone Rows for Philharmonic Hall

In 1965, the Maestro had just finished changing his shirt at intermission, when he heard over the loudspeaker in his dressing room the Big Ben motive summoning the audience to their seats for the second half of the program. He asked me, "Why do we have to listen to that same old formula? This is the twentieth century; let's get with it and update. I know what, twelve-tone rows! See what you can do about it." And so began an enjoyable jaunt for me to explore which rows could be included. Of course the Second Viennese School had to be represented, but I also included what, in those days, was considered to be its polar opposite, Stravinsky, and, by extension, selections from LB's music. These were recorded in a studio, and, I am pleased to say, were used for forty years, discontinued at the end of 2005. In fact, I am the only composer in history who had been played daily in any concert hall in the world. (Of course, it's not my music, but that's another story.)

Here is the formal description I wrote, as printed in a 1965 NYP program when the tone rows were newly minted.[1]

The four-tone chimes that preceded concerts and recalled audiences to Philharmonic Hall after intermission has been replaced by five sets of tone rows taken from the music of Schoenberg, Bernstein, Webern, Berg and Stravinsky. Three rows are played at a leisurely pace ten minutes before starting time, repeated at a moderate pace three minutes before, then played twice quite fast one minute before. The process is repeated during intermission. It will take five weeks to get through the fifteen rows, then the cycle will be repeated. The rows are in the following order:

Set I
Schoenberg—"Waltz" from Piano Suite, Op. 23
Bernstein—"Quiet" from *Candide*
Webern—Symphony, Op. 21

Set II
Berg—Violin Concerto
Bernstein—"Kaddish," Movement 1
Webern—Piano Variations, Op. 27

Set III
Schoenberg—Wind Quintet, Op. 26
Stravinsky—*Agon*
Webern—String Quartet, Op. 28

Set IV
Schoenberg—Variations for Orchestra, Op. 31
Bernstein—"Dirge" from "The Age of Anxiety"
Stravinsky—*Threni*

Set V
Berg—*Lulu*
Bernstein—The "Galop" from *Fancy Free*
Webern—Cantata No. 1, Op. 29

Each set is played on a celesta and recorded onto tape cartridges that are triggered by remote control. Because of the nature of the instrument, some rows have necessarily been compressed into one or two octaves.

* * *

I always took great delight in watching audiences scurry back to their seats. What a rush I had experiencing that power!

In general, LB was not sympathetic to the twelve-tone school. Between 1958 and 1971, he did program six works of the Second Viennese School. Symptomatic of his disinclination to do any more such pieces was the first and only time I ever witnessed a concert performance that did not go full steam ahead. On 13 October 1966, on a program that included the Beethoven *Fidelio* Overture and the "Eroica" Symphony, LB had to stop Schoenberg's Chamber Symphony No. 2, Op. 38 dead in its track because the New York Philharmonic had lost its place. He started all over again and it went smoothly. Embarrassing, perhaps, but no one seemed to notice.[2]

Lenny's views on so-called serialism were cited in a letter to me, 5 November 1970:

A propos tone rows: it occurred to me that I've used twelve-tone rows to show:

1. Hysteria ("Galop" from *Fancy Free*)
2. Boredom ("Quiet" from *Candide*)[3]
3. Dislocation ("The Age of Anxiety"),
4. Blind groping (ditto)
5. Dogmaticism (*Mass*)
6. Despair (*Mass*)

Does this seem to say something about the serial world?

My response should have been, "Maybe it does; but it also says something about you."

His use of tone rows was basically effectuated in a melodic context; only slightly in the Schoenberg manner, but never serialistically in the Boulez fashion. As he indicates above, the purpose was either (a) to display discomfort, violence or other such unrest—in other words, a theatrical device—as in the "Dirge" from "The Age of Anxiety" (pyramid building to reveal weight) or (b) to contrast atonality (irresolution) and tonality (resolution) as in "Kaddish," movements 1 and 2 (some Alban Berg–like dodecaphony) and in the *Dybbuk* ballet, which opens with a row in a male vocal duet, but quickly dissolves into folklike tunes. However, the row is broken up and scattered elsewhere in the ballet.

In June 2007, I wrote to Zarin Mehta, manager of the Philharmonic, suggesting that the Bernstein tone rows alone be revived as a tribute during the fall 2008 LB festival. The Philharmonic did, sort of, take this suggestion to heart. But instead of using tone rows, they chose to serenade the audience with "Maria" and "Tonight" from *WSS.* What Broadway show tunes had to do with the Philharmonic is beyond me, to say nothing of the fact that Lenny would have cringed at such a decision.

Then on 26 February 2009, Sedgwick Clark wrote the following blog entry on MusicalAmerica.com:

> **Bells of the Hall.** By now everybody has read that [Alice] Tully Hall's Second Coming is the bee's knees. But what about the icing on the cake: the intermission bells? No, I'm not kidding. Remember those exotic intermission bells at Philharmonic (now Avery Fisher) Hall? In 1965 Leonard Bernstein wanted a new signal for the audience to return to its seats, so he asked his assistant, the composer Jack Gottlieb, to select some felicitous twelve-tone rows as prompters. "I chose rows written by the second Vienna school, Stravinsky, and Bernstein," Jack recounted earlier this week, "and recorded them on a celesta for Lenny's approval." After Bernstein retired as music director in 1969 and George Szell, who detested twelve-tone music, became interim "music advisor," the bells were replaced by what sounded like foghorns. Soon after Pierre Boulez became music director in 1971, I urged him after a concert to reinstate the bells. Boulez hadn't known about them, but he must have approved of Jack's recording because they reappeared not long afterwards. They disappeared again at some point after Boulez's departure, but now someone at Lincoln Center has had the brilliant idea to revive them at the newly reopened Alice Tully Hall. Bravo! Long may they resound.

That someone was engineer Peter Daryl Bornstein; but, alas, they resounded only for the one night.

Some higher-up power at Lincoln Center must have agreed with George Szell's assessment.

Original-itis: Nielsen and Gould

Glenn Gould was a luminous pianist, but quite messy about his appearance. I remember Felicia Bernstein's cutting his hair and grooming him in the Osborne apartment. At the NYP Thursday evening preview of 5 April 1962, LB had intended to talk about Danish composer Carl Nielsen, but canceled it and spoke, instead, about Gould's unorthodox concept for the Brahms D-Minor Piano Concerto, and their disagreement about the interpretation. It was a disclaimer and a performance that still lingers in our collective musical consciousness, a kerfuffle primarily whipped up by Harold Schonberg's *New York Times* snide review. The critics were not supposed to cover the Thursday previews, but they were there the next day when LB happened to deliver the same statement.

Nielsen's *Masquerade* Overture (led by John Canarina, an assistant conductor) and Symphony No. 5 were on the program. I do not know if LB meant his talk on Nielsen and originality to be complete; but here it is:

> Before we play the Nielsen symphony, I want to share some scattered thoughts with you. In tonight's program notes, you will find Nielsen referred to as an "original" composer, with the implication that in his originality lay his basic importance. I don't quarrel with this: on the contrary, it started me thinking about this whole subject of originality in music. We have all heard "original" music that made no real impression on us—music that is "different" for the sake of being different. That's one of today's most fashionable diseases—original-itis. And yet, on the other hand, almost no music that we call great, or feel to be important, has ever failed to carry a quality of originality with it. Where do we draw the line? Obviously, at the point where we are moved or stimulated. Short of that point, originality is a vain pretension—beyond that point, it is gravy.
>
> This judgment necessarily governs the choice of all new music that we present on our programs: does it stimulate? Does it move us? Now the Nielsen symphony is anything but new music, being forty years old; and yet it is new to these audiences, and in certain ways still sounds new as well. Of course, all great music sounds eternally new: a Schubert song, a Bach prelude, sound as fresh as if they were hot off the press; but Nielsen sounds new in the sense it still has an experimental ring to it, a kind of daffy, willful, capricious feeling. And yet, even when you examine those caprices in detail, those obsessive peculiarities, you find that they are not, taken separately, all that original in themselves.

In the light of these undelivered remarks about Nielsen's Symphony No. 5, it is noteworthy to read LB's jottings on the title page of Nielsen's Symphony

LB and Glenn Gould at a recording session.

No.3 ("Sinfonia Espansiva"). He traced a kind of genealogy from Schumann's Symphony No. 3 ("Rhenish"), as the begetter of the second movement from Brahms Symphony No. 2, which begat Nielsen's Symphony No. 4, which begat something in Mahler and Shostakovich (neither of the latter two are spelled out). He then described the Nielsen No. 3 as follows:

> Phrase lengths. Mad; seemingly arbitrary, but once studied, clear & right.
>
> Harmonies: ditto. Constantly unpredictable: surprising, unexpected.
>
> But melody not distinguished. Therefore, hard to play.
>
> Tonal scheme: strange, deliberate, very important, especially relationships between movements & polar points. Therefore, hard to listen to.
>
> (For "therefore," he used the geometric three-dot triangular symbol.)

For the sake of the record, here is what Bernstein did say at the concerts, which led to all the brouhaha:

Don't be frightened. Mr. Gould is here. He will appear in a moment. I'm not, um, as you know, in the habit of speaking on any concert except the Thursday night previews, but a curious situation has arisen, which merits, I think, a word or two. You are about to hear a rather, shall we say, unorthodox performance of the Brahms D-Minor Concerto, a performance distinctly different from any I've ever heard, or even dreamt of for that matter, in its remarkably broad tempi and its frequent departures from Brahms' dynamic indications. I cannot say I am in total agreement with Mr. Gould's conception, and this raises the interesting question: "What am I doing conducting it?" I'm conducting it because Mr. Gould is so valid and serious an artist that I must take seriously anything he conceives in good faith and his conception is interesting enough so that I feel you should hear it, too.

But the age-old question still remains: "In a concerto, who is the boss; the soloist or the conductor?" The answer is, of course, sometimes one, sometimes the other, depending on the people involved. But almost always, the two manage to get together by persuasion or charm or even threats to achieve a unified performance. I have only once before in my life had to submit to a soloist's wholly new and incompatible concept and that was the last time I accompanied Mr. Gould. But, but this time the discrepancies between our views are so great that I feel I must make this small disclaimer. Then why, to repeat the question, am I conducting it? Why do I not make a minor scandal—get a substitute soloist, or let an assistant conduct? Because I am fascinated, glad to have the chance for a new look at this much-played work; Because, what's more, there are moments in Mr. Gould's performance that emerge with astonishing freshness and conviction. Thirdly, because we can all learn something from this extraordinary artist, who is a thinking performer, and finally because there is in music what Dimitri Mitropoulos used to call "the sportive element," that factor of curiosity, adventure, experiment, and I can assure you that it has been an adventure this week collaborating with Mr. Gould on this Brahms concerto and it's in this spirit of adventure that we now present it to you.

What I find captivating is how the actual talk on Gould/Brahms links up to the intended talk on Nielsen: they both question the dividing line between vain pursuits of originality and what moves the listener; and they both attest to the value of experimentation, but doubt the inherent truth of the maxim "Art for art's sake."

In any case, it has been said that "fallout from the event was a factor that led Gould to withdraw from public performances" in favor of making recordings in private.

Turning Pages

(From the ten-CD set New York Philharmonic Bernstein LIVE, *1951–81, released in 2000)*

Anyone who has ever turned pages for a pianist in a public concert can attest to how much of a nerve-racking big deal it can be. (The trick is to turn at the *beginning* of the last bar on the page.) My ordeal took place on 29 July 1959 at an outdoor concert in Lewisohn Stadium, New York City, during a performance of Beethoven's Triple Concerto, with Bernstein as pianist (the program booklet misspells his name as Bernsten), concert master John Corigliano and lead chair cellist Laszlo Varga comprising the triple threat. High-anxiety time; but happily, I did not screw up. Four years earlier I had turned pages for pianist Aaron Copland at a Brandeis University concert playing his own *Emily Dickinson Songs* (I don't recall the singer; it may have been Eunice Alberts or Phyllis Curtin). To paraphrase a famous Lincoln quote, "The occasion was piled high with difficulty"; but I rose to the occasion.)

Although the orchestra was billed as the Stadium Symphony Orchestra, it really was the New York Phil in disguise. I sat next to LB, who played, surprisingly, under the baton of Josef Krips. (The only other time I can recall Bernstein as pianist in tandem with another conductor, after he became famous, was the premiere of his "Age of Anxiety" Symphony with Koussevitzky and the BSO. A joke about Krips was his bragging about how he championed contemporary music. "Look," said he, "I can conduct in 7/8 time: one-two-three-four-five-six-sev-en.") Less than a month later, however, Bernstein would take over the conducting assignment of the Beethoven concerto, synchronous with his star turn at the piano, during the unprecedented nineteen-week tour by the orchestra to the Near East and Russia. I do not recall turning pages for concerts during that historic trip, but it seems to me I must have since only the first movement of Bernstein's conducting score is marked. The remaining movements are left untouched, implying that he conducted while playing from a piano score. The broadcast of the recorded performance heard on this set was made upon the orchestra's return to the USA.

Not the least of the many perks that came my way was the opportunity to observe him in the process of planning NYP concert programs. Typically, in pencil he would juggle blocks of composers and timings of pieces on long yellow lined sheets, a tricky balancing act of old and new. Many considerations had to be taken into account: obvious ones such as the availability of soloists or having enough rehearsal time (there never was enough) or the more hidden agenda of fulfilling long-lived loyalties ("settling scores"?) to composers. Sometimes these yellow sheets would be embellished with doodles, added during interrupting phone calls, drawings that could have given Jungian psychologists a run for their money.

The initial formation of his 1959 survey of "The Avant-Garde" (his introductory talks are a distinctive feature on this CD set), included ideas for "New Sounds in the Orchestra," a mix of Beethoven, Xenakis and Ligeti on the first half with Zino Francescatti as soloist after intermission. Or "The Electronicists," listing Davidovsky and Varèse, balanced by Mozart, with soloist Malcolm Treger? Or "Music of Chance," with Vivaldi and Tchaikovsky for the opening, but Cage, Feldman, Brown and an improvisation by the orchestra postinterval? Whatever the final decision—and there were the to-be-expected headache compromises—his goal always was to stimulate his audiences, in the process moving them emotionally, and to accomplish this in the course of five rehearsals and four performances.

In his unjustly criticized Thursday evening previews, during which Bernstein spoke, it was patently obvious that audiences savored his urbane talks. He would explain for example, Carl Nielsen was an original (see "Original-itis") or why the reputation of Robert Schumann as a pedestrian orchestrator was bunk or how American composers Irving Fine, Ned Rorem and William Russo were (are) "pleasant moderns." (One presumes that the music of certain other composers was appraised as being "unpleasant.")

In July 2000, almost a half-century after some of these concerts took place, I was asked to listen to advance pressings of all the selections that made it onto the set (and others that did not) for my reactions. Frankly, I am not a fan of all the works that have been included, but what a phenomenal showcase this is of both conductor and orchestra. (Hate the sin, but love the sinner?) To have followed the performances for the most part with LB's own marked scores, stored in the NYP Archive, made it truly an extraordinary experience. It was as if I were not only in the hall with him, but standing by his side on the podium, turning pages again! After a performance series was over, these scores were reverently bound in dark green with the title, composer and LB's name embossed in gold on the cover. The flyleaf papers are an elegant design of red capillaries and green corpuscles. Michael Zito, of the Rex Bookbindery in the Bronx, New York, personally picked them up and lovingly hand-delivered them upon completion. These never would have been treated any other way.

6 Spinning Platters

The LB Discography

(Based on a Prelude, Fugue and Riffs *article, Spring/Summer 2002)*

LB believed in the efficacy of calendar dates. In 1943, he made his historic debut with the New York Philharmonic on the fourteenth of November, a date in 1954 on which he made his equally historic television debut. It also was the birth date of his compeer and mentor, Aaron Copland. Bernstein would have also appreciated the significance of his having been born in the eighth year (known as the octennial) of the 1910s, for it was in 1958, shortly after his fortieth birthday, that he formally became music director of the New York Philharmonic and when he hired me. My assistantship ended in 1968, Bernstein's fiftieth birthday year. When I rejoined his employ in 1977, the music quotient of my work took ascendancy as I was empowered to become his editor.

Among the publications I edited were three editions of so-called complete catalogs (nicknamed the Red Books) spaced at ten-year intervals. The first of these in 1978, celebrating his sixtieth birthday, had a discography of Bernstein as composer. Due acknowledgment was given to the Rev. J. F. Weber, a Catholic priest and expert on liturgical music, who had published a sixteen-page Bernstein discography in 1975. During this decade, a more thorough tabulation was compiled by Byron Bray, a Columbia Artists Management representative and close friend of Bernstein's secretary, Helen Coates.

However, it was Miss Coates, in those precomputer days, who from the beginning had laboriously typed in all such data into loose-leaf notebooks. The second edition of the Red Book in 1988, observing the seventieth birthday, added a videography to the discography. But again these were only inventories of Bernstein as composer since, as I noted at the time, "Bernstein as conductor during this time period has been prodigal in the field of recordings; it will be necessary to compile a separate discography/videography. . . ."

Soon after this edition had appeared, the phone rang at home just as I was walking in exhausted from an overseas trip. It was David Diamond, fulminating in his notorious "diamond-in-the-rough" mode over my having omitted the fact that the very first commercial recording Bernstein ever made was as a pianist in the Diamond Prelude and Fugue in C-Sharp Major.[1] Yes, it was the first; and we should note that, although more projects were in the works, fate sadly decreed Bernstein's last recording be *The Final Concert* at Tanglewood on 19 August 1990.

Diamond's attitude always left a lot to be desired, and what could not be cured had to be endured. To quote him: "I continue to speak out with disturbing candor. . . . I criticize . . . vituperatively and add a few more enemies to an already long list."[2] The following story from Ellen Adler is not untypical: Tennessee Williams was hosting a party in his New York City apartment. A blizzard had caused a blackout, and everything was illuminated by candlelight. Ellen asked Williams' boyfriend if LB had arrived as yet. "No," said he. "Is my mother [Stella Adler] here?" she inquired again. "No." While looking down, as she was taking off her wet shoes, she heard a distinctive husky voice: "What a wonderful thing to be young, to go a party and meet your boyfriend and your mother." She looked up and was startled to see Greta Garbo. When Lenny arrived, Ellen rushed over to tell him the great (an anagram of Greta) Garbo was there. Lenny clutched his forehead and exclaimed, "Omigod!" They were introduced and exchanged glowing mutual appreciation, one for the other. LB went on, "We share more than our mutual admiration; we have a friend in common." "Who is that?" asked she. "David Diamond," said he. To which she replied, "Who?" In typical fashion, the despicable DD had invented the relationship. LB growled, "I'm going to murder him."

A third edition of the Red Book, in 1998, celebrating what would have been LB's eightieth birthday year, was subtitled *Volume I: Life, Musical Compositions and Writings* because, to self-quote again, "The Bernstein discography and videography has become so immense that it requires a separate volume. We

Four composers with Ellen Adler: LB, Manos Hajidakis, JG and Calvin Hampton. Port Said Cabaret, West Twenty-ninth Street, New York City.

hope that volume 2 will be ready for release in the year 2000. . . ." Well, volume 2, two years late, was not so far off the mark. As Lillian Hellman put it—in the mouth of her eponymous hero from the Bernstein-Hellman operetta *Candide*—"We promise only to do our best and live out our lives. Dear God, that's all we can promise in truth" (a passage, by the way, that has made it into the fifteenth edition of *Bartlett's Familiar Quotations*). At last we broke the octennial cycle, and I was thankful we did not have to wait for the year 2008 to present this discography to the public, all 124 pages of it!

The number of Bernstein recordings is, to say the least, impressive. The only other conductors who have come close are Herbert von Karajan and Neville Marriner. Although there are gaps (to be discussed), the total count is 826. Kudos for our breakthrough are due first and foremost to James H. North, who generously allowed us to extract the Bernstein quotient from his index of all New York Philharmonic recordings, an extraordinary achievement. Grateful acknowledgment also goes to Florian Conzetti, who did the lion's share of computer input under the watchful eyes of Amberson vice presidents Marie Carter and Craig Urquhart and our executive vice president, Harry J. Kraut.

Catalogs from record companies were reviewed, riffled and raided—notably, the Phonolog monthly listing used by record stores and the indispensable Schwann catalog. It is particularly fascinating to examine original time sheets from the 1940s for the earliest Bernstein sessions on 78 rpm for the RCA-Victor label. Blitzstein's *Airborne Symphony*, recorded 30 October 1946 at the Lotos Club in New York City, took only three hours to complete; but Stravinsky's much smaller *Octet*, recorded 11 August 1947 at Tanglewood, took almost five. On the log for Stravinsky's *L'histoire du soldat* there is a note: "The noises heard on all sides are not system noises, but mechanism noises from bassoons which could not be eliminated." Salaries for the recording of Gershwin's *An American in Paris* (6 December 1947, at the Manhattan Center) totaled $3,949.75; the lowest amount paid an individual was $68.75. Among the musicians that day were oboist Ralph Gomberg, brother of Harold Gomberg (famed oboist of the New York Philharmonic); clarinetist David Oppenheim, who five years earlier had recorded Bernstein's Sonata for Clarinet and Piano with the composer; and celesta player Howard Shanet, who later wrote a notable history of the Philharmonic. Copland's *Billy the Kid* (11 June 1949) is stamped: "Also made on 7 [-inch] 45 RPM." Bernstein's own "Jeremiah" Symphony was recorded 14 February 1945 with the Saint Louis Symphony Orchestra, and according to the time sheet, the session took place in the Municipal Auditorium. However, this 1932 building was renamed in the 1940s as the Kiel Opera House (after a Saint Louis mayor) and is so noted herein. Nowadays the auditorium is known as the Savvis Center.

This is an example of the persnickety kind of detail and sleuthing that one has had to undertake. Not only do performing arenas change names, but so do record companies. "In the beginning" there was Columbia Records, which begat CBS Records, then Sony and, of this writing, Sony Classical. But whatever the name, the largest bulk of Bernstein recordings were created for the company between the 1950s and '70s, numbering over five hundred compositions. Dan Shiffman, our resident computer guru at the time, faithfully oversaw the relocation of the data to cyberspace. Indeed, the flexibility of the cyberworld is the ideal environment for a discography, making it possible to keep pace with the rapidly changing formats and labeling numbers endemic to recordings. Because record companies are always exploring ways to exploit their holdings, many of the titles with Bernstein as conductor have been repackaged in differing and dizzying combinations, most recently remastered and marketed by Sony Classical as *The Bernstein Century*. This becomes a convoluted ordeal for indexers. Bernstein as narrator was first recorded on the Decca label as a Book-of-the-Month Club series. These symphonic analyses, made with the Stadium Concerts Symphony Orchestra (the New York Philharmonic in disguise) feature the Tchaikovsky "Pathétique," Schumann No. 2, Dvořák "New World," Brahms No. 4 and Beethoven "Eroica"—subsequently released on the Deutsche Grammophon label. Other narrations include titles from the Omnibus series, such as Beethoven's Fifth Symphony and *What Is Jazz?* (CL-919) and *The Humors of Music* (MS-6225). To all this we add Bach's *St. Matthew Passion* and *The Music of Charles Ives*, issued with discussions of Beethoven Symphonies Nos. 3 and 5 on CBS Special Service Records. And there are still others: Stravinsky's *Petrouchka* and the Berlioz *Symphonie fantastique*, the Nielsen "Espansiva" Symphony as well as an interview with Bernstein about his own recording output. The second matter is more tricky as it concerns Bernstein as composer: works conducted by others. What we have done is to add a section called Selected Discography, which was finished in 1998 with the help of Maria Bedo for the third edition of the Red Book. But it was never used in that publication in anticipation of what we thought was going to be volume 2. Please note that this section is not all-inclusive nor is it up-to-date. Therefore, such 2001 releases as the Boston Symphony Orchestra's 1949 premiere of Bernstein's "The Age of Anxiety" with the composer as pianist under the baton of Serge Koussevitzky or violinist Joshua Bell's recording of *West Side Story Suite* will not be found here. Hopefully, it will be possible to bring this resource up to speed, but this may well turn out to be a pipedream. After all, *West Side Story* albums and single songs continue to rain and reign. Some formatting problems also remain, but we have been anxious to get going onto the World Wide Web. Happy hunting to all!

Jack's Picks

(A list of my favorite LB recordings, 1988)

I was asked to name my ten favorite recordings of Bernstein as composer and ten more of him as composer for the LB Web site. Trying to select such a list is a bit like asking a jellybean addict to choose from a candy store full of goodies. Gosh, which flavors? They're all jellybeans, for pity's sake! Okay, here are my choices, but not in any particular order.

BERNSTEIN AS CONDUCTOR

1. Mahler: Symphony No. 9 with the Berlin Philharmonic (live recording 1979)

   DG 435378-2

Searing, red-hot. More electric than the one LB did with the New York Philharmonic. Could it be that his one and only time with this orchestra in Berlin, the former seat of anti-Semitic horror, was the subtext and that the players were giving their all for a Jewish conductor and, yes, a Jewish composer?

2. Beethoven: String Quartet, Op. 131 with the Vienna Philharmonic Orchestra (VPO) (1979)

   DG 435779-2

   At the time he made this recording, LB considered it the best of his work with the VPO. One can hear why: the delicate finesse of a complete orchestral string section playing music originally written for only four players, is phenomenal. (And, besides, I wrote the jacket notes.)

3. Berg: Three Orchestral Pieces, Op. 6 with the New York Philharmonic

   Special Editions NYP 9708/09, vol. 4, disc 8, cuts 3–5

   Alas, you have to buy an expensive five-volume package of *The Historic Broadcasts, 1923 to 1987*. But it's well worth it. This performance belies the myth that LB was *totally* unsympathetic to music of the Second Viennese School.

4. Strauss: *Der Rosenkavalier*, G. Jones, L. Popp, C. Ludwig, P. Domingo, W. Berry, VPO and the Chorus of the Vienna State Opera

   Columbia M4X 30652

   Bernstein, the consummate theater man, led and preserved far too few repertoire operas: *Carmen, Cavalleria rusticana, Falstaff* (delicious!), *La bohème, Tristan und Isolde*—and this glorious document, which helped to remind the Viennese of their lost traditions.

5. Schumann: The Four Symphonies, Vienna Philharmonic

   Sony, *The Bernstein Century* DGG B001227209

   LB believed in the original versions and never tampered with them, as have so many other conductors. His belief in the rightness of the orchestration is here for all to hear.

6. Stravinsky: *Pulcinella Suite,* Concerto for Piano and Wind Orchestra, *Symphony of Psalms*, New York Philharmonic, Seymour Lipkin, piano soloist

   Sony Classical: *Leonard Bernstein, The Royal Edition* SMK 47628

   A early disc, but fascinating for its mix of the sacred and the profane.

7. Brahms: Serenade No. 2 in A for Orchestra, Op. 16, New York Philharmonic

   Sony Classical: *Leonard Bernstein: The Royal Edition* SMK 47536

   The perfect listening piece for long, sensuous weekends in countryside forests and pastures.

8a. Tchaikovsky: Symphony No. 4/Overture to *Romeo and Juliet*, New York Philharmonic

   DG 429234 2

8b. Tchaikovsky: Symphony No. 5/Overture to *Hamlet*, New York Philharmonic

   Sony Classical SMK 47635

   Two cups o' *tchai* (Russian for "tea") with Shakespearean sweeteners.

9. Copland: Sonata for Piano, *Billy the Kid*; Bernstein: *On the Town Dances* and *Seven Anniversaries for Piano*

   RCA Gold Seal *Leonard Bernstein: The Early Years*, vol. 1

   No one, but no one plays the Copland sonata with so much insight. But why didn't LB also record Copland's Piano Variations, his so-called party piece?

10. Shostakovich: Symphony No. 1 and Symphony No. 7, Chicago Symphony Orchestra

    DG 427632-2

    Fireworks, blazing brass, 105 (or more?) musicians playing as one.

That finishes the first ten, but where's the Haydn, Mozart, Sibelius, Berlioz, Ravel, Schuman (William, that is), Prokofiev, Harris, Foss, Ives and . . . and . . . and . . .?

BERNSTEIN AS COMPOSER, SOMETIMES AS CONDUCTOR

1. *A Quiet Place*, at the Vienna State Opera with C. Ludgin, B. Morgan, J. Brandstetter, P. Kazares, J. Kraft, T. Uppman, et al., ORF Orchestra, conducted by LB (1986). DG 419 761-2

   Not successful on stage, this is haunting on disc. Obviously, you are not distracted by the scenery and you are able to concentrate only on the music. Superbly written for the voice, but perhaps overorchestrated.

2. The original cast albums of the musicals (do these count as four picks?):

   A. Roz Russell (*Wonderful Town*) is a hoot as a zoot suiter. More spontaneous than the TV remake. MCA 0881-10050-2 9 (originally on Decca)

   B. I much prefer Barbara Cook and Co. (*Candide*) to *any* of the later versions. Sony Broadway SK 48017

   C. Now if only the cast of *West Side Story* (Lawrence, Rivera, Kert, et al.) could hook up with the orchestra of the so-called opera cast version. *That* would be an album to behold! Columbia CK 32603 & DG 415963-2

   D. As for *On the Town*, try the newer Broadway production (Daly, Hampson, Von Stade, et al.) with the reworked, spiffy orchestrations by Bruce Coughlin (pronounced as in "cough"). DG B00001614

3. *Prelude, Fugue and Riffs*, Simon Rattle and the London Sinfonietta, Michael Collins, clarinet EMI 886802

   Swings like a jam session. I prefer it to LB's own version with the VPO.

4. Overture to *Candide, Facsimile, Fancy Free, Symphonic Dances* from *West Side Story*,

David Zinman, Baltimore Symphony Orchestra. London 452 916-2

I am not crazy about LB's *Candide* Overture with the NY Philharmonic. Too frenetic. Sometimes it takes an outsider to see the forest for the trees, and Zinman delivers.

5. *Mass*, soloists, Norman Scribner Choir, Berkshire Boy Choir, orchestra of the original production led by LB. CBS M2K 44593

   LB sometimes bemoaned the fact that others did not record his music because they figured, Why bother? They were correct for a long time in this instance until more recent versions came out on the Naxos label (8559622-23) and on Chandos Records (CHSA5070-2).

6. *Dybbuk*, full ballet, LB and the New York City Ballet Orchestra with baritones David Johnson and John Ostendorf. Sony SMK 63090

   Because I consider it to be LB's shining masterpiece, a perfect blend of intellect and emotion. I do wish, however, that Jonathan Sheffer's 1998 outing with the now defunct EOS Orchestra could have been preserved.

7. The Three Symphonies: "Jeremiah" [Tourel], "The Age of Anxiety" [Foss] and "Kaddish" in one package. New York Philharmonic, LB. CBS SMK 47162 (with *Serenade* [Stern], *Chichester Psalms* and *Prelude, Fugue and Riffs*)

   I pick this version over the Israel Philharmonic Orchestra only because you could get more for your money.

Well, I snuck in five extra titles in this second half. May you enjoy all this music and treasure it as I always shall.

Beethoven: String Quartet Op. 131

(Jacket note on Deutsche Grammophon LP, 1979 and CD, 1981)

When Dimitri Mitropoulos made his American conducting debut with the Boston Symphony Orchestra, in January 1937, Bernstein was a sophomore at Harvard University. He remembers the time well because it was the midyear examinations period at the university. But it also was his turn to attend a Boston Symphony concert. As a student, he could afford only to share a subscription (every other week) to the orchestra's concerts; and Mitropoulos' debut happened to fall on Bernstein's week. The Beethoven Op. 131 String Quartet, played by the Boston Symphony strings, was included on that occasion, and Bernstein found the experience unforgettable. Shortly thereafter, the student came to know the conductor, who presented him with what were in those days steel air-check records played at 78 rpm. They could be listened to only a few times, for they wore out quickly; and, indeed, that is exactly what happened in this case.

But, more significantly, in 1946, Mitropoulos let Bernstein (by this time a professional conductor) borrow his score, which showed exactly where the cellos were to be doubled by the double basses. These doublings were discreet and strategic, and Bernstein notated them in his own miniature score. It was then that Bernstein first presented his performance of the piece, using these doublings, with the New York City Symphony Orchestra. At that time, as in the performance with the Vienna Philharmonic, not a single note, dynamic, or scoring detail of Beethoven's was changed, other than the addition of those doublings.

Although there are precedents for conductors performing string quartet literature with string orchestras (Mahler, Furtwängler and others), not every quartet lends itself to this treatment. Op. 131 succeeds in this medium because the inner voices are more audibly delineated when played by a full body of strings. Not only is the counterpoint clarified, but many of the awkwardnesses with which four individual players have to struggle in this quartet (as well as the other late Beethoven quartets) are eliminated. However, other hazards arise, such as the need to play cadenza-like passages precisely in unison by eighteen first violins or twelve cellos.

But the virtuosity, warmth and built-in chamber music experience of the Vienna Philharmonic lessen such difficulties. Besides, the composer's thought process is projected as more unified under the guidance of a single conductor than in an ensemble of four independent minds that strive to become of one mind. Bernstein considered this recording to be a culmination of his work with the Vienna Philharmonic, who have here managed superbly the almost impossible task for a string orchestra to perform a late Beethoven string quartet.

José as Tony?

(from an interview with Alison Ames, 1 August 2008)

Since the *West Side Story* recording by opera singers and the composer as conductor was being made in the United States, Alison Ames took over the role of Hanno Rinke, the artists and repertoire representative at Deutsche Grammophon (DG) in Germany. It started out as a project in peril when the third or fourth candidate to sing the role of Tony had fallen by the wayside. Neil Shicoff was the ideal choice, but Shicoff realized he would have had only one free day after finishing his first operatic recording, Verdi's *Rigoletto*, and reluctantly had to refuse. Plácido Domingo had been suggested, but LB vetoed him on the grounds of his Spanish accent. (I can hear the Reader say: "So how come . . . ?")

What to do? An emergency meeting took place at the old Amberson office on West Fifty-seventh Street. In addition to Alison, there were John McClure, Bernstein's former producer and engineer at Columbia Records, John Mauceri, a trusted conductor colleague, and Harry Kraut, his manager. They plumbed the tenor listing in the annual *Musical America* volume and came up empty.

Harry then mentioned that LB had been interested in José Carreras, but everyone else naturally questioned, Why him? because the Maestro had not been satisfied with Domingo as a possibility. Wouldn't Carreras present the same accent objection? Nevertheless, Harry said LB had heard him in London and would want him.

It turned out that Carreras was available and happy to do it. So he was flown in from Greece, where he had been on vacation. Since it was last minute, he was unable to make the rehearsal the night before the recording date at Bernstein's Dakota apartment. On top of everything else, the airline had lost his luggage. Alison had to buy him some clothing. Wait, the story gets better.

It was only on the day of the recording in RCA's Studio 4 on West Forty-fourth Street that Bernstein met Carreras, apparently for the first time. Alison was baffled as to why LB was so curt to the singer, totally unlike his typically welcoming self. As the recording sessions went on, and things were not going well—due mainly to the Maestro's frustration with the Carreras accent—Alison asked Harry where exactly did LB hear the tenor in London. At the English National Opera, Harry responded. What opera was he in? *Siegfried* was the answer. What? José Carreras singing Wagner? That did not make sense.

Alison did some quick thinking, and remembered that Siegfried at the ENO was sung [in English] by an English-born tenor with the Spanish-sounding name of Alberto Remedios. LB could not remember the name, so when Harry tossed out the name of José Carreras, LB must have replied yes. But could he have not previously known the Carreras voice? Why wasn't he skeptical? Why had no one bothered to double-check that Carreras was an unlikely heldentenor? Most likely this blunder was due to the frenetic state of affairs, and that the session could not be canceled without great financial loss. Even though the recording became a best seller, especially in Europe, DG did not recoup its expenses. The cost for copying the parts alone for the full (not the typical Broadway pit constituency) orchestra set the company back $75,000.

The full score was also in bad shape. The common practice for Broadway pit orchestras is to use a piano-conductor score that indicates in condensed form which instrument plays what. Bernstein had never before conducted the show score, and this was a four-day session being televised as a documentary by the BBC. Nerves were raw; tensions high. The orchestra players were spectacular—for me the best thing on the recording by far—but there were stretches of blank score that only had the instruction of "repeat bars such and such" or some other kind of shortcut. The copyists had all they could do to get the parts in shape; but The Man on the podium was at a disadvantage, deprived of actual notes on the page. At one point he understandably boiled over and cursed out the copyists, but I could feel his eyes burrowing deep into me. This all happened on camera, the full-blooded version broadcast in England, but edited out of the U.S. airing.

The circumstances of the unfortunate Carreras mix-up have been related on the Internet following a conversation Ms. Andrys Basten, a photographer, had had with Jerry Hadley, the benighted tenor—and to whom Alison much later had told the story of her suspicions. Hadley had wanted to do it, and later on, in fact, did record the title role of *Candide* with LB. According to Basten's account, Harold Moores, a well-known London record dealer, claimed that LB had indeed heard Remedios, forgot the name and could only inform DG it was of Spanish origin. How Moores knew about this is anybody's guess; but since Alison had been recounting the story for years to sundry folk, she could well have been the conduit.

I mention Jerry Hadley because when it came time for LB to do the *Candide* recording in 1988, there were some echoes of the *West Side Story* experience. Almost everyone in the cast was keeling over like flies because of a flu outbreak. Again there was panic about how to proceed. Alison told Harry Kraut that the only way was to lay down orchestra tracks and have the singers come in later to dub their songs. Harry said LB would never concur—too commercial for the lofty likes of the Maestro. But when LB was asked, he was relieved and agreed.

Certainly Bernstein could be a practical man; but there were times when he was not. Rather smitten with the pianist Justus Frantz, he insisted that DG engage Frantz to record the Schumann Piano Concerto with him. The pianist was not up to the challenges; but LB praised him, nevertheless. Hans Weber, DG's recording producer—he had worked with von Karajan and Kubelik as well as LB—was overheard to paraphrase the bromidic "Love is blind," as "*Liebe macht taub*," "Love is deaf."

7 Teaching and Television

Candide Goes to College

(Originally written for the concert performance of 10 November 1968, Philharmonic Hall, NYC, and updated for the New York City Opera playbill, performances of Candide *in 2008.)*

When I was a music major in college, I wondered what it would have been like to have known Mendelssohn, Liszt, Mahler and Gershwin. I found out.

It is the last of the graduate students' monthly get-togethers with Leonard Bernstein; and it has been a most instructive, but unorthodox, encounter. The scene is a college classroom on a muddy campus in Waltham, Massachusetts. Within a few years the young Brandeis University will replace the classroom's three-story house with the more lasting Slosberg Music Center. But it is 1954 and we are in a reconverted framework building called Roberts Cottage. Seated at the piano is a nervous student composer (yours

Harold Shapero, Arthur Berger, Lillian Hellman and Irving Fine at Brandeis University, 1954.

truly) with an audience of his peers and faculty composers Harold Shapero, Arthur Berger and Irving Fine. However, the focus of attention this evening is on a special guest, playwright Lillian Hellman. She is here at the invitation of Mr. Bernstein, the peripatetic professor of this particular seminar.

The student is about to perform an operatic excerpt of his, based on a chapter subtitled "What Happened to Candide and Martin in France" from the 1759 novella *Candide* by Voltaire (pen name for François-Marie Arouet). In this incident, Candide is bilked of his gold by a fake Cunegonde working in cahoots with swindlers acting as a maid-in-waiting, an abbé and policemen. About to be hauled off to—as they say in French—*prison,* Candide buys off his persecutors and Martin remarks, "I am more of a Manichaean than ever."

The performance over, dutiful applause, and Professor Bernstein comments to dramatist Hellman, "Quite a different approach, isn't it?" She agrees, and the two collaborators of a work-in-progress—a comic operetta called *Candide*—go on to discuss problems in general about which stylistic route to travel from Westphalia to Eldorado and back. It is an engrossing dialogue capped by composer Bernstein, performing for the first time in front of an audience what was—at that time—the opening number, "The Best of All Possible Worlds" and the Old Lady's Tango, "I Am Easily Assimilated." The latter he sings (well, a *kind* of singing) in a distinctive Jewish-Polish accent. (It is the same voice Bernstein uses as Raja Bimmy, the carnival barker in the "Real Coney Island" sequence from the May 1961 studio-made "Original Cast Recording" of *On the Town*, where he is credited as Randel Stirboneen, an anagram of his name.)

Bernstein's unique teaching manner has already crystallized by this time, prior to his television exposure. Who else would attempt to conduct a college course for a full semester based on a not-yet-completed theatrical endeavor? Composers, as a rule, are notoriously guarded about their unfinished works; but here is an instance where a developing musical work becomes a kind of textbook syllabus. One assignment has been to write battle music. But how? Ominously, as Prokofiev did in *Alexander Nevsky*? Or victorious bombast à la Tchaikovsky's *1812 Overture*? A month later, various student attempts have been tried, mostly abortive. Then Bernstein presents his solution: a deceptively simple takeoff on a march-step that mocks tonic and dominant relationships. (The second section of the Overture to *Candide* includes this march parody.) All told, a revealing lesson.

Another enlightening session concerns the knack of the song cue, how to sneak music in, over and under spoken words. One source of pedagogical inquiry is a lecture-demo on how Beethoven used melodrama in *Fidelio*. The most potent musical examples, however, are vividly illustrated in an analysis of scenes from Marc Blitzstein's opera *Regina* (based on Hellman's *The Little Foxes*). Blitzstein himself is another seminar guest. One is haunted by the memory of the two Steins—Bern and Blitz—performing fragments of *Regina* with unabashed enthusiasm.

Certainly Blitzstein had some influence on the theater works of Bernstein. But more than melodic associations, Blitzstein's insights also are an inspiration in how to frame a song within a dramatic context and how to use background music under dialogue. Furthermore, the styles of both composers are suffused with a healthy eclecticism; and in *Candide*, Bernstein luxuriates in this propensity. The globe-trotting plot allows him to poke fun at national musical forms, a subject that had intrigued him ever since his Harvard University honors thesis, "The Absorption of Race Elements into American Music." Thus we have a conglomeration of tango, polka, mazurka, barcarolle, Neapolitan bel canto, Germanic chorale, an extravagant coloratura aria that mocks the French "Jewel Song" from *Faust*, a Venetian waltz (not to be confused with the *Viennese* style used for the "Paris Waltz," which is confusing enough) and a schottische. About these last two dances: in "What's the Use?" (the waltz), the trumpet riff that demarcates each verse is a direct quote from Jean-Baptiste Arban's famous set of variations on *Carnival of Venice*.

Candide begins bucolically at the Baron's castle in Westphalia where "Life Is Happiness Indeed." The Baron's son Maximilian (from Latin, "the greatest," as he so regards himself), his perhaps chaste sister, Cunegonde (Latin, *cunnus*, "vulva") and his bastard cousin, Candide (Latin, *candidus*, "white," hence a blank slate) are under the tutelage of Dr. Pangloss (from Greek, *pan*, "all" and *glossa*, "tongue"; in other words, a windbag). Without putting too fine a point on it, Bernstein, in setting the word *happiness*, stresses the last two syllables. In fact, in the score itself there are two broken lines that draw a phallic outline from Candide's "hap-" to the simultaneous utterance of "-piness" by Cunegonde and the servant-girl Paquette (French for "daisy"). Alas, our hero, about to be caught in flagrante delicto with Cunegonde, is banished, and goes forth into the world. His adventures encompass an outrageous journey that finally—like Dorothy in Kansas—brings him back home. Or, to put it another way, if he had ever lost his virginity, he finds it again.

Voltaire similarly lashes out in all directions and at human folly. Transforming all this farrago into music, Bernstein had said:

> We play hopscotch with periods, jumping around in musical style . . . with Voltaire's jumping around in locale . . . But as much as we jump, we never approach any contemporary or near contemporary period.

(Truth to tell, he does play around with a twelve-tone row, an inside joke used to satirize boredom, in the ensemble song "Quiet."). He continued,

> The particular mixture of styles and elements that goes into this work makes it perhaps a new kind of show. . . . There seems to be no really specific precedent for it in our theater, so time will tell.[1]

Indeed, time *has* told. The original Columbia cast album established an enormous cult following, particularly on college campuses. In fact, it may well be the only show recording that achieved greater popularity than its original stage production. Another kind of record that *Candide* holds are its many book rewrites and differing song orders—too dizzy-fying to survey here.

* * *

There are composers who allege in their curriculum vitae that Bernstein was their teacher after showing him only one or two compositions for critique. I can make the same claim. There are others who say they were his conducting students on the basis of being auditors at his Tanglewood classes. But this does not necessarily make for a teacher-student kinship. LB showed his early work to Copland, but I would not describe that as the same relationship Copland had with Boulanger. With me it was always an uptight affair, and became increasingly so with the passage of time. It was when he got no further than the first bar of a new song of mine that I decided not to share my efforts thereafter. It was too agonizing. Of course I sought his unconditional praise, but never received it. He did give me helpful notational tips (how to jot down a quarter-note rest in three quick strokes) or he pointed out bad word-setting, which should have been obvious, but was not (my emphasis on the first syllable of "scarlet"—in the phrase "lips like a scarlet thread" from the Song of Songs—turned the beloved's mouth into a scar).

He performed only one piece of mine, and that was at the piano with mezzo Nancy Williams on the occasion of my fiftieth birthday concert when he premiered a song I wrote in memory of Felicia, a setting of Stephen Spender's moving poem "I Think Continually." Afterward, Joan Peyser, who was finishing her biography of LB, hosted a reception for me. An enlarged photo of LB greeted the guests as they entered her home, which I thought was rather tacky for what was supposed to be my night. LB never showed up and I'm sure it irked her no end. When her notorious biography came out, a page devoted to me made no mention of the fact that I am a composer.

LB and JG at author's fiftieth birthday concert, Merkin Hall, New York City, 1980.

Mary V. Ahern

Some of the raw facts about Mary Virginia Ahern are (1) she, as one of the Robert Saudek Associates, coproduced ten of television's *Omnibus* series and more than fifteen other programs featuring LB with the New York Philharmonic; (2) she subsequently served as acquisition specialist at the Motion Picture, Broadcasting and Recorded Sound Division at the Library of Congress, where she dramatically helped to increase their holdings; and (3) she was the first curator at the Museum of Television and Radio in New York City.

But this is only her résumé. As of this writing, now in her late eighties, Mary is the most fully engaged, politically savvy, flaming liberal Irish Catholic I have ever known. Here is one of various examples: In 1963 she set out to vote in a special election held to oust New York City's Tammany boss Carmine DeSapio, which Ed Koch won by a very slim margin. Mary knew

LB, Mary Ahern, Robert Saudek and JG.

her vote was going to count, but at the sign-in desk she was told that she was not registered. She went ballistic: "I have proof where I live; what proof do you have?" The "goons" called over a cop, but luckily Assemblyman Bill Passannante, passing by, knew Mary, and she got in her vote.

Mary was waiting at the airport in Hyannisport, when an airline employee informed her that Senator Ted Kennedy had driven off with a gaggle of kids in a station wagon and had inadvertently left one behind. Would Mary mind taking care of the child until the senator returned? She did and so did he. (Incidentally, Kennedy died on what would have been LB's ninety-first birthday.)

Witty and chock-full of smarts, Mary entertains her friends at the Cosmopolitan Club when she is in New York City. She broods over the leadership of her church and is a stickler for facts. So she knew how to take on LB when he was wrong about something. Engaged to help out on a Young People's Concert featuring Liszt's *Faust Symphony* and based on Goethe's classic poem, she challenged him that it was not a pact made between Mephistopheles and Faust, but a wager. Mary was about to give up because he was so stubborn; but ultimately he went to the original German poem and Mary won that bet.

They had been introduced to each other by Broadway producer Paul Feigay, who had produced *On the Town* and was an assistant producer to Robert Saudek on *Omnibus*. Feigay took Mary to meet LB at lunch, where she recalls his swallowing a raw egg. For LB's first *Omnibus* program, the justly famous one based on Beethoven's sketches for Symphony No. 5, she was the one who came up with the idea that the first page of the score be painted on the floor. Mary continued to work with LB on his six televised lectures at Harvard and with the Boston Symphony Orchestra providing illustrations. Theirs was a long-lasting and mutually trusting relationship.

The various adult televised shows I was involved with were arduous, but they also were exhilarating. (See the beginning of "Bette Davis Sat on My Lap"). Even more than that. On "The Creative Performer" show, I got to meet the Greatest of the Great: Igor Stravinsky.

"To Jack Gottlieb, my best greetings. Sincerely, I. Stavinsky, Hollywood, February 1960."

In preparation for the program "The Drama of *Carmen*," LB and Mary were stumped about how to find a copy of the original opéra comique version. I was the one who knew that Jennie Tourel had it. During that telecast, the French mezzo-soprano Jane Rhodes lifted her arms during the "Seguidilla," revealing the European standard for feminine grooming. Marveling at the sight, a cameraman was heard to wonder aloud, "I thought we were doing *Carmen*, not the *Barber of Seville*."

For the program "The Music of Johann Sebastian Bach," a typist inadvertently typed the name of a performing group as "The St. Thomas Goy Choir." Perfect.

How Mimi Got On the Waterfront

On 29 May 2008, Turner Classic Movies was showing the Alfred Hitchcock classic *Psycho*. I wanted to see it again, if only to prove to myself that I could now view it with equanimity. I managed fine. Immediately thereafter, on came a flick new to me called *Screaming Mimi*, starring Anita Ekberg as an exotic dancer; Gypsy Rose Lee, who runs the chintzy El Madhouse nightclub in which Ekberg does her stuff; and Red Norvo, the jazz vibraphonist, among its mixed bag of characters. This 1958 film had to be almost the worst movie I've ever seen, if not the worst. It was new to the channel, and Robert Osborne, the host, said that Columbia Pictures had little faith in it, as well they should have, but, he noted, that it had become a cult classic because of Ekberg who portrayed a kind of female Norman Bates.

Here I am lying in bed watching this morass, when suddenly, in the background, I hear something familiar. At first I couldn't believe my ears, but it would not stop. Lo and behold, they were using the love theme from Bernstein's 1954 score for *On the Waterfront*. As it continued on its seedy way, other huge chunks of LB's music played underneath. In fact, the more it went on, the more *I* became a screaming mimi.

The music man in charge of this incredible mess was one Mischa Bakaleinikoff, who did a lot of schlock B-pictures in mid-twentieth century, more often as a conductor than as a composer. (His brother Constantin was a music director at RKO.) For a good laugh, look up Mischa's filmography online. For that matter, you will have an even bigger laugh by reading the synopsis of the film. Evidently one of Bakaleinikoff's duties was to take stock material that Columbia Pictures owned. He probably wrote some original bridge material, but most of his work was a cut-and-paste job. Then to add insult to injury, in 1959, he reused the same love theme from *On the Waterfront* in a B-picture western, *Gunmen from Laredo*.

Only four years after Bernstein's magisterial score was heard on screen, Harry Cohn, or some other power that was, had relegated it to the trash heap. Luckily, LB had rescued it in the nick of time to transform it into a concert suite. (I worked with him on making corrections in the score.) The contract between Columbia Pictures and LB allowed him to extract a concert suite, but of no more duration than twenty minutes. Moreover, he was only paid the paltry sum, even in 1954 dollars, of fifteen thousand dollars.

On 11 April 1955, he wrote to Helen Coates,

> I am furious about the Academy Awards, especially since *Waterfront* took all the awards, but the music one. It is obviously politics, and I don't care, except that it would have jacked up my price for the next picture to double. And that is important. Oh well.

On 26 April 2002, I wrote the following letter to the editor of the *New York Times*, which they chose not to print:

> The implication that Leonard Bernstein delivered his score to Elia Kazan for *On the Waterfront* before he had even viewed the film ["Making Complex Stories Simply"] not only makes no sense, it is also untrue. In Bernstein's article "Upper Dubbing, Calif." (originally written for the *Times* and later reprinted in his first book *The Joy of Music*), the composer recounts his struggle sitting 'day after day at the movieola, running the

print back and forth' to complete his collaborative contribution to the movie. To say that the score was a suite is also nonsense. The suite was fashioned in 1955, one year after the film was released.

Young People's Concerts

(My note as editor for the revised and expanded edition of the book, 1992, reissued 2006)

Decades have elapsed since Leonard Bernstein last presented a televised "Young People's Concert" with the New York Philharmonic. From 1958 to 1972, Bernstein wrote and appeared as commentator, piano soloist, and conductor in fifty-three different concerts designed for young people (loosely defined as ages eight to eighteen). Bernstein's teaching skills and vivid personality soon became nationally known. Through print, audio, and visual media, he helped convert an entire generation of casual American music listeners into avid music lovers. His articulate and lucid talk was a most uncommon attribute for a musician, who—as the saying goes—usually prefers to "let music speak"—or should one say "sing"?—"for itself."

As a high school student he received a solid grounding in Latin (where else, but at the Boston Latin School?), and he was known to correct other people's grammar in the midst of heated discussion, usually to their chagrin. His natural affinity for foreign languages helped him communicate, in varying degrees of fluency, in German, French, Italian, Spanish, Yiddish, and Hebrew. His study was filled, floor to ceiling, with dictionaries, etymological works, and phrase books of all kinds. His familiarity with literature was almost frightening in its scope; and his passion for unconventional word games, like cutthroat anagrams and convoluted British-magazine crossword puzzles—the harder the better—almost bordered on the religious. At one time he had in his home an electronic box that randomly flashed on four letters at a blink, in unending different combinations. The purpose of his box was not to recognize the actual words that might have accidentally appeared, but instantaneously to infuse meaning into all the *non*-words through anagramming and supplying missing letters. Another game he played with companions, often during long car rides, was called "Mental Jotto," in which the challenge was to discover five-letter words through mental anagramming. He almost always won. [He would come up with anagrammatic phrases such as, "She married her admirer"; "He's got bread on his beard"; "Be silent: Listen!"; and "An orchestra is not a carthorse." His friends were challenged to do the same; and one of the better anagrams was by filmmaker Franco Amuri, who turned Gershwin's "The Man I Love," into "Leave Him Not," by G. H. Swinger.] LB clearly was a musician whose interest and gifts ranged far beyond purely musical matters. A born teacher and eloquent spokesman on many wide-ranging issues, cultural and otherwise, he was intoxicated with words.

The popularity of the "Young People's Concerts" (YPCs) made best sellers of the first two editions of the book based on them. Nothing like them had been seen before 1958, and nothing since 1972 has come close to the record of their stunning achievement. There were other televised New York Philharmonic YPCs during and after the same fourteen-year Bernstein period, made by other personalities; but none of them captured the public fancy with the same colorful impact. (To be fair, these other conductors did not have the time to develop a following, nor were they a music director of the Philharmonic. Nevertheless, on 2 October 1994, Edward Rothstein of the *New York Times* made a whopping error in stating that "each [LB] script was reviewed by a team of assistants, including at various times Aaron Copland, Dean Dixon, Yehudi Menuhin, Peter Ustinov and Michael Tilson Thomas.")

The Bernstein analyses and commentaries were, of course, more than ad-libbed introductory program notes to works being performed by the orchestra. Each concert was a carefully scripted event, eventually transcribed onto a teleprompter. Bernstein's practice was to write a first draft in pencil on yellow legal pads. They were then typed and distributed in a format with wide margins (computers were not then prevalent) designed for committee conferences. With producer-director Roger Englander, a team of production assistants met with Bernstein in his home to review, discuss, clarify, time, and help rewrite portion of the script where needed. In addition to Englander, the team usually consisted of Mary Rodgers, John Corigliano, Elizabeth "Candy" Finkler, Ann Blumenthal and the author. Possible cuts were suggested by The Man himself, and often these had to be taken due to the time constraints of the approximately fifty-five minutes made available for airtime. (A total of about five minutes had to be allotted to opening and closing credits and the commercial break for the hourlong concerts.) He called these excisions "poss cuts." New materials were dubbed "addburgers."

The family-type script meetings were mini-workshops, and were as exciting and fulfilling as the concerts themselves. There was a lot of easygoing give-and-take, with Bernstein welcoming the banter and commentary of his production team. But it must be emphatically stated that every word ultimately was his own. Given his impatience with misuse of language, it was a very rare instance, indeed, when he made an error. Therefore, when that did occur, it was a memorable happening. I recall, from 1969, one such rarity. During our meetings on the script for "Berlioz Takes a Trip," Maestro B. referred to a female wolf, a fantasy creature in the mind of Berlioz's hero in *Symphonie Fantastique,* as a "wolverine." But I protested, "How could a team of Michigan football players be known as a team of female anything?" He dismissed this objection cavalierly. The next day, however, he gave me a handwritten note. Apparently troubled by my comment, he had looked up the word, and *wolverine* turned out to be a badgerlike animal, not at all in the wolf family. It was replaced in the script with "wolf-girl." His note to me read,

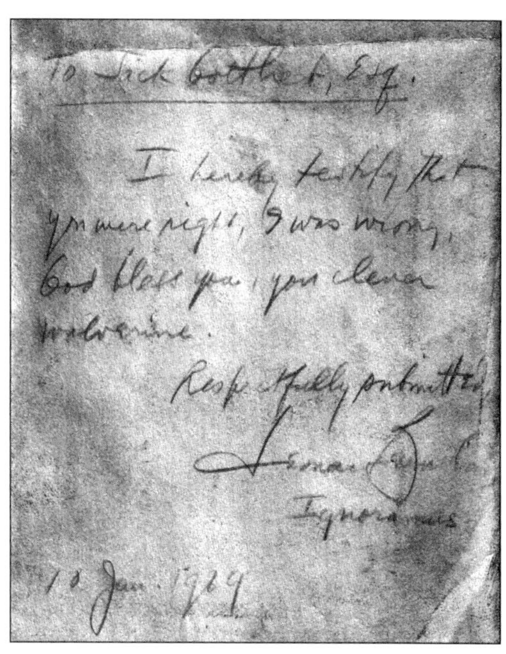
To Jack Gottlieb, Esq.
I hereby testify that you were right, I was wrong, God bless you, you clever wolverine.
Respectfully submitted,
Leonard Bernstein
Ignoramus
10 Jan. 1969

LB thinks it over, and the wolf is no longer at the door.

> To Jack Gottlieb, Esq.
> I hereby testify that you were right, I was wrong. God bless you, you clever wolverine.
> Respectfully submitted,
> Leonard Bernstein, Ignoramus
> 10 Jan., 1969

I have it among my most prized papers.

In his original foreword, Bernstein makes mention of the problems that arise in transferring scripts that are spoken aloud to a medium that is read in silence. Not the least of these is what to do about musical excerpts that are intended to be heard live. Many of the concerts have been made available for home video libraries. Bernstein said that "examples and records have the advantage of letting you play them over and over again . . . as you cannot do, of course, on television"—a statement, of course no longer valid. Now, using video formats and DVDs, it is equally possible to stop, reverse, and go forward—to play the music "over and over again for enjoyment and study." Nevertheless, the written page has the advantage of allowing readers of music to have hands-on "enjoyment"; and perhaps nonreaders of music will be motivated to "study." It becomes a matter of participatory involvement on the reader's part, something like the physical performances of the orchestral musicians who played the original concerts. In other words, his book challenged the reader not only to be a couch potato.

The 1960s were a time of great social upheaval, with a moral character quite unlike that of previous decades. Television itself was among the major factors contributing to the unrest: you only have to recall the funeral of John F. Kennedy and the Democratic National Convention in Chicago. The mystique of the 1960s, the decade of the Beatles, was closely allied with the so-called drug culture: LSD, Timothy Leary, flower children, hippies, and all the rest. In "Berlioz Takes a Trip," Maestro B. refers to psychedelic "trips" and hallucinogenics. But compared with a later generation's acquaintance with angel dust, crack, and the like, the earlier decade's dalliance with drugs almost verges on romantic innocence. Nevertheless, in the latest edition, it was decided to leave in all dated reference. Not every young reader may be familiar with the music of the Kinks, or with the Beatles, although music like theirs is continually being revived.

With the passage of time, it is now possible to get an overview of Leonard Bernstein's musical mission. Those common themes that carried over from show to show, year to year, have been noted. Although he did feature program music (i.e., music with a story) in various concerts, one senses that he did so with reluctance—his main mission being to inculcate purely musical values, as opposed to extra-musical ideas, into budding minds. A script such as "Igor Stravinsky Birthday Party" was a retelling of the *Petrouchka* ballet story. But the story Berlioz reveals in *Symphonie fantastique is* pertinent because the concept of the idée fixe is a neat way of explaining the variation principle in musical composition. In his first book, *The Joy of Music*, Bernstein talks about the "Music Appreciation Racket" and of his desire to find a "happy medium" between that racket and "purely technical discussion." If ever anyone did find that happy medium, it must have been he.

8 Postlude

(I began this piece in the air via Continental Airlines on my way to Seattle, 20 March 1991.)

Am I closer to him up here with the angels? It's more than five months since his death, and I've been resisting writing this down until now. Something I noticed on the way to the funeral—a word he used to anagram into "real fun." Everyone—and I mean everyone—had this terrible need to articulate "the last time I saw" or "spoke to him." I suppose we tend to do this each time someone we have known dies. It is a way of sharing, of commiserating. But this was different. It had a kind of heightened urgency, even theatricality. Some of it, I'm sure, was identifying with a piece of immortality, that by publicly declaring the last contact one had with him, one had secured protection for one's own demise. He was going to pave the way for us, and make our eventual entrance into the "great unknown" easier. But a bigger part of it had to be that so many of us were going to lose a valuable entrée to the "great known" here and now. Screw the future! What was going to happen to the present? We would not so much remember him as we would not be able to forget. Ultimately, of course, it was more about us than it was about him.

Two days before he died was my sixtieth birthday. That was hard enough to bear. I'd gone for a swim, coming home at 3:00 p.m. The phone rings. Rob Lind at the office is asking if I'm coming in. Should I go along with the usual charade? But I can't sustain it. "Come on, Rob, I know you've got cake and champagne there." "Yes, we do, so please come down." "Okay." I arrive to have good-natured conviviality with five business colleagues.

Now the office phone rings. It's Phillip Allen saying the Maestro wishes to speak to me. I should have taken the call privately, but pick it up in front of the others. I hush up the gathering, there's a pause, and LB gets on to give me birthday greetings. His voice is as deep as always, but also strangely hollow. I say to him, "Give me a present." He answers, "What's that?" "Let me come see you." "What good would it do?" Those were the last words I had from him. Not quite "the seven last words," but five will have to do. You see, here I go acting like all the others, doing the last-time-I-saw-I-spoke-to-him routine. Well, not quite. The last time I actually saw him alive was at the Dakota the night after his last concert, 19 August at Tanglewood. Earlier that year, he had given me a brass statue of a cowboy with a removable hat. Now he wanted me to bring it to Tanglewood to Texan conductor Carl St. Clair as thanks for taking over the conducting of his *Arias and Barcarolles* at the concert, a conducting effort too much for LB to handle. Perhaps because he had not orchestrated it.

Anyhow, he was upset with me because I hadn't brought the cowboy statue to Tanglewood. Messages via the assistants (especially P.) got lost in transit. It was not clear that I was to bring it along. But I was bothered that Lenny had forgotten he had given me the objet, which had been given to him by some sexy car driver or other. When I told him that night that the last thing I wanted to do was to upset him, especially at such a time of obvious illness, he recalled he had given the statue to me and that he would never have asked to have a gift returned. But I insisted he take it. He refused; and sitting back in his swivel chair, scotch in hand, he suggested that the next time I was in Times Square that I could pick up a duplicate at some souvenir store and send that one on. A rather infuriating instruction since it presupposed (1) I would know where to get such presumably "shoddy goods," at least in his eyes, and (2) that it was presumed to be a cheap gift for all concerned. At this point I was really pissed off and left the "bone of contention" there at the apartment for Craig to mail out to Mr. St. Clair.

I was reading the Week in Review of the Sunday *New York Times*, 14 October 1990, and came to a startling headline: "Final Bow for the Maestro?" The announcement that he was to retire from conducting had been released the prior Tuesday. The Amberson office staff had been partially alerted the week before that. In any case, I was flabbergasted, having been guardedly kept away from him by his manager, for eight weeks. Instructions from Harry Kraut to "have no contact with him." Foolishly, I stuck to the admonishment and have regretted it ever since. I condemn myself for having obeyed that order, especially when there were others who did not. Tricia Andryzewski, his newish secretary since Helen Coates died in February 1989, took me aside to say she felt particularly bad about keeping her lips sealed, especially to me.

Secrecy was also due to dodging pressure from the press. Earlier on, LB had had a stay at Lenox Hill Hospital where he was registered as Franco Levy. Now he was told by his doctor, Kevin Cahill, to keep visitors, even family, to a minimum. His regimen was to be exercise and massage. He was allowed one drink before dinner, but food had to be high protein (Ensure), along with various antidepressants and painkillers. In his date book, for 5 January 1990, he lists his various ailments: right elbow bursitis, anal bleeding, indigestion, no appetite, postnasal pus, bronchial junk, arthritis in the pinkie fingers, lethargy, sciatica.

So, as I am sitting there reading the *Times* article, the phone rings again. This time it's Julia Vega, who appears once more in this memoir: "Did you hear about Mr. Bernstein?" "No, Julia." "He died." That was it. Short and direct. For the first time in my life, the floor gives way and a rush of dizziness floods my head. Quite literally, my senses reel just short of fainting. "Oh, no!" I scream. "You must be strong," she advises in her best Roman-Catholic Chilean voice.

He died at 6:15 p.m. I get the call one hour later, put on a tie and jacket, and feel conscious of being outside my body as I walk over from my apartment on West Seventy-ninth Street to the Dakota on Seventy-second Street. I go up, as usual, the back way into the kitchen. Julia tells me to "go in and see Mr. Bernstein." I go to his bedroom. There his body, clothed in yellow pajamas, lies "in state," blanket covered from chest level down. A round, oblong pillow has been placed under his chin to keep the head erect. (Julia gave me the pillow afterward. It was covered in what looked like a tallit [a Jewish prayer shawl, white with black stripe fringes]. I slept with it for a while until it began to fray.)

A pin spot from the ceiling illuminates his head. The scene is vaguely stagey. I stand there weeping. Phillip Allen, an assistant, comes rushing in. Why can't I be left alone? He embraces me in a tearful bear hug. I'm weeping a cliché-ridden, "Oh, Lenny, I'm sorry . . . ," the same words I cried over my own father's body. Nothing original, nothing extraordinary. I reach out and rub his hand. The skin is grayish and cold, but smooth as marble. I have never touched a dead body before. Another first in my life with him. Hah!

The image that will always remain with me, however, was to see him hauled out in a body bag through the kitchen and out the rear entrance of the apartment like a sack of potatoes. It was unspeakable. Julia and I witnessed this perfunctory act, an everyday occurrence in the lives of the two service men. The family was in the library.

* * *

The funeral was a private affair that took place two days later in the apartment, jammed with family, friends, and sundry others. I can still hear his mother quietly sobbing. C., an employee, and L., a musician friend, were standing in front of the coffin, chatting away as if it were a cocktail party. I got up and asked them to step aside. Burtie, his brother, told the assembled that "my brother, Lenny, who was always larger than life, turned out to be smaller than death."

Afterward, coming downstairs, there was a large crowd, TV cameras from CNN, and reporters gathered outside the Dakota. Someone shoved a mike in my face for comments, which I waved away, not that they knew who I was. The funeral procession drove down Seventy-second Street and turned onto Columbus Avenue where, at Sixty-ninth Street, was Stanley Drucker, the New York Philharmonic clarinetist, standing silently at attention like a beefeater at Buckingham Palace. Then Lincoln Center, Lenny territory, the flags at half-mast in his honor; and out to Brooklyn, where we passed construction workers tipping their hard hats in recognition; and finally onto the grounds of Green-Wood Cemetery in Brooklyn.

At the grave site, where Felicia had been buried in 1978, two occurrences stood out for me as each of us shoveled in a spadeful of dirt onto the coffin: Bob Kirkland, an LB confidante, tossing in Catholic prayer beads and whispering to me, "It's for extra insurance." Most affecting of all was his sister Shirley putting a penny in her mouth, then disgorging it onto the coffin. (Lenny usually was given a "lucky penny" from a family member or associate before each concert.) It was Shirley's way of wishing "bon voyage" to her brother on his way toward eternity. (She joined him and her sister-in-law in the site eight years later.). A penny already had been put in the pocket of the conducting tails in which he was buried, along with, in the casket, a piece of amber, one of his custom-made batons, the French Legion of Honor lapel floret, and a pocket score of Mahler's Symphony No. 5, a lovely gesture decided upon by Craig Urquhart, his assistant. His children threw in a copy of *Alice in Wonderland*, just about his favorite book, which he almost knew by heart. As one wag later put it, "All that was missing was a bottle of Ballantine scotch."

LB gravesite, Green-Wood Cemetery, Brooklyn, New York.

Each time I visited the cemetery over the nineteen years since his death, usually with Julia Vega and Charlie Harmon, there have been tokens of remembrance left by others on his gravestone. Besides the Jewish tradition of courtesy stones left by visitors, items have included coins, calling cards, pieces of music and other random objects. A more recent visit took place on 11 June 2009, when Julia, dead at the age of ninety-one, was buried elsewhere in the cemetery. This sat heavy on me. She was such a nurturing presence in my life for fifty-one years and, despite her stern backbone, so goodhearted a soul, it was as if I had lost my godmother. Lenny was still "here and now" as long as Julia was alive. She would give him wise counsel during his sleepless nights. They were born the same year; her father's name was Jeremiah. I recited the Kaddish prayer next to her coffin and to all those assembled at her graveside. To make sure LB could hear it all the way from the hollow where she was buried to the top of the hill where he lies about a quarter mile away, I declaimed it very loudly. It was my way of saying good-bye to him at long last.

Jack in the Back Photo Gallery

LB greeting Pablo Casals. NYP president David Kaiser in foreground, UN aide Franco Passigli on the far side of Casals. United Nations, October 1958.

Surprise birthday party for Felicia Bernstein on 6 February 1962 at Café La Mama, NYC. *Facing camera, left to right:* Ellen Adler, Cornelia Foss, Phyllis Newman, Felicia Bernstein. JG in back of Felicia, Jerome Robbins and Nora Kaye in the rear, and Mendy Wager in the crook of LB's arm.

Dressing room in Carnegie Hall, 1960(?): LB embracing Gloria Vanderbilt, Jule Styne and Betty Comden in back of them, Jennie Bernstein in fur coat and Jennie Tourel in front.

LB with Glenn Gould and Igor Stravinsky, on the TV show "The Creative Performer," January 1960.

Front, left to right: LB, Jennie Tourel and Paul Hindemith. *Rear:* JG and Bruno Zirato. Carnegie Hall, February 1959.

Backstage at Tchaikovsky Hall, Moscow, 1959. Dimitri Shostakovich in left background, JG behind him with Maxim Shostakovich. Boris Pasternak in right foreground, Carlos Moseley on left.

LB with Harry Belafonte and Nat King Cole. Rehearsal for JFK Inaugural Gala, Washington, D.C., January 1961.

January 1959 rehearsal for an episode of the TV show *Lincoln Presents*: "Jazz in Serious Music." Members of the NYP: Al Brunning at far left, Jack Fishberg (holding violin) on right, stagehand Pete Regan in back with JG.

Part Two

MY NOTES ON LB'S NOTES

More formal writings about the Maestro's compositions based on previously printed concert programs, recording jackets, essays, and forewords to scores.

9 Chamber Music

"You wash my back and I'll wash yours."
– from a ditty by LB

Arias and Barcarolles

(Based on the introduction to the Boosey & Hawkes piano-vocal score, 1991)

Arias and Barcarolles is both a memory piece and a rumination on the nature of love. Its two piano premieres were dedicated to the memory of friends from the world of piano: (1) Jack Romann, the artists' representative of Baldwin Piano Company, and (2) Ruth Mense-Cohen, staff pianist of the Israel Philharmonic Orchestra. The main title and the dedications are based on the composer's personal experiences; but the life cycle events that are recalled are universal, though not necessarily sung in chronological order: birth ("Greeting"), childhood ("Little Smary"), the mystery of creativity in conflict with mundane affairs ("Love Duet"), inconclusive liaisons ("The Love of My Life"), wedding ("Oif Mayn Khas'ne"), married life ("Mr. and Mrs. Webb Say Goodnight") and death ("Nachspiel").

On 5 April 1960, Bernstein appeared as pianist-conductor, with members of the New York Philharmonic, in a concert of the Mozart Piano Concerto in G Major, K. 453 and Gershwin's *Rhapsody in Blue* at the White House. Afterward, President Eisenhower said to Mr. Bernstein, "I liked that last piece you played. It's got a theme. I like music with a theme, not all them [*sic*] arias and barcarolles." This artless phrasing imbedded itself in the composer's memory to be utilized twenty-eight years later, in 1988. The terms *arias* and *barcarolles* are, of course, most often associated with high-brow European opera. Therefore, Eisenhower's ingenuous comment was a low-brow American suspicion of European musical traditions. *Arias and Barcarolles*, nevertheless, wryly and resolutely makes use of the European art-song tradition.

The individual dedications are initials and idiosyncratic acronyms that refer to family members, friends and colleagues, all of whom had loving relationships with Bernstein in varying degrees. The opening "Prelude" suggests, however, that relationships are not always blissfully peaceful. Although the two singers imperturbably assert "I love you . . . ," the piano underpinning is a musical maelstrom. Perhaps this stark juxtaposition is a reinvention of Virgil's evergreen aphorism, *omnia vincit amor* (love conquers all things). But over the words the composer has indicated a marking of *non espressivo* (or *neutral*), which implies the phrase is meant, instead, to be ironic commentary.

A similar kind of irony purveys the seemingly charming "Love Duet." (for JAVE: Jamie Bernstein and David Thomas). Here the word *melody*, and its pronominal *it*, can be regarded as metaphors for *relationship*, at least as it pertains to the singers. As in the "Prelude," there is an undercurrent of unrest here, in what appears initially to be a picture of conventional domesticity. There is no such hidden agenda in "The Love of My Life," (to SWZ, for KO: Stephen Wadsworth Zinsser and Kurt Ollmann) a cry of regret over lost and/or missed opportunities in affairs of the body, and presumably, of the heart.

An earlier version of "The Love of My Life" was to be "Sticky Talk," a telephone conversation, which had lines such as, "Go away and leave me alone," "We gotta have a long talk about it," "Don't talk, you'll spoil it," "Why does it have to be your way?" "I have someone on the other line," and "But I *did* call you; no answer."

"Little Smary" (for S.A.B.: Shirley Anne Bernstein) by Jennie Bernstein is a recollection of a story often told to the composer by his mother when he was a child. This childhood bedtime tale is counterpoised with the adult pillow talk of "Mr. and Mrs. Webb Say Goodnight" (for Mino and Lezbo: Michael Barrett and Leslie Tomkins) an imagined vignette between Charles Webb, dean of the Indiana University School of Music, and his wife, Kenda. (Another Bernstein memory work, the opera *A Quiet Place*, had its first workshop readings at the university.) Actually, this duet is partially a quartet as both pianists briefly participate in roles as sons of the Webbs. (At a rehearsal, I proposed that LB not double the first appearance of a vocal line in the piano—at bar 146—since it diminished its effectiveness. He readily accepted the suggestion.)

When Bernstein's son, Alexander Serge, was born in 1955, the proud father wrote "Greeting" (for JG: Jack Gottlieb) as a kind of thanksgiving prayer. (It was revised in 1988. As mentioned earlier, a lullaby he wrote on the birth of his elder daughter, Jamie, later was used as the basis for the number "Quiet Girl" in the musical comedy *Wonderful Town*.)

The choice of the Yiddish poem "Oif Mayn Khas'ne" (for MTT: Michael Tilson Thomas) by Yankev-Yitskhok Segal alludes, perhaps subconsciously, to Bernstein's early career conflict with his father. Like the elders in the Yiddish poem, Samuel J. Bernstein was initially dubious about his son's musical aspirations. (He once supposedly replied to an interviewer's question about his opposition to his son's career, "How did I know he was going to be Leonard Bernstein?") The composer omitted an ironic couplet about the young fiddler from the original Yiddish poem (which comes after the line about "radishes from the garden"), a sneering comment on the untutored musician's knowledge: "He's a card-playing scholar, cunning in card science subtleties, interpretations and grammar." But the poem's main appeal to the composer had to be in its depiction of music's magical and youthful power to transform hidebound elders into wild paganistic enthusiasts (as the elder Bernstein was eventually transformed by his son's music-making).

The dedication history for "Nachspiel," the final portion, is quite convoluted. It was published separately as a piano piece in the publication of *Thirteen Anniversaries*, written in memory of Ellen Goetz, a friend. Originally, however, it was a song called "First Love (for My Mother, March 1986)."

My First Love, Jennie B.,
Eighty-eight, young to me.
My second love is eighty-eight too.
Eighty-eight keys that sing to you . . .
[Interlude]
Thus do I dedicate Eighty-eight
To my first two loves.

In *As and Bs,* it is at first dedicated "In memory of Jack Romann" who had died of AIDS. On the manuscript, this was crossed out and changed to "In memoriam, all my friends who died of AIDS." However, the final print inscription reads simply "In memoriam. . . ." Although one could make a guess, the composer's motivation for modifying this last entry is not known.

As a wordless *Nachspiel*, this simple Schubertian waltz provides a fitting conclusion to the last major work of the composer.

Dance Suite

(From the Boosey & Hawkes study score, 1992)

I. Dancisca (for Antony)
II. Waltz (for Agnes)
III. Bi-Tango (for Misha)
IV. Two-Step (for Mr. B.)
V. M T V (for Jerry)

Dance Suite is the last Bernstein work to be written, mostly in late 1989. It was premiered as part of the fiftieth anniversary gala of American Ballet Theatre at the Metropolitan Opera House, New York City, on 14 January 1990. This lighthearted divertissement was not danced, even though that was the original intention of the ballet company. A choreographer began work on it, but apparently it was felt that the movements were too short for danceable development. It was presented instead on stage, in front of the traveler curtain, as an independent instrumental work. The performers were the Empire Brass Quintet, to whom the suite is dedicated "with affection": Rolf Smedvig and Jeffrey Curnow, trumpets; Eric Ruske, horn; Scott Hartman, trombone; and Sam Pilafian, tuba. The first movement alone was doubled simultaneously with the Quintet members by the ballet orchestra in the pit.

Each movement is dedicated to a choreographer-friend: Antony Tudor, Agnes de Mille, Mikhail Baryshnikov, George Balanchine and Jerome Robbins. More than a *pièce d'occasion*, the work has other layers of meaning, as each movement had its origin in other formats. These are mostly anniversary pieces composed for family and friends.

The portmanteau word "Dancisca" is the title for what was originally a piano piece. Written for the composer's granddaughter, Francisca Ann Maria Thomas, "For my Rhymy Girl, with thanxgiving and love, Tata," it was completed "21 Nov. '89."

The ironic "Waltz," which sometimes is in 3/4 time (alternating with common time) has wry overtones. Dated "22 Nov. '89," it was conceived as "the NEA Forever March," after the composer refused the National Medal of Arts from President Bush. A grant from the National Endowment for the Arts to Artists Space, a nonprofit gallery in New York City, had been revoked because of its AIDS exhibit, "Witnesses: Against Our Vanishing." This was unacceptable to Bernstein, whose lyrics for the march were:

Everyone got a medal but Bernstein,
The President gave twelve medals,
Not to Bernstein.
Well, actually there showed up only ten to toast,
'Cause one of the dozen couldn't make it,
And the other was just a ghost.
But ten out of twelve is better than most,
And the President was a very lovely host.
So everyone had a great time but Bernstein.
The Lord be praised!

The "Two-Step" was at first "A Spiky Song," written for the composer's grandson, Evan Samuel Thomas: "Two weeks old, from his loving Granddaddy, 28 Oct. '89." ("Spike" was the name given to Evan prior to his birth by his father, David Thomas.) Its words include:

Hooray, ni-hao, Little Spike.
So glad, thank God,
Didn't call you Mike(ae)l, Stephen, Paul, . . .
Hip, hip, loud cheers, little tyke.
Welcome, warning:
Livin' ain't a bike ride, . . .
Hooray. Thank heaven for Evan.

The bitonal "Bi-Tango" is based on a "Birthday Serenata" composed for a violinist friend, Paul Woodiel, "17 Nov. '89" with words in Spanglish for "Señorito Pablito."

"M T V" is not exactly a tribute to the ubiquitous Music Television station. The middle section was also a song, written for the mother of the Bernstein grandchildren, Jamie Bernstein Thomas: "7.II.86, for Jamie, to be continued . . . Love, LB." This one was inspired (if that is the appropriate word) when

Bernstein watched an episode of *Miami Vice* on TV. The composer's lyrics for it were loosely based on actual dialogue. The words are found partly in the manuscript, and have been in part recalled by conductor Michael Barrett, as:

> He said: You wash my back and I'll wash yours.
> With the baby lyin' in a shoe-bag on the floor
> So she stabbed that rapist crime for crime.
> He was a small-time stand-up comic anyway,
> Very small-time.
> Now ain't that nice?
> Miami Vice.

Touches

Chorale, Eight Variations and Coda for Piano

Touches begins with a bluesy chorale that is virtually identical to a *Virgo Blues* written for Jamie Bernstein's twenty-sixth birthday in 1978. The full work was completed as the required piece for all entrants to learn in the Sixth Van Cliburn International Piano Competition of 1981. Soon thereafter, LB had a notion to convert it into a movement of a larger piano work. What did I think? I told him I regarded it as mostly sufficient unto itself. However, I did sense it could have used an additional variation better to prepare the coda. The lack of a build-up to this ending meant that it came at us "socko," too abruptly. He agreed with me. Since the music of *Touches* reminded me of variations in *Dybbuk,* I even suggested that he raid *Dybbuk* as an impetus toward writing the proposed additional variation.

Eight months before he died, he asked for my opinion about an orchestration that had recently been made—not by him—of *Touches.* He knew I was not happy with a transcription that had been made of *Arias and Barcarolles,* a version that vitiated the hard-edge, percussive character of that original piece. But this was not the case with the transcription of *Touches,* accomplished by conductor-composer Rudolph Palmer—all in all, a nice surprise.

A statement by Aaron Copland, after he had transmuted his 1930 *Piano Variations* into the *Orchestral Variations* of 1957, succinctly sums up what make such successful transmutations:

> My purpose was not to create orchestral sounds reminiscent of the quality of a piano, but rather to re-think the sonorous possibilities of the composition in terms of orchestral color. This would have been impossible for me to do when the work was new, for at that time the piano tone was an integral part of its conception. But with the perspective of twenty-seven years it was a comparatively simple matter to orchestrate as I have in the past, using the original as a piano sketch with orchestral possibilities.[1]

One month later, when I wrote a memo inquiring what Lenny planned to do about writing the additional section, his reply was a vague, "We'll see." Alas, by then he was suffering multifarious ills, and never got around to it.

10 Choral Works

"Singing a joyous, crazy song of courage."
– Lillian Hellman

A Choral Quilt

(Note to score, March 2008)

A quilt is often referred to as a comforter; and it is in this sense of warmth and protection that I designed a musical quilt of Bernstein songs. It is something I had been wanting to create for many years ever since I realized there was an ongoing thread of comfort, home and family weaving in and out of his theater works. Covering a long span within his composing life from 1950 to 1976, the order of titles is:

"Take Care of This House" from *1600 Pennsylvania Avenue* (1976, lyrics by Alan Jay Lerner)	The White House
"My House" from *Peter Pan* (1950, LB)	Shelter
"Make Our Garden Grow" from *Candide* (1956, Richard Wilbur)	Farmhouse
"There Is a Garden" from *Trouble in Tahiti* (1951, LB)	Schoolhouse ("love will teach us")
"Somewhere" from *West Side Story* (1957, Stephen Sondheim)	Elysian Fields (greenhouse)
"Almighty Father" from *Mass* (1971, LB and Stephen Schwartz)	House of God

Of the six songs that make up the quilt, two are choral to begin with; but they are not exact replicas of the originals. Adaptations of various kinds have been made; and only the last two numbers are presented in full. Shortened versions of the other selections are basically due to the lead-in factor of going from one number to the next. I use a stitching technique in which one lyric or musical segment either overlaps or anticipates the following one:

> Take care of this house→Build my house of wood→We'll build our house and chop our wood and make our garden grow→There is a garden / harmony and grace/ a quiet place→There's a place for us / peace and quiet→And fill with grace all those who dwell in this place.

There is no doubt in my mind that Bernstein was the one to pressure his lyricists to come up with the words for what he might have called "that hymn we've been putting off." I can also imagine that cynics night well dismiss these sentiments as sentimentality. Nonetheless, the composer was a man not only driven by the belief that we can envision a better world, but by the Hebraic precept of *tikun olam*, that we are obligated to repair it.

I could have included the song "Eldorado," from *Candide*; but that piece is more about fantasy than is the prayerful vision of "Somewhere," a justly famous anthem that never says "I wish" or "we hope." It insists, instead, on declaring "there is" and "there will be." Hence Micah's prophecy that "every man shall sit under his vine and fig tree" must ever be the goal of life's journey.

I do not know if I will be around to celebrate the centennial of Lenny's birth. I can only trust that my gift—in this which would have been his ninetieth year—will prove to be a worthy addition to American choral literature, and that it will have a life of its own from now until then and for decades thereafter.

The Lark and *Missa Brevis*

for Full Chorus of Mixed Voices or Septet of Solo Voices, a cappella

(*From various writings, in 1964 and 2002*)

Part I French Choruses (with drum)

1. Spring Song
2. Court Song
3. Soldier's Song

Part II Latin Choruses (with bells)
1. Prelude
2. Benedictus
3. Sanctus
4. Requiem
5. Gloria

"The girl was a lark in the skies of France, high over the heads of her soldiers, singing a joyous, crazy song of courage." So goes the description of Joan of Arc in Lillian Hellman's adaptation of Jean Anouilh's 1953 *L'Alouette.*

In 1955, while in the midst of working on a musical version of Voltaire's *Candide* with playwright Hellman, Bernstein composed these French and Latin choruses as incidental music to the play. The opening was on 28 October 1955 at the Plymouth Theater in Boston. The cast included Julie Harris as Joan, Boris Karloff (Cauchon), Christopher Plummer (Warwick) and Theodore Bikel (Robert De Beaudricourt). The first New York performance was on 17 November at the Longacre Theater.

Since the drama was about the trial of Joan of Arc (1412?–1431), Bernstein's music was deliberately evocative of the medieval era.[1] However, the French choruses are settings of French chansons that date from after Joan's execution:

1. "Spring Song" is based on "Revency de printemps" by Claude Le Jeune (1528–1600), called "shepherd's song" in the printed play version:

   See the springtime comes [in French]
   O praise the Lord, Alleluia! Amen. [in Latin]

2. "Court Song," on "Fi, mari de vos tre amour":

   Fie, my husband, on your love. For I have a lover, noble and charming. And I love him completely. Fie my husband! For I have a lover, noble and charming. He serves me night and day. And I love him completely. Fie my husband!

3. "Soldier's Song," on "Vive la Jeanne":

   Long live Jeanne, pretty Jeanne,
   Jolie, jolou, jola, la, la
   Jeanni, Jeannou, Jeanna, na, na.
   O pretty, pretty Jeanne.

Although the printed score separates the French from the Latin choruses, in the play they are interwoven as follows:

Act I: Prelude (*Exaudi*), "Spring Song" (or "shepherd song")/Alleluia, "Court Song," Benedictus.

Act II: "Soldier's Song," Sanctus, Requiem, Gloria.

I. Prelude

Before the curtain rose, a setting of a psalm text was heard: *Exaudi orationem meam, domine* ("Hear my prayer, O Lord, and give ear unto my cry"), the same Latin text (Psalm 39, verses 13–14) used by Stravinsky to open his *Symphony of Psalms*. When the curtain rose, the music changed to a motet on words from the Mass: *Qui tollis peccata mundi* ("You who take away the sins of the world, have mercy on us.")

II. Benedictus

Blessed . . . Hosanna in the highest! In the name of the Lord!

III. Sanctus

Holy, holy, holy, Lord God of Hosts,
The heavens and earth are full of Your glory.
Hosanna in the highest.

IV. Requiem

Grant eternal rest to them, O Lord,
And let everlasting light shine upon them.
Lord, have mercy. Christ, have mercy. Lord, have mercy.

V. Gloria

Glory to God in the highest!
Glory to our most glorious king.
Glory to our most renowned king.
Elect of God.

* * *

The sprightly "Spring Song" begins with a clapping rhythm that Bernstein was later to use with such exhilarating effect in "America" from *West Side*

Story. Depending on the context, it is either a *huapango* rhythm (meter) of 6/8 constantly alternating with 3/4 or a hemiola device. It is put to use here in a fugal manner, with the first two entrances in imitation welcoming "*le printemps*," while the second pair of entrances imitate each other in a retrograde version of the first pair. Two more entries (as in the other, two bars apart) are also in canonic form. All six voices then explode in a joyous outburst of triads moving in contrary motion above parallel fifths sometimes resulting in bi-tonal clashes. The countertenor interrupts this festivity with a freely expressive utterance, in Latin, praising God for the good season. In even note values, this solo becomes a cantus firmus to the next section, in which the fugal tune, by three, then six voices, is now sung on the syllable "la" in nonimitative counterpoint (Ex. 10-1):

Example 10-1

A final section, a variation of the opening and also truncated, is completed by an *amen* cadence in the countertenor (Ex. 10-2). This cadence, a favorite motive of the composer, is also the prominent motto motive for the first movement of his "Jeremiah" Symphony (Ex. 10-3):

Example 10-2

Example 10-3

In the filigreed "Court Song," on top of a drone bass (à la bagpipe) a melismatic troubadour melody (about "noble love") is sung by the first soprano. As in the "Spring Song" (at the end of the second section), there are scale chain effects, going from one voice to the next, which conclude the first part. The second part is an inexact repetition, with the soprano melody now echoed in canon by the countertenor.

The "Soldier's Song" is appropriately martial, enhanced by drum and fife (i.e., whistling). There is only one tune ("Long live the beautiful Joan") repeated twice in ever-increasing density of texture: two voices, then all seven in a lower octave succeeded by the tutti chorus in an upper octave. The composer used an old folk song for this marching ditty of the faithful: "Vive la Grappe."

Whereas the French choruses are popular in flavor and belong to the character of Joan, the Latin group is considerably more austere, concerning her king and inquisitors. The opening Prelude, the music of which is repeated in the final Gloria (forming a set of musical parentheses) is a somber invocation. There are cross relations and harmonic clusters that are severe and hard (Ex. 10-4), perfectly attuned to the role of Joan's judges:

Example 10-4

The second section of the Prelude, a new segment on the words "*qui tollis peccata mundi*," is in quiet contrast—a three-part canon in strict second-species counterpoint. Again the countertenor enters on the final cadence points of the choir.

The second Latin chorus, a Benedictus, starts in recitative style by the countertenor echoed by the women's voices rapidly singing triads. A main section in presto tempo ensues. very much in fourteenth-century conductus style, first in the Mixolydian mode and then in the Lydian. The exultant shout at the end ("Blessed be he who comes in the name of the Lord") spills over into bells whose sounds overlap in a kind of ecstatic improvisation.

The Sanctus (No. 3) is closely related to the Benedictus, using the same conductus style in the choir, alternating with the recitatives (first *senza misura*, then in tempo) in the countertenor. The "moll-dur" aspect of the modal content is strongly pronounced: B-flat followed by B-natural and back again.

A tiny Requiem (No. 4) consists of two motivic phrases repeated four times. The first is an open fifth in the men's voices that dissolves into a slightly chromatic cadence, which is then held while the women sing the second phrase of an abbreviated litany above it (in octaves). It is ascetic and simple. without any superfluous embellishments.

The final Gloria begins with the aforementioned Prelude material. Instead of a second section ("Who takes away the sins of the world") there is a fanfarelike coda (Ex. 10-5)—a harmonic phrase in contrary motion, reminiscent of the opening "Spring Song," repeated three times (see also Ex. 10-1):

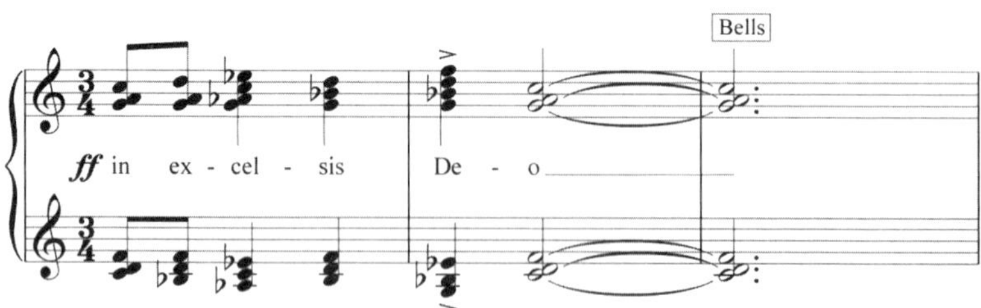

Example 10-5

Two sets of bells one in each wing, playing ad libitum notes, punctuate these phrases; and repeated triads in E-flat (with an added supertonic) passionately bring the choral suite to completion.

Missa Brevis (1988)

For A Cappella Mixed Chorus (or Octet of Solo Voices)
and Countertenor Solo with Incidental Percussion

(Based on Choruses from *The Lark*, 1955)

1. Kyrie Eleison (with 2 timpani)
2. Gloria (with bells)
3. Sanctus

3A. Benedictus (with bells, cymbals, tam-tam)

4. Agnus Dei

4A. Dona Nobis Pacem (with tabor, hand drum, tambourine, etc.)

The eminent choral conductor Robert Shaw attended one of the first performances and suggested to Bernstein that the music would make an effective *Missa Brevis*. Thirty-three years later, in honor of Maestro Shaw's retirement as music director of the Atlanta Symphony Orchestra, Mr. Bernstein followed up on the suggestion, which he had wanted to do all along.[2] In so doing, the two men continued an association that began with Shaw's recording of selections from Bernstein's *On the Town* in 1944.

The version of *Missa Brevis* recorded by Shaw with the Atlanta Symphony Chorus on the Telarc label did not include certain liturgical passages from the Gloria and Agnus Dei. For the publication of the score, the composer, assisted by George Steel [a protégé of LB's who has since been named director of New York City Opera] amplified the score to accommodate these texts.

A White House Cantata: Scenes from *1600 Pennsylvania Avenue*

(Written in 1997, unpublished)

The 1972 musical "About the Problems of Housekeeping," *1600 Pennsylvania Avenue* was really about theater and all the baggage that went along with the collaborative efforts of authors, production team and actors. In contrast, the 1997 concert scenes extracted from the show: *A White House Cantata* is all about music and lyrics with none of the storm and stress that went into the show's plot strategems, characterizations and philosophical stance.

This is not the place to explore the tortured history of *1600 Pennsylvania Avenue*. For those who are interested, this has been well documented by the show's latter-day enthusiast, Erik Haagensen.[3] However, a brief overview is in order to place some perspective on a project that had more "downs and downs" than "ups and downs."

Covering the first hundred years of the American presidency, from George Washington to Theodore Roosevelt, the musical was a passing parade of episodes in presidential careers alternating with vignettes of the backstairs staff at the White House. One pair of white actors played all the presidents and first ladies, while another pair of black actors depicted all the head servants through the century. To bind these disparate elements, a play-within-a-play format had these same performers occasionally step outside of their roles and portray themselves as actors rehearsing the show. The authors' intention was to symbolize democracy as a process always in rehearsal, always striving to perfect itself. The device did not work, and none of these commentary scenes are part of the cantata.

The critical reception to the initial production, as well as to the 1992 revival attempts, disparaged Lerner's book while praising his lyrics. Less attention was paid to the score, which, nevertheless, was favorable. Indeed, Bernstein recycled certain numbers in some of his later works, where they took on a life of their own. However, *A White House Cantata* offers a rare chance to peruse and pursue the music with fresh ears, unencumbered by stage trappings and the traps of the political stage. A short analysis of each scene, mostly from a musical perspective, follows.

Act One

1. Prelude: The pitch of middle C, four beats to a bar, is repeated without variance as it goes through a harmonic journeys from the bottom to the top of different chord structures. A precedent for this kind of reiterating artifice is to be found in Chopin's "Raindrop" Prelude, but like that famous piano piece, the cantata's moving opening is more than an intellectual exercise. In fact, the music was reused by the composer in his *Songfest*, where it became a backdrop for Walt Whitman's poem "To What You Said." Keen listeners will detect the opening motive of the melody as the same notes that begin "Tonight" from *West Side Story*.

2. "Ten Square Miles"/"If I Was a Dove": Bernstein has the congressional delegates plead their respective colonies as the rightful seat of the nation's capitol in an overlapping fugal petition. President Washington sweeps away all such partisan posturing in a snappy march tempo. The motive that begins this march: a triplet plus quarter-note, is eventually scattered about until it completes a twelve-tone row on the words, "I'm not disinclined." This motive will figure prominently in later scenes. The blustering mood then changes to a haunting echo-call from the trackers of Lud, the escaped slave. The tritone effect is reminiscent of a similar chordal sound in the chase scene from Britten's *Peter Grimes*.

3. "Welcome Home, Miz Adams": An amusing a cappella chorale that derives much of its humor from sudden changes in tempo. The middle solo section ("You'll be mighty glad to learn"), in a quasi-pentatonic mode, is suggestive of a folk-song idiom.

4. "Take Care of This House": Starting with a pre-verse section that repeats the opening of "Ten Square Miles," the verse proper is sung to a filigree accompaniment of thirty-second notes. The inspirational refrain, launched by the motive mentioned above in No. 2, is the best known song from the musical.

5. "The President Jefferson Sunday Luncheon March": Unlike the "boots tramping" trudge of No. 2, this march, opening with vocal fanfares, is an debonair two-step, the kind Bernstein subsequently used in the Finale of his *Divertimento*. The cadence of the main tune with its penultimate 3/2 bar, as well as an "oom-pah" section of alternating 4/4 and 3/4 times, help to keep the party-goers slightly off balance.

6. "Seena": With its resonance of phrases from *On the Town*, this blues-y, lyrical ballad is an extended song form: A/A repeated in a new key/B, an enlarged bridge section based on motives from A, returning to A once again.

7. Sonatina ("The British"): The Alberti bass of a polite drawing-room keyboard tinkles away in wry Clementi style over which the British officers volley bon mots at each other à la W. S. Gilbert. Gradually the opening strain of the drinking song "To Anacreon in Heaven," which was

to become "The Star-Spangled Banner," is heard in its authentic original version. This is followed by a concluding segment wherein the British rail against divine intervention for the sudden downpour of rain that stops the burning of the city of Washington. Incongruously, the protest is heard in a pseudo–Middle Eastern mode: an altered scale of a raised 4th step and a flattened 7th step. Perhaps this is a musical joke, juxtaposing a Jehovian God against the "By Jovian" conviviality of the scene.

8. "Lud's Wedding": Dignified invocations by the Reverend in a 7/4 meter give way to less proper decorum, first in the form of a cakewalk and then a lively calypso chorus. The latter, distinguished by a repeating pattern of 3+3+2 beats per bar, is anachronistic for its time period; but the dancey tune is a welcome foil between the extended scenes that precede and follow it.

9. "The Monroviad"/"The Mark of a Man": The title, which could be defined as "the state of President Monroe's mind," had to be an invention of the composer. The scene, best described as pillow talk, begins as a recitative by Monroe and leads to a lulling plea from his wife to "go to sleep." The interchange becomes more heated as Eliza sardonically refers to society's treatment of its black members as "that little white lie." Monroe's protestations of non-guilt only arouses Eliza to more righteous indignation to which Monroe now must respond with "go to sleep." A concluding soliloquy, "The Mark of a Man," eloquently defines Monroe's dilemma, as it reaches one peak with a trumpet solo and then a higher one with a partial recall of the anthem "Take Care of This House."

10. "This Time": A kind of mirror image of the preceding duet, now a dialogue between the servants Lud and his wife. Seena, filled with apprehension at the prospect of resettlement in Liberia, fears for their safety. Her melody ("You ain't comin' back"), reappeared in Bernstein's opera *A Quiet Place* ("Mommy, are you there?"). Its melancholic strain, à la Edvard Grieg, climaxes on a four-note motive that will be the opening for the cantata's Finale. Lud anguished reaction is heard as a reminiscence of "Seena." As he declares his deep allegiance to the house, a more complete account of the anthem peals forth.

11. "We Must Have a Ball": A foppish President Buchanan responds to government problems by sweeping them under a rug of elegant waltzes—

shades of recent "gates" in American history. An introductory section (A) rotates in rondo style first with a melody (B) built on rising chords based on the whole-tone scale, and then with a secondary C section.

Act Two

12. "Welcome Home, Miz Johnson": A reprise of No. 3. This time, however, the humor is muted as Seena refers to the grief of Mrs. Lincoln, who is still in mourning for her assassinated husband.

13. "Bright and Black": A mock memorial service for the stereotypical figure of Uncle Tom is in progress. Like the traditional New Orleans funeral parade, which moves to a solemn tempo on the road to the cemetery and then switches to a jaunty ragtime beat on the way back, this also begins lugubriously and ends in triumphant jubilation. An early sketch for the tune, written years prior to the show, was set to a Bernstein lyric "It's the Jews," a sardonic rebuttal to anti-Semitism.

14. "Duet for One": Long before she was known as the addle-pated Mrs. Bucket (pronounced "bouquet"!) on the acclaimed English television comedy *Keeping Up Appearances*, Patricia Routledge triumphed as the original first ladies in *1600 Pennsylvania Avenue*. This virtuoso number was her shining moment, during which she changed faces in kaleidoscopic fashion from the southern Julia Grant to her successor, the northern Lucy Hayes. Like some crazed "Jacquel'yne Heidi," she brilliantly transformed herself from gentility to bitchery.

15. "The Money-Lovin' Minstrel Parade": High jinks pervade the four segments of this takeoff on a peculiar nineteenth-century American entertainment. As in "Gee, Officer Krupke" from *West Side Story*, Bernstein mines the conventions of vaudeville for ironic commentary. A precursor of Lerner's caustic "Pity the Poor" is to be found in Marc Blitzstein lyric from *Regina*: "For the half-poor are poorer than poor/ Unhappy, unloved, unsure." In "The Grand Old Party," Lerner's pun on "bald eagle" is priceless: "Got de U.S. by the bal— d'eagle." But it was unclear that the minstrel show was a jab at the GOP because there was no context; the book was in such a shambles. The composer plucked the GOP music to help fashion the independent concert overture *Slava!*

16. "To Make Us Proud": The finale opens with the same chords as those that began the cantata. Like the finales to his Symphony No. 2, "The Age of Anxiety" and his operetta *Candide*, Bernstein's stirring, unapologetic paean to patriotism moves in a dignified slow tempo, this time in 5/4 time. The music later became the source for a separate choral work, the *Olympic Hymn*, set to a German text and then in English by Richard Wilbur. Is this evolution or convolution?

11 Dance and Theater Works

"He may be heaven's gift to music, but he's nervous indigestion to me."
– *Collier Magazine,* 13 October 1945

On the Town and *Fancy Free*

(From the program book "Concordia Celebrates Leonard Bernstein," 7 June 1991)

In the 1950s there was a television game show, emceed by Robert Q. Lewis, Bert Parks and others, called *Masquerade Party*. Through a series of questions, a panel of so-called experts (Ogden Nash, Faye Emerson et al.) tried to identify celebrity guests who were in facial disguises (rubber masks) and costumes. On 16 May 1956, there appeared two mystery guests in sailor garb, Felicia and Leonard Bernstein.[1] The ballet *Fancy Free* (premiered 18 April 1944) and its spin-off Broadway musical *On the Town* (13 December 1944) had by then, in one decade, become imbedded in American folklore; and the sailors theatricalized in both works had become integral to the Bernstein legend in the making. All the same, the panel was not able to identify them.

Although the ballet was the nucleus of the musical, the latter's story and score were utterly different, particularly in their romanticism. A sailor and his two shipmates pursue, discover, lose and recover an idealized female (the wartime pinup "Miss Turnstiles"), their search shaped by rhythms of daily living that imperceptibly meld into dance patterns. Bernstein wrote the following note about the "Three Dance Episodes" for its concert hall premiere, which he conducted:

> It seems only natural that dance should play a leading role in the show *On the Town*, because the idea of writing it arose from the success of

the ballet *Fancy Free*. I believe this is the first Broadway show ever to have as many as seven or eight dance episodes in the space of two acts; and, as a result, the essence of the whole production is contained in these dances. I have selected three of them for use as a concert suite:

I. *Dance of the Great Lover* (from the "Dream Ballet," Act II)
II. *Pas de Deux* (from the "Lonely Town" Ballet, Act I)
III. *Times Square Ballet* ("Finale," Act I)

That these are, in their way, symphonic pieces rarely occurs to the audience actually attending the show, so well integrated are all the elements by the master direction of George Abbott, the choreographic inventiveness of Jerome Robbins, and the adroitness of the Comden-Green book. Their use, therefore, as concert material is rather in the nature of an experiment. The story is concerned with three sailors on 24-hour leave in New York, and their adventures with the monstrous city which its inhabitants take so for granted.

I. *Dance of the Great Lover*: Gabey, the romantic sailor in search of the glamorous Miss Turnstiles, falls asleep on the subway and dreams of his prowess in sweeping Miss T. off her feet.

II. *Pas de Deux*: Gabey watches a scene, both tender and sinister, in which a sensitive high school girl in Central Park is lured and then cast off by a worldly sailor.

[Apparently, in those more innocent days, the park was more receptive to "sensitivity."]

III. *Times Square Ballet*: A more panoramic sequence in which all the sailors in New York congregate in Times Square for their night of fun. There is communal dancing, a scene in a souvenir arcade, a scene in the Roseland Dance Palace. Cuts have been made in the music of those sections relating directly to the plot action.[2]

Only eight months passed between the premiere of *Fancy Free* and the creation-to-opening of *On the Town*. Although some of the music was retrieved from the proverbial composer's trunk, it still was an astonishing feat, especially compared to current-day averages of musical evolving over the course of years. It certainly was a hectic time, as was the rest of Bernstein's musical life. He would not have had it any other way. Ever on the go, he was quoted as saying, "I've always found the train a good place to write music. It was on the train that I wrote 'New York, New York.' No, it wasn't the subway. I happened to be riding past the farms of Nebraska at the time."[3]

One is reminded of the train rhythms that stimulated musical ideas in Gershwin for *Rhapsody in Blue*, while he was en route to Boston. Complementing the whirlwind pace of the writing was the joy Bernstein must have had doing it.

In the summer of 1944 both he and Adolph Green, his close friend and collaborator, shared the same room when each had minor surgery at Doctors Hospital in Manhattan. They planned to work on the show during their recuperation. LB was in for a deviated septum and Green had to undergo a tonsillectomy. (According to the *On the Town* souvenir book, all six collaborators: Comden and Green, producers Oliver Smith and Paul Feigay, Bernstein and Robbins also shared the same age of twenty-six!) The writing continued in a madcap atmosphere that did not sit well with the medical staff, one of the nurses saying about Bernstein, "He may be heaven's gift to music, but he's nervous indigestion to me."[4] The show was actually in rehearsal before the score was finished. It opened on December 26 for a run of 463 performances. Bernstein even appeared once on stage in the nightclub scene, as a "drunk" extra, and once again with conductor Dimitri Mitropoulos as his "drinking partner"! The musical was, indeed, a gleeful romp for both writers and audience. In fact, John Chapman of the *Daily News*, the only reviewer to pan it originally, did a complete

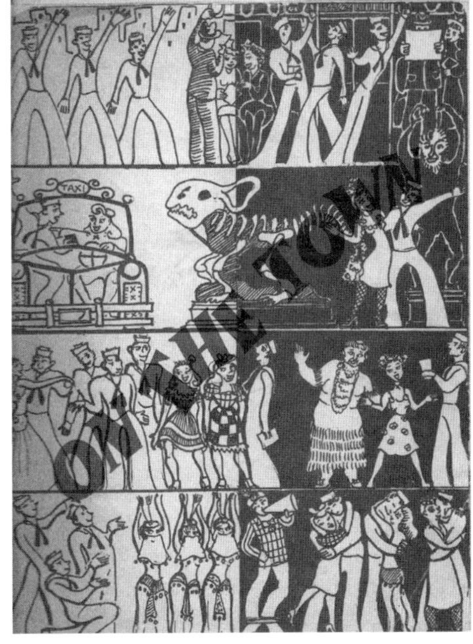

Souvenir book cover for the original production of On the Town.

turnabout six months later (5 August 1945) when he described it as "fresh, funny, . . . filled with private pranks."

The 1949 MGM movie of *On the Town*, which Gene Kelly considered his favorite, established a number of precedents: the first musical to be filmed, even though in part, on location (NYC); the first to command the high fee it received even before it went into its Broadway rehearsals, and the first to be sold for the highest amount paid until then for a musical. Louis B. Mayer, who had bought the property, did so with reluctance for the considered it to be "smutty;" and because it dared to show a black girl dancing with a white man, he thought it was "Communistic." But perhaps the most astounding "first" of all is that the movie barely used any of the composer's music—only parts of two dances and three songs; and even these were abridged or adapted. As usual, Bernstein was busy elsewhere, and therefore had given artistic control to his collaborators. Apparently, the score with its spiked rhythms, pungent harmonies and unconventional melodies, was considered too long-haired (i.e., not commercial enough) for mainstream America. Even the poignant ballad "Lonely Town" was dropped, the only song in the entire Bernstein catalog that Frank Sinatra, one of the sailors, ever recorded independently. Nevertheless, the film was a smash; and its success inspired a slew of similarly plotted movies, including a kind of sequel by Comden and Green, the 1955 *It's Always Fair Weather* (three solders, this time around).

In the world of popular musical theater, sailors have had a theatrical lineage from Gilbert and Sullivan's *H.M.S. Pinafore* (a work Bernstein produced during his late teens while at summer camp) to the Robin, Grey and Youmans musical *Hit the Deck*. But *Fancy Free* was something else. Although there were European ballets that previously had used sailors, such as Balanchine's *The Triumph of Neptune*, to a score by Berners, and Massine's *Les Matelots*, score by Auric, *Fancy Free* was the first to combine classical ballet with a jazz idiom. Bernstein claimed he was not thinking jazz when he wrote it, but that was how "it came out, had to be. Those who try to write music that is deliberately American seldom succeed. Some have used Indian themes or Puritan hymns or Negro tunes, but where these are deliberately 'tacked on' they are not more than extraneous tinsel."[5] *Fancy Free* was, in addition, probably the first dance piece to show off sailors in an overtly erotic way. Earlier, paintings by Paul Cadmus—*Shore Leave* (1933), *The Fleet's In* (1934) and *Sailors and Floozies* (1938)—with their frank carnality of casual pickups, had caused a public furor. Sailors were supposed to swab decks, hoist sails, or polish brass. To picture them as uninhibited sex subjects, as well as objects, was unpatriotic. But Cadmus also portrayed specific individuals rather than uniform group solidarity. (Why is it that nuns and sailors always seem to appear in public in pairs?) This zeroing-in on separate characters and their specific emotional makeup was also indigenous to the Robbins choreography, perhaps its most endearing aspect. Each sailor's exhibitionism is particularly spotlighted in the ballet's "Three Dance Variations": virtuoso athleticism in the "Galop," sinuous insinuation in the "Waltz," and bump-'n'-grind sensuality in the "Danzon." To the extent their randiness may be mirrored in the sound, it is held in check by a restraining trumpet solo in the midsections of each variation.

LB wrote a lyric for the tune of what became the "Danzon." Here is the opening:

> A thousand years ago
> They danced it soft and slow,
> The little Indians were dancing sweet and low
> In Rio Bamba!
>
> But when the Spaniards came
> They found it much too tame,
> And since that day the dance has never been the same
> In Rio Bamba!
>
> And then they heard the beat
> Of Africano feet,
> And now the dance is full of Africano heat
> In Rio Bamba!

A proletarian ballet (more hoi polloi and less hoity-toi), *Fancy Free* has sustained its enduring popularity and repertory status. Bernstein's lusty music, with its signature drum rim shots, is impudent and tough, but also a poetic distillation of life in a great city, especially apparent in the piano-concertante writing. Listen to the brash opening piano solo riffs and their transformation into a New York kind of blues in the closing "cadenza." In his program note for the "Three Dance Variations," the composer wrote:

> From the moment the action begins, with the sound of a juke box wailing behind the curtain, the ballet is strictly young America of

> 1944. The curtain rises on a street corner with a lamp post, a side street bar, and New York skyscrapers pricked out with a crazy pattern of lights, making a dizzying backdrop. Three sailors explode on the stage, they are on shore leave in the city and on the prowl for girls. The tale of how they first meet one, then a second girl, and how they fight over them, lose them and in the end take off after still a third, is the story of the ballet.[6]

The juke-box sound is a fragment of the song "Big Stuff," words by the composer, first recorded by his sister Shirley, later by Billie Holiday, and then by Dee Dee Bridgewater. The set was by Oliver Smith, a key personage in the creation of the ballet and the musical. Bernstein knew him as the set designer for the de Mille–Copland ballet *Rodeo*; and it was through Smith that Robbins met Bernstein a month before his historic debut with the New York Philharmonic. According to the composer, Robbins "had some notion about three sailors on shore leave and girls and fun." As early as 1938, at Camp Tamiment in the Poconos, Robbins had choreographed a sailor dance called *At the Anchor.* Work on the new ballet was carried on via telephone, telegraph and disc recordings (made on the piano four hands with Aaron Copland), sent through the mails because Smith went to Mexico, Robbins was on tour with Ballet Theatre, while Bernstein was based in New York with side trips to Boston and Pittsburgh, where the premiere of his first symphony, "Jeremiah," took place in January 1944. As Smith tells it,

> We first talked it over and then were off. Oh, I guess Lenny did send Jerry a record or two, and I wrote them both a couple of letters about the sets, but that long distance collaboration is the bunk. When we finally got together again each of us had completed his job and all that remained was to draw the loose ends together.[7]

As recently as 22 April 1991, Smith spoke about the halcyon days of Ballet Theatre to the *New York Times*: "I have great affection for that era. . . . there was an atmosphere of joy and innocence to the New York of *Fancy Free*."

Like *Trouble in Tahiti*, the ballet is in seven scenes. This results in a symmetrically balanced form, the first three scenes on one side of a central arch, the last three on the other side. The centerpiece, the Pas de Deux, is a symphonic expansion of the song "Big Stuff."

I. Opening Dance	II. Scene at the Bar	III. Enter Two Girls
	IV. Pas de Deux	
V. Competition Scene	VI. Three Variations	VII. Finale

Facsimile

(Columbia Records LP jacket note, 1965)

After the phenomenal success of *Fancy Free* in 1944, Ballet Theatre commissioned another dance work from the creators, Leonard Bernstein and Jerome Robbins. *Facsimile*, their new work, written in only three weeks during the summer of 1946, was premiered October 24 at the Broadway Theater, with a cast including Robbins, Nora Kaye and John Kriza, and the composer as conductor. The settings were by Oliver Smith and the costumes by Irene Sharaff. Later, Bernstein fashioned a "Choreographic Essay" for orchestra alone, differing mainly from the ballet-proper in its final section. This version was first presented on 5 March 1947 with the Rochester Philharmonic and is dedicated to Jerome Robbins.

If the music had been written twenty years later, it might have used the language of the discotheque, for the then postwar scenario concerns the desperation of people seeking meaningful and real relationships in their "go-go" way. They find, instead, only a facsimile of companionship, ultimately leading to boredom and to the rediscovery of the painful inadequacies of their loneliness. This theme Bernstein was to explore further in his symphony "The Age of Anxiety" and his opera *Trouble in Tahiti*. *Facsimile*'s action occurs, significantly, not in a metropolis but on a beach, that place to which one supposedly escapes from the city. But the emptiness of existence is made even more poignant, in this barren spot, for the "unintegrated personalities" stripped of all the trappings and camouflages of urban life.

The music, on the other hand, is anything but unintegrated, with much of the thematic material deriving from the opening oboe phrase followed by an elegiac flute melody. These brooding segments figure prominently throughout the work. The score divides into four sections, played without pause in one movement, which closely mirror the stage action.

I. *Solo*: The Woman is by herself, idly and vainly trying to pass the time.

II. *Pas de deux*: She meets the First Man, who is also restless. They carry on a flirtation (waltz), which leads to a quick and abrupt sensation of passion. But their false lovemaking causes them to withdraw into themselves more than ever (muted strings with two solo violins and solo viola).

III. *Pas de trois*: The Second Man comes on the scene (scherzo, with concertante piano solo passages). This is a signal for the other two to bestir themselves out of a need to see how much emotional mileage they can get out of the situation. All three indulge in "Fun and Games." the woman playing one man off against the other. It begins with a facade of jocularity, but turns into a triangle situation filled with the expected accusations, denunciations and threats. The three are now sure that they are "really living," only to realize, suddenly, that they really could not care less. In the ballet this is unexpectedly pinpointed by the woman shouting, "Stop!" An embarrassed pause follows, the men standing by helplessly.

IV. *Coda*: Awkwardly the men leave. The woman is alone as at the beginning, no more fulfilled than she was before. This is reflected in the music, which ends on an inconclusive treatment of the tonic triad.

Symphonic Dances from "West Side Story"

(From the New York Philharmonic program note "A Valentine for Leonard Bernstein," 13 February 1961)

This is from the very first program note I ever wrote on LB's works. It was for a Pension Fund concert under the direction of Lukas Foss. Not mentioned is the contribution I made to the shaping of the work, one of the most popular in LB's catalog. The orchestrators, Sid Ramin and Irwin Kostal, were mulling over how to end the piece with the composer and came up empty because they had exhausted the dance sequences. This was when I suggested that they conclude with the song "I Have a Love," even though it is not a dance. They concurred.

The four shows *On The Town*, *Wonderful Town*, *Candide* and *West Side Story* show a progressive line of stylistic integration in Bernstein's compositional development. An ever-advancing economy of musical means and tightening of structure proceeds from one show to the next. It was almost predictable from this trend that when *West Side Story* hit Broadway like a bombshell, in September 1957, it would be hailed as a landmark in American theater. It was, indeed recognized as a major leap toward an original kind of theatrical conception. Bernstein had speculated much earlier that a genuine, indigenous form of American musical theater would eventually arise out of what has been known as musical comedy. Many people think that, in *West Side Story*, this theory began to be implemented. Elements from the European and American musical stage traditions were fused into an original art form that is neither opera nor musical comedy.

From the Old World came complicated vocal ensembles, such as the Quintet in act 1; the use of music to project the storyline forward (as in the duet "A Boy Like That"); the dramatic device of leitmotifs like the one associated with the reality of gang violence, as in the "Prologue" (Ex. 11-1),

Example 11-1

or the one associated with the diametrically opposite vision of togetherness, as in the "Finale" (Ex. 11-2).

Example 11-2

In addition, from the European tradition came the deductive-inductive species of developing musical materials, by basing much of the *West Side Story* score on transformations of the interval, tritone interval, or by immediately developing the opening statement of any given song with melodic or rhythmic variation.

From the New World came idiomatic jazz and Latin timbres and figurations (much of the dance music); a fluid and constant change from word to music and from scene to scene, such as the second-act ballet that goes from accompanied spoken word into song into dance and back again; and most important, the kinetic approach to the stage—communication through choreographic music—delineated, in concentrated form, by these *Symphonic Dances*.

Why are these dances called "symphonic"? Simply because the dance music, even in its original format, is symphonically conceived. Relatively few thematic ideas that are combined with each other and metamorphosed into completely new shapes are all that is necessary to meet the varying dramatic requirements. This is music on its own terms, music that does not have to depend upon presupposed knowledge of the unfolding events.

However, for those who might be interested in knowing what transpires on stage during the course of the dances, the following summary outlines the principal sections of the music (arranged so that one section flows into the next without a break, and ordered according to alternating high and low levels of emotional intensities):

Prologue (Allegro moderato): The growing rivalry between two teenage gangs, the Jets and the Sharks.

"Somewhere" (Adagio): In a dream ballet, the two gangs are united in friendship.

Scherzo (Vivace e leggiero): In the same dream, they break through the city walls and suddenly find themselves in a world of space, air and sun.

Mambo (Presto): In the real world again; the competitive dance at the gym between the gangs.

Cha-Cha (Andantino con grazia): The star-crossed lovers Tony and Maria see each other for the first time; they dance together.

Meeting Scene (Meno mosso): Music accompanies their first words spoken to one another.

"Cool,", Fugue (Allegretto): An elaborate dance sequence in which Riff leads the Jets in harnessing their impulsive hostility, figuratively "cooling their jets."

Rumble (Molto allegro): Climactic gang battle; the two gang leaders, Riff and Bernardo, are killed.

Finale (Adagio): Maria's "I Have a Love" develops into a procession, which recalls the vision of "Somewhere."

The score calls for an unusual array of percussion instruments: xylophone, vibraphone, chimes, glockenspiel, cymbals, tenor drum, snare drum, bass drum, jazz snare drum, four tuned drums, maracas, guiro, gourd, jazz traps, timbales, three tuned tom-toms, conga drum, bongos, finger cymbal, tambourine, tam-tam, wood block, triangle, three pitched cowbells and police whistle.

Recording session of *Symphonic Dances from "West Side Story"*, Manhattan Center, NYC, 6 March 1961. *Standing, left to right:* unknown, Irwin Kostal, Buster Bailey (NYP percussionist), Sid Ramin, JG. *Seated:* John McClure (recording engineer), LB and Russell Stanger (assistant conductor).

West Side Story Fact Sheet

(Guide and commentary written for the LB Web site)

Story Sources

It is widely known that *West Side Story* (*WSS*) is based directly on Shakespeare's *Romeo and Juliet* (*R&J*). Far less well known is the fact that Shakespeare based his play (1594) on other material, particularly a narrative poem by Arthur Brooke entitled *The Tragicall Historye of Romeus and Juliet* (1562). The theme of two lovers thwarted by circumstances beyond their control, however, had long before been established in Western legend: Troilus and Cressida, Tristan and Isolde, to name only two such pairs. In more recent times, American folklore had assimilated the myth into the feud between the Hatfields and McCoys. Brooke's description of *R&J* as an "vnfortunate coople" displays a puritanical streak:

> louers, thrilling themselves to vnhonest desire, neglecting the authoritie and aduise of parents and frendes.

Shakespeare transcended the question of morality, though he borrowed freely from the earlier poem, and in fact, he replicated Brooke's actual words in at least three instances. But Brooke pales by comparison. Shakespeare rapturously expanded the soliloquies, and fashioned new personages endowing them with nobility.

Although there are many borrowings of plot and content from *R&J* to *WSS*, Arthur Laurents, author of the book for the musical, did not verbally borrow from Shakespeare. But just as Shakespeare transformed Brooke's

> drunken gossypes, superstitious friers, vnchastitie, the shame of stolne contractes hastyng to more vnhappye deathe,

so Laurents replaces the second half of Shakespeare's play, which he tells us,

> rests on Juliet's swallowing a magic potion, a device that would not be swallowed in a modern play.

He continues,

> In the book (why are the spoken words for a musical show called this?) . . . the dialogue is my translation of adolescent street talk into theater: it may sound real, but it isn't.

That he succeeded, and did so brilliantly, is attested to by his companion-in-arms, Alan Jay Lerner:

> Arthur Laurents' book, with its moving retelling of the Romeo and Juliet tale . . . is a triumph of style and model of its genre. As a fellow tradesman, I was filled with the deepest admiration.

Interestingly, in two of his post-*WSS* screen plays, Laurents subliminally returns to the *R&J* theme. In *The Turning Point* (featuring Mikhail Baryshnikov and Leslie Browne in the Pas de Deux from Prokofiev's balletic treatment of *R&J*) he explores the conflict between marriage and career. In *The Way We Were*, the conflict is between political activism (embodied by the Jewish girl, portrayed by Barbra Streisand) and social passivity (her gentile lover, Robert Redford).

Was this *Way We Were* in some way a recall of the original idea for *WSS*? Jerome Robbins had at first envisioned Juliet as a Jewish girl and Romeo as an Italian Catholic. The action, set during the Easter-Passover season, was to have occurred on the Lower East Side of New York City. Hence the title might have been *East* Side Story. (Another working title was *Gangway!*) That was in 1949. Six years later, Laurents and Leonard Bernstein were working (independently) in Hollywood, where they conferred on the aborted project. The newspapers were filled with reports of street riots by Chicano Americans in Los Angeles. Those headlines turned the trick, triggering the imaginations of the collaborators. The locale swiftly shifted to New York's West Side, and in 1957 *WSS* exploded onto the American stage. In the decades that have passed, *WSS* has become a contemporary classic.

The Operatic Trap

Soon after its premiere, Bernstein wrote about the lengthy gestation between the show's conception and birth: "All the peering and agony and postponement and re-re-rewriting turn out to have been worth it." Part of that agony was the decision

> not to cast "'singers": anything that sounded more professional would inevitably sound more experienced, and then the "kid" quality would be gone.

How can this statement be reconciled with his 1985 "operatic" recording? Critic David Stearns, among others, addresses the issue of Opera versus Broadway. Actually, the problem is less an issue in recorded sound than in live sound. If we did not know it were Kiri Te Kanawa, "International Opera Star," on the recording, would the issue have been raised? Nevertheless, there are concerns about form, if not singers. Music history has demonstrated over and over that one man's dissonance later becomes another's consonance. That which seemed impossible—even to its authors—in 1957, has now become acceptable. It may be box office poison to describe a musical as opera; but operatic tendrils have by now become so intertwined with Broadway techniques that we have become the beneficiaries of a new music theater hybrid.

Still, in 1949, Bernstein voiced apprehension of "making a musical that tells a tragic story in musical comedy terms . . . never falling into the 'operatic' trap." That trap must be the vise (as well as the vice) of vocal pyrotechnics for its own sake, without moving the story forward. Bernstein does avoid that trap in *WSS*. For example, one of the most operatic moments is the duet between Anita and Maria: "A Boy Like That/I Have a Love." This denouement is, in the words of Stearns, "Anita's fateful change of loyalties from which the rest of the drama unfolds." Bernstein evolves one song out of the other through a kind of musical wizardry. Thus when Anita fulminates against the killings, we hear what will turn into Maria's eloquence, using precisely the same pitches and almost the same rhythm. The seed has grown to tower over the ground in which it was planted.

While there is hope in *WSS*, there also is despair, and this, too, is reflected, in musical terms. Throughout the entire score the interval of the tritone is prominently displayed. (Theorists from the past have nicknamed the tritone *Diabolus in musica,* "Devil in music"). It was considered the most "dangerous" interval. Its unstable, rootless quality (C, for example, to F-sharp consists of three whole-steps, hence tritone) was the perfect musical distillation of the unstable relationship between Tony and Maria, and for the rootlessness, and the resulting ruthlessness, of the Jet and Shark gangs.

Careers

Bernstein had said the show could not "depend on stars, being about kids." Hundreds of young hopefuls auditioned for the original production. Of the forty "kids" who landed the jobs—for most, their Broadway debut—many went on to a wide variety of show business or related activities. Perhaps not all their pathways were to greater glory, but without *WSS* their careers would probably have taken considerably longer to blossom. Furthermore, some of them continued to maintain relationships with their *WSS* colleagues on a personal and/or professional basis. The most astonishing career to be launched from the *WSS* pad was that of its lyricist, Stephen Sondheim, considered by many to be the most significant composer-lyricist of our time. If there is an indigenous American "operatic" style of today, Sondheim must be regarded as its standard-bearer. The operatic innovations introduced by the *WSS* creative quartet: broader song dimensions, simultaneities in complex counterpoint, and so on became grist to the Sondheim mill. But, strangely, not one Sondheim show has ever advanced the choreographic inventiveness of Jerome Robbins in *WSS*. (Has any show?) Unlike Bernstein, Sondheim is not a composer for the dance.

Symphonic Dances from "West Side Story" was premiered by the New York Philharmonic on 13 February 1961, but the conductor was Lukas Foss. Bernstein was named music director of the Philharmonic one year after the opening of *WSS*, and although he later performed and recorded "Dances" with the orchestra, he never, prior to the 1985 recording, conducted a performance of the show. (He was in the pit to conduct the so-called Overture—a compilation of tunes not made by him—for one of the early Broadway revivals.) But why should someone whose career has been so diversified concentrate on one all-consuming project, a Broadway run? It was only very late in his life that Bernstein conducted a live theater performance of his *Candide*, and never of *Wonderful Town* or *Mass*, either. His recording of *On the Town*, made long after its premiere with, among others, three of the original cast members, is the first show album ever to be put onto disc by its composer. But one historical first has yet to occur in the annals of recorded Broadway musicals: a full original-cast album conducted by its composer.

The Movie

The Academy Award for Best Picture of 1961 went to the movie version of *WSS*. It earned a total of ten Oscars. Although Bernstein did not suffer the indignity of the mayhem perpetrated on his score in the movie of *On the Town*, the movie of *WSS* did make some minor alterations. "I Feel Pretty" was transferred to an earlier scene, the bridal shop. The location of "Gee, Officer Krupke" was interchanged with "Cool." Sondheim also wrote new lyrics for "America," performed by all the Sharks and their girls (in the stage version it is presented by four girls only).

These changes were judged to be necessary to sustain an onrushing sense of doom. After all, the movie was not interrupted by an intermission during which an audience could recover form the devastation wrought by the danced "Rumble." Onstage, the bubbly "I Feel Pretty," at the beginning of act 2, was a kind of extension of intermission babble. Good theater, but not good movie.

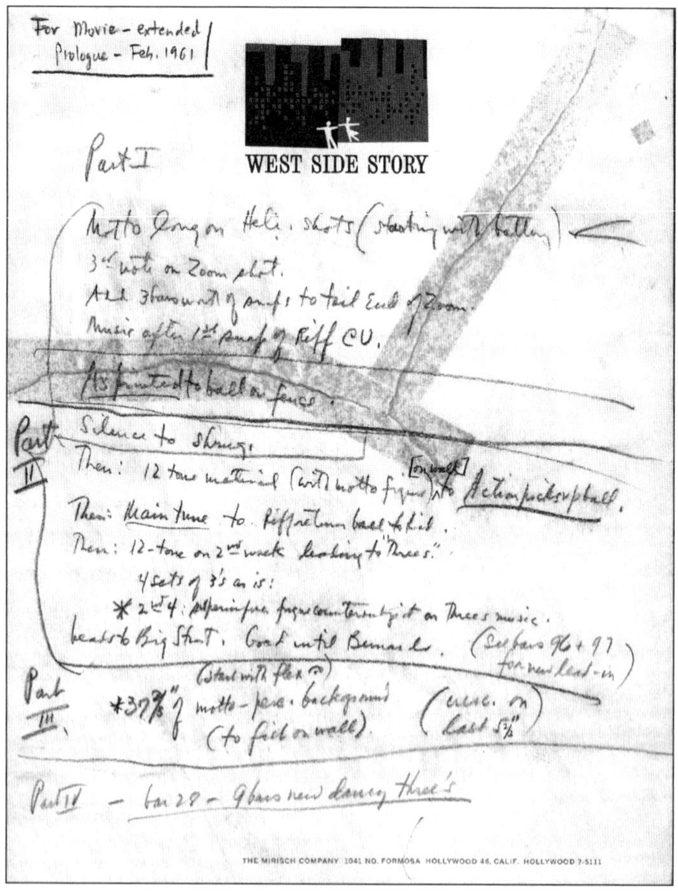

Discarded note in LB's hand for changes to the WSS movie Prologue, 1961.

The Dubbers

The singing voices of Richard Beymer (Tony, in the movie) was that of Jim Bryant, a Hollywood jazz and commercial arranger and bass fiddler, chosen because his singing timbre matched Beymer's spoken sound. Similarly, Betty Wand, a mezzo-soprano, was hired to do some, but not all, of Rita (Anita) Moreno's singing. Wand later sued to get a percentage of the movie-album sales, a dispute settled out-of-court. But the most convoluted dubbing problems were those for the voice of Natalie Wood (Maria).

Marni Nixon was employed on a day-to-day basis (no contract was signed) to do only the high or sustained notes that Wood's less disciplined voice could not manage. And, indeed, the songs were recorded in that manner, with Wood being continually told how "wonderful" she was. While this was going on, Nixon was being told that she would do the full soundtrack, which was hard to believe under the circumstances. But this delicate and deliberate game of musical pawns was played to ensure there would be no clash between star and studio until Wood's visuals had been completely filmed. When she was finally "in the can," Wood was informed that Nixon had been elected. Wood's reaction was understandable anger. (Later on when she filmed her role in *Gypsy*, no substitutions were made for her singing voice.) Nixon's job then became much more complicated than her dubbing of Deborah Kerr in the filming of *The King and I.* There, everything had been carefully worked out in rehearsal, with Nixon physically standing next to Kerr at all music rehearsals. But since Wood had already been filled with musical inaccuracies, Nixon had to compensate for them. On long shots there was no problem, but on close-ups she had to hedge it one way or another. (In fact, Nixon even dubbed Wood's speaking voice at the very end: "Don't you touch him! Te adoro, Anton.") Due to the web of deception, Nixon felt she deserved a cut of the movie-album royalties. Neither the movie or the record producers would bow to her demands. Bernstein broke the stalemate by volunteering a percentage of his income, a gesture of loyalty-royalty because Nixon had been a performer-colleague of his at New York Philharmonic concerts. (Marni Nixon can be heard singing on the NY Philharmonic's *Bernstein Live!* CD set.)

DID YOU KNOW THAT . . . Irving Shulman wrote the novelization of Arthur Laurents' "book" in which he provided family names for the characters: Tony (Anton) Wyzek, Maria (and Bernardo) Nuñez, Riff

Lorton, Chino Martin, Anita Palacio, and (now it can be told) Glad Hand was "christened" Murray Benowitz!

DID YOU KNOW THAT . . . *WSS* has been translated into Japanese, Serbo-Croatian, Hungarian (in two versions), Swedish, Norwegian, Danish, Dutch, Finnish, German, French, Russian, and not so surprisingly, into Spanish, twice?

DID YOU KNOW THAT . . . Marilyn Horne not only was the voice of Dorothy Dandridge on the film soundtrack of the Bizet–Oscar Hammerstein *Carmen Jones*, but also sang "Love, Look Away" on the soundtrack for the movie of Rodgers and Hammerstein's *The Flower Drum Song*? And also on the 1985 *WSS* recording, singing "Somewhere."

DID YOU KNOW THAT . . . The music for "One Hand, One Heart" was originally earmarked for Bernstein's *Candide,* with a whole other set of lyrics? And that it has become almost as popular as "Oh, Promise Me" in wedding ceremonies? Or that the music in the second movement of Bernstein's *Chichester Psalms*, set to warlike words form Psalm 2, was a rejected Jets' war song called "Mix"?

DID YOU KNOW THAT . . . The musical *The Fantasticks* is also based on *Romeo and Juliet*?

DID YOU KNOW THAT . . . Not one of the Oscars won by *West Side Story* included the composer, who was deemed "ineligible" because his music was not written for the film?

DID YOU KNOW THAT . . . Although in the stage version "Cool" is sung by Riff, on the screen it was delivered by a newly invented character named Ice—get it?

DID YOU KNOW THAT . . . Both the movie and original Broadway cast albums of *WSS* earned Gold Record status, sales of over one million?

DID YOU KNOW THAT . . . Ramin and Kostal also helped Bernstein prepare the concert work *Symphonic Dances from "West Side Story"*, and that they performed the same valued function for the composer's opera *A Quiet Place*?

12 Jewish Works

"I'm no longer sure what the question is, but I do know that the answer is yes.*"*
– Leonard Bernstein, Norton lecture

Chichester Psalms

(Written for the premiere; New York Philharmonic program note, July 1965)

Every summer the Cathedral of Chichester, in Sussex, England, joins choral forces (all male) with its neighbors, the Winchester and Salisbury cathedrals, to produce a music festival. (Chichester has a great musical tradition, stemming from its famed organist-composer of the early seventeenth century, Thomas Weelkes.) For its 1965 festival, the dean of Chichester, the Very Reverend Walter Hussey, commissioned Leonard Bernstein to write a new work. Completed on 7 May 1965, *Chichester Psalms* was the composer's first work since the "Kaddish" Symphony of 1963.

Like its predecessor, *Chichester Psalms* is a choral composition in Hebrew. There are other resemblances as well, but while the earlier work was an expression of despair and anguished hope, the later work is one of serenity and childlike humility. Despite the choice of psalms that concern war and peace, the "I and Thou" image is preeminent, and it has influenced the mood of much of the music.

The opening chorale (Psalm 108) is a majestic introit, using compelling intervals of the seventh (Ex. 12-1), and it appears again, like a signpost, at the end of the first movement and at the start and end of the last movement.

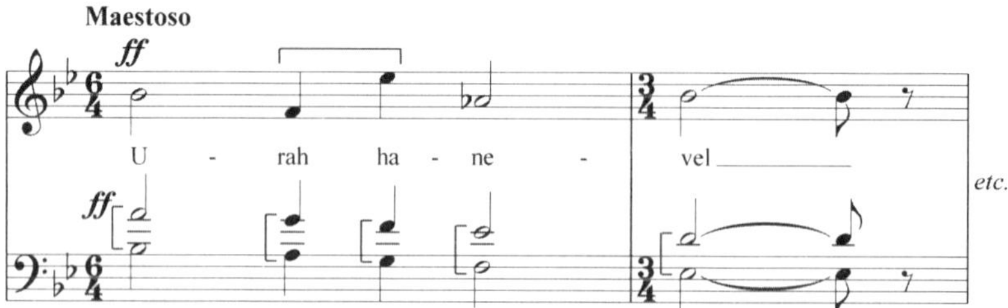

Example 12-1

The phrase calls to mind the affirmation of "Veni creator spiritus" that begins Mahler's Symphony No. 8. It leads directly into a joyful, dancelike setting of Psalm 100 (Ex. 12-2) in a fast and constant 7/4 meter (cut-time plus 3/4). (Similarly, "Kaddish" begins with an "Invocation" followed by an Allegro in 7/8.)

Example 12-2

The second movement begins with a lyric, almost naive, solo (Psalm 23) by a boy alto, accompanied by simple intervals on the harp (suggesting David, the shepherd boy):

Example 12-3

This folklike melody is repeated by the women in canon, but is suddenly interrupted by a ferocious outburst by the men, "Why do the nations rage?" (from Psalm 2, Verse 1–4), in dramatic opposition to the previous pastoral mood:

Example 12-4

The violence moves into the distance, but it continues softly and insistently while, above it. Psalm 23 is resumed, the singers "blissfully unaware of the threat" (as noted by the composer). Their innocent melody gradually subdues the menace of the psalm, but even under their final long note the orchestra whispers a reminder of the disturbance, so that the movement ends on an equivocal note. (In "Kaddish" the chaos of the "Din-Torah" movement, in like manner, is calmed down by the ensuing lullaby of "Kaddish" 2.)

The third movement is also reminiscent of "Kaddish": an orchestral meditation introduces the Finale. Unlike the symphony, however, the instrumental reverie in this instance is preparation for a warm, comforting (rather than a jubilant) conclusion in song form. The "peacefully flowing" melody (Ex. 12-5) is sustained by the unusual meter of 10/4, divided into patterns of three plus two beats.

Example 12-5

* * *

On 11 May 1965, Bernstein wrote the following letter to the dean of Chichester Cathedral:

> My Dear Mr. Hussey:
>
> The Psalms are finished, *laus Deo*, are being copied, and should arrive in England next week. They are not yet orchestrated, but should be by June, and you should receive full score and parts in ample time for rehearsal. Meanwhile, the choral preparation can start forthwith.

I am pleased with the work, and hope you will be, too; it is quite popular in feeling (even a hint, as you suggested, of West Side Story), and it has an old-fashioned sweetness along with its more violent moments. The title has now been changed to "Chichester Psalms" ("Youth" was a wrong steer; the piece is far too difficult). The work is in 3 movements, lasting about 18½ minutes, and each ~~comprise~~ movement contains one complete psalm plus one or more verses from another complementary psalm, by way of contrast or amplification.

Fragment from LB letter to Dean Walter Hussey, Chichester Cathedral.

I am pleased with the work, and hope you will be, too; it is quite popular in feeling (even a hint, as you suggested, of *West Side Story*), and it has an old-fashioned sweetness along with its more violent moments. The title has now been changed to "Chichester Psalms" ("youth" was a wrong steer, the piece is far too difficult). The work is in 3 movements, lasting about 18 minutes, and each movement contains one complete psalm plus one or more verses from another complementary psalm, by way of contrast of amplification. Thus,

I. Opens with chorale (Ps. 108, vs. 3) evoking praise; and then swings into Ps. 100, complete, a wild and joyful dance, in the Davidic Spirit.

II. Consists mainly of Ps. 23, complete, featuring a boy solo and his harp, but interrupted savagely by the men with threats of war and violence (Ps. 2, vv. 1–4). This movement ends in unresolved fashion, with both elements, faith and fear, interlocked.

III. Begins with an orchestral prelude based on the opening chorale, whose assertive harmonies have now turned to painful ones. There is a crisis; the tension is suddenly relieved, and the choir enters humbly and peacefully singing Ps. 131, complete, in

> what is almost a popular song (although in 10/4 time!). In this atmosphere of humility, there is a final chorale coda, (Ps. 133, vs. 1), a prayer for peace.

I hope my score is legible. In order to help with the Hebrew text, I shall enclose a typewritten copy of the words (the Hebrew words of Ps. 2 are a tongue-breaker!). The score contains exact notes on the pronunciation. As to the orchestra, I have kept to your prescribed forces, except that there will be a large percussion group necessary (xylophone, glockenspiel, bongos, chimes, etc.; in addition to the usual tympani, drums, cymbals, etc.). Also, I am sure more strings will be necessary than the number you list—especially low ones. Certainly one bass will not do the trick. One of three trumpets must be very good indeed, in order to perform several difficult solo passages. There is also an extensive harp part.

One last matter: I am conducting a program of my own music with the N.Y. Philharmonic in early July, and I have been asked if I could include the Chichester Psalms. I realize that this would deprive you of the world premiere by a couple of weeks; do you have any serious objections? [N.B. He had also asked for a similar relinquishment from the Boston Symphony Orchestra to give the premiere of the "Kaddish" Symphony in Israel.]

In any case I wish you well with the piece; and I may even take your performance as an excuse to visit Sussex in late July. I should dearly love to hear this music in your cathedral.

Faithfully yours,
Leonard Bernstein

The world premiere took place on 15 July 1965 at the New York Philharmonic. Two weeks later, on 31 July, the first performance of the version originally conceived by the composer for all-male choir took place at Chichester Cathedral. The sound of Hebrew words sung in an Anglican church accompanied by, among other things, bongos should have been exceptional; but the performance was rocky. In a letter dated 3 August 1965, written from the Savoy Hotel in London, LB wrote to Miss Coates:

The Psalms went well, in spite of a shockingly small amount of rehearsal. The chorus was a delight. They had everything down pat, but the orchestra was swimming on the open sea. They simply didn't know it. But somehow the glorious acoustics of Chichester Cathedral cushion everything so that even mistakes sound pretty.

Part I.

Psalm 108, verse 2 (Maestoso ma energico):

Urah, hanevel, v'chinor!	Awake, psaltery and harp!
A-irah shachar!	I will rouse the dawn!

Psalm 100, entire (Allegro molto):

Hariu l'Adonai kol ha-arets.	Make a joyful noise unto the Lord all ye lands.
Iv'du et Adonai b'simcha.	Serve the Lord with gladness.
Bo-u l'fanav bir'nanah.	Come before His presence with singing.
D'u ki Adonai Hu Elohim.	Know ye that the Lord, He is God.
Hu asanu, v'lo anachnu.	It is He that hath made us, and not we ourselves.
Amo v'tson mar'ito.	We are His people and the sheep of His pasture.
Bo-u sh'arav b'todah,	Enter into His gates with thanksgiving,
Chatseirotav bit'hilah,	And into His courts with praise,
Hodu lo, bar'chu sh'mo.	Be thankful unto Him, and bless His name.
Ki tov Adonai, l'olam has'do,	For the Lord is good, His mercy is everlasting, and
V'ad dor vador emunato.	His truth endureth to all generations.

Part II.

Psalm 23 (Andante con moto, ma tranquillo):

Adonai ro-i, lo echsar.	The Lord is my shepherd, I shall not want.
Bin'ot deshe yarbitseini,	He maketh me to lie down in green pastures,

Al mei m'nuhot y'nachaleini,	He leadeth me beside the still waters,
Naf'shi y'shovev,	He restoreth my soul,
Yan'heini b'ma'aglei tsedek,	He leadeth me in the paths of righteousness,
L'ma'an sh'mo.	For His name's sake.
Gam ki eilech	Yea, though I walk
B'gei tsalmavet,	Through the valley of the shadow of death,
Lo ira ra,	I will fear no evil,
Ki Atah imadi.	For Thou art with me.
Shiv't'cha umishan'techa	Thy rod and Thy staff
Hemah y'nahamuni.	They comfort me.

Psalm 2, verses 1–4 (Allegro feroce):

Lamah rag'shu goyim	Why do the nations rage,
Ul'umim yeh'gu rik?	And the people imagine a vain thing?
Yit'yats'vu malchei erets,	The kings of the earth set themselves,
V'roznim nos'du yachad	And the rulers take counsel together
Al Adonai v'al m'shicho.	Against the Lord and against His anointed.
N'natkah et mos'roteimo,	Saying, let us break their bands asunder,
V'nashlichah mimenu avoteinu.	And cast away their cords from us.
Yoshev bashamayim	He that sitteth in the heavens
Yis'hak, Adonai	Shall laugh, and the Lord
Yil'ag lamo!	Shall have them in derision!

Psalm 23, continued (Meno come prima):

Ta'aroch l'fanai shulchan	Thou preparest a table before me
Neged tsor'rai	In the presence of mine enemies,
Dishanta vashemen roshi	Thou anointest my head with oil,
Cosi r'vayah.	My cup runneth over.
Ach tov vachesed	Surely goodness and mercy
Yird'funi kol y'mei hayai,	Shall follow me all the days of my life,
V'shav'ti b'veit Adonai	And I will dwell in the house of the Lord
L'orech yamim.	Forever.

Part III.

Psalm 131, entire (Peacefully flowing):

Adonai, Adonai,	Lord, Lord,
Lo gavah libi,	My heart is not haughty,
V'lo ramu einai,	Nor mine eyes lofty,
V'lo hilachti	Neither do I exercise myself
Big'dolot uv'nifla-ot	In great matters or in things
Mimeni.	Too wonderful for me.
Im lo shiviti	Surely I have calmed
V'domam'ti,	And quieted myself,
Naf'shi k'gamul alei imo,	As a child that is weaned of his mother,
Kagamul alai naf'shi.	My soul is even as a weaned child.
Yahel Yis'rael el Adonai	Let Israel hope in the Lord
Me'atah v'ad olam.	From henceforth and forever.

Psalm 133, verse 1:

Hineh mah tov,	Behold how good,
Umah nayim,	And how pleasant it is,
Shevet achim	For brethren to dwell
Gam yachad.	Together in unity.

Concerto for Orchestra (*Jubilee Games*)

(Note for the premiere performance and recording)

It was eighteen years after LB's death that I again heard a live performance of this concerto, which probably says something about its durability. Gustavo Dudamel led the work with the Israel Philharmonic Orchestra on 15 November 2008 in Carnegie Hall, as part of an expansive three-month NYC citywide Bernstein Festival. Dudamel almost made it work and Lenny would have been delighted. (However, I am not sure how he would have felt about occupying the planet at the same age and at the same time as the sensational Dudamel.) He sometimes was wistful about the fact that few other conductors were playing his music, a reluctance on their part undoubtedly due to taking on such a challenge when the composer himself had his own built-in and wide-ranging venues. It was another story, however, when it came to performing standard symphonic repertoire. LB basked in being king of the hill and was not particularly close to other conductors.

I never regarded the affectionately named "Jew Games" as one of his stellar achievements mainly because of the tangled history of its construction. The original version, called simply Jubilee Games, *was in two movements, "Free-Style Events" and "Diaspora Dances" (where the number eighteen plays a significant role). Dedicated to the Israel Philharmonic Orchestra for its jubilee (fiftieth) year, it was premiered on 13 September 1986 by the IPO in Avery Fisher Hall, New York City. In my estimate, it should have remained a two-movement work because of a musical connection not found in the other two movements of the final version. Although few listeners would recognize it, the first movement concludes with the gang whistle from* West Side Story, *the last three pitches of which are further expounded in the original second movement (confirming LB's encoding of the* WSS *gang whistle as a cryptic shofar call). While "Mixed Doubles," one of the subsequent added movements, does maintain the concept of games and play, the musical link is missing.*

On 15 December 1986, Opening Prayer*—a work which opened the then refurbished Carnegie Hall and was performed by the New York Philharmonic with baritone Kurt Ollmann—was transplanted into* Jubilee Games, *where it became the second movement and was retitled "Benediction." (The Carnegie Hall program booklet for the 2008 performance mistakenly and amusingly reproduced the Hebrew lettering backward, as if it were romanized). This second version was first played by the IPO on 31 May 1988 at the Frederic Mann Auditorium in Tel Aviv.*

But the Games *continued to grow even after that. In December 1988, while vacationing in Key West, LB wrote a piece for recorder called* Variations on an Octatonic Scale. *Written at the request of Helena Burton, daughter of Bernstein's future biographer—it was given a reading in January 1989 by members of the New World Symphony in Miami, in a version for flute and cello. After hearing it, Bernstein quickly rethought the set of variations in orchestral terms and, in expanded form, this became "Mixed Doubles," the new second movement of the retitled Concerto for Orchestra (*Jubilee Games*), while the old second movement, "Benediction," became the fourth movement. This third and final version was performed by the IPO on 24 April 1989 in Tel Aviv.*

The composer conducted all the reworkings; but for the sake of the historical record, it was Sid Ramin who orchestrated "Diaspora Dances"—of course under the supervision of LB in the same pre and post conferences that had been their practice in past collaborations from West Side Story *to* A Quiet Place. *This is acknowledged in the score, but has not appeared on program or jacket notes.*

I worked with LB mainly on notating the aleatoric first movement. My hand appears on the first and last four pages of the manuscript. In the early 1960s, following the example of improvisatory experiments by composer Lukas Foss, LB had fiddled with music of chance, using the New York Philharmonic as his guinea pigs. Some observers would argue that LB's concert pieces generally were more the creations of a consolidator than an innovator, but he was always eager to try out new ideas and inventions. One of the latter trials employed a machine called the Synclavier, used in "Free-Style Events" to play back previous sections of the performance through loudspeakers simultaneously with the live orchestra's continuing improvisations. This monster contraption was installed in LB's country studio supposedly to help out during the composing process; but like Audrey 2, the plant in Little Shop of Horrors, *it overtook the place to the extent that a hole had to be knocked out of the roof. LB quickly became distracted and frustrated by the gizmo (as he did with most electronic devices) and gave up on it.*

In 1991, when Deutsche Grammophon posthumously released the work's recording (LB's last), it contained a booklet titled "Leonard Bernstein Conducts American Compositions." American, yes; but with its Biblical inspiration and dedicatory impetus, the concerto does leap across national boundaries. However, any recording of the piece cannot ever do it full justice. One reason why Dudamel nearly made it work in 2008 is that he and the IPO turned it into a visual as well as an auditory treat by regulating the improvisation traffic and the odd pairings.

* * *

Concerto for Orchestra

According to the Biblical injunction of Leviticus 25:8–17, every fiftieth year is to be observed by sounding the shofar, or ram's horn. One kind of shofar, the *yovel* (the source of the English word *jubilee*), later came to refer to the jubilee year and was celebrated by "proclaiming liberty throughout the land onto all the inhabitants thereof," the cherished inscription on the American Liberty Bell. Jubilee was to take effect by allowing farmlands to lie fallow, by releasing all those imprisoned for nonpayment of debts and by freeing all bondsmen, who were to be returned to their families in dignity and peace. Is it any wonder that the idea of jubilee has had special meaning in the history of African Americans?

Bernstein follows this command quite literally. In the first movement, "Free-Style Events," the orchestra players shout (or, in one instance, whisper) the word *sheva* (Hebrew for "seven") seven times, every four bars. (According to the passage in Leviticus, in fact, the jubilee was to be proclaimed after every seventh cycle of Sabbatical years; the choice of notes for these seven-note scales or mode groupings, is left to the immediate choice of each individual orchestra member, limited only by certain prescribed registers. However, the meter, phrase structure, direction and duration of the pitches and dynamics are fully notated. This aleatoric aspect of the movement could be regarded as a symbol for the celebration of freedom that jubilee connotes.

One bar after the final *sheva* the players, having observed the biblical mandate, proclaim *hamishim* ("fifty"), at which point the entire brass section bursts forth with shofarlike fanfares. Each brass instrument, in roughly cued staggerings, lets loose in versions of the four horn signals prescribed by tradition: *teki-ah* (blast), *shevarim* (breaks, in a tone of lament), *teru-ah* (series of short staccato blasts) and *teki-ah gedolah* (big blast). This section is the first time in the movement that actual pitches are provided by the composer. However, they are not to be performed in synchrony, which makes for a second kind of "free style."

The horns-of-plenty are followed by a section in 7/8 time, carrying forward the numerological spirit of the games. While the strings skitter about with rapid seven-tone scales and modes, the winds echo the shofars in *pianissimo*. These fragments gradually dissipate, as the brass family begins a chorale in 7/8 (of course!) and then in 7/4 time. Again, the chorale notes are optional within given registers. In the midst of the chorale a taped reprise of the opening section, ending with *hamishim* is heard. Here the third kind of improvisation occurs, strictly "pure," with no written instructions, eye-to-eye between conductor and orchestra. The final section is a tutti version of the chorale with a tape recording of the shofars superimposed and "signed" with the gang whistle from *West Side Story*, although one is hard-pressed to make out the quote.

The second movement of Bartók's Concerto for Orchestra, "*Giuoco delle copple*" (Play of Couples), is elicited in the second movement of Bernstein's concerto. "Mixed Doubles" is a theme with seven (please note!) variations. In keeping with the gaming liveliness of the first movement, "mixed doubles" is also a sports allusion to tennis, and is manifested by mixing pairs from different families of instruments for the first three variations, and combinations from within the same families for the last four variations and coda. After the strings present the theme, the pairings for the variations are: (1) flute and horn, (2) trumpet and double bass, (3) clarinet and trombone, (4) mallets and timpani, (5) two solo violins, (6) alto flute and bass clarinet, (7) oboe and bassoon, followed by the coda, viola and cello. The movement concludes with a unison G by all soloists who have played in the movement except percussion. According to the composer, "The theme, its variations and the coda are constructed on an octatonic scale from *Dybbuk* (1973)." This scale alternates whole and half steps, producing a Near Eastern, possibly Hebraic coloration. At the end of the movement the composer inscribed words from Psalm 118 on the manuscript: *Hodu ladonai ki tov* ("Give thanks unto the Lord, for He is good").

Throughout the third movement, "Diaspora Dances," *gematria* (the practice of assigning numerical values to each letter of the Hebrew alphabet; from the Greek, meaning "geometry") is applied. The movement begins with a lively dance tune in 18/8 time, with whispered, vocalized interjections of *chai* and *chayim* ("alive" and "life"). The unusual choice for meter is explained by the *gematria* equation of *chai* equaling eighteen, the value of the two Hebrew letters comprising the word. *L'chayim*, the traditional toast-salutation at joyous events, is doubly significant for the IPO because it was born in 1936, and thirty-six is double-*chai*, twice "alive." Thirty-six is also the number of just men present in each generation for whose sake, according to the mystics, God allows the world to continue.

The dance tune is divided into two groups of nine beats each (totaling eighteen!), first played against a double-quick version of itself. Then 9/4 becomes the underlying metrical block of varying divisions of thirty-six: two bars of eighteen eighths, four bars of nine eighths, three bars of eight plus one of the twelve, and so on. A solo violin bridge passage, seeded by the concluding motto of the first movement, leads to a new Hassidic-like tune in the meter of 2/4 alternating with 3/8 (together 7/8, reminding us of the sevens in the first movement). This music utilizes *gematria* manipulations, including elements such as six bars of 3/8 time (equaling eighteen beats), among others. New developments of the opening material pile up in contrapuntal profusion, leading surprisingly to a jazz-spirited coda, an exuberant (and American) affirmation of life and jubilee-joy.

"Benediction," the last movement, opens with brass flourishes that vaguely recall the first movement. The main theme is played by the wind instruments and then reiterated by the strings. Against a background of sustained strings, a baritone voice intones the ancient threefold blessing (in Hebrew, from Numbers 6:24–26):

> May the Lord bless you and keep you.
> May the Lord make his face to shine upon you and be gracious unto you.
> May the Lord lift up his countenance upon you and give you peace.

The composer's comments:

> The first movement, "Free-Style Events," is musical athletics, with cheers and all. It is also charades, anagrams, and children's "counting-out" games. But mainly it is celebratory, therefore spontaneous, therefore aleatoric, ranging from structured improvisation to totally free orchestral invention "in situ." It is thus inevitable that the movement will vary considerably from one rehearsal to another. But it is formally controlled, at least in terms of beginning-middle and end, by prerecorded tape-reprises. The "Diaspora Dances" of the third movement are "free-style" only in a socio-cultural, geo-Judaic sense, and hence necessarily eclectic in style, their musical connotations ranging from the Middle East back to Central European ghettos and forward again to a New Yorkish kind of jazz music. *Horas* are strictly excluded, as is whatever could slither in under the rubric of "Disco."

Dybbuk

(Deutsche Grammophon LP jacket note, 1981)

If I had to select one piece of his from the Bernstein catalog, this one would be my desert island choice. Alas, mine is not an enthusiasm much shared by others, which I find incomprehensible. For me, the score displays the skill and imagination of a composer at the peak of his powers. Motivic manipulations, counterpoint and orchestration coalesce into a singular and original sound filled with heat and logic, passion and calculation. The sensibility is not American sounding. Instead the composer integrates both the folk-song idiom and the Talmudic deliberations of his Eastern European forebears. He draws upon the numerology of Kabbalah, finding musical equivalents to letters of the Hebrew alphabet, and presents us with a forceful drama quite unlike any other work by him or, for that matter, by anyone else. This is a masterpiece and its place in the sun will some day arise.

* * *

Suite No. 1 from *Dybbuk*
Invocation and Trance
The Pledge
Kabbalah
Possession
Pas de Deux
Exorcism

Suite No. 2 from *Dybbuk*
The Messengers
Leah
Five Kabbalah Variations
Dream (Pas de Deux)

There is a Yiddish folk song, of late-nineteenth-century origin, that poses the old philosophic riddle of existence: *freygt di welt an alte kashe* ("the world asks an eternal question"). To this there is only the answer "*tradi ridi ram*" or perhaps, "*tridi dam*," which, like all other possible replies, means nothing—the riddle remains unsolved. The same inquiry was made in purely instrumental terms by Charles Ives in his 1908 work *The Unanswered Question*. Leonard Bernstein appropriated Ives' title for his 1973 Harvard University lectures; and he makes prominent reference, whether consciously or not, to the Yiddish folk song in his *Dybbuk* ballet of 1974. The composer's evident metaphysical preoccupations of the early 1970s thus found both verbal and musical expression.

At the end of his lecture series, Bernstein stated that "Ives's 'Unanswered Question' has an answer. I'm no longer sure what the question is, but I do know that the answer is *yes*." With these words, he affirms his belief in tonality as the "Poetry of Earth" for all music. In *Dybbuk*, the Jewish song materials can be understood as the "poetry of earth," deeply rooted in the soil of eastern European folklore. There is much of this kind of music in the First Suite, and it can be found in the Second Suite in the lilting section entitled "Leah."

Poster for original New York City Ballet production of *Dybbuk*, 1974.

But there is another kind of music in the score, displayed more prominently in the Second Suite, which might be understood as the "poetry of air." With its mysterious manipulations and unpredictable rhythms, it soars like a projectile. It seems to avoid key centers, either through the use of serial techniques or through the use of so-called symmetrical scales (stepwise progressions that alternate half and whole steps, resulting in eight-note scales, rather than the more familiar ones of seven or twelve). Although symmetrical scales *are* tonally oriented, they are of such mercurial character that any one of the eight different pitches could function as the key center.

Earth and air: these are the principal elements of *Dybbuk.* Bernstein, in his own program note, has himself noted such dualities in the drama by Shlomo Ansky (1863–1920), on which the ballet is based, calling it a story of "Good and Evil, Ends and Means, Male and Female, Justice and Necessity, Self and Society . . . and especially the duality of the so-called True World as opposed to *this* world in which we seem to reside." A dybbuk (from the Hebrew) in Jewish folklore is the disembodied spirit of a dead person which seeks entry into the body of a living being. In Ansky's play, two young men have pledged the marriage of their offspring if one should have a son and the other a daughter. This has indeed happened, but the pledge has not been honored. When the action begins, one man has died, leaving a son, Channon; the other has forgotten the pledge, and has arranged for his daughter Leah to be married to a wealthy suitor. Channon, of course (the Heavens have willed it), does fall in love with Leah, and she with him.

In despair, he invokes the mystical powers of the forbidden Kabbalah and dies in the process, his spirit returning as a dybbuk to enter into Leah. She, being possessed, speaks his words, and in his voice. A rabbinic court is held in order to exorcise the dybbuk; but Channon will not be dissuaded from claiming his bride; and in this final exorcism, he takes Leah with him, so that they are united in death. The "unanswered questions" of Ansky's drama are eventually resolved, albeit in a mystical way. But are there resolutions in Bernstein's musical transformation? Suite No. 1 ends, in the nether regions of the orchestra, with a repeated tritone—C sharp and G—the most equivocal of all intervals. Suite No. 2 concludes with a pensive metamorphosis of the tone row that opens the ballet, followed by a final chord constructed of five pitches from the aforementioned symmetrical scale, still another irresolute conclusion. Like the folk song, we remain—to quite a lyric from Bernstein's *Mass*—in a state of "possibly yes, probably no."

The Texts in Suite No. 1

There are Hebrew texts interspersed throughout the ballet, which are sung by a tenor-baritone duo representing variously the voice of the community, the pledge between the two fathers, and the presence of the Other World. These episodes are all gathered in Suite No. 1.

Invocation and Trance. Excerpts from Havdalah (literally, "separation"), the concluding service of the Jewish Sabbath, a bittersweet ceremony.

Baruch Atah Adonai	Praised be You, O Lord
Eloheinu melech ha-olam	our God, King of the Universe,
hamav'dil ben kodesh l'chol	who has made a distinction between holy and ordinary,
ben or l'choshech	between light and darkness,
ben Yisrael	between the people Israel
ben la-amim	and the other nations,
ben yom shvi-i	between the seventh day
l'shei-shet y'mei hama-aseh . . .	and the six working days . . .
Amen.	Amen.

This prayer establishes the basic duality of the work. (Ansky had originally called his play *Between Two Worlds.*)

The Pledge. The text is from the Bible (1 Samuel 20:4), the famous oath of allegiance between David and Jonathan.

Mah t'omar nafsh'chah	Whatsoever thy soul desireth,
v'e-eseh lach.	I will do it for thee.

Kabbalah. Also from the Bible (Song of Solomon 4:1).

Hinach yafah rayati . . .	Behold, thou art fair, my love . . .
einayich yonim . . .	Thine eyes are as doves . . .

This love lyric is interrupted by the mention of the heroine's name, Leah. Each of the three Hebrew letters of her name is then manipulated by Channon (here musically) according to the practice of Kabbalah, through which he arrives at the devastating conclusion that those letters (*lamed, alef, hei*) can be read as "not God" (*lo Adonai*)! (In the original ballet, this is the last of a set of six variations and is subtitled "The quest for secret powers." For concert purposes, the first five, strictly instrumental variations have been included in Suite No. 2.)

Pas de deux. A canonic setting of part of the "Kaddish" text (the ancient doxology), containing repetitions which might be considered a kind of "speaking in tongues." Stuttering iterations of the letter *lamed* (as in the word *l'olam*, "forever," but also the first letter for Leah!)— *l', l', l', l'*– produce this effect.

Yit'gadal v'yi'kadash	Magnified and sanctified
sh'mei raba	be His great name
b'al'ma div'ra chir'utei	throughout the world which He hath created according to His will,
v'yam'lich mal'chutei	and may He establish His kingdom
b'hayeichon uv'yomeichon	during your life and during your days,
uv'hayei d'chol beit Yis'raeil	and during the life of all the house of Israel,
ba-agala uviz'man kariv,	speedily, and at a near time,
v'im'ru: Amen.	and say ye: Amen.
Y'hei sh'mei raba m'varach	May His great name be blessed
l'alam ul'al'mei al'maya.	forever and to all eternity
Yit'barach v'yish'tabach	Blessed and praised
v'yit'pa-ar	and glorified

v'yit'roman v'yit'nasei . . .	and exalted and extolled . . .

Exorcism. The hollow knocking on wood, heard at the start, introduces the solemn ritual, a sound universally associated with the invoking of transmigrated souls from the world beyond. The text is a Biblical curse, taken from Deuteronomy 27:22.

Arur shocheiv im achoto	Cursed by he that lieth with his sister
bat aviv	the daughter of his father,
o vatimo.	or the daughter of his mother.
V'omar kol ha-am	And all the people shall say:
Amen.	Amen.

After this is sung, allusions are made to a number of traditional Hassidic tunes, including "V'taheir libeinu," which asks God to "purify our hearts to serve you in truth." This can be regarded as a double-edged musical sword since it is also saying: "Cast out the demons from within!"

Hashkiveinu ("Cause us")

(From the article "The Choral Music of Leonard Bernstein: Reflections of Theater and Liturgy," American Choral Review, *Summer 1968)*

Incredibly, this, the only work LB wrote directly for the synagogue (in 1945), was never recorded until 2003, on a CD I coproduced: Leonard Bernstein: A Jewish Legacy *(Naxos 8.559-407). It was particularly meaningful for me since the cantor who commissioned it, David Putterman, also commissioned two works from me; and Max Helfman, who led the premiere, was my beloved first composition teacher. On the following page are all three collaborators in the Park Avenue Synagogue sanctuary, New York City.*

Twentieth-century music is noted for its frequent use of symmetrical or mirror form. Such different composers as Hindemith,[1] Bartók,[2] and Berg[3] have shown a propensity for forms that proceed from a certain axis or arch with a retrograde of notes, sections or tonalities. Less frequently, the same formal arrangement appears in isolated works of others: in Britten's *Turn of the Screw*, in Stravinsky's *Canticum Sacrum*, and so on. Other composers—notably Webern and Messiaen—have been profoundly concerned with interior symmetric techniques (e.g., hexachordal constructions or mirror scales and rhythms) that have had direct bearing on the external organization of their works.

Although symmetry is aesthetically best comprehended (i.e., most immediately) in the visual or plastic arts, since it naturally belongs to the spatial rather than the temporal realm, it serves a purpose in music as a means of organization.

Bernstein has also taken advantage of such artistically satisfying organization principles in his "The Age of Anxiety," in *Trouble in Tahiti*, and in his *Hashkiveinu.*

Left to right: LB, Cantor David Putterman and Max Helfman on the pulpit of Park Avenue Synagogue, New York City, 1945.

The three-part division of the choral composition *Hashkiveinu* is clearly dictated by the text of the prayer on which it is based. The words are quiet and meditative in the first and last sections and vociferously dramatic in the middle, reflected directly by the music. The outer sections are both concerned with the Hebrew word *shalom* ("peace"), the first in the form of an invocation:

> Cause us, O Lord our God, to lie down in peace . . .

and the second in the form of a benediction:

> Blessed be Thou, O Lord, who spreadest the tabernacle of peace over us . . .

The composer sets both of these with the same, simple expressive idea—almost like plain chant (preceded by bi-tonal introductory chords):

The two outer sections are in the form of a two-fold canon.

The pedal point of the organ[4] on the one note of E makes the entire section deliberately static and rigid, so that, despite the polyphonic texture, the result is heterophonic. Symbolically, this mirrors the stability of the fundamental concept of *shalom.*

Example 12-6

In dramatic opposition to its surroundings, the arch section is highly rhythmic and vigorous. However, the harmonic content remains, as before, relatively static. The text includes the pleading petition to "remove from us every enemy, pestilence, sword, famine and sorrow." This prompts a jagged, syncopated phrase:

Example 12-7

The entire section divides into three subsections. The first is in the Lydian mode built on C, and is based on the rhythmic profile of Example 12-7. The second subsection starts in E minor and then shifts to the Lydian mode constructed on E, and the melodic line (with new words) is the same as the first subsection. The final subsection, in the Mixolydian mode on A, contains an augmentation of the rhythmic motive heard before (in the chorus), and a variation of the motive in its original rhythm (in the organ):

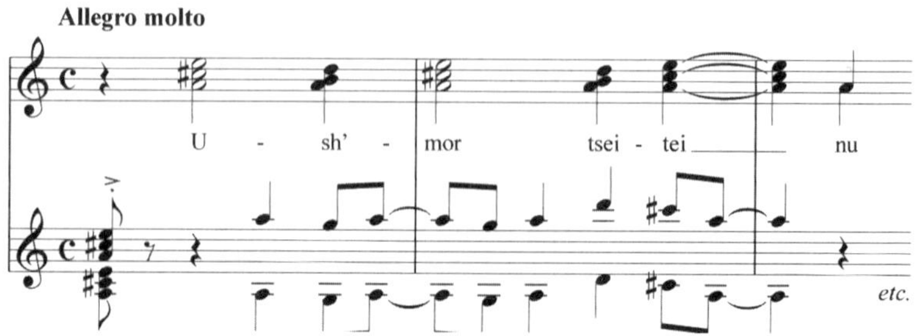

Example 12-8

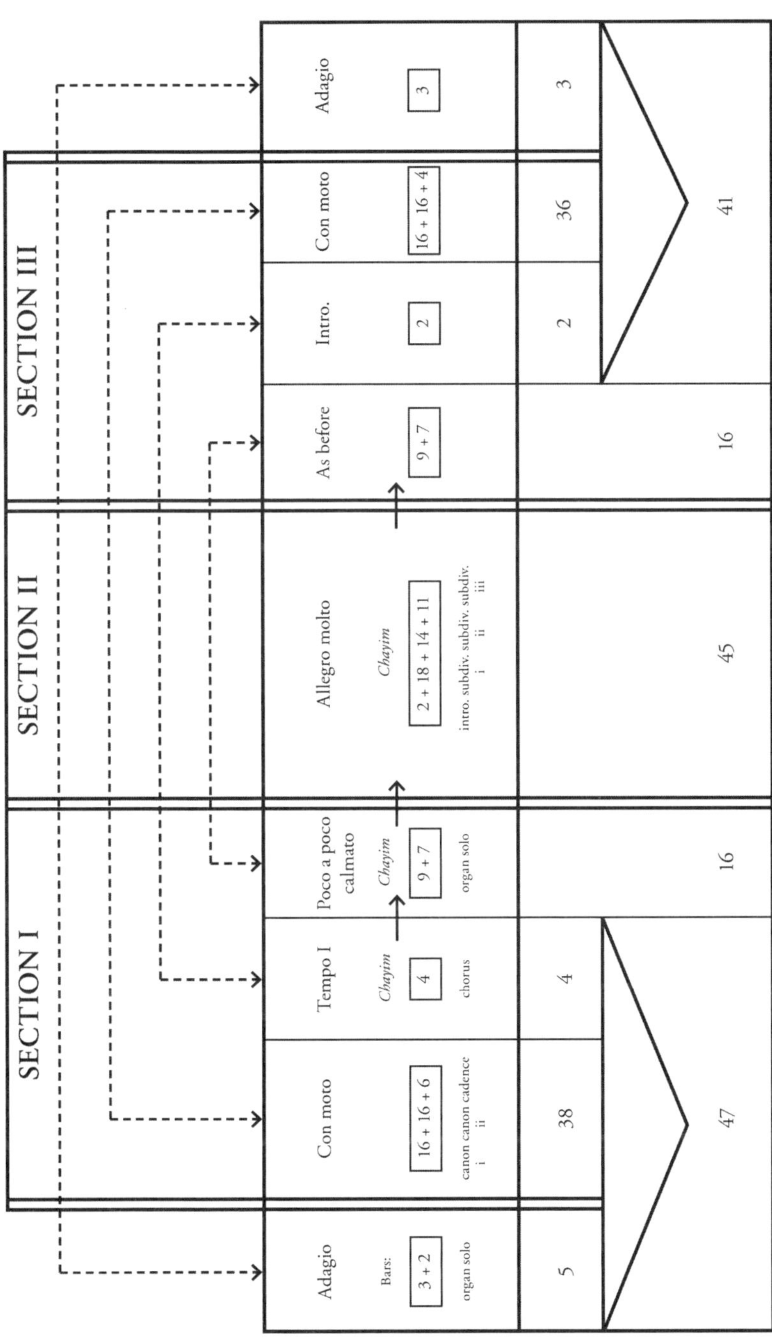
SECTION I
SECTION II
SECTION III
Adagio
Bars:
3 + 2
organ solo
5
Con moto
16 + 16 + 6
canon i canon ii cadence
38
47
Tempo I
Chayim
4
chorus
4
Poco a poco calmato
Chayim
9 + 7
organ solo
16
Allegro molto
Chayim
2 + 18 + 14 + 11
intro. subdiv. i subdiv. ii subdiv. iii
45
As before
9 + 7
16
Intro.
2
2
Con moto
16 + 16 + 4
36
41
Adagio
3
3

Example 12-9

The keystone section goes directly back to the symmetrically balancing final section, shown in the schematic outline, Ex. 12-9.

From this outline, the tripartite division is made apparent from the outer to the inner design. Within the adagio phrases on either end, which serve as supporting pillars to the architectural plan, each of the three sections clearly splits into three small subdivisions. These are delineated by the tempo markings. Such an architectural balance, coupled with the rigidity of harmonic, melodic and rhythmic design, lends a kind of classical stature and nobility to this Sabbath prayer. Synagogue music generally places more emphasis on melody than any other musical dimension.

There are similarities between *Hashkiveinu* and the "Jeremiah" Symphony. Both are in the tonal area of E (in the case of the former this may be defined more accurately as the Phrygian mode); both open with the same bi-tonal chord construction (triads a half-step apart. with the median as the common tone); both resolve the ambiguous nature of this bi-tonal effect at the end (i.e., in *Hashkiveinu* the F-minor triad combined with the F-major triad at the start suggests the Phrygian mode, but an F-sharp in the final chord changes this to a definitive E major); both are built in three large parts (or movements): slow-fast-slow; and both use jazzy rhythms in the fast parts. In fact, there is almost a direct quotation from the "Profanation" movement of "Jeremiah" (Ex. 12-10) in the middle section of *Hashkiveinu* (Ex. 12-11):

Example 12-10

Example 12-11

Finally, the symmetrical formal implications in "Jeremiah" become the distinctively explicit characteristic of the choral work—most probably through the influence of the balanced periods of Hebraic liturgic writing noted for its literary parallelisms.

Hashkiveinu was first performed on 11 May 1945, at the Park Avenue Synagogue of New York, which commissioned it.

Hashkiveinu

Hashkiveinu, Adonai Eloheinu,	Cause us to lie down, O Lord, our God,
l'shalom v'-ha-amideinu,	in peace, and raise us up,
Malkeinu, l'-chayim.	Our King, to life (renewed).
Uf'-ros aleinu sukat sh'-lomecha	And spread over us the shelter of Your peace,
v'tak'-neinu b'eitsah tova mil'-fanecha,	and guide us with Your good counsel,
v'-hoshi-einu l'-ma-an sh'mecha,	and save us for Your name's sake,
v'-hagein ba-adeinu.	and protect us.
V'-haseir mei-aleinu oyeiv, dever,	And remove from us enmity, pestilence,
v'-cherev, v'-ra-av, v'-yagon,	and war and hunger and anguish,
V'-haseir satan	And remove the evil inclination
milfaneinu u'-mei-achareinu.	from before us and from behind us.
U'-v'-tseil k'-nafecha tastireinu.	For God, You are our Watchman and Deliverer,
Ki Eil, shom'-reinu u-matsileinu,	For God, a gracious King and merciful are You,
Ki Eil, Melech chanun v'-rachum Atah,	And guard our going out and coming in
U'-sh'-mor tseiteinu u'-vo-ei-nu,	to life and to peace,
l'chayim u'-l'-shalom,	From this time forth and forever more.
mei-atah v'-ad olam.	
Uf'-ros aleinu sukat sh'-lomecha.	And spread over us your tabernacle of peace.
Baruch Atah Adonai,	Blessed are You, O Lord,
hapores sukat shalom aleinu,	who spreads the tabernacle of peace over us

v'-al kol amo Yisrael,	and over all His people,
v'-al Y'-rushalayim.	and over Jerusalem.

Symphony No. 1, "Jeremiah"

(Prefatory note to the full published score)

The date of Bernstein's bar mitzvah is unknown. Temple Mishkan Tefila, his synagogue then located in Roxbury—now in Chestnut Hill—Massachusetts, does not have records that go back that far. However, we can make some deductions about when it took place. Bar mitzvah dates are usually based on the first Sabbath after a boy's thirteenth birthday. Since LB's—25 August 1931—was on a Tuesday, the first Saturday thereafter would have been 29 August. It is doubtful that the ceremony took place on that Sabbath since it was still before Labor Day, the so-called end of summer. The family spent its summers in Sharon, Massachusetts. Sam Bernstein, his father, most likely waited until the following Saturday when everyone was back in town (i.e., Boston).

In either event, the bar mitzvah Bible reading for 29 August 1931 would have been Deuteronomy 30:19–20 through 31:9, followed by the reading from Prophets: Isaiah 61:10 through 63:9. The readings for 6 September 1931 would have been Deuteronomy 32:1, and from Prophets II Samuel 22:47–51.

Whichever day it may have been, the passages from Prophets are chanted the same way, according to cantillation symbols atop and under the Hebrew text that indicate musical motives that then combine into full melodic sentences. Bernstein used these motives as the basis for the second movement of "Jeremiah," his Symphony No. 1.

If such an initiation into manhood could predict one's future—almost astrologically—through the particular Bible reading, the passage for the 6 September rite is hardly indicative for LB as it is filled with texts about war and vengeance—even though the reading does contain words about singing "praises unto Thy name."

More to the point, the cantillation motives that generate the melodic material in Bernstein's first symphony could have suggested any other prophet as his inspiration. Why did he choose the gloom and doom of Jeremiah? The probable explanation is twofold: (1) war clouds were beginning to smother Europe and news of Jewish suffering was traveling back to America; and (2) the Jewish fast day of Tisha b'Av (the ninth day of the month of Av) that commemorates Jewish tragedies, takes place in August. It could well be that as part of his bar mitzvah studies and at his father's urging, the composer had to attend synagogue services on that solemn 1931 fast day where he would have heard the intonation of Lamentations (Eicha in Hebrew), the basis of the symphony's last movement, the original sketch of which was written only eight years after his bar mitzvah.

* * *

There is a fascinating exchange of letters between Bernstein and Copland about the "Lamentation" movement that reveals Copland's ambivalence about Jewish content and about overdoing a "richness of feeling."

In August 1939, LB wrote that

Eventually the song will become one of a group, or a movement of a symphony for voice & orch., or the opening of a cantata or opera, unless you give me a very bad verdict . . .

Copland's response in September reads, in part,

There are certain drawbacks, of course, in adopting a Jewish melos. People are certain to say [Ernest] Bloch. . . . As far as I can judge by your music thus far, you are hopelessly romantic as a composer. It was clever to have adopted the "Jewish" manner in this piece. (I don't mean to imply that this was more than subconscious.) But somehow, someday, that richness of feeling that I call romantic will have to be metamorphosed so that it comes out more new-sounding, more fresh.

* * *

The three symphonies of Leonard Bernstein are concerned with the loss and retrieval of faith, a faith not so much in God as in humankind itself. In Symphony No. 1, "Jeremiah" (1942), the crisis is joined: faith has been shattered, symbolized by the destruction of the Temple in Jerusalem, with only consolation for a finale. With Symphony No. 2, "The Age of Anxiety" (1949), the search for faith begins again, this time ending in a kind of Hollywood hope, more hollow than holy. A compromise resolution to this search comes with Symphony No. 3, "Kaddish" (1963). Yet even this renewal of faith is tempered at the end by the knowledge that faith must be accompanied by pain.

But in 1965, with his *Chichester Psalms*, Bernstein suggests that faith might be grasped through the vision of childlike innocence, that perhaps knowledge itself is pain. Indeed, this notion is as old as the Bible. In Ecclesiastes, verse 18, we read, "For in much wisdom is much grief; and he that increaseth knowledge increaseth sorrow."

Bernstein's entire spiritual journey is summed up in *Mass*, his theater piece of 1971. Here the search starts in innocence, gradually adding the trappings of over-encumbered dogma, only to collapse at the end under its own encumbrances. As at the conclusion of "Kaddish," *Mass* finishes with the phoenix of hope in humanity—not in divinity—rising from the ashes of faith's conflagration.

The composer, in an interview in Berlin in August 1977, when "Jeremiah" was being recorded by him for the third time, addressed this issue:

> Although everything I write seems to have literary or dramatic underpinning, it is, after all, music that I am writing. Whatever happens in the music happens because of what the music does, not because of the words or the extramusical ideas. In a sense, I suppose, I am always writing the same piece, as all composers do. But each time it is a new attempt in other terms to write this piece, to have the piece achieve new dimensions, or even acquire a new vocabulary.
>
> The work I have been writing all my life is about the struggle that is born of the crisis of our century, a crisis of faith. Even way back, when I wrote "Jeremiah," I was wrestling with that problem. The faith or peace that is found at the end of "Jeremiah" is really more a kind of comfort, not a solution. Comfort is one way of achieving peace, but it does not achieve the sense of a new beginning, as does the end of "The Age of Anxiety" or *Mass*.

But how is the nebulous idea of "faith" actually transmitted through the music? At the time "Jeremiah" was written, Bernstein wrote, "The symphony does not make use to any great extent of actual Hebrew thematic material" (see the full statement, page 255).

Actually, the composer was not aware that there was more influence of liturgical motives upon the music than he consciously knew. This is certainly a testament to his upbringing as a Jew both in the synagogue and at home, particularly through the example of his scholarly and God-loving father.

The opening theme of the first movement is derived from the High Holy Day liturgy, heard for the first time as part of the Amidah ("standing") prayers, or eighteen blessings. This compilation of fixed benedictions, recited at all services, Sabbath or holiday, with varying interpolations, constitutes the second most important Jewish prayer after the monotheistic creed of Sh'ma Yisrael ("Hear, O Israel"). This theme nourishes the growth of the entire movement.

The Scherzo ("Profanation") theme from the second movement that Bernstein refers to is based on cantillation motives used during the chanting of the Bible on the Sabbath, especially the Haftara ("concluding") portion. The motives are well known to those who chant Bible passages in preparation for bar mitzvah.

In the "Lamentation," the third movement, the "liturgical cadence" the composer mentions is a sequence of motives derived from the *kinnot* ("dirges") chanted on Tisha B'Av (The Ninth Day of the month of Av), an observance of mourning for the lost Temple. These *kinnot* are, of course, sung to the words of the biblical Lamentations of Jeremiah, and Bernstein uses motives as chanted by Ashkenazic ("Germanic") Jews. Other subconscious sources include various penitential modes, as well as free cantorial improvisation. Significantly, the conclusion of the Lamentation recalls the Amidah theme from the first movement, indicating that the foreboding prophecy has been fulfilled.

* * *

The original program notes for the world premiere in 1944 included the following comments by the composer:

> In the summer of 1939 I made a sketch for a "Lamentation" for soprano and orchestra. This sketch lay forgotten for two years, until in the spring of 1942 I began a first movement of a symphony. I then realized that this new movement, and the scherzo that I planned to follow it, made logical concomitants with the "Lamentation." Thus the symphony came into being, with the "Lamentation" greatly changed, and the soprano supplanted by a mezzo-soprano. The work was finished on 31 December 1942 and is dedicated to my father.
>
> The symphony does not make use to any great extent of actual Hebrew thematic material. The first theme of the scherzo is paraphrased from a traditional Hebrew chant, and the opening phrase of the vocal part in the "Lamentation" is based on a liturgical cadence still sung today in commemoration of the destruction of Jerusalem by Babylon. Other remembrances of Hebrew liturgical music are a matter of emotional quality, rather than of the notes themselves.
>
> As for programmatic meanings, the intention is again not one of literalness, but of emotional quality. Thus the first movement ("Prophecy") aims only to parallel in feeling the intensity of the

prophet's pleas with his people; and the scherzo ("Profanation") to give a general sense of the destruction and chaos brought on by the pagan corruption within the priesthood and the people. The third movement ("Lamentation"), being a setting of poetic text, is naturally a more literary conception. It is the cry of Jeremiah, as he mourns his beloved Jerusalem, ruined, pillaged, and dishonored after his desperate efforts to save it. The text is from the book of Lamentations.

Symphony No. 3, "Kaddish"

(Jacket note for the first recording, Columbia Records, 1964)

To the Jews of the world, the word "Kaddish" ("sanctification") has a highly emotional connotation, for it is the name of the prayer chanted for the dead, at the graveside, on memorial occasions and, in fact, at all synagogue services. Yet there is not a single mention of death in the entire prayer. On the contrary, it uses the word *chayei* or *chayim* (life) three times. Far from being a threnody, the Kaddish is a compilation of paeans in praise of God, and, as such, it has basic functions in the liturgy that have nothing to do with mourning.

This doxology (the first two sections) is written in a mixture of Hebrew and Aramaic, the vernacular language at the time of Jesus. In fact, it could be said that the doxology became the basis for the Christian Paternoster (Lord's Prayer). Originally, in the period following the destruction of the Second Temple (AD 70), fragments of the Kaddish used to be recited by a preacher at the end of a discourse when he was expected to dismiss an assembly with an allusion to the Messianic hope. It was not until the twelfth century, however, that the prayer reached its present-day form, and through folklore came to be associated with mourning.

The last verse is completely in Hebrew, and in contrast to the almost delirious effusiveness of the doxology, it is, along with the preceding (partially Aramaic) verse, a quiet plea for peace (*sh'lamah* or *shalom*). Thus, praise and peace arc the two salient features of the text—not death.

The words of the complete prayer are the sung portions of the symphony, heard three complete times. (The speaker's text is separate.)

Bernstein exploits the dualistic overtones of the prayer: its popular connotation as a kind of requiem, and its celebration of life (i.e., creation). He does this both in his speaker's text and in his music. The choice of a woman as the speaker [in the original version] and also as a soloist—singing sacred words that are traditionally reserved for men in the synagogue—is in itself a dualistic decision. The woman represents, in the symphony, that aspect of man which knows God through intuition, and which can come closest to the Divine, unlike the strictly male principle of organized rationality. (Bernstein

Example 12-12

used the same device in his Symphony No. 1, "Jeremiah," in which the Prophet's Lamentation is sung by a mezzo-soprano.)

But the dualism is even stronger than this. The speaker mourns, in advance, man's possible imminent suicide. At the same time she observes that man cannot destroy himself as long as he identifies himself with God. Hence, man as creator, as artist, as dreamer (as, therefore, a divine manifestation), could be immortal.

Musically this dualism is illustrated by the dramatic contrast between intensely chromatic textures (which border on the edge of atonality) and simple, expressive diatonicism. For example there is a particularly anguished outburst by the speaker in the middle of the Din-Torah (trial scene or "judgment by law") in which she accuses God of a breach of faith with man.[5] It is commented upon by agonized nontonal music that culminates in an eight-part choral cadenza of vast complexity (Ex. 12-12). But immediately after this, the speaker begs God's forgiveness and tries to comfort Him; and the ensuing lullaby is explicitly tonal, with gentle modulations.

Again, at the climax of the symphony (in the Scherzo) another painful spoken moment, musicalized in extreme, angular motives, is followed by a gradual clarification and resolution into G-flat major. The crucial word of the speaker at this point is "believe." Similarly, it would seem that the composer's credo resides in his belief in the enduring values of tonality.

The symphony opens with an Invocation, mainly for the speaker, with a choral and orchestral background that is both disturbing and contemplative. This background music begins with a low indeterminate humming by the chorus; it then introduces two of the main motives of the entire symphony:

Example 12-13 Example 12-14

—and one of the main themes, which Bernstein calls the "Kaddish Tune":

Example 12-15

A very brief, muted passage by the chorus, singing words of the prayer for the first time, switches abruptly to a savage allegro: "Kaddish" 1, an irregularly metric movement (actually, it is part 2 of the first movement) that the composer associates with David dancing ecstatically around the Holy Ark. A twelve-tone row, used only melodically:

Example 12-16

—and a subsidiary, declamatory theme:

Example 12-17

—are the principal new components. All of the given elements now build up to a climax of frantic choral shouts on the word *amen*, at which point the speaker interrupts. A short choral coda concludes the movement.

The Din-Torah (part 1 of movement 2) begins with solo percussion canons and the chorus humming the "Kaddish Tune," over which the speaker hurls her accusations at God. The height of her torment (the conflict of love and anger) is punctuated by an orchestral eruption, containing new musical ideas which are virtually expressionistic in their disjunct counterpoint. One of the new ideas is still another tone row based on a chain of fourths[6]:

Example 12-18

The anguish is increased by a grotesque, quasi-jazzy development. leading to an even more desperate outburst that eventually explodes in the chaotic cadenza cited earlier.

"Kaddish" 2 (part 2 of movement 2) is the tender lullaby, in a slow undulating 5/8 time, for soprano solo with choral responses by the women. Bernstein refers to this section as the "Pietà."

Part 1 of movement 3: "Kaddish" 3, a presto scherzo, is the crux of the symphony, both musically and textually. In it every motive or theme already cited (with the exception of the last) is subjected to almost every kind of musical operation, in combination and succession: exact and inexact imitations, diminutions, augmentations, inversions and retrogradations. This treatment might be called manipulation, rather than development. By such usage of musical formulas, first exposed by itself, the composer points up the speaker's ironic commentary. In the melodrama she passes through a painful crisis to a deep acceptance of reality, which is neither resignation nor wishful dreaming. This process is musically mirrored in the evolution of the original tone row into a purely diatonic, folklike melody. (See the essay that follows this, from *Perspectives of New Music*.)

The Finale (part 2 of movement 3) begins with an orchestral meditation, organized mainly on the second tone row (the chain of fourths), but also recalling in tranquility the "Kaddish Tune" and the diatonic melody of the Scherzo. This has its counterpart in the speaker's final meditation, which signals the start of the jubilant final fugue, for all the vocal forces. There is a triumphant, dance quality about the first half of this fugue, in 7/8 time, which is reminiscent of "Kaddish" 1. In the remaining half, the chorus exults in contrapuntal *amens* that spill over themselves and are consummated in two striking glissandi before the end. [Not in the revised version.] Thematic allusions from the entire symphony punctuate these *amens.*

On 22 November 1963 Bernstein had come to the orchestration of the final Amen section of the symphony when, abruptly, fate commanded the dedication: "To the Beloved Memory of John F. Kennedy."

Kaddish

(*In the Sephardic pronunciation*)

Yit'gadal v'yit'kadash sh'mei raba	Magnified and sanctified be His great name
B'al'ma div'ra chir'utei,	Throughout the world which He hath created according to His will.
V'yam'lich mal'chutei,	May He establish His kingdom

B'chayeichon uv'yomeichon,	During your life and during your days,
Uv'chayei d'chol beit Yis'rael,	And during the life of all the house of Israel,
Ba'agala, uviz'man kariv,	Even speedily, and at a near time,
V'im'ru amen.	And say ye, Amen.
Y'hei sh'mei raba m'varach	May His great name be blessed
L'alam ul'al'mei al'maya.	For ever and to all eternity.
Yit'barach v'yish'tabach v'yit'pa'ar,	Blessed, praised and glorified,
V'yit'romam, v'yit'nasei, v'yit'hadar,	Exalted, extolled and honored,
V'yit'alei, v'yit'hallal,	Magnified and lauded
Sh'mei d'kud'sha, b'rich Hu.	Be the name of the Holy One, blessed be He.
L'eila min kol bir'chata	Though He be beyond all blessings
V'shirata, tush'b'chata, v'nechemata,	And hymns, praises and consolations,
Da'amiran b'al'ma,	That can be uttered in the world,
V'im'ru, amen.	And say ye, Amen.
Y'hei sh'lamah raba,	May there be abundant peace
Min sh'maya v'chayim aleinu,	From heaven, and life for us
V'al kol Yis'rael,	And for all Israel;
V'im'ru, amen.	And say ye, Amen.
Oseh shalom bim'romav,	He who maketh peace in His high places,
Hu ya'aseh shalom aleinu,	May He make peace for us
V'al kol Yis'rael	And for all Israel;
V'im'ru, amen.	And say ye, Amen.

Leonard Bernstein: "Kaddish" Symphony

(Review from Perspectives of New Music, *Fall–Winter 1965)*

The American press reactions to Leonard Bernstein's Third Symphony for orchestra, chorus, boys' choir, speaker and soprano solo—subtitled "Kaddish"—read like notices of a controversial Broadway play: "mustn't be missed, the hit of the year" and "the worst tearjerker since the heyday of the Second Avenue Yiddish melodrama." Such opposite views are almost to be expected about the work of a composer who has openly declared all his music to be inherently theatrical. However, the preponderance and type of vituperation that has been heaped upon the symphony leads one to suspect that it was the personality, rather than the music, that was being judged. Admittedly, all criticism, in one way or another, takes personality into account; but the extra-compositional activities of Bernstein have tended to impel critics to launch certain kinds of vendetta against him, and have not prompted genuine artistic evaluation of his works.

In Israel, the world premiere of "Kaddish" was enthusiastically received by the press (with one exception) despite the most forbidding obstacles to performance: the absence of any real choral tradition, prima-donna complications, and the unfamiliarity of the participants with the medium and the idiom. True, Bernstein is a kind of hero in Israel and "Kaddish" is a Jewish piece and all minorities are supposed to "stick together." However, he does not appear on television there—it is nonexistent anyhow [*at that time*]—and so there was no such direct way to "offend" the critics, because of any imagined usurpation of their duties. But, more seriously, the Speaker's text of the symphony, written by the composer, contains such blasphemies that the zealots were expected to rise in violent protest. In fact, it was feared beforehand that the orthodox Jews of Jerusalem's Meah-Shearim quarter would throw stones, as they have been known to do, a fear that was dissipated quickly when assurance was given that exactly because of their orthodoxy they never attend such frivolities as concerts. On the contrary, the "blasphemies" were recognized as indigenous to Jewish thought by, among others, such an eminent author as Max Brod. Against all expectation, certain American writers took umbrage at these same irreverences. The image of the Lord cannot be defiled by an accusation such as: you are a "Tin God"! (Interestingly, the critic of the *Christian Science Monitor* was one of the few to react favorably, while some Jewish critics were the most vitriolic.) But was this genuine moral indignation or merely an excuse for a tirade?

This Speaker's text dominates the symphony and is woven into the fabric of the music (although some listeners have expressed the desire to hear the music without it. I, for one, find a few of its passages "purple" and some of its similes obvious). Even so, it is not the main characteristic of the whole by any means, despite the overweening journalism that appraised it intensively while glossing over the music. On the other hand, the music does reflect the text, but not in its Jewish aesthetics. Just as the Speaker is torn between love and anger, and just as the Kaddish prayer itself celebrates life, but is popularly known as the Judaic "requiem," so the music has dichotomous elements. It ranges from one extreme to the other, from folk-like tunes to aleatoric components; from tonality to atonality; from a neo-Bellini melody to jazziness; from simple neoclassicism to complex expressionism. This seesaw points up a paradox for many composers: a desire to communicate, but only on one's own terms, those that may tend to alienate many listeners. But "Kaddish" also points toward a solution to the problem. The layman's response to it, while not unanimous, was certainly fervid, in spite of the "advanced" methods used. Unburdened by mannerisms and labels, one is free to experience "an evening in the theater." Nor does one have to be concerned that one moment sounds like Copland and another like Berg.

Indeed, "Kaddish" asks why it is not possible to build upon the example of others, to consolidate the multifarious styles of contemporary music. It also poses the question of why a composer's refusal to follow a particular stylistic tendency is automatic reason for critics to dismiss his work. Is it no longer possible for a work to be considered on its own merit, or in relation to its composer's other output, rather than on its generalized "political" allegiances?

For example, the following passage appears in a brochure about the 1964 Fromm Foundation commissions at Tanglewood: "The judges' definition of 'originality'—one of the traits sought—excluded a number of young composers who write in the tradition of Howard Hanson and Samuel Barber and of the nineteenth-century romanticists before them."

How curious!—since one of the most romantic features of romanticism is the desideratum of "originality" at all costs. Certainly the powers that be do not accept every work written in an advanced idiom, though it may fulfill the basic minimum requirements. Thus, idiomatic emphasis is not necessarily a guarantee of worth; and, what is more, it is no guarantee of originality either.

"Kaddish" cannot be classified either as "avant-garde," though it employs advanced techniques, or as "reactionary," though it is occasionally evocative of other times. But to understand the unique way in which it does create from these disparities a wholly original Gestalt, it is necessary to consider Bernstein's particular "middle-of-the-road" compositional approach.

Here, the word *theater* is the principal clue. A manifestation (albeit a minor one) of Bernstein's theatrical impulse is found in the way many of his works open with solo instruments, a "curtain-raiser" feature which demands the listener's attention. "Kaddish," for example, starts with the "instrument" of the Speaker, against a background of indeterminate humming by the chorus. Such an attention-getting procedure is a significant indication of a theatrical quality embodied in the music itself; for theatrical music, like theater itself, always has an audience in mind. Like theater, it must tempt, tantalize, and persuade a listener to its point of view; and in order to do so, it must draw upon a wide range of musical resources, often taking the best of the tried and the true. In other words, it must, by its very nature, be eclectic, which is an apt description of Bernstein's oeuvre.

The usual critical conclusion that a necessary condition of eclectic tendencies is a lack of strong personal expression is not only debatable, but in Bernstein's case, fallacious.

To be sure, it cannot be denied that in his music the shadows of Strauss, Berg, Hindemith, Stravinsky, Gershwin, Copland, and others (some of whom are eclectics themselves, in varying degrees) weave in and out. For example, the resemblance is obvious between a phrase from "Kaddish" (Ex. 12-19) and one from Copland's *Appalachian Spring* (Ex. 12-20). But it is more to the point that the "Kaddish" melody—which appears toward the end of the third movement—is a direct outgrowth of its own original, primary source.

Example 12-19

Example 12-20

The first motive heard in the symphony (Ex. 12-21) then becomes the bass line at the beginning of "Kaddish" 1 (Ex. 12-22). The rest of "Kaddish"

1 is, in turn, based on a twelve-note ostinato, evolved out of the triadic implications of the previous example (Ex. 12-23).

Example 12-21

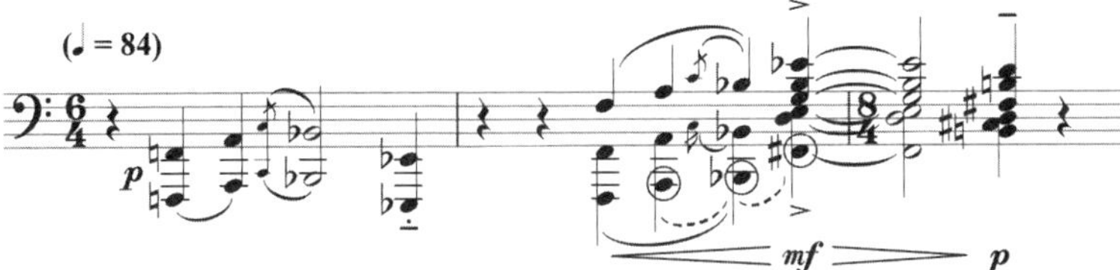

Example 12-22

Example 12-23

As the Speaker goes through a kind of trauma in the third movement, one that ultimately resolves itself through a catharsis based on faith, so this ostinato pattern exfoliates from utter chromaticism to complete diatonicism. The first six notes (transposed, Ex. 12-24) through expansion (Ex. 12-25) finally result in Ex. 12-26:

Example 12-24

The accompanying scalar bass line, in turn, becomes the progenitor of yet another tune, treated in five-part canon and sung by the Boys' Choir at the end of this same Scherzo movement (Ex. 12-27).

Example 12-25

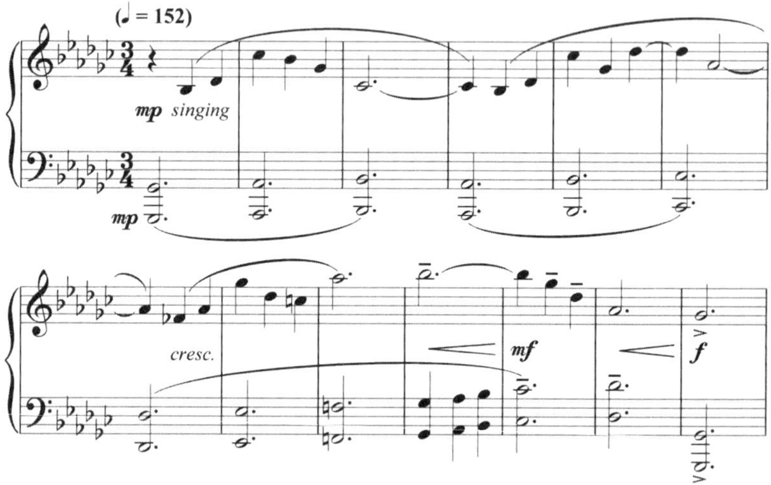

Example 12-26

Example 12-27

Thus, even though occasional resemblances to foreign sources may occur in passing, the music is wholly unified. Bernstein was certainly aware of the melody's kinship to the Copland theme; but besides the good sense of its contextual evolution, there is the implication that he found it helped to satisfy the musical struggle and the triumph of tonality.

Leonard Bernstein: A Jewish Legacy

(Written for the Milken Jewish Archive Label, CDs distributed by Naxos International. I served as coproducer and also participated as pianist.)

(*Notes on the recording, 2003*)

Israelite Chorus, from incidental music to *The Firstborn*

Premiere recording; premiere: 29 April 1958, New York City

The Firstborn, a verse drama by Christopher Fry, was produced by Roger Stevens in conjunction with the America-Israel Cultural Foundation, in tribute to the state of Israel's tenth anniversary. The first public hearing of this choral work was given at an American Jewish Congress fund-raising dinner at the Essex House in New York City on 22 April 1959. The music was on tape, which was how it was presented during its Broadway run and, later, in Israel. Sets were by Boris Aronson. (The world premiere of the play, with music by John Hotchkis, was in 1948 at the Edinburgh Festival.) Fry's play is set in Egypt at the time of the Exodus account of the plagues visited by God upon the Egyptians, including the death of the firstborn Egyptian males, which finally induced the pharaoh to declare the release of the Israelite slaves. Among the distinguished cast were Anthony Quayle (who directed and also played the role of Moses), Katharine Cornell, Torin Thatcher (as Seti, the pharaoh), Mildred Natwick, and Michael Wager, a close friend of the composer's who persuaded Bernstein to write the music in the first place. In addition to the choral number, there was a solo song by the pharaoh's daughter with lute accompaniment: "Teusret's Song," words by Fry, sung live by Kathleen Widdoes. The "Israelite Chorus," based on incidents described in Exodus 12, is marked "allegro ruvido" (rude, noisy), which describes the piece precisely, with its choral canonic imitations in an Israeli horalike dance rhythm, shofarlike horn calls, three sets of wild hand-drum rhythms, and a screaming clarinet at the end—a whoop of joy anticipating the freedom that lies ahead for the Hebrew slaves.

LB never held out much hope for the production. On 22 May 1958 he states he will waive royalties, and that "the whole thing was silly anyway." (Letter to HGC).

(*Sung in Hebrew*)
Go, children of Israel, from Egypt to life.
Go toward the north, my brothers, to life.

Invocation and Trance, from *Dybbuk*

Premiere recording of piano-vocal version; premiere of orchestral version: 18 May 1974, New York City
Conducted by the composer, choreography by Jerome Robbins

For rehearsals of a ballet, a short score or piano reduction is required of the composer— sometimes, as in this case, reduced from full orchestra to two pianos, not necessarily intended for concert performance. This piece, however, is equally effective in both full orchestral dress and the stripped-down dual keyboard format. Based on the famous Yiddish play *The Dybbuk*, by S. Ansky (Shloyme Zanvi Rappaport), Bernstein's ballet version uses Hebrew texts selected by the composer. They are sung intermittently throughout the ballet by a tenor-baritone duo representing the voices of the two shtetl (East European market town) communities of Brinnits and Miropolye, in the Pale of Settlement (the area in which Jews were permitted to live) within the Czarist Empire at the turn of the twentieth century. Texts used in the ballet are taken from the Bible—the oath of allegiance between David and Jonathan; Song of Songs; and the curse found in Deuteronomy (27:22), and from "Kaddish," the established Jewish doxology extolling God's greatness. The excerpt recorded here opens the ballet. The text is from the *havdala* ("distinction") ritual that concludes the Sabbath—a bittersweet ceremony in its farewell to the peace and restfulness of the day. There is a musical reference in this opening scene to a late-nineteenth-century folksong, *Di alte kashe* (the perennial question about existence, to which the only answer is "*tradi ridi ram*").

(*Sung in Hebrew*)
Praised be You, O Lord, our God, King of the universe, who has made a distinction between holy and ordinary, between light und darkness, between the people Israel and the other nations, between the seventh day and the six working days. Praised be You, O Lord, who distinguishes between holy and ordinary. Amen.

"Psalm 148" (1935)

Words in a rhyming adaptation, common to many old Psalters.
Premiere recording, not previously performed in public.

There was considerable thought given whether or not to include this early composition on the recording since it gives no indication of Bernstein's eventual compositional style. Yet it does reveal the musical environment to which he was exposed as a youngster in his family's congregation—specifically the music of Cantor Solomon Braslavsky. In 1962 Bernstein subsidized the publication of Braslavsky's setting of a central prayer from the High Holy Day liturgy, *Un'tane tokef* ("Let us declare") in appreciation of the man who had meant so much to him in his youth. We hear some of that Braslavsky influence in this psalm setting, which in turn refers to von Weber, Mendelssohn, and other Romantic composers. The work begins with grave chords, à la Handel, but with Wagnerian harmonies. There is even a hint of Rossini in the allegro agitato section. The manuscript is dated 5 September 1935. Bernstein rediscovered the piece in the mid-1980s and he expressed an affection for its innocent sweetness, even though he recognized its Victorian excesses. At the time, he suggested that because the text was in praise of animal life, England's Prince Charles might be interested in somehow using it in his patronage of wildlife conservation.

"Reena" (1947)

Premiere recording of the choral version

This piece, in a different version, appeared on *Jewish Holiday Dances and Songs* (Vox), a 78-rpm recording produced by dancer Corrine Chochem, and also included settings by Milhaud, Castelnuovo-Tedesco, Diamond, Eisler, Toch, Trude Rittman—who later arranged Bernstein's music for *Peter Pan*—Wolpe, and Kosakoff. It was conducted by Max Goberman, who subsequently conducted the original production of *West Side Story*. No score survives. The version presented here was transcribed from the original recording, but choral forces have been substituted where the original scoring included strings. The tune is known according to the lyrics—*yesh lanu mayim, mayim b'sason* ("we have water, water with joy")—an expression of thanksgiving by the early *chalutzim*, the pioneering Jewish settlers in Palestine.

Three Wedding Dances, from *Bridal Suite* (1960)

Premiere recording

These dances are excerpted from a *pièce d'occasion* written for songwriter-lyricist Adolph Green and actress-comedienne Phyllis Newman upon their marriage. Part 1 opens with piano secundo playing Bach's C-Major Prelude from the *Well-Tempered Clavier*, while piano primo simultaneously plays "Just in Time" from the Comden-Green, Jule Styne score for *Bells Are Ringing* (along with a touch of Rimsky-Korsakov's *Scheherazade* and the Strauss *Don Juan*). Part 2, comprising the three dances, is subtitled "Bell Book, and Rabbi" (*pace* John Van Druten). The three dances comprise "The First Waltz" (Canon) in which "he leads" and "she follows." Nine bars later the order is reversed, and then, five bars after that, the theme is marked, "Who is this third voice?" No. 2 is a "Cha-Cha-Cha," and No. 3 is a "Hora" (the popular Israeli dance) marked "Fast and Jewish."

"Y'varech'cha" from Concerto for Orchestra (*Jubilee Games*)

Premiere recording of the final section in the organ version; premiere: 15 December 1996, NYC

Kurt Ollmann, baritone, with the New York Philharmonic, conducted by the composer

Originally conceived as *Opening Prayer*, a work written to inaugurate the newly renovated Carnegie Hall, this piece is now the concluding fourth movement—known as "Benediction"—of Bernstein's Concerto for Orchestra (*Jubilee Games*). This is certainly consistent with the text—the threefold priestly benediction (Numbers 6:24–26), the conclusion of the traditional morning service liturgy. The free-floating vocal line and the serenity of the organ's sustained harmonic structure (an F-sharp minor triad against an F-sharp major triad, underpinned by a pitch of D-natural) present a counterbalance to the agitated aural environment of Bernstein's setting of "Vayomer Elohim," included on this recording.

(*Sung in Hebrew*)
May the Lord bless you and keep you.
May the Lord make His face shine upon you, and be gracious to you.
May the Lord turn His face toward you and give you peace.

***Halil* ("Flute"): Nocturne for Flute, Percussion and Piano**

Premiere recording of chamber version; premiere of orchestral version, 27 May 1981

Jean-Pierre Rampal, flute, with the Israel Philharmonic Orchestra, conducted by the composer

("Halil" is pronounced with the gutteral "ch" as in "Bach.")

The composer says, "This work is dedicated to the Spirit of Yadin and to His Fallen Brothers." The reference is to Yadin Tannenbaum, a nineteen-year-old Israeli who, in 1973, at the height of his musical powers, was a tank leader in the Sinai. Bernstein was reluctant to reveal that the pyrotechnical cadenza section depicted the slaughter of the Israeli soldier, but critics were quick to note this programmatic aspect of the work. But it is all organically integrated, and as he notes, the work is "like much of my music in its struggle between tonal and non-tonal forces. In this case, that struggle as involving wars and the threat of wars, the overwhelming desire to live, and the consolation of art, love and the hope for peace. It is a kind of night-music that, from its opening twelve-tone row to its ambiguously final cadence, is an on-going conflict of nocturnal wish-dreams, nightmares, repose, sleeplessness, night-terrors and sleep itself, *Death's twin brother*. I never knew Yadin Tannenbaum, but I know his spirit."

"Simchu Na" (1947)

Premiere recording of the choral-piano version.

This is a setting of a well-known Hebrew song by Matityahu Shelem (Weiner, both words and music), which, like so many songs of the early idealistic adherents of the Zionist movement who came to Palestine to settle and rebuild the land, has achieved folksong status. This arrangement was done for the Pacific Symphonietta and Chorus at the invitation of dancer Corrine Chochem for her album *Four Horah Dances* (Alco Records) and was conducted by film composer Victor Young. The original 78-rpm recording also included settings by Jewish composers Milhaud, Diamond, and Toch. The piano-choral transcription from that recording was realized in 1954. The sheet music indicates that this was accomplished by R.K., the initials of Reuven Kosakoff (1898–1987), a composer devoted to Jewish-related works. No original score survives.

(*Sung in Hebrew, arr. by L. Bernstein*)
Let us celebrate and throw off our burden!
It's a joyous holiday for us; a great day for us.
We have created something out of nothing
With the hand that sows and plows.
Flint rocks and stones flow with abundant waters;
Strength, might and courage.
Awake, awaken and be revived among the sickle bearers!
Persist in work and toil;
The strength of our spirit should not fall,
Awaken, awake!
Translation: Eliyahu Mishulovin

"Oif Mayn Khas'ne" (At My Wedding), from *Arias and Barcarolles*

Poem by Yankev-Yitskhok Segal (1896–1954)
Premiere: 9 May 1988, New York City
Mordechai Kaston, baritone; the composer and Michael Tilson Thomas, piano

Bernstein's choice of this Yiddish poem alludes, perhaps subconsciously, to his early conflict with his father over his career choice. Like the elders in the poem, Sam Bernstein was initially dubious about his son's musical aspirations. The poem's main appeal to the composer had to be its depiction of music's magical and youthful power to transform hidebound elders into frenzied enthusiasts. Of particular interest is the composer's commentary in the piano parts. At the words *nor a vunder* ("what a wonder"), the organlike piano parts are marked "*pp*, a vision." At a *lebediker bronem* ("a living wellspring"), the cadence is annotated with the word *amen*. At *un dos fidele hot gekusht* ("and the little fiddle kissed"), piano primo is marked "fiddly" against piano secundo's descriptive "waltzer," while the last bar carries the indication "*ff* frantic."

(*Sung in Yiddish*)
At my wedding a jolly red-haired musician
Played on the smallest quietest fiddle.
He played a lament, An old time sad song.
Old musicians marveled silently: From where did he pick this up, this young redhead?

When, after all, he spends his nights and days in the villages,
Plays at drunken peasant parties,
And, after all, he can barely read a line of Hebrew.
He sleeps on a hard couch,
And he eats wherever he happens to be,
As when a village girl gives him radishes from her garden.
But what a wonder and a dream it was to look at him: The shoulders and the head, nose and ears laughed magically with joy and sorrow.
And his entire thin bony face
Welled up like a spring flowing with life.
At my wedding this youngster played
So that people were lifted from their seats,
Feet wanted to take off, Ears were sharpened like spears;
And with the little fiddle he caressed, tore, and bit out pieces,
Till it was painful, and it pinched
Into the blood of the taut arteries,
Until the old ones pleaded: "Have Mercy!"
Translation: Eliyahu Mishulovin

"Vayomer Elohim" (ca. 1989)

Premiere recording; not previously performed in public

This setting was found posthumously among Bernstein's papers in a folder marked 1989, but the musical atmosphere suggests his style in *Dybbuk* (1974). Only ten bars long, this rumination on the mystery of creation is, by extension, a tone painting of artistic creativity, suggesting something formed out of nothingness.

(*Sung in Hebrew, Genesis 1:3*)
And God said, "Let there be light," and there was light.

"Yigdal" (1949)

Premiere recording

In 1950, an important anthology of Jewish songs, *The Songs We Sing*, was published by the United Synagogue of America, the lay umbrella organization of the Conservative movement. The collection was compiled and edited by Harry Coopersmith, music director of the Board of Jewish

Education in New York City. Bernstein's setting, as a round, of this well-known hymn text appears in section 3, entitled "Favorite Songs—Old and New." Some instrumental touches have been added for this recording to augment the accompaniment.

(*Sung in Hebrew*)
Exalted be the Living God and praised, He exists, unbounded by time is His existence.

***Four Sabras* (ca. 1950)** [recorded by JG]

The sabra is a cactus-type plant with tough thorns on the outside and sweet flesh inside. In common usage, it is applied to native-born Israelis. The sabras in this piece are (1) Ilana, the Dreamer; (2) Idele, the Hassidele (little Jew, the little Hassid); (3) Yosi, the Jokester; and (4) Dina, the Tomboy Who Weeps Alone.

On the cover page of the original manuscript, the title is given as *Six Sabras,* with an indication of two possible additions—a kibbutznik (member of a collective agricultural settlement) and an [Israeli] Boy Scout, without names—but these two pieces were not composed. Some detective work has been necessary in order to determine even the approximate date of composition. The title page is stamped Israeli Music Publications (IMP), suggesting that the piece might have been requested by that publisher—possibly as a set of children's piano pieces or, conversely, that it was simply a handy piece of paper found by Bernstein when he was conducting in Israel in 1948. He was there again in 1950, briefly in 1953, and then not until 1957. In any case, it can be established that these vignettes were written prior to 1956, since Ilana, the first portrait, became "Candide's Lament" in Bernstein's celebrated score for *Candide.* (It was also known as a piano piece written for an anniversary occasion for a friend, Cesarina Riso.) No. 2, "Idele," recalls Mussorgsky's "Samuel Goldenberg and Schmuyle," from *Pictures at an Exhibition.* Bernstein's version of "Samuel Goldenberg" is a *rav*—a rabbinical-type teacher who Talmudically intones lessons to Bernstein's version of "Schmuyle"—known as "Idele" (Yudel, the name of Bernstein's paternal grandfather). "Idele" is otherwise distracted—i.e., the pianist's right hand—while the *rav* continues to drone on in the left hand. No. 3, "Yosi," may refer to a friend of Bernstein's, Yossi Stern, an Israeli artist known for his incisive drawings. The rhythms are reminiscent of the "jump" sequence from *West Side Story*'s "Dance at the Gym." The middle lento section of No. 4, "Dina," found a later echo in the score for *On the Waterfront.* Appended to "Dina" is the commentary "It's going to happen, disappointment. Why couldn't it have happened? Take comfort in imagining how it might have been. But it isn't true."

"Silhouette" (Galilee) (1951) [*see* Song Album, *chapter 15*]

Hashkiveinu (1945)

Premiere recording

The liturgical text Hashkiveinu is recited at all evening services, with some text variation between the weekday recitation and that on Sabbaths and other holy days. The version here is for Sabbath eve, and Bernstein's three-part division in the music is dictated by the text's structure. As part of a letter to his secretary, Helen Coates, dated 3 March 1945, Bernstein wrote a poem entitled: "On Not Having an Idea in My Head for a Setting of Hashkiveinu!"

> Oh deign, foolish Muse
> To sit upon my shoulder,
> I've got to sing a Blues
> Ere I am one week older.
> The trouble of the Jews
> In my dear guts does smolder
> But spark is the fuse:
> My writing arm grows colder
> I ask not stupid Muse
> For a *Tristan and Isolde*,
> Just a small Berceuse?
> But ere I'm one week older!

Evidently the composer was answered by his Muse, since the work was premiered ten weeks later.

(For a translation, see *Hashkiveinu*, pages 251–252.)

13 Commentaries

Warm-worm-word-cord-cold
– A game of word golf, a.k.a. word chain

Symphony No. 2, "The Age of Anxiety"

(From an essay originally titled "Symbols of Faith in the Music of Leonard Bernstein."[1])

The latter half of this article (not reproduced here) appeared in a chapter on Bernstein in my first book, Funny, It Doesn't Sound Jewish. *At first I had intended to investigate puns and anagrams in LB's music. Since he was so addicted to—and a master of—wordplay, I thought there had to be a musical equivalency in his compositions. It proved to be a futile undertaking. Is Stravinsky's "Greeting Prelude" a pun on "Happy Birthday"? When the pitches of Gershwin's melody for "I've Got Rhythm" are immediately reversed in "I've got music," is that an anagram?*

The late Bruno Walter once was asked what he considered to be the essential difference between Bruckner and Mahler. Walter replied that "Bruckner had found his God, but Mahler was always looking." Like Mahler, Leonard Bernstein in his symphonic works has been in the pursuit of theological meanings, but for our time. In the preface to the score of his Symphony No. 2, "The Age of Anxiety" (1949), after the poem by W. H. Auden, he states: "The essential line of the poem (and of the music) is the record of our difficult and problematical search for faith. . . . " But faith in whom or what? A deity, humanism, existentialism, dogma, self-reliance? Describing the last two sections of his symphony, the jazzy "Masque" and the "Epilogue," Bernstein goes on to say how all the energy expended in the "Masque" results in a new freedom "to examine what is left beneath the emptiness. What is left, it turns out, is faith. The trumpet intrudes its statement of 'something pure.'" But what is this "something pure"? We are still left hanging. It is a vague comment, uncharacteristic of Bernstein. In 1977, on the jacket notes for the more recent recording of "The Age of Anxiety" (DG 2530969), he offers more precise guidance:

> Faith . . . turns out to be in your own backyard, where you least look for it, as in this glass of orange juice I am holding in my hand. There is God in the orange juice, for sunshine is there, earth, vitamins. . . . It's really a Buddhistic idea. God in everything.

That is helpful, but still it does not totally ring true, given the composer's non-Asian background.

In the same preface to the symphony, Bernstein suggests that a fresh look be taken at the music by going back to the Auden poem. Perhaps Auden's words could offer clues. Bernstein had said,

> No one could be more astonished than I at the extent to which the programmaticism of this work has been carried. . . . I was . . . writing a symphony inspired by a poem and following the general form of that poem. Yet . . . I discovered detail after detail of programmatic relation to the poem—details that had "written themselves," wholly unplanned and unconscious.

The last part of the original "Masque" by Auden finds the character Rosetta observing Emble, a drinking companion who has passed out on her bed. She says,

> We're so apart
> When our ways have crossed and our words touched
> On Babylon's Banks . . .[2]

An allusion to Psalm 137: "By the waters of Babylon, there we sat down and wept"? Rosetta goes on:

> . . . You'll build here, be
> Satisfied soon, while I sit waiting

On my light luggage to leave if called
For some new exile . . .

Another clue: "exile." Further on, she continues:

. . . I'd hate you to think
How gentile you feel . . .

And still later:

You're too late to believe. Your lie is showing,
Your creed is creased. But have Christian luck.
Your Jesus has wept; you may joke now,

Then, in the following lines, Rosetta changes from the second person singular, and now speaks in the first person plural:

. . . for we are His Chosen,
His ragged remnant with our ripe flesh
And our hats on, sent out of the room
By their dying grandees and doleful slaves,
Kicked in corridors and cold-shouldered
At toll-bridges, teased upon the stage,
Snubbed at sea, to seep through boundaries,
Diffuse like firearms through frightened lands, . . .
But His people still.

An obvious reference to the Diaspora of the Jewish people. Then in a subsequent passage:

. . . Though I fly to Wall Street
Or Publisher's Row, or pass out, or
Submerge in music, or marry well.
Marooned on riches, He'll be right there
With His eye upon me. Should I hide away
My secret sins in consulting rooms,
My fears are before Him; He'll find all.

Ignore nothing.

This specifically suggests Psalm 139:

Where could I go to escape from You?
Where could I get away from Your presence?
If I went up to heaven, You would be there,
If I lay down in the world of the dead, You would be there.
If I flew away from beyond the east
  or lived in the furthest place in the west,
You would be there to lead me,
You would be there to help me. (vv. 7–10)

The concept of the omniscient and omnipresent God may be a Buddhistic idea, but it is also deeply embedded in Jewish theology.

But if this were not enough to convince us of the poet's intention, Auden's "Masque" concludes with:

Though mobs run amok and markets fall,
Though lights burn late at police stations,
Though passports expire and ports are watched,
Though thousands tumble . . . *Sh'ma Yisrael,*
Adonai eloheinu, Adonai echad.

Judaism's declaration of monotheism: "Hear O Israel, the Lord our God, the Lord is One!" And then, *attacca*, we are into Auden's "Epilogue."

Bernstein's "Epilogue," with that "something pure" idea in the trumpet, thus demands to be reevaluated. Exactly what is that idea? Four notes formed into two intervals of the fourth:

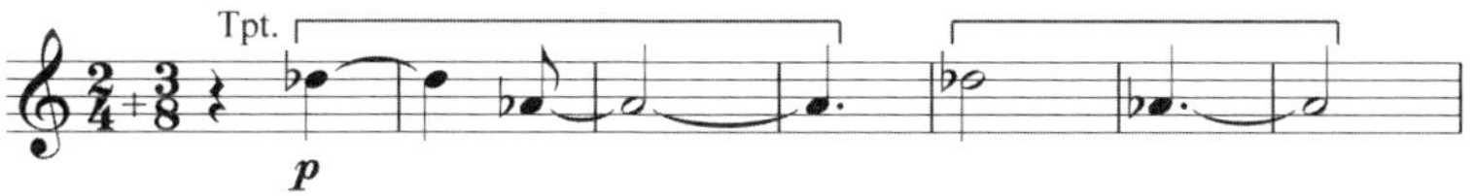

Example 13-1

balanced by another set of four notes made up of two more fourths:

Example 13-2

In terms of Judaism, what else could this be but a musical pun on the "Name of the Four Letters," the Tetragrammaton — the four letters that form the Hebrew name for the Divine Being:

(reading right to left)

hei	**vav**	**hei**	**yod**
ה	ו	ה	י
A-flat	D-flat	A-flat	D-flat

These are consonants. With vowels added to them, the name becomes

יְהֹוָה

transliterated as Ye-ho-vah, hence the name Jehovah.

In the mystical practice of the Kabbalah, the letter *yod* (י) is considered to be the supreme point of the letter *vav* (ו). They are manifestations of the same divine emanation. The two D-flats correspond, then, not to two letters (*yod* and *hei*) but to two revelations of one concept.

The Hebrew etymological root of Ye-ho-vah is *hayo* (from *l'hiyot*, "to be" or "to exist"). "He was, He is, and shall be," an expression of eternity, in Hebrew is sounded as

Hu hayah, Hu hoveh, Hu yih'yeh.

From these tenses, an ideogram evolved for another name of God: Yahveh.

But the word "Yahveh" is never invoked or pronounced by an observant Jew. The ineffable name is not uttered in Hebrew as it appears to the eye. Instead, the word "Adonai," meaning "Lord," is substituted for it, often followed by the word "Elohim"—Adonai Elohim ("Lord God") or "Eloheinu"—Adonai Eloheinu ("Lord *our* God"). Bernstein's musical equivalent of the "something pure" is thus triumphantly proclaimed, at the conclusion of the symphony:

End of "The Age of Anxiety."

Everything points to it: Auden's words, Bernstein's heritage, the notes themselves, including a penultimate one-quarter measure denoting the word *echad*: "One!" a full measure containing one chord. Perhaps the choice of the pitch names D-flat and A-flat (enharmonically written as C-sharp and G-sharp) are an unintentional abstraction of the name ADonAi. But, more convincingly, they could be a pun on one of the names Auden uses for God: "our colossal father" and "our lost DAD."

The acceptance of faith in "The Age of Anxiety" is not blind. In the heart of the composer it is always the Jewish faith, pure and simple. (Perhaps not so simple.) Bernstein, deliberately or unintentionally, cannot be otherwise.

The Chain-Reaction Principle: A New Approach to Tonality?

(Based on New York Philharmonic program notes, 14 November 1988 and 15 July 1996, concerning the works "The Age of Anxiety" and Serenade*)*

As a program annotator of LB's music, I sometimes had to suffer arrows thrown at me by the critical press. Alan Rich took me to task for the following essay, saying, "Is it really possible that Mr. Gottlieb . . . can let himself believe that the twelve-tone system cannot sustain a large musical form as logical as that of a Mozart symphony?"[3] *I am not aware that anything I stated below denies this possibility since I was referring to the concept of bigness in* tonal *music. Rich generally has been a notorious gadfly of Bernstein. So it was puzzling to me that the editors chose to include him in the 2008 volume called "Leonard Bernstein, American Original," where he continues to snipe away at the Maestro. Equal opportunity be damned!*

One of the major reasons for the decline in the output of large new symphonic works since the 1920s has been the dissolution of tonality. What does this mean? As long as a musical structure could be delineated by the developmental drive toward one or another tonal area, it was possible to create large forms. With the increasing density of chromatic alterations and modulations into other keys, the forms also became more and more complex until they reached a bursting point. Tonality ultimately had to tear at the seams of its confinement, and explode into so-called atonality.

Correspondingly, symphonic forms were deflated, never since fully recovering from the shock and renewing themselves with their old vigor. Composers have had to rethink the concept of bigness, especially in tonal music. Bernstein's stab in this direction could be called "melodic concatenation." In this procedure, melody proceeds and develops like a chain-reaction, with later elements relating indirectly to earlier ones through a series of linkages each dependent upon a preceding component. Theoretically, such music could go on infinitely, in an unending spinning-out, one idea always suggesting the next. A prime figure could evolve into an accompaniment figure with a new prime figure about it, and so on—continually shifting the emphasis from foreground to background or middle ground. The form thus arises out of itself, as if containing a self-charging battery. An example of this metamorphosis, using the "Word Gold" game, would be "warm-worm-word-cord-cold."

But such evolving form would eventually exhaust itself, like a battery that has played out. It is up to the composer, of course, to determine what that point of exhaustion may be, and in this there lies the exciting challenge of every piece being uniquely formed according to its melodic components. (The technique is not to be confused with Schoenberg's concept of "continuous variation," in which all material relates *directly* to a primary source, the row.)

Bernstein's commentary on "The Age of Anxiety" describes the characters of Auden's poem conversing in "a kind of symposium on the state of man," which is echoed in Plato's title of *Symposium* from which the music for *Serenade* draws its inspiration. One dictionary definition of symposium is "a drinking party with music and conversation" (from the Greek *syn* "with" + *posis* "a drinking"). Whether in a twentieth-century Third Avenue bar (Auden) or in ancient Athens (Plato), such discussions, tempered as they are by drink, never proceed from alpha to omega. Often they jump about, sometimes reiterative, sometimes off on a tangent.

The Bernstein musical process mirrors such symposia. In "The Age of Anxiety" he tells us that in section titled "The Seven Ages," there is a series of variations in which "each variation seizes upon some feature of the preceding one and develops it, introducing, in the course of the development, some counter-feature upon which the next variation seizes."[4] In his notes to *Serenade*[5] he also informs us that "the 'relatedness' of the movements does not depend on common thematic material, but rather on a system whereby each movement evolves out of elements in the preceding one." However, the evolutionary process is also at work within the movements.

The music of the opening bar (Lento), initiating a lyrical fugato subject ("Phaedrus"), turns into a jaunty theme (Allegro marcato) that ushers in the second part of the first movement ("Pausanias"). In this latter guise, elements of the "Phaedrus" theme are incorporated into an extended solo from which there emerges a *grazioso* grace-note motive of descending ninths. In turn, the gossamer second movement ("Aristophanes") spins off from the grace-note idea. At the midpoint of this song-form movement a "singing" melody, treated canonically, is introduced. "Erixymachus," the mercurial movement that follows, is fueled by this canon, taking off like a rocket. A perky three-note motive, which opens and closes the scherzo, is then metamorphosed by the solo violin into an eloquent statement for the movement ("Agathon") that ensures.

On top of an undulating underpinning based on "Phaedrus" material, the solo violin soars above the staff with the three-note motive in expressive slow motion. In the middle section of "Agathon," a new chromatic theme is heard which becomes the basis for the long and serious first part of the final movement ("Socrates").

The second part of the last movement ("Alcibiades") is not tied down to the domino principle of thematic relationships. Instead, it bursts upon the scene as a jubilant rondo, dramatizing the interruption made by Alcibiades and his chums on Socrates and his dinner guests in Plato's *Symposium*. But within the rondo, the evolutionary process reasserts itself; and it does so most effectively by returning to familiar material: the music that began the *Serenade*. Having thus come full cycle, the entire work is uniquely formed by the dictates of its melodic components.

Elements of melodic concatenation had appeared in the earlier scherzo movement of "Jeremiah." They later cropped up in *Symphonic Suite from "On the Waterfront"* and in "Kaddish." By inventing a way of giving new life to tonal forms, through the aegis of such evolved melody, Bernstein has truly given substance to the old aesthetic argument that form is synonymous with content. This may be his most significant technical contribution to the mainstream for, as far as I can determine, no other composer has so rigorously applied this particular stimulus to the resuscitation of tonal structure.

14 Overtures and Entertainments

"If I am elected to this high office . . ."
– Standard phrase for a political orator

A Musical Toast

(From the Boosey & Hawkes study score, 1980)

After attending the premiere of my sacred service Love Songs for Sabbath, *André Kostelanetz commissioned a work from me. It was his hope that this new piece would repeat the success he had had with* Lincoln Portrait, *the commission he had given Copland. This time, however, instead of continuity being provided by a narrator, the idea was to use the actual voices of famous statesmen, in this case, mostly the voices of FDR and JFK.* Articles of Faith, *the resulting work, was premiered by the Detroit Symphony led by Sixten Ehrling. It was not well received and Kostelanetz abandoned it.*

There is a game musicians play in which they compete in fitting triple-trochaic musical names to George Gershwin's "Fascinating Rhythm." (It can also be done to Richard Rodgers' "Some Enchanted Evening.")

(– ∪/– ∪/– ∪)

Example 14-1

"André Kostelanetz" is often the name that sets the game in motion. (Other names that come to mind include Antonin Dvořák, Gregor Piatigorsky,

Zino Francescatti, Tossy Spivakovsky, Michael Tilson Thomas, "Slava" Rostropovich, Igor F. Stravinsky, and so on.)

It is this gameful spirit that infuses Leonard Bernstein's tribute to Maestro Kostelanetz, *A Musical Toast*. It may seem strange to write a memorial tribute in a "party" vein, rather than an elegaic one; but the composer is simply complying with the wish of Kostelanetz who, in his Last Will and Testament, left these instructions:

> If there is contemplated a gather of my family, friends and associates in New York City, or elsewhere, I direct that such a gathering shall be a cheerful get-together.

Thus, a toast is in order, an orchestral toast by the composer in affectionate memory of his distinguished colleague and friend. After a short fanfare in 7/8, there emerges a figure comprising the aforesaid three trochees:

Example 14-2

—and the party is on.

First performed 11 October 1980 at Avery Fisher Hall in New York City by the New York Philharmonic Orchestra under the direction of Zubin Mehta and repeated on the same occasion under the composer's direction.

Divertimento for Orchestra

(Note for the 25 September 1980 premiere by the Boston Symphony Orchestra)

I supplied the title for this work, and my hand appears on a few pages of the manuscript. I sat with LB at the first rehearsals of Divertimento *in the side balcony of Symphony Hall in Boston. This was so he could freely give me notes without distracting the orchestra. I remember that toward the end of the Mazurka, the small oboe quote from Beethoven's Symphony No. 5 elicited laughter from the orchestra. The experience of being in the same place he had been as a student at Harvard University, so many years later, certainly was a sentimental journey for him as was the visit we paid to Randall Thompson in Cambridge—an homage to his Curtis Institute teacher, whose sweet Symphony No. 2 was an LB favorite.*

The captivating Waltz (in 7/8 time) has taken on an independent life of its own. The composer wrote a lyric to the tune for daughter Jamie's twenty-eighth birthday in September 1980, calling the song "Revanche" ("Revenge"). With the tempo mark of "Allegretto, senza rancor," it begins: "Shit-a-brick, time is running out on me/I must get moving fast undoubtedly." More than this not need be provided.

* * *

I. Sennets and Tuckets
II. Waltz
III. Mazurka
IV. Samba
V. Turkey Trot
VI. Sphinxes
VII. Blues
VIII. In Memoriam; March: "The BSO Forever"

Divertimento is an expression of Bernstein's love affair with the city of his youth and its symphony orchestra, for whose centennial celebration in 1980 the work was written. It is a nostalgic album filled with affectionate memories of musical growing up in Boston, particularly his hearing live symphonic music for the first time in Symphony Hall under the direction of Arthur Fiedler, the late and beloved conductor of the Boston Pops (which may account for the lighthearted nature of the work).

Divertimento is a series of vignettes based on two notes: B, for "Boston," and C, for "centennial." This tiniest of musical atoms is used as the germinating force for all the thematic ideas. Most of these generate brief dances of varying character, from wistful to swaggering, from dodecaphonic to pure diatonic.

The opening vignette, "Sennets and Tuckets" (a Shakespearean stage direction for fanfares), was originally to have been the entire composition, but such an abundance of transformations flowing from the B–C motive suggested themselves to the composer that he found himself with an embarrassment of riches. Nevertheless, the dimensions of the separate pieces are as modest as the motive itself; and while there are eight of them, each lasts only a minute or two.

The work was completed in Fairfield, Connecticut, during August 1980, and the orchestration was completed in the nick of time for the premiere performance on 25 September, Seiji Ozawa conducting the Boston Symphony Orchestra in Symphony Hall, Boston. *Divertimento* is scored for conventional orchestra with the addition of a euphonium doubled by the tuba player, and a battery that includes Latin percussion instruments. Otherwise, the instrumentation is for the normal orchestral complement, featuring various soloists and small groups: a Waltz for the strings alone, a Mazurka for double-reed woodwinds with harp, a Blues for the brass and percussion, and so on.

The movements contain allusions to standard repertoire, some quite obvious, others rather more secret messages for the players themselves. The opening section of the final March, a quiet meditation for three flutes, is marked in the score "In Memoriam," recalling the conductors and members of the Boston Symphony Orchestra no longer with us.

Overture to *Candide*

As you see below, the 7th doesn't belong only to Candide. And since when is it a leitmotif for Candide at all?

So stated LB in a note sent to me from the Beverly Hills Hotel in September 1960, with the above comment concerning my note for the Candide *Overture, and which was scribbled on a program face sheet for a 30 August concert with the NYP in San Diego. On it LB drew four handwritten two-bar music quotes from (1) the opening of the* Candide *Overture, (2) what became known as "Candide's Lament," (3) the love theme from* On the Waterfront *and (4) "Somewhere" from* WSS.

My reply in 2009 may be a bit late in coming, but sorry, sir, I still have to disagree. First off, where did I say it was exclusive to Candide and where did I use the word leitmotif? *What I did say was "the interval of the minor seventh plus major second serves as a motto and a basis for musical development throughout." To be specific, Candide selections generated by—or imbedded with—those intervals include "The Paris Waltz," "You Were Dead, You Know," the "Quartet Finale" to Act I and "Make Our Garden Grow." Those, along with your citation of "Candide's Lament," make for a total of five numbers animated by the eloquent motif, more than enough evidence. By the way, are you aware that "Bon Voyage" also comes out of the Overture?*

(*Program note for premiere of the concert version, New York Philharmonic, 26 January 1957*)

When the Lillian Hellman–Leonard Bernstein rendering of Voltaire's satire *Candide* opened in New York in December 1956, there was a considerable debate as to what label should be attached to it—was this a musical comedy or an operetta? Two months previous to the opening, the composer had presented his criteria for what constitutes either of these forms during an *Omnibus* television show about musical comedy. Any musical stage piece that employed the American vernacular in a verbal sense (i.e., slang or familiar speech patterns), and in a musical sense (i.e., jazz) was, according to Bernstein, a musical comedy. If the situation and characters were remote or exotic then it was an operetta. By these standards, *Show Boat*, *The King and I* and *My Fair Lady* are all operettas, whereas *DuBarry Was a Lady* (despite its foreign setting), *Guys and Dolls* and *Gypsy* are "pure" musical comedies.

Candide is operetta in the vein of Offenbach and Gilbert and Sullivan. Its music has all the wit, élan and sophistication that are associated with that genre. This is immediately apparent in the Overture (who ever wrote a special overture—in sonata-form, no less—for a musical comedy?). It begins with a fanfare built on the intervals of a minor seventh, followed by a major second—typically Bernstein, which serves as a motto and a basis for development, throughout the entire operetta.

This seventh sets up an expectation of B-flat major, but, instead, the musical line suddenly stumbles, like a pratfall, into E-flat major, in what follows. [Carlos Moseley, NYP manager, objected to the word *pratfall*.] This, in the body of the show, becomes "Battle Scene" music. Next, a lyrical contrast from the duet "Oh Happy We" is stated. This entire section is then repeated with lighter orchestration (note the devilish glee of the solo violin) and is succeeded by a brilliant codetta derived from the end of the aria "Glitter and Be Gay." The Overture concludes with a shower of musical sparks utilizing fragments of everything already heard.

Prelude, Fugue and Riffs

(From the Boosey & Hawkes full score, 1950, and a Columbia LP jacket note, 1964)

When I first heard this piece in the late 1950s on a live recording disc in LB's Osborne studio, I went berserk. I listened to it over and over until the needle almost wore through the vinyl. It packs such a wallop that it is regrettable the performing forces prevent it from having more live hearings that it assuredly deserves. Although a few big band troupes still exist in the nostalgia mode, this dynamo work is not their kind of thing; and when scheduled for performance elsewhere in the concert world, it requires hiring players outside of conventional orchestral personnel. Bernstein had said that he had the most difficult time writing this piece. However, I heard him say this long before writing such later works as Mass *and* Dybbuk.

The following note was written for the LP recording with Benny Goodman; and when it was reprinted in a concert program, I was raked over the coals in the press for having the temerity to say the work "is a higher form of composed jazz," ignoring concert-hall compositions by Duke Ellington and others, which certainly was not my intention at all.

Originally commissioned by Woody Herman for his Thundering Herd dance band, *Prelude, Fugue and Riffs* was to be part of a series of jazz works that already included Stravinsky's *Ebony Concerto*. The work was completed in November of 1949, but Herman never performed it, nor did he pursue the series project any further. The work lay dormant until 1952, when Bernstein revised it for a smaller, pit-size band in order to incorporate it, as a ballet sequence, in *Wonderful Town*. Known as the "Courtroom Ballet," the new version did not survive its out-of-town performances since it did not fit in with the decidedly lighter surroundings. However, a bit of the music remained in the show in the "Conquering the City" and "Conversation Piece." Since its first performance on the television show *What Is Jazz?* (1955) by Bernstein with Goodman—to whom it is dedicated—it is not often performed [as stated above] because of its very special requirements of the "big band" sound, a phenomenon that more or less died out with World War II.

Despite its misfortunes, it is one of the most notable achievements in Bernstein's output, since it represents a kind of summation of his musical philosophy. It is virtually his only significant composition that is absolute music—without any literary or dramatic implications. Also, it is one of his few works that emphasizes contrapuntal movement over harmonic texture, and it is one of the very first attempts to write an indigenously American jazz composition from the "classical" standpoint. Unlike some other works, *Prelude, Fugue and Riffs* is not just jazz-influenced and it does not just use jazz techniques. It is a higher form of composed jazz. To borrow a word from jazz argot, it is music that "swings."

This "swinging" approach might be defined as controlled spontaneity. Since there is a controversy as to whether any composed, rather than improvised, music can be called jazz, it is all the more meaningful when a work in this genre gives the impression of being improvised. This is accomplished in the Prelude, for brass and rhythm, by a fluid alternation between a strict dance beat (although it is metrically highly irregular) and a loose, free beat

LB's latter-day insert into *Prelude, Fugue and Riffs.*

(marked: "with drag"). This might be termed the "hot" versus the "blue." Both meter and tempo are unpredictable in the forward flow, which adds to the subtlety and understatement characteristic of swinging jazz.

The spontaneity is all the more remarkable in the Fugue, for saxophones, since this is, of course, one of the most intellectual—and, therefore, anti-improvisational—musical procedures. By the use of very perky, almost spastic, rhythms, especially in the counter-subject material, Bernstein creates the impression of extemporaneous playing. Finally, the Riffs (for everyone plus the solo clarinet with backing from the piano), repeated rhythmic figurations, are what might be called written-out improvisations, most fully accomplished through the virtuoso display of the two fugue subjects stated simultaneously with the Riff ostinati. The complete independence of these integrated contrapuntal voice lines brings about the traditional "jam session." [The work was later transcribed for clarinet and orchestra by Lukas Foss. The title has become the name of the Bernstein Newsletter.]

On 1 May 1963, LB added a two-bar insert to the last movement, better preparing the approach to the wide-open wailing section that followed.

Slava! A Political Overture

(Program note for the premiere performance)

When Mstislav Rostropovich ("Slava" to his friends) invited Leonard Bernstein to help him launch his inaugural concerts as music director of the National Symphony Orchestra, he also asked him to write a rousing new opening piece for the festivities. This overture is the result. The world premiere took place on 11 October 1977 with Rostropovich conducting his orchestra at the Kennedy Center for the Performing Arts in Washington, D.C.

The first theme of *Slava!* is a vaudevillian tune redolent of political campaign high jinks. Theme two, which prominently features the electric guitar, is a canonic tune in 7/8 time (both themes based on songs from *1600 Pennsylvania Avenue*). A very brief kind of development section follows, after which the two themes recur in reverse order. Near the end they are combined with a quotation (proclaimed by the ubiquitous trombones) from the "Coronation Scene" of Mussorgsky's *Boris Godunov*, where the chorus sings the Russian word *slava!* meaning "glory!" In this way, of course, the composer is paying an extra four-bar homage to his friend Rostropovich.

The original version has a tape of election conventioneering. The recording session was held at a studio on the East Side of New York City, near the United Nations building, with LB, Michael Wager, Adolph Green and Patrick O'Neal as orators who shout typical clichés: "If I am elected to this high office . . . ," "The people of this nation are sick and tired . . . ," "Never again shall we submit to . . . ," "Permit me to quote the words of . . .", "I give you the next president. . . ." All of these slogans get lost in the roar and cheers of the crowd.

Although the composer has called this piece an overture, it has been found to be equally effective as the conclusion of a program, or even, if the occasion warrants, as an encore.

15 Songs

"Thou glittering bauble, fame!"
–J.M. Barrie

"Captain Hook's Soliloquy"

(Unpublished note, August 1996)

In 1950 Bernstein wrote incidental music for a Broadway production of *Peter Pan* starring Jean Arthur as Peter and Boris Karloff as Captain Hook. The first performance took place 24 April at the Imperial Theater in New York. The music was orchestrated by Hershy Kay and conducted by Ben Steinberg. There were, in addition, instrumental leitmotifs, for characters such as Tinker Bell, written by (Ms.) Trude Rittman.

Neither Arthur nor Karloff were singers, and so Bernstein's contributions consisted of only four songs (both words and music) for other characters: three for Wendy and one for the Mermaids, as well as two choral numbers, sung by the pirate band. For the road company production, which took place the following year, the composer had an opportunity to write an additional solo number since the role of Hook was to be performed by a trained singer: Lawrence Tibbett, whose last appearance at the Metropolitan Opera was in March 1950. On 22 October 1951, LB wrote Miss Coates, "Tibbett is having trouble, hoarseness, since he is not accustomed to eight performances per week." Tibbett never actually performed the new aria; and, in fact, the production was abandoned midway in its tour.

"Captain Hook's Soliloquy" was not heard for twenty-four years (!) until the revue *By Bernstein*, 23 November 1975 at New York's Chelsea Theater. On his manuscript, dated 13 October 1951, LB changed from pen to pencil, made evident by his side comment: "Sorry, Cuernavaca is out of ink." Unlike

Barrie, he provided a pungent, agitated orchestral introduction laced with various animal sounds, as Hook "gazes quietly into the twilight, undisturbed by the orchestra goings-on." Otherwise, he set the Barrie text quite literally, here given with Barrie's witty stage directions:[1]

> HOOK (*communing with his ego*). How still the night is; nothings sounds alive. Now is the hour when children in their homes are a-bed; their lips bright-browned with the good-night chocolate, and their tongues drowsily searching for belated crumbs housed insecurely on their shining cheeks. Compare them with the children on this boat about to walk the plank. Split my infinitives, but 'tis my hour of triumph! (*Clinging to this fair prospect he dances a few jubilant steps, but they fall below his usual form.*) And yet some dusky spirit compels me now to make my dying speech, lest when dying there may be no time for it. All mortals envy me, yet better perhaps for Hook to have had less ambition! O fame, fame, thou glittering bauble, what is the very—; (SMEE, *engrossed in his labours at the sewing-machine, tears a piece of calico with a rending sound which makes the Solitary think for a moment that the untoward has happened to his garments.*) No little children love me. I am told they play at Peter Pan, and that the strongest always chooses to be Peter. They would rather be a Twin than Hook; [Bernstein added: "They'd rather be a Smee than Hook;] they force the baby to be Hook. The baby! That is where the canker gnaws.

LB repeated and chose to end on a cadenza of "thou glittering bauble, fame." Could this, perhaps, be regarded as a kind of auto-psycho commentary on the part of the composer?[2]

Song Album

(From the foreword of the second edition, 1988. Two later volumes, Leonard Bernstein Art Songs and Arias, 33 selections for medium voice and 29 for high voice [2007] *contain additional and useful notes by Richard Walters.)*

I Hate Music! **A Cycle of Five Kid Songs (1943)**

First performance: 24 August 1943
Jennie Tourel and the composer, Public Library, Lenox, Massachusetts

Tourel's New York recital debut at Town Hall included the cycle. The date is significant since it was the night before Bernstein's unprecedented debut with the New York Philharmonic, 13 November 1943. Barbra Streisand has recorded the first song, omitting the second *a* of Barbara. Song No. 4 of the cycle is sometimes known as "A Riddle."

***La Bonne Cuisine: Four Recipes* (1947)**

First performance: 10 October 1948

Marion Bell, soprano and Edwin MacArthur, piano, Town Hall, New York City.

Émile Dumont's *La bonne cuisine française* (*Tout ce qui a rapport à la table, manuel-guide pour la ville et la campagne*) ("Fine French Cooking (Everything That Has to Do with the Table, Manual Guide for City and Country") was first published in 1899. "Plum Pudding," adapted by the composer from a larger recipe, appears under *Mets anglais* ("English Dishes"). "Queues de boeuf"("Ox-Tails") is taken whole. "Tavouk Gueneksis," a Turkish delight, is also complete, and comes from the section *Patisserie et confiserie turques* ("Turkish Pastry and Sweets"). Two ingredients of the original recipe are missing from the musical setting of "Civet à toute vitesse" ("Rabbit at Top Speed"): *muscade* ("nutmeg") and *un verre d'eau-de-vie* ("a glass of brandy"). During his lifetime, the volume sat on the Bernstein kitchen shelf along with other cookbooks.

(*Literal translation by Ron Mendelsohn*)

I. "Plum Pudding"

250 grams of Malaga grapes, 250 grams of Corinth grapes (Corinth grapes); 250 grams of beef kidney fat, and 125 grams of bread crumbs (of bread crumbs!). 60 grams of powdered or brown sugar; a glass of milk; a half glass of rum or brandy; 3 eggs; a lemon! powdered nutmeg, ginger, cinnamon, mixed (all together about half a teaspoon); half a teaspoon of finely ground salt.

II. "Queues de boeuf" (Ox-Tails)

Ox-tails is not a dish to be scorned. First of all, with enough ox-tails you can make a tolerable stew. The tails that were used to make the stew can be eaten, breaded, and broiled, and served with hot or tomato sauce. Ox-tails is not a dish to be scorned.

III. "Tavouk Gueunksis"

Tavouk Gueunksis, breast of hen; put a hen to boil, and take the white meat and chop it into shreds. Mix it with a broth, like the one for Mahallebi. Tavouk Gueunksis, breast of hen.

IV. "Civet à toute vitesse" (Quick Stew)

Should you be in a hurry, here's a method for preparing a rabbit stew that I recommend! Cut up the rabbit (hare) as for an ordinary stew: put it in a pot with its blood and liver mashed. A half pound of breast of pork, chopped; twenty or so small onions (a dash of salt and pepper); a liter and a half of red wine. Bring this quickly to boil. After about fifteen minutes, when the sauce is reduced to half of what it was, apply a fire to set the stew aflame. When the fire goes out, add to the sauce half a pound of butter, worked with flour . . . and serve.

Two Love Songs, on Poems of Rainer Maria Rilke (1949)

First performances: No. 1, 13 March 1949; No. 2, 13 March 1963
Jennie Tourel and Alan Rogers, Philharmonic Hall, New York City

In 1908, Rilke (b. Prague, 1875–d. Valmont, 1926) was secretary to the sculptor Auguste Rodin in Paris. That was the year when Jessie Lemont, herself a poet, met Rilke. Ten years later, her translations from the original German poetry of Rilke first appeared in print in the United States.

"So Pretty" (1968)

Words by Betty Comden and Adolph Green
First performance: 21 January 1968
Barbra Streisand and the composer, Philharmonic Hall, New York City

The premiere was at a rally-concert called "Broadway for Peace," regarding American involvement in the Vietnam War.

"Piccola Serenata" (1979)

First performance: 27 August 1979
Christa Ludwig, soprano and James Levine, piano, Salzburg, Austria

Written on the occasion of Karl Boehm's eighty-fifth birthday: "with affection from his admiring colleague," and completed in Munich, 25

August 1979, Bernstein's birthday. The nonsense words imply Hassidic vocalizations—perhaps a bit ironically?

"Silhouette" (Galilee) (1951)

Words by the composer
First performance: 13 February 1955
Katherine Hanse, soprano and Evelyn Swarthout, piano, National Gallery of Art, Washington, D.C.

Another birthday piece, this one for Jennie Tourel on her forty-first. The song incorporates an old Lebanese folk song, the Arabic words of which are paraphrased in the preceding English phrases: "The boys in the dark olive groves assemble." His imagery depicts a peaceful, late afternoon scene in northern Israel. Bernstein can be heard singing this tune in the 1967 documentary film *Journey to Jerusalem*.

"A Simple Song" and "I Go On," from *Mass* (1971)

Text by Stephen Schwartz and Leonard Bernstein
Alan Titus, baritone, opening of the John F. Kennedy Center for the Performing Arts, Washington, D.C.

These two selections and the *Candide* songs in this album are the only ones to have been written originally for male voice. "A Simple Song" is sung at the beginning of *Mass* by the Celebrant, who is dressed plainly in jeans. By the time he sings "I Go On," he has become constrained by robes symbolizing the onus of traditional rituals and values.

"Take Care of This House," from *1600 Pennsylvania Avenue* (1976)

Words by Alan Jay Lerner
First performance: 24 February 1976
Patricia Routledge, soprano and Ken Howard, baritone, Forrest Theatre, Philadelphia

Sung by John and Abigail Adams (the "upstairs" residents of the White House), followed by Lud and staff (the "downstairs" folk). The show surveyed various presidents and first ladies and was written on the occasion of the American bicentennial year. The song also was performed at the presidential inaugural concert of Jimmy Carter.

"It Must Be So," from *Candide* (1955)

Words by Richard Wilbur
First performance: 29 October 1956
Robert Rounseville, tenor, Colonial Theater, Boston

To judge from this elegy, the peripatetic Candide must also be pathetic. In the original Lillian Hellman version, "It Must Be So" was first heard after the destruction of our hero's homeland, Westphalia, and after the alleged loss of his beloved Cunegonde. A second verse, "It Must Be Me," was subsequently heard after an earthquake in Lisbon. We are pleased to report that Candide recovers from both calamities.

"My House"; "Peter, Peter"; "Who Am I?"; "Never-Land" from *Peter Pan* (1950)

Words by the composer
First performance: 24 April 1950
Marcia Henderson as Wendy (for the first three songs), Stephanie Augustine and Eleanor Winter as the Mermaids (for *Never-Land*), Imperial Theater, New York City

In this original production of James M. Barrie's play, neither Peter Pan or Captain Hook sang any songs, although Hook did participate in the "Plank Round," a pirate chorus. Presumably, Jean Arthur, the movie actress who portrayed Peter Pan, could not carry a tune.

Songfest

(Written for the piano-vocal score, 1977)

Since this note was written, two of the poets have died: Gregory Corso and June Jordan. We had the pleasure of meeting Ms. Jordan at one of the New York Philharmonic performances, and I recall how excited she was to be part of the program. Incidentally, the Cummings estate has stated that their preference is for the poet's name to have initial caps, like any other poet. Although I dearly love each of these poem settings, I am not altogether convinced that the work is as equally effective when heard as a whole. Perhaps this is could be attributed to its length or because the final Edgar Allan Poe piece was the last section to be written and seems to be more last-minute driven than inspired.

Originally commissioned to be a work in celebration of the American bicentennial year (1976), *Songfest* could not be completed in time. Although the commission was vacated, the idea persisted, to draw a comprehensive picture of America's artistic past, as seen in 1976 through the words of thirteen poets embracing three hundred years of the country's history. The subject matter of their poetry is the American artist's experience as it relates to his or her creativity, loves, marriages, or minority problems—blacks, women, homosexuals, expatriates—within a fundamentally Puritan society.

An insight into the composer's thought process during the two years of building *Songfest* may be gained from considering the variety of possible titles he contemplated: *An American Songfest*, *Six Characters in Search of an Opera, Notes Toward an American Opera, The Glorious Fourth*— with both patriotic and musical import—*Mortal Melodies, A Secular Service* and *Ballet for Voices*, among others. Furthermore, each of the three sextets (Nos. 1, 4 and 6) contains a key poetic phrase that provides other insights: "a real right thing" (O'Hara), "if you can't sing you got to die" (Cummings) [The setting is also available in a version for men's ensemble.] and "a mortal melody" (Poe).

The strongest binding musical force in the cycle is that of unabashed eclecticism, freely reflecting the pluralistic nature of our most eclectic country. The composer believes that with the ever-increasing evidence of this unfettered approach to writing new music, typical of many other composers today, we are moving closer to defining "American music." In a musical world that is becoming ever more international, the American composer—to the extent that his music can be differentiated as "American"—inevitably draws from his own inner sources, however diverse and numerous they may be.

The world premiere of the full *Songfest* took place on 11 October 1977, the composer conducting the National Symphony Orchestra of Washington with singers Clamma Dale, Rosalind Elias, Nancy Williams, Neil Rosenshein, John Reardon and Donald Gramm. Five of the songs had been performed previously: the Aiken, Corso, Millay and de Burgos settings were premiered on 24 November 1976 with the New York Philharmonic; and the Bradstreet trio was first presented at the presidential inaugural gala of Jimmy Carter on 19 January 1977, and was dedicated, on that occasion, to Mrs. Carter. The entire work, however, has been dedicated by Bernstein, "To My Mother."

The score calls for the following instrumentation, in varying combinations from song to song: piccolo, two flutes, 2 oboes, English horn, E-flat clarinet, two B-flat clarinets, bass clarinet, two bassoons, contra-bassoon, four horns, three trumpets, three trombones, tuba, piano, celesta, electric keyboard and bass guitar, harp, timpani and twenty-five other percussion instruments, along with the usual body of strings. A brief description of each song follows:

"To the Poem" (Frank O'Hara, 1926–66): A proclamation of and for unpretentious art, done as a kind of satire on patriotic hymns. The composer ironically misplaces syllabic accents of certain words (e.g., "some*THING*" and "ele*GANT*"). Furthermore, he uses a full brass section at the precise moment when O'Hara's words tell us, "not need*ING A* mil*I*ta*RY* band."

"The Pennycandystore Beyond the El" (Lawrence Ferlinghetti, b. 1919): A frustrated sexual encounter in childhood recalled from the adult's point of view, this is a hushed, jazzy scherzo that uses strict twelve-tone technique and whizzes by like a roller coaster.

"A Julia de Burgos" (Julia de Burgos, 1914–53): The poet qualifies as an American citizen since she was from the Commonwealth of Puerto Rico. In angry words (sung in Spanish) she expresses her self-conflict about the dual role she plays as a conventional woman and as a liberated woman-poet. (Her poem antedates by two decades the so-called women's liberation movement.) The music is sharply rhythmic, almost a dance.

"To What You Said . . ." (Walt Whitman, 1819–92): A recently discovered poem about the poet's homosexual secret, and never published in his lifetime. Over a continuous *ostinato* middle C, this setting comes closest in the cycle to being simply a "song," what the French would call *une mélodie.*

"I, Too, Sing America" (Langston Hughes, 1902–67) and "Okay 'Negroes'" (June Jordan, 1936–2002): Perhaps the first attempt ever to combine poems by two different authors. The Hughes poem (an indirect allusion to Whitman's lifelong theme of "singing America") concerns the black artist seeking a forum in which to glorify his identity. The Jordan poem seems to mock these attitudes in words about the new "black" as opposed to the outdated concept of the "Negro." The offspring of this poetic marriage is a kind of operatic recitative with scat singing.

"To My Dear and Loving Husband" (Anne Bradstreet, c. 1612–72): Unlike the position taken by Julia de Burgos, Anne Bradstreet expresses her dual role of being a woman and a poet as one that can work harmoniously. Although contemporary American poetry is blessed with many women poets (Sylvia Plath, Muriel Rukeyser, et al.) how extraordinary it must have been to be a female voice in the wilderness of pre-Colonial America. The composer has said that if he had written this as a solo piece, the naiveté of the poem would have made the setting sentimental. By making it a trio, the sentimentality is avoided, and the poem becomes more sophisticated. However, this is not a *Rosenkavalier* kind of female trio with three independent thoughts, but, rather, a multilayered abstraction of one individual's feelings.

"Storyette H.M." (Gertrude Stein, 1874–1946): The initials specifically refer to the painter Henri Matisse, but the story, in general, refers to impossible marraiges. Musically, it is delivered as a deadpan duet with a *perpetuo moto* accompaniment, both of which mirror the poet's distinctive manner.

"if you can't eat you got to" (E. E. Cummings, 1894–1962): The Bohemian artist in a casual mood, speaking of his poverty, his lifestyle, and his artistic compulsion. The music swings in the old radio way of the Mills Brothers, a team of four black men who specialized in making instrumental effects through purely vocal means.

"Music I Heard with You" (Conrad Aiken, 1889–1973): A remembrance of bereaved love. More than any of the songs heard thus far, this one adheres closest to the tradition of art-songs. The unusual factor here is that both diatonic and twelve-tone sections coexist and interlock.

"Zizi's Lament" (Gregory Corso, 1930–2001): The expatriate in Belly-Dance Land. The young poet identifies with the aging North African entertainer; and the music is, indeed, a kind of symphonic belly dance overladen with melancholy and bitter humor.

"What Lips My Lips Have Kissed . . ." (Edna St. Vincent Millay, 1892–1950): Haunted by forgotten lovers, the poem is not only moving, but sensual in its heartbroken way. The setting is an adapted song-form: A, A1, A2, B, A3, based on a plaintive rising melodic figure. The composer has been heard to say that this is his favorite song in the cycle.

"Israfel" (Edgar Allan Poe, 1809–49): The title is the name of the Muslim angel of music (from the Koran) who will blow the trumpet on Judgment Day, and who despises an unimpassioned song. The poet utters paeans to this immortal spirit, at the same time conceding the inevitable mortality of his own songs. All this is in the ornate antebellum manner of which Poe was a master, and the music is similarly florid and virtuosic in its praise of the creative muse.

APPENDIX ONE
YOUNG PEOPLE'S CONCERTS

The following essays were printed as pamphlet-guides for school teachers during the 1964, 1965 and 1966 New York Philharmonic Young People's Concerts seasons, which were at first sponsored by the Bell Telephone Hour and later prepared for the Bell System by TV Guide *magazine. In their words: "Since 1924, these celebrated concerts have been designed to introduce children to the enjoyment of good music, to give them factual information about music and musicians, to stir their imaginations and open new horizons. We hope this booklet will help you further your students' interest in the enjoyment of good music." This many decades later, I am struck by how much my writing echoes Bernstein's style of communication.*

Popular Musical Misnomers

(Written for the YPC program "What Is Sonata Form?" 6 November 1964)

Perhaps the most significant contribution Leonard Bernstein has made to American music education, through his New York Philharmonic Young Peoples Concerts, has been his crusade to demolish and bury forever the myth of so-called music appreciation. This is the myth that proclaims such dicta as "music is like the gentle rippling of a meadow brook"—or "music is a revolutionary call to arms." Since his very first program in 1958 titled "What Does Music Mean?" Mr. Bernstein has stressed that this lazy approach to musical understanding not only has been an easy way out, but also has been an obstacle to the grasping of a most elusive art. His concern has been with promoting the far more difficult course of understanding music solely in musical terms. For him music is a language unto itself, with its own vocabulary, grammar and syntax; a language that is incapable of being translated into anything that is extra-musical. Musical meaning is communicated only through musical materials by themselves, not through poetic descriptions of those materials.

In accordance with this philosophy, Mr. Bernstein's first Young People's Concert of this season will deal with what may appear to be a forbidding subject, but one that is, nevertheless, explicitly musical: "What Is Sonata Form?" To illustrate this he has chosen the first movement of Mozart's extraordinary last symphony, No. 41 in C Major (K. 551)—popularly known as the "Jupiter." Mozart wrote the score in 1788, three years before his death.

It is doubtful that Mozart would have approved of the nickname that was appended to his symphony after his death; it is such titles that helped give impetus to the music appreciation myth. Let us see how apt (or inept) is the name "Jupiter" for this symphony (a title that was also used, by the way, for Haydn's Symphony No. 13 in D Major). The subtitle has been ascribed to J. B. Cramer, a publisher and pianist who was a contemporary of Beethoven (and who, also, supposedly entitled the latter's "Emperor" Concerto). Perhaps the noble ideas of the first movement suggested the name; but, according to Eric Blom, the second theme (in G major) of the first movement was borrowed by Mozart from one of his comic arias (also written in 1788): "Un bacio di mano," K. 541. The aria contains the following words, "You are a little dense, my dear Pompeo; go and study the ways of the world." This human criticism seems rather curious as a source for what is touted to be a *super*human work. It has been said that the triplets that begin the symphony suggest the lightning bolts by Jove; but their classic regularity seems to belie the Sturm und Drang qualities that one associates with such awesome phenomena.

More than any of these considerations are those that result from guilt by association. *Jupiter* implies the majestic grandeur of a Beethoven symphony, a titanic struggle (incidentally, Mahler called his Symphony No. 1 the "Titan" *after* he had composed it). This is not the character of Mozart's masterwork. Lofty it is, serene and pure; but it cannot be regarded in terms of deep conflicts and stormy tensions. Furthermore, it is hardly possible to consider the second movement (a lovely songlike Andante) or the third (a charming, graceful Minuet) as even distant relatives of the gods of Mount Olympus.

Possibly the most famous example of a misnomer subtitle is the one given (by some unknown publisher) to Beethoven's Piano Sonata, No. 2, Op. 27: the "Moonlight." This title added to the image of the long-suffering, long-haired artist longing for unrequited love. To him came angels, descending from heavenly portals, into his leonine head in order to dictate the notes through his quill—while disturbing strands of moonlight filtered through the casement. [The Austrian film *Eroica* is only one instance that gives sustenance to this nonsense.] The fact that the composer may not have had sufficient illumination in which to write does not seem to have occurred to the perpetrators of the legend. It is said that Beethoven thought of the moonlight on the Lake of Lucerne as his inspiration; but, as far as is known, he never actually visited the lake. More important than any of this, is that the moonlight is meant to apply only to the first movement of the sonata. What of the other two? Following the line of argument, if the first movement is about moonlight, then the third could be called, let's say, the "flaming meteor." The familiar title does a distinct disservice to the sonata as a whole. Many people are not aware that there is more than just the one movement, and only through all three can one experience a satisfying artistic whole.

Other examples of misemphasis subtitles are: Haydn's "Surprise" Symphony (based on a surprise outburst that occurs only in the slow movement), his "Clock" Symphony (again the slow movement, and a title which could just as easily be given to the slow movement of Beethoven's Eighth Symphony) and his "Bear" Symphony (from the dronelike sound of the last movement). Tchaikovsky's Third Symphony is known as the "Polish" only because the last movement is marked as *Tempo di Polacca*.

Besides moonlight, other misnomers have been derived from Mother Nature. One of the best known is the "Raindrop" Prelude of Chopin. By thinking of the repeated note in this piece as a musical depiction of rainfall, the listener loses the far greater pleasure of discovering how the one note changes character through its varying harmonic contexts. Similar mis-appellations to other Chopin pieces are the "Butterfly" and "Winterwind" etudes. The "Sun" Quartets (Op. 20) of Haydn have nothing to do with heat or light; they were so named because of a sun-burst engraving on the title page of an old edition. Further confusion is created by the title of still another Haydn Quartet, Op. 76, the "Sunrise."

Then there is the "Case of Mistaken Identity." Robert Schumann wrote glowingly of Mendelssohn's Third Symphony, the "Scotch," that it "places us under Italian skies." He had been informed he was listening to the Fourth Symphony, the "Italian." This, mind you, from one of the great musicians of all time! Tchaikovsky's Second Symphony, the "Little Russian," has nothing to do with diminutiveness: it is a reference to that part of Russia better known as Ukraine. The *Harmonien Messe* (No. 5 in B-Flat) by Haydn is not a "Harmony" Mass, but a "Wind-Band" Mass. The "Coronation" Mass of Mozart has nothing to do with the crowning of a king, but with the crowning of a statue of the Virgin. On the other hand, his "Coronation" Piano Concerto was written for the crowning festivities of Leopold II.

Still another category of misleading titles is the "Ethos-Pathos" School. It is the department of appassionatas, pastorales, romantiques and pathétiques. For this we usually have the composer to blame. Such affectations from contemporary composers, for example, smack of pretentiousness. But not always, as witness the "Classical" Symphony by Prokofiev (the last movement of which the Philharmonic will also perform on this program). One of the first pieces to be written in the so-called neo-classic style (1917), the title of this contemporary masterpiece is *musically* pertinent. Prokofiev deliberately, and amusingly, acts the role of a modern, sophisticated European in the Viennese court of Empress Maria Theresa. On the other hand, for the nineteenth-century composer, who used these titles legitimately, an overabundance of similarity gets in the way. For example, one must be careful to qualify a reference to a piece called "Tragique." Does one mean the Fourth Symphony of Schubert, the Fifth Symphony of Bruckner, the Sixth Symphony of Mahler, or even the "Tragic" Overture of Brahms?

No, Mozart's "Jupiter" should not be listened to in terms of its misnomer. With Mr. Bernstein, on November 6, explore the beauty and wonder of its first movement simply as one of the supreme achievements of the classical sonata form.

Some Pitfalls of Pigeonholing

(Written for the YPC program "Farewell to Nationalism," 30 November 1964)

Besides the accident of birth, can the nationality of composers stem from political regimes, naturalization changes or natural climate influences?

Political Regimes

Many references list Smetana as a Czech composer; but others claim he was Bohemian. Bohemia, at the time he was born, was part of Austria. Since Czechoslovakia did not exist when he was alive, what to call him? Austrian, Bohemian or Czech, or all three? And, moreover, what exactly is a Bohemian? (To top it all off, *smetana* means "sour cream" in the Czech language.)

Nowadays, if you were to say of someone, "He's such a footloose type, a real Bohemian!" you would probably receive a bemused smile. For this label has become a quaint euphemism, at one time replaced by the more indigenous American tag, "beatnik." What, after all, do the happy peasants of Bohemia's meadows have to do with the coffeehouse devotees of New York's Greenwich Village?

Actually, Bohemia was originally part of the Holy Roman Empire, later a crown land of Austria. It received political autonomy in 1860, but since World War I it has been part and parcel of Czechoslovakia [today, the Czech Republic and the Slovak Republic].

Despite the political changes (or perhaps because of them) a Bohemian came to represent the vagabond gypsy—one who led a fancy-free life unbound by bourgeois family-society. (The Bohemian image was enhanced by the Henry Murger's stories of *Scènes de la vie de bohème* in 1849 and immortalized by Giacomo Puccini's ever-popular opera *La bohème* in 1896.) Hence the derivation of the appellation—transplanted from the streets of Prague to the Squares (Washington and Sheridan, that is) of New York—and, for that matter, to the gabled roofs and cobbled streets of "gay Paree" and elsewhere.

Settling the question of nationality-pinpointing is not a simple matter. Every student of European history has been confronted by the bewildering array of different names given to one country at different times. Germany, for example, was a hodge-podge of hundreds of states before 1797, which Napoleon reorganized into the Confederation of the Rhine. After the Congress of Vienna in 1814, it became the Germanic Confederation, consisting of Prussia, part of Austria and many smaller states such as Bavaria and Saxony. During the late nineteenth century, Austria-Hungary had become as large as the by then unified Germany. But after World War I, Austria-Hungary was split into separate countries, and Yugoslavia and Czechoslovakia were carved out of its former territory. And since World War II, Germany was divided again [now united].

How does one classify Mozart, born in Salzburg in 1756? Was he Bavarian, Austrian or German?

Naturalization Changes

Another problem of pigeonholing is caused by switches in citizenship. Take the case of a Russian composer. Although Russia was already geographically stabilized in the nineteenth century, her composers helped to advertise her culture to the rest of the world for the first time. Ironically enough, perhaps the most Russian of them all—Tchaikovsky—was not recognized as a cultural ambassador by his colleagues Balakirev, Cui, Borodin, Mussorgsky and Rimsky-Korsakov (a.k.a. The Five). He was too cosmopolitan for their tastes.

If the Five were alive today, no doubt they would have felt the same about another famous Russian, Igor Stravinsky. And perhaps they would have a point, since Stravinsky's music has steadily progressed away from its earlier folk origins, reflected by his adopted homelands of France and the United States. Similarly, one refers to the "American" period of the great Viennese composer Arnold Schoenberg, the time when this composer made a so-called return to tonality. In both cases, therefore, a stringent labeling by singular national origin is not a simple matter. These composers, and others, cannot be easily compartmentalized.

W. H. Auden was born in York, England, in 1907, but has been a U.S. citizen since 1946. Is he an American poet? T. S. Eliot was born in Saint Louis, Missouri, in 1888, but he has been a naturalized British subject since 1928. Is he an *English* poet?

Climate Influences

These pitfalls of classification may seem like just so much hair-splitting; but it is a psychological truism that a country's topography profoundly affects an artist's work. Yet, even here, caution should be exercised. For example, it is fashionable to say that the music of Jean Sibelius is "bleak and cold"—like his country, Finland. Or, one says that the "sunny Mediterranean" climate of Spain is mirrored in the music of Manuel de Falla. But, then, how does one account for the jolly, "warm" folksiness of the Norwegian, Edvard Grieg—or, the other side of the coin—the somewhat forbidding "frigidity" of the Italian, Ferruccio Busoni?

Is the somber *View of Toledo* by El Greco emblematic of "hot" Spain? Do the sparkling greens of John Constable's Landscapes conform to his native "fog-bound" England?

Artists are not creatures who fall into neat categories of *any* order—including, oftentimes, their nationality. (There is much of the French sound in that most typical of all Americans, George Gershwin.) Mr. Bernstein's program on nationalism undoubtedly will help some of his listeners to avoid the all too frequently used—and unfortunately all too convenient trap of—pigeonholing.

Musical Child Prodigies

(Written for the YPC program "Young Performers," 28 January 1965)

We are all familiar with the exploitative parent and following type of dialogue from a book or movie.

> Son (at piano, almost weeping): "Papa, my arms ache from scales. May I go out and play?"
>
> Father (rapping the boy on the knuckles): "Practice, or else no supper for you!"

While there is some real-life truth to this Dickensian scene, it has become so commonplace in the public eye that it is often assumed all child prodigies go through such torture. The aggressive, possessive mother and the ruthless, self-aggrandizing father are almost recognized as stock characters out of a melodrama. Actually, however, there have been enough devoted child-parent relationships among the lives of our leading artists to temper this distorted image.

Intelligent parental judgment, a balanced education and a wise social rearing have been the hallmarks of most successful careers that have evolved. And yet, even this restrained, sometimes overpurposeful and careful approach (the opposite extreme, occasionally, of the "slave driver" parent) has had backfiring results.

Josef Hofmann, one of the great all-time pianists, made his debut with the Boston Symphony Orchestra at the age of ten. Shortly thereafter, his appearances were suspended on the theory that this was the only way for him to mature properly. He did not publicly perform again until he was seventeen. Later, Hofmann considered those seven years wasted. It was a normal experience for him to play for people, not for the four walls of a studio. The intended corrective measure actually placed him at a disadvantage when he finally reappeared. Instead of growing up with his public, and perfecting his pianism along with their reactions (but not as a tryout platform), he had to face the "show us" attitude, and dispel the fact that he was not just a ten-year-old flash in the pan. With such a handicap, he deliberately tamed the passionate side of his musical nature and, for a while, met with a cool reception.

The performing musician is by definition a social creature, unlike the composer. He has to be heard by others in order to function. He carries on a kind of love affair with his listeners and thrives on their affectionate response or learns from their rejection. It would seem logical, therefore, that a child prodigy would best develop in an educational situation that capitalizes on this inherent need. Instead of emotional isolation and pampering, he or she could be inspired by concert experiences in the most impressionable years. Having tasted the applause of an adoring audience, and having been moved by them, he/she could progress continuously and productively as a human being, not as a freak.

This fact has been recognized to an extent, in New York City, by virtue of its high schools of Music and Art and of Performing Arts. Since the American educational system is oriented to competitive conditions, the gifted child would benefit from such pressure. Always he would have to be "on his toes" in order to keep up with his peers. In such an environment he would not stand out as a sideshow exhibit.

The child prodigy is not intrinsically one-sided. Above all other considerations, he has the same needs and drives as anyone else. He should be recognized exactly for what he is—a youngster with special abilities—and allowed to grow up with other equally blessed children. Unfortunately, even for those parents who realize this fact, the outlets for its implementation are all too few in number and too limited in location. However, there are encouraging signs. A number of universities have built performing arts centers, which could be attractive lures for prodigious musicians who would ordinarily just be conservatory bound. Equally promising is the reverse development of conservatories (such as Juilliard and Hartt) that have changed their academic status and have been incorporated as colleges.

The Art of Shooting an Orchestra

(Written for the 1965 Young People's Concerts with Leonard Bernstein on CBS-TV)

On 23 September 1962, an historic event took place in the world of television—a two-hour live telecast of the opening night at Philharmonic Hall in New York's Lincoln Center. That night, over 23,500,000 viewers saw Leonard Bernstein begin the concert with the Gloria from Beethoven's Missa Solemnis. *As producer Robert Saudek said, "We want the cameras to act as the 'eyes' of the viewer, letting him see things just as if he were there himself. We don't want to bring Lincoln Center to him—we want to bring him to Lincoln Center."*

"The Art of Shooting an Orchestra" is an account of the technique involved in telecasting an orchestral performance. It proposes that a television director is a kind of conductor himself who interprets music in his choice of camera shots.

There's more to a televised orchestral performance than meets the eye. Television is not only a medium that creates the illusion of intimacy, but it also offers unique interpretive values in combination with orchestral music. In fact, it can be said a new art form has evolved: the "shooting of an orchestra."

Actually, there are two schools of thought about how to televise symphonic music. The first might be called the passive approach. It maintains that the camera should register only the conductor's back, with the orchestra facing him, retaining the popular impression of an orchestra in a concert hall.

The second school, the active approach, proclaims that the camera should never be still—that as music moves forward in time, so should the picture. But since a televised concert is neither a concert hall performance (even though it may originate from a hall) nor an exercise in camera expertise, a compromise is made—the moderate approach. It is a sensitive blend of the two schools that forms the basis of the directorial method for shooting orchestral music.

To elicit an inspired camera performance of a symphony, a knowledgeable TV director must do as much advance planning and rehearsing as the orchestra's conductor himself. It is planning on two levels. First, the director's visualization of the orchestral score is determined by his knowledge of the music itself and by what it says to him emotionally and intellectually. In this regard, he may be regarded as a conductor in his own right, motivated by his own artistic attitude. On another level, the TV director must intelligently pre-plan his camera shots in order to achieve an interesting and—indeed—moving interpretation of a musical program. A haphazard, random selection of pretty pictures of violins and bows or strummed harps is not a realization of the vitality inherent in the medium.

Thus, early in his preparations, he is faced with many decisions. How should he show, for example, the entrances of the "Ode to Joy" tune in the finale of Beethoven's Ninth Symphony; or how best can he intensify the struggle between soloist and orchestra in their byplay with the "full moon and empty arms" tune of Rachmaninoff's Second Piano Concerto? Should the camera sweep of a full line of double basses be made in spurts—or in a controlled, even progression? How are the camera cues anticipated—by split-second timing or by a slower preparation of upbeats? Will a close-up of the flutist's pursed lips distract the viewer? What kind of lighting will best underline the music of the French horn section, not merely show faces? At what height? Position? Profile or head on?

A rather ticklish problem involves the placement of the conductor on the screen. Since television has the unique advantage of allowing an audience to see the conductor's face, the question is: When? Too often such a shot is used as a time-killer for music that is relatively indefinable as clear-cut instrumentation. But there is no denying the dramatic impact of the conductor's facial expression. It helps communicate a message to the orchestra as much as his hands. Often, too, it helps create unusual interest for the home viewer. A climactic moment in a Strauss tone poem, for example, takes on a new dimension when we see the conductor's features set it up, achieve it, and leave it.

Like the conductor, a TV director also has personal feeling to project in his work—his "style." Intensification, enhancement, cultivation, illumination—all these become crucial as the director works hand in hand with the conductor. However, due to the exigencies of rehearsal time and expense, as well as the fact that the conductor cannot be in the control room with the director, there is little opportunity for detailed consultation. The director must, in the final analysis, project his own musical sensibility.

In the television control room, the director deploys a group of technicians as if he were captain of a ship. Each of his crew, to whom he directs screening orders, mans a specific station. On one side sits his associate director (AD), who helps in assigning specific cameras, in the studio or hall, to specific shots.

During the telecast, the AD cues all the advance shots a step ahead of the game. Since there are a limited number of cameras to work with, this becomes a matter of careful strategy to make sure a camera is free of one shot in time to get in position for its next one.

On the other side of the director is the technical director (TD), the man in direct charge of (and in telephone communication with) the camera crew. His main function is to signal the various cameramen on orders from the director.

Additionally, there may be a third assistant needed to help the director keep in touch with the printed music score and its progress. The captain, with many things to think about, often needs this navigator to keep his ship on course.

The director, in his control seat, now concentrates on the visual interpretation of the music, measure by measure, with all the studio equipment and technicians at his disposal. . . . a slow dissolve (fade-out) from one camera shot to another, during a legato or lyrical passage . . . a series of quick camera *cuts* (separated shots) from one instrument or section to another during staccato or dramatic music . . . traveling (*trucking* or *panning*) the camera along several neighboring instruments to follow the progress of a melody . . . tightening into a close-up (*dolly-in*) approximating a crescendo, or going away from it (*dolly-back*) . . . a *split screen* view to emphasize a contrapuntal section of a *superimposition* for harmonically complex passages . . . a dramatic overhead shot with the tower camera or the tractorlike television crane . . . or crawl into the heart of an orchestra with the "creepie-peepie" portable camera. And so on through the intricacies of the score.

Thus the television director "conducts" his aides and cameramen, giving shadings to the performance, and enhancing the enjoyment of music.

Television's contribution to symphonic music, as you may now see, is more than mere reportage. It is an agent for increasing understanding, for making a musical event more meaningful and exciting. A televised concert demands greater attention than the same concert on radio or recording, and in reliable hands, it can be just as rewarding. With more frequent programs, undoubtedly the unique worth of televised concerts will become more generally acknowledged. [Wishful thinking?]

Perhaps we can look forward to an interesting possibility: the day may come when a television director's talents in "shooting" a performance of Beethoven's Fifth Symphony will be as heatedly argued as we not debate a conductor's interpretation of it—all for the good of music.

Alas, since LB's time, concerts of orchestral music have dwindled almost to the vanishing point. PBS has been stalwart in telecasts of the Metropolitan Opera, especially alluring under the leadership of Peter Gelb. There are documentaries on cable stations such as Ovation, but these are not viewed by the same size audience that were turned on by the YPCs on the national networks in their heyday.

Unknown Musical Works

(Written for the program "A Tribute to Sibelius," 19 February 1965)

For approximately the last thirty years of his life, it was rumored that Sibelius had written an Eighth Symphony, perhaps even more. The mystery was enhanced by the godlike aura that surrounded him while he was in retirement and by his emergence as the internationally-known symbol of Finland.

However, all the rumors proved unfounded. After his death, no new compositions were discovered among his effects. Strange, that for one-third of his life he did not compose. Yet, Gioachino Rossini, after having written *William Tell* in 1829, closed his career as an opera composer at the age of thirty-seven. He had almost forty more years left, although toward the end of his life he did write some smaller works including a series called *Sins of Old Age*. In our own time, the American composer Charles Ives stopped composing many years before he died. [The same can be said of Aaron Copland.]

Surely none of these stoppages in creative activity were due to a wish to rest on one's laurels. No true artist is ever so content. (As a matter of fact, there were few laurels set on the brow of Ives, at least during his lifetime.) Nor can the advance of years be used as an excuse. Some of our greatest composers were vigorously active in their later years: Verdi, Strauss, Vaughan-Williams and Stravinsky.

Had Sibelius exhausted his creative resources? Was he intimidated by the burgeoning eruptions of "modern music" that inundated him in the twenties? (He was, after all, a child of the romantic nineteenth century.) Or was the process of composing too fatiguing? Not many people realize that it usually takes many hours to orchestrate a few seconds of music, to say nothing of composing it in the first place and making a legible copy. [This situation has improved somewhat in the computer age.]

But the most fascinating of all the speculations is whether Sibelius actually destroyed, for whatever reason, any music he might have written after 1929. This is not an unreasonable assumption, when it is remembered that Brahms in all likelihood destroyed about one-third of his total output. Paul Dukas also was known to have burnt a quarter of a century of his works and, more recently, the German composer Carl Orff had built his reputation on works written after the mid-1930s; renouncing his earlier pieces. Other composers and artists in other media have been similarly and severely critical of their creative output.

Sibelius undoubtedly had the courage to reject that which did not come up to his own standard of artistic merit and integrity. Therefore, we need not further consider music of his that might or might not have been written. What we should be concerned about, however, is his extant music that is not known. Generally this is music of a vocal nature that has been relegated to a position behind his instrumental works. There are, for example, as many as 12 choral works with orchestra in his catalogue that remain unperformed and unrecorded. [I do not know if this remains true since this essay was written.]

And in this respect, other noted composers share his fate. How many people have ever heard the purely orchestral works (besides the *Siegfried Idyll*) of Wagner? There are nine overtures, three marches and one symphony. Who knows the Mass of Puccini; the twelve early symphonies of Mendelssohn; Mahler's cantata *Das klagende Lied*; the opera *The Invisible City of Kitezh* that Rimsky-Korsakov considered his best; the Second and Third symphonies of Shostakovich; or the partially atonal cantata by Prokofiev called *Seven, They Were Seven*? What of the concertos and other major violin works by Lalo besides *Symphonie espagnole*? Of the sixty-seven operas of Donizetti, why are only about eight ever performed?

The list of unknown musical works is endless, and probably for the good reason that many of them are mediocre and better left unsung. But certainly not all. It would be fascinating to attend a music festival devoted to performances of only these unknown works.

Pity the Poor Composer?

(Written for the program "Musical Atoms, A Study of Intervals," 29 November 1965)
(not previously published)

How often have we heard the pat phrase, "Nobody really appreciates you until after you're dead." For some reason, composers and painters are particularly subject to this sorry platitude. Yet the careers of the composers represented at this concert: Wagner, Brahms and Vaughan Williams, appear to belie such a notion. And the same may be said for a goodly number of other composers; they were famous in their day and they *were* appreciated. Therefore, how to account for this romantic flim-flammery that has prevailed for lo these many years?

It is, first of all, a product of self-indulgent nineteenth century romanticism, sustained by Victorian biographies. Oh, how the poor artist suffers! No one understands Dr. Faustus; he is so far ahead of his time. He struggles in a cold attic; but strangely, he always can afford a piano, if not food. He is constantly beleaguered by bill collectors and a shrew of a wife (to say nothing of an occasional peccadillo with a contessa or two, thrown in for good measure).

But up to the nineteenth century a composer was still regarded as a kind of medieval guild member and servant— either of the church or royalty. Only with the advent of Beethoven do composers break through this "bondage" and assert their independence. (It was this titan, not Goethe, who happened to be with him, who dared refuse to take off his hat to Archduke Rudolph.)

Accompanying this declaration of rights was the emergence of "individual style," above all else. And such rugged individualism has lingered on to this day of utter conformity, where styles have meshed and lost the sharp edge of uniqueness. Even in this age of copyrights and protection societies, composers themselves tend to perpetrate hard-luck stories. It helps to feed their typical neuroticism, if not their stomachs, an unneurotic composer being a rarity.

The sad news is that many composers are unsung simply because they are not good enough. But to be an unknown genius is another matter. One can hardly be masterful without word of it spreading about town sooner or later. A distinction must be made, however, between fame and economics; money and reputation are not necessarily handmaidens. Schubert (who never made much and never wanted much) and Mozart (whose wife, incidentally, *later* profited) both ended up penniless; but they were revered in their day nevertheless. Although phenomenal interest ensued in Bartók's music only after his death, he was certainly not totally ignored during his lifetime; and Ives, whose vogue has only recently ascended, was a well-off insurance man. Stephen Foster and Mussorgsky died in charity wards, but "Oh! Susanna" was a popular classic shortly after its creation, and *Boris Godunov* made a hit with its first audiences.

Of course the vagaries of time are unpredictable, and retrospective appraisals can occur only with the passing years; and, alas, for every well-known Cesar Cui or Anatoli Liadov, there is a lesser-known contemporary named Alexander Borodin or Modest Mussorgsky. And yes, Bizet did die broken-hearted over the failure of *Carmen*; and Erik Satie was a victim of his own eccentricities.

Now look at the other side of the coin. National heroes: Verdi, Sibelius, Grieg, Smetana, Rimsky-Korsakov, Glinka; darlings of the salon: Liszt, Chopin, Rachmaninoff, Mendelssohn (a banker's son); wealthy theater personalities: Offenbach, Rossini, Puccini, Gershwin, Strauss, Stravinsky, Britten.

Further evidence. Bach: progressive economic growth from Arnstadt to Leipzig and acknowledged master of his world. Handel: a sometime opera impresario, occasionally rich. Gluck: internationally known before his death. Haydn: thirty years with an understanding patron, Esterhazy—then, Salomon. Beethoven: not wealthy, but a wily negotiator with publishers and a legend in his time. Berlioz: at first had to write hack journalism, but gained government grants later, and became a notorious avant-gardist. Schumann:

led a comfortable Bürger existence, from teaching, his journal *Neue Zeitschrift* and his wife's concert tour income.

As for Wagner, we know that he made an imbroglio of money matters, but we also know that he was an extravagant spender. Mad King Ludwig of Bavaria ultimately made him secure. Furthermore, he left a large inheritance, and even today his grandchildren continue to benefit from his fame and name at Bayreuth. Controversies over his music and writings made him a *cause célèbre* while he was still around to enjoy it.

Brahms, like Schumann, was a solid bourgeois type, successful enough to maintain himself at whatever level he chose. Academic honors were showered upon him, and the ordinary citizens of Vienna respectfully tipped their hats to him in the street. In fact, by the time he wrote his Fourth Symphony he was fairly well off, and he could have been rich. However, he was so scrupulous about his work that he destroyed many pieces that publishers would have given their eyeteeth to include in their catalogs. Brahms is quoted as having said, "The hard thing is not to compose, but to let the superfluous notes fall under the table."

And Vaughan Williams' life was as respectable as a dignitary of state. He was the son of a well-to-do clergyman, and he went through a pleasant middle-class upbringing. Not only did he receive a doctorate in music—no mean accomplishment for a Britisher—but he also was the recipient of the Order of Merit and other honoraria. In fact, he achieved a status of unofficial composer laureate in his country. Never lacking for a performance or a shilling, he is generally conceded to be one of the few great English composers.

The movements from the two Fourth symphonies on this program both are solid, meaty fare, like main courses. Their sturdy qualities represent "elder statesmen" composers of similar stature and nobility; not only in the actual music, incidentally, but also in their respective girths. A description of the music of Brahms could well apply to Vaughan Williams: "like a gypsy woman dancing in a tight corset, latent heat beneath a formal exterior."

Lest it be construed that the lot of a composer is generally a happy one, a disclaimer must be made that even some of the most esteemed ones of our time rarely make more than five thousand dollars a year from royalties. However, this does not mean that the piper never gets paid. Almost, as if by definition, history cannot ignore a musical giant (although quasi-giants may get lost in the shuffle); and, what's more, there is a fifty-fifty chance that his pockets will jingle with sounds other than musical.

Strictly Musical? (1966)

(not previously published)

This was written during the early splurge of James Bond films, with particular reference to Dr. No *from 1962. At the time, there was a joke going around about Luigi Nono, the avant-garde Italian composer—something to the effect that the response to the Italian's refusals was the obedient German, Wolfgang Jaja.*

Mention the words *motive*, *interval*, *tune*, *compose*, *instrument*, *scale*—in one breath, and you will most likely be regarded as a musical expert. But witness this tongue-in-cheek bit of prose (with apologies to 007):

> What would be the *repercussion* of Dr. Nono's *motive*? Jaja Bond mused on this as he *tuned* up the motor, pumped the *pedal* and *composed* himself for the ordeal ahead. Was the fiend *instrumental* in the caper? Were the *scales* of justice loaded in the *crook's* favor? Did he escape in that split-second *interval* between time lock clicks? These not so *minor* questions beset our *sharp*-minded agent as the *rhythm* of the tires set up a *counterpoint* to the "tuh-puck-a-tuh" *cadence* of his heart*beat*. Jaja wondered if he would ever be allowed a *measure* of peace and *harmony*. The *strain* was too much; and the *damper* his brow became, the more he contemplated the cool *tonic* at his private club. Anything to take the *flat* taste out of his mouth. Suddenly, there was a *dissonant* screech, a *canon* shot, and around the curve . . .

You take it from there. Words obviously must be understood in some context. But the foregoing illustration also makes one ask if there is any word at all that belongs exclusively to musical terminology, and can be used in no other context. Of course! is the immediate reaction; what about "clarinet"? True, we recognize *clarinet* as a music word, but its root, *clarino*, gave us the expression, the clarion call! This is made even *clearer* (pardon the pun) by the fact that the clarino was an early Italian trumpet. The French *trompe* can be likened to "an elephant's proboscis," and gave us the word *trumpet*. And *horn* (which, after all, was wrenched from some poor animal in caveman days) comes from the French *cor*, which owes its namesake to Latin, as in *cornu copiae*—or cornucopia, the cone-shaped horn of plenty. *Cornu* can be traced back to an ancient Hebrew measure of capacity *kor*. *Oboe* derives from the French *hautbois* (highwood) and *hautboy*, incidentally, is also a variety of strawberry.

Thus, methods of producing sound or the shape of materials determine names of instruments, Mr. X did not, for instance, pick the word *xylophone* out of the blue. *Xylo* is Greek for "wood" and *phone* means "sound."

We have barely begun to scratch the etymological surface. Music words also shift meanings from one culture to another, from one age to the next. The word *intermezzo*, which might be associated with Brahms' lyrical and melancholy piano pieces, was at first the title of a light, comic entertainment inserted between operatic acts. Over the years the word was corrupted into an almost opposite meaning. Similarly *melodrama*, which these days evokes shades of "Curses! Foiled again!" originally designated in operas those sections of words spoken over or between music.

The ancient Greek *symphonia* defined "sound" *phonein* "in unison" *sym*. In the Middle Ages the drum, hurdy-gurdy and bagpipe were all called *symphonia*, whereas in the seventeenth century the term *sinfonia* signified an introductory piece or overture—ultimately developing into the present-day "symphony." Interesting, isn't it, that from an archaic meaning of "one sound" this word evolved into a modern meaning of a myriad of sounds?

Terpsichore, the Muse of Dance, had her roots in *terpsis* (joy) and *khoros* (a place). Although choreography is the obvious modern result, the Latin offshoot *chorus* was, in the beginning, a dance with singing. Members of the chorus in *Oedipus Rex* were meant to be dancers also, but today it would be quite a sight for an oratorio society to do an interpretive dance while it sang Handel's *Messiah*.

As a matter of fact, music (*mousike*) itself owes its parentage to the nine Muses, while museum (*mouseion*) was the sanctuary of their efforts. These creative creatures were the active practitioners of *ars* (art): a way of being, a skill—hence, a talent. The uncreative ones were *iners*: inactive, as in *inertia*.

The question might be: Are there *any* musical terms that arose out of a strictly musical background? Even "Do-Re-Mi" comes from the syllables of a medieval Latin hymn (at first *Do*, from *Dominus*, was called *Ut*):

UT queant laxis REsonare fibris,
MI gestorum FAmuli tuorum,
SOLve polluti LAbii reatum.

One possible exception might be "counterpoint," from *punctus contra punctum*, "point against point," notes punched out by monks on their parchment. But a *counterpoint* is also a quilted coverlet.

Here is a tiny lexicon of terms and their nonmusical sources:

1. Clef: Latin, *clavis*, key
2. Composition: Latin, *componere*, to put together
3. Instrument: Latin, *instruere*, to build or equip
4. Minuet: French, *menuet*, smallish, pretty
5. Opera: Latin, *Ops*, Goddess of Harvest, implying work or labor
6. Rhythm: Greek, *rhythmos*, measured motion
7. Scale: Italian, *scala*, a ladder
8. Waltz: German, *waizen*, to roll about

One of the most interesting terms is *accompaniment*, related to *companion* and *company*, from the Latin, *panis*. An accompanist, literally, shares bread! And did you know that *tarantella* came from music purported to cure the bite of a tarantula?

Music genealogies are as complicated as family trees. In this brief search for an infant word that is born of purely musical parents, and has no further connotations, one is hard pressed to find any progeny other than *melody*, from Greek *melos* and *ode*, both meaning "song." But watch out; the latter word may have originated from the *singing* sound produced when a substance is superficially scorched, or "singed."

Anyone for a game of chicken versus egg?

The author and LB.

APPENDIX TWO
BERNSTEIN: A BRIEF OVERVIEW

(*Based on an entry for the* Dictionary of Twentieth-Century Music, *E. P. Dutton & Co., Inc.*)

First written in 1964, this obviously is not a complete overview of LB's life. It does not refer to his writings, honors, latter-day televised concerts, master classes, and political activism. Instead, it concentrates on his compositions (with the exception of piano pieces and other small works). Although it contains information that appears elsewhere in this volume, I include it as a useful reference that offers succinct descriptions of LB's school of thought and composition style.

During his ten-year tenure (1958–68) as the music director of the New York Philharmonic, Leonard Bernstein conducted approximately two hundred different contemporary works. This was an enviable record, and it corroborates the conductor's reputation as a champion of new music. However, a closer examination of his programs reveals that he did not display mach sympathy toward the Second Viennese School and its twelve-tone derivatives. He offered, rather, a token amount—about ten such works in all. His métier was mostly the so-called French school of Stravinsky (although not the late period), Copland and other disciples of the teacher Nadia Boulanger.

Surprisingly, very little support was given to the younger generation of today's composers of any nationality or persuasion. One would have expected more of him in view of his own youth and spirit of adventurousness. This was considerably less true when he headed, in his twenties, the New York City Center Orchestra (1945–48), performing numerous works of musicians his own age and which paralleled his aesthetic outlook.

The significance of this is that when he assumed the Philharmonic post at the age of forty, his musical predilections were, for the most part, determined, and he carried along with him the composers he had previously brought to public attention. Like any other artist, Bernstein has been a mirror of his education and teachers. His programs and compositions are an index of this truism. In fact, he has been fiercely loyal to his background.

Bernstein's father, Samuel J., a Russian-Jewish immigrant, did not fully encourage his son's musical ambitions. Although he was not a child prodigy, his gifts developed rapidly, after the age of ten, when a piano was introduced into the household quite by chance. Despite his father's opposition to artistic aspiration—understandable in view of the lowly esteem held by musicians had in the "old country"—the elder Bernstein instilled in his son a profound love of Jewish tradition and learning, which later imbued many of his most important compositions. The youth received further indoctrination from his rabbi, H. H. Rubenowitz of Temple Mishkan Tefila, Roxbury, Massachusetts. The rabbi's sermons, in particular, enthralled him. Their dramatic timing and clear expository style became a hallmark of Bernstein's television programs, for which he alone has written the scripts.

A further ramification of the parental-child conflict were the close-knit ties Leonard made with his younger sister and brother, Shirley and Burton. The staying power of these early allegiances became the pattern for other relationships, including professional ones. In fact, associations with many of his most intimate colleagues began when he was in his twenties and even earlier.

Since he is probably the first musician of international repute who is wholly the product of American schooling, his teachers are of primary importance to his history. Phillip Marson, his English teacher at the Boston Latin School, from which he graduated in 1935, introduced him to the wonder of language. Bernstein is fluent in four languages other than his own (as well as a smattering, of others), important to any musician's growth. Furthermore, he delights in solving difficult word puzzles and etymologies. The philosopher David W. Prall, at Harvard University, helped broaden his literary interests, which in turn affected him as a composer with a penchant for literary texts or some form of programmatic allusion.

At Harvard, he studied counterpoint with A. Tillman Merritt, composition with Walter Piston and orchestration with Edward Burlingame III. At this time his first significant theatrical efforts took place: as the composer of an incidental score for Aristophanes' *The Birds* (Hindu ragas, which he then first heard and was fascinated by, figure in this student work), and as the director of *The Cradle Will Rock* by Marc Blitzstein, whose distinctive use of melodrama (i.e., spoken words and music) influenced Bernstein's own theater works. After graduating cum laude in 1939, he matriculated, with the help of Dimitri Mitropoulos, at the Curtis Institute of Music (until 1941) where his teachers were Fritz Reiner in conducting (a restraining force), Randall Thompson in orchestration and the pianist Isabelle Vengerova. Piano studies had begun much earlier in Boston under Helen Coates (who later became his secretary) and Heinrich Gebhard.

Initially urged by Mitropoulos to become a conductor, Bernstein pursued further study in the summers of 1940–43 at the Berkshire Music Center, where he soon became assistant to the director, Serge Koussevitzky. A benevolent alliance resulted, and Koussevitzky (like Samuel Bernstein, a Russian Jew) became a kind of musical father. Indeed, Bernstein assimilated some of the older man's extravagant conducting mannerisms, as well as his sense of mission. He succeeded Koussevitzky as head of the conducting department of the center (1951–55). Before then, however, Artur Rodzinski had selected him to be assistant conductor of the New York Philharmonic in 1943. On 13 November, the twenty-five-year-old conductor made an unprecedented and successful debut with the orchestra, when he suddenly took over for the ailing guest conductor Bruno Walter.

The Horatio Alger aspect of this debut ("son of immigrant rises to the top of his chosen profession in the land of opportunity") had a sensational effect, and Bernstein's services henceforth were much in demand—conducting orchestras (sometimes doubling as piano soloist) the world over. Obviously, glamour alone was not enough to sustain such a whirlwind career; and yet for the next fifteen years it became a liability as much as an asset. Critics asked how was it possible for a native son to function in a field that had been the domain of foreigners. They were dismayed by his excessive choreographic tendencies on the podium (which have been tempered by increasing maturity); and they were perturbed that a "dignified" musician be a popularist, writing for the commercial stage as well as a so-called serious composer of the concert hall. Yet it was just this antiestablishment behavior, as well as unique ability, that was and continued to be Bernstein's main strength. Contrary to the opinion that if he had only concentrated on just one musical discipline to the exclusion of any other he would be a greater musician, the fact is that he would not be Leonard Bernstein.

For four years (1951–55) Bernstein taught on a part-time basis at Brandeis University; but his natural talents as a teacher found its greatest fulfillment when in October 1955 he began his remarkable music series on television. These unparalleled programs were directed towards adults first on seven *Omnibus* shows in such diverse subjects as jazz, grand opera and musical comedy, then exclusively with the New York Philharmonic (until 1962) in fifteen programs exploring, humor, rhythm, romanticism in music, and so on. Also with the Philharmonic, starting in 1958, he undertook four annual televised Young People's Concerts. He has rarely resorted to appreciation gimmicks or to talking-down on these programs, always dealing with the actual stuff of music. Evidently this approach found great favor since it earned Bernstein the sobriquet of "Music's most articulate spokesman," and since his first book, *The Joy of Music* (1959), which contained the seven *Omnibus* scripts, became a best seller.

At the same time the author was accused of "mit-cultism" or the promotion of a middlebrow American society seeking instant culture. But it was his contention that in an age of rapid communication and expanding population the aristocracy of art can no longer be tolerated, thus agreeing in part with the philosophy of Marshall McLuhan.

* * *

As a composer, Bernstein has the distinction of being the first American who is equally at home in the popular theater and the concert hall (although Gershwin was the first to be successful in this respect, he was not as technically accomplished, especially in the formal construction of his serious works). Bernstein has been a consolidator, rather than an innovator; and as such he is a true eclectic. His prominent influences have been Stravinsky, Copland and Shostakovich, while the lesser ones include Strauss, Mahler, Hindemith and Berg. Added to this mixed bag is the whole tradition of jazz and Latin American idioms that permeate his works, and there are occasional twelve-tone procedures (but always in the context of tonality, which the composer feels "is built into the human organism"). Perhaps his eclecticism is due to his enormous conductorial repertory and direct experience with learning what is effective and what is not. When a question of stylistic influence does arise, it usually can be traced to primary sources, earlier in the work, which are Bernstein's own. Even in his neo-Hindemithian work the Sonata for Clarinet and Piano (the first piece of his to be published) the composer's personality emerges in its asymmetric jazzy passages, although there is an element of Shostakovich in the "Jeremiah" Symphony, the personality is markedly stronger. Here he calls upon his adolescent memories of Jewish prayer cadences, bar mitzvah cantillation and traditional Biblical chant.

Complete individuality emerges in the ballet *Fancy Free* which, with its piquant evocation of forties jazz, is a set of seven vignettes organized into a unified rondo design. Its musical comedy transformation, *On the Town,* is the first Broadway production to contain seven or eight dance episodes within the standard two-act format. The composer's second ballet, *Facsimile*, is actually an A-B-A symphonic movement in which all the melodic material grows out of the opening phrases. Both ballets are thematically integrated, an unusual feature of a medium not noted for such tight construction.

In some ways, the most typical of Bernstein's output is the concise and appealing *Prelude, Fugue and Riffs* for big band. Both this and the clarinet sonata are the only two compositions that do not involve extramusical ideas. Significantly, Bernstein had one of his hardest struggles in completing this jazz piece, even though it is characteristically dancelike. However, it was choreographed much later than some subsequent compositions, which is surprising since most of his concert-hall works have been borrowed for ballets. Rhythmically the composer generally has been strikingly inventive with a fondness for syncopations, cross-rhythms and asymmetrical meters in slow as well as fast tempos. His orchestration displays a prominent use of solo piano, of brass in high registers and of a large, virtuoso percussion section (with as many as two dozen instruments in one work).

His second symphony, "The Age of Anxiety"—a work, like *Facsimile* and the one-act opera *Trouble in Tahiti*, concerned with the neuroses of contemporary society—cultivates a kind of chain-reaction procedure. There are variations not so much on one theme as progressively evolving, each out of some aspect of the preceding one.

The film score for *On the Waterfront* expanded upon this technique of melodic concatenation. Using few thematic ideas, the scenes are masterfully underpinned and interrelated. Particularly memorable is a fugato for percussion, pointing up the violence in the scenario, which gradually evolves into a love theme. In the orchestral suite that the composer extracted from the film, this love music suffers from being overly repetitious both as an entity and within itself.

The concatenation method is further refined in the five-movement *Serenade*. Although this violin concerto is inspired by a literary source, it is perhaps the least theatrical of Bernstein's concert hall pieces. Or, to put it another way, it is a "pure" work that need not rely on any program. The challenge of a solo string pitted against a string orchestra is successfully met, and the slow "Agathon" movement is one of the most moving in the entire violin literature.

Trouble in Tahiti, a satire on suburbia composed to Bernstein's own libretto, is symmetrically organized into seven scenes. Its imposition of musical comedy mannerisms upon an operatic frame is only partially convincing. When this was reversed, operatic practice in a Broadway context, as in *West Side Story*, the attempt was wholly successful.

The exuberant *Wonderful Town*, his second musical comedy, has an infectious spontaneity which may be because of its being written in little more than one month. (This was helped along by using the melody of the Irish folk tune "The Siege of Ennis" as the basis for the song "My Darling Eileen.") Bernstein always works best under pressure or in meeting a deadline. Almost all the compositions already mentioned were accomplished in this way. It may explain why he assumes so many varied projects—as a modus operandi.

In *Candide* the composer took on a completely different genre. Here he could indulge his eclectic proclivities to the hilt. The global locales of this operetta allowed him to parody many different national styles—a subject that had intrigued him ever since his Harvard honors thesis, "The Absorption of Race Elements into American Music." This is probably the most admired work by the cognoscenti. The Overture has also become a repertory piece.

It is revealing that Bernstein worked on *Candide*, with all its artifice, and on the verismo content of *West Side Story* simultaneously. This, his most popular accomplishment, may be regarded as a theatrical milestone, perhaps one of the first genuinely American operas. By coming to grips with the most vital social problems of midcentury urban life, via a modern interpretation of the Romeo and Juliet story, he molded the best of established European operatic custom with the fluidity of the American stage.

The third symphony, "Kaddish," is actually an ambitious oratorio using large choral and orchestral forces, as well as a controversial spoken text written by the composer. Like *West Side Story*, it dramatizes the torment and unrest of the present-day world. The anguish is also present in the conflict between atonality and tonality. The preoccupation with Jewish texts continues, two years later, in the attractive *Chichester Psalms*. Quite unlike the bulk of "Kaddish," however, this is an optimistic and uncomplicated homophonic work. The opening and chief motif pays homage to the similarly affirmative opening of Mahler's Eighth Symphony.

Melodically and thematically, Bernstein places much architectonic importance on such short motives as well as on intervals. A whole work may exploit a basic generative interval (perfect fifth in *Wonderful Town*, minor seventh in *Candide*, tritone in *West Side Story*). Moreover, there are certain motivic configurations that he uses constantly which calls attention to an axiom of the style: an ascending or descending interval tends to be preceded or followed by a single step up or down. Of the 384 possible motives that can result from this formula (in which the interval of the second is the constant and those of the third through the seventh are the variables), there are particular favored combinations: descending, fa-mi-do, do descending to mi-re, and so on.

2009 Postscript: In a foreword to "The Age of Anxiety," Bernstein confessed, "I have a deep suspicion that every work I write, for whatever medium, is really theater music in some way." Obviously this holds true spectacularly for his *Mass: A Theater Piece for Singers, Players and Dancers* (for the opening of the John F. Kennedy Cultural Center in Washington 1970), and the opera *A Quiet Place* (1982), but it can be equally applied to other late works such as *Songfest* for six singers and orchestra (in celebration of the bicentennial of the United States in 1977); *Slava! A Political Overture* (1977), *Divertimento* and *A Musical Toast* (both 1980), three works for orchestra; *Halil*, Nocturne for Solo Flute and small orchestra (1981); Concerto for Orchestra (*Jubilee Games*) (1986–88); and *Arias and Barcarolles* for two singers and piano duet (1988).

Like a true showman, Bernstein never lost sight of reaching an audience's approval. In the fall of 1969 he may have relinquished his directorship of the New York Philharmonic so as to concentrate more on composition, but he never abandoned his conducting activity—going on to triumph as guest conductor of the Vienna Philharmonic. In his words: "To live with myself I must continue to do everything better than I've done it before." On a 2009 *Great Performances* telecast on the life of conductor Herbert von Karajan, Christa Ludwig, the mezzo-soprano who worked with Bernstein in his later years, said, "Von Karajan made music; Bernstein was music."

ACKNOWLEDGMENTS

All thanks go to the following:

Leonard Bernstein's children: Jamie, Alexander and Nina. They read the first draft of the book and only corrected errors of fact. There were some details of opinion they disagreed with, but they did not ask for any modifications. I am ever grateful for their loyalty, which is on the same wavelength as their father's.

The personnel of the The Leonard Bernstein Office: Paul Epstein, Craig Urquhart, Marie Carter, Eleanor Sandresky, Garth Sunderland, Michael Sbabo, Milka DeJesus and Josh Carr. They not only provided source material but also offered guidance and technical support. I may be the senior member on staff, but their combined knowledge and skills have sometimes made me feel like a junior partner.

The archivist/historians at the New York Philharmonic Archive: Barbara Haws and Richard Wandel, who gave of their services generously and often. The Bernstein conducting scores, stored under their loving and faithful care, have been digitized for online viewing.

The Music Division at The Library of Congress: Susan Vita, Elizabeth Auman, Raymond White and, especially, Mark Eden Horowitz, Senior Music Specialist. The vast collection of Bernstein papers have been magnificently maintained by this gifted librarian.

The dedicatees of this book: Daryl Bornstein, Charlie Harmon, John Walker and Craig Urquhart, who have remained devoted colleagues over the course of several decades.

Mavens of the recording industry: John McClure, former chief engineer for Columbia Records, and Alison Ames, former A&R Representative for Deutsche Grammophon Records.

Friends of Felicia and Leonard Bernstein: Ofra Bikel, Gail Jacobs, Louis D'Almeida, Ellen Adler and Shirley Gabis Perle.

My friends: Dr. Caldwell Titcomb, Dr. Philip E. Miller, Michael Leavitt, Paul McKibbins, Eric Gordon, Evan D. Lewis, Jon D. Popiel, Joshua Breitzer, and my neighbors, Dr. Sung Lee and Anita Siegel, who came to the rescue more than once.

The team at Amadeus Press: John Cerullo, my indefatigable publisher, Iris Bass, meticulous copy editor; Diane Levinson, for publicity and marketing; and, in particular, Jessica Burr, editor, who always kept me on target.

NOTES

INTRODUCTION

1. Barry Seldes, *Leonard Bernstein: The Political Life of an American Musician* (Berkeley: University of California Press, 2009); Boris Morros, *My Ten Years as a Counter Spy* (London: Werner Laurie, 1959).
2. *The Jewish Week* (25 June 1993).
3. Quoted in *Stars of David* by Abigail Pogrebin (New York: Broadway Books, 2005).
4. *The Jewish Week* (14 November 2008).

CHAPTER 1

1. A title that LB first considered was, no less, in Latin, *De Rerum Musica*, guaranteed to frighten off all buyers. Others included *The Language of Music* and *A Sheaf of Notes*. Alternative titles for the YPC book were *The Young Listener*, *For Young Ears*, and *The Youthful Music Lover*.
2. Hans W. Heinsheimer, *Best Regards to Aida* (New York: Alfred A. Knopf, 1968), 255.
3. Friedman was also a lawyer for Aaron Copland and William Schuman. Schuman's biographer, Joseph Polisi, mentions disagreeable experiences Schuman had with Heinsheimer, even describing him as a bully.
4. Humphrey Burton, *Leonard Bernstein* (New York: Doubleday, 1994), 186.
5. Tallulah Bankhead, *Tallulah: My Autobiography* (New York: Harper & Brothers Publishers, 1952), 2.
6. Hewitt was interviewed by Blitzstein's biographer Eric Gordon in 1988.
7. Shirley, a theatrical and literary agent, never married. She did have a lengthy affair with Jules Dassin, the movie director and actor.
8. Hugh Fordin, *The Movies' Greatest Musicals* (New York: Frederick Ungar Publishing Co., 1984,) 258.
9. Ibid., 239.
10. Among them were Mark Stringer and Stephen Somary (both conductors), Jeff Voorhees and Angus Whyte.

11. This would be *Everybody's Favorite Piano Pieces*, a collection LB traveled with, fondly remembered from his youth.
12. *New York Magazine* 9, no. 9:51.
13. Schuyler Chapin, *Leonard Bernstein: Notes From a Friend* (New York: Walker & Co., 1992), 164.
14. Of course it does. "My New Friends," a 1979 song, was an open declaration: "Come on in, At last the door is open/Come right on in, My new friends,/You've been waiting so long there outside . . ."
15. Greg Lawrence, *Dance With Demons: The Life of Jerome Robbins* (New York: G. P. Putnam's Sons, 2001), 87.
16. Humphrey Burton, *Leonard Bernstein*, 437 and 438.
17. Review of *Dutch*, a biography of Ronald Reagan by Edmund Morris, *The New York Times* (22 October 1999).
18. Joan Peyser, *Bernstein: A Biography* (New York: William Morrow, 1987); quotes, respectively, on 231, 229 and 211.
19. Meryle Secrest, *Leonard Bernstein: A Life* (New York: Alfred A. Knopf, 1994), 96.
20. John Gruen, *Callas Kissed Me . . . Lenny Too!: A Critic's Memoir* (powerHouse Books, 2008), 199.

CHAPTER 2

1. Letter from LB to Burton Bernstein, 14 April 1960.
2. *Bartlett's Book of Anecdotes*, rev. ed.
3. Reprinted in the book *Leonard Bernstein: American Original* by Burton Bernstein and Barbara Haws (New York: HarperCollins, 2008) from an *Esquire* magazine article in 1961.
4. Whenever he was due to play a concerto in public, LB would warm up with a slow-tempo version of the Robert Schumann Toccata, Op. 7, a fiendishly difficult piece.
5. Excerpt from "Bobby and Jackie and Jack" from the show *Merrily We Roll Along*. In *Assassins*, Sondheim has the character of Sam Byck speak aloud letters he is writing to LB.

6. Both of LB's writer-colleagues on *WSS* found Bernstein the man to be fodder for their invention. Arthur Laurents exploited the Black Panther affair in a play of his that had a short run, *The Radical Mystique*. Laurents also wrote *Madwoman of Central Park West*, a solo vehicle for Phyllis Newman, which had two LB songs.
7. Chapin, *Leonard Bernstein: Notes From a Friend*, 169.
8. Ibid., 168.

CHAPTER 3

1. Alex Ross, *New Yorker* (15 December 2008).
2. None of the set of *Four Anniversaries* was source material for other pieces.
3. See the review from *Perspectives of New Music* (1965) in chapter 12.
4. John Mauceri, *Celebrating West Side Story* (Winston-Salem: North Carolina School of the Arts Press, 2007), 10.
5. Burton Bernstein, *Leonard Bernstein: American Original*, 79.
6. Jack Gottlieb, *Funny, It Doesn't Sound Jewish: How Yiddish Songs and Synagogue Melodies Influenced Tin Pan Alley, Broadway, and Hollywood* (Albany, NY: SUNY Press, 2004), 181–84.
7. Vivian Perlis, ed., *Copland: 1900 Through 1942* (New York: St. Martin's Press, 1984), 339.
8. Winthrop Sargeant, *New Yorker* (12 January 1963).
9. See "A Jewish Legacy," in chapter 12, for details.
10. *Tsuris* is Yiddish for "troubles."
11. Said "visa" allowed Mlle. Abarbanell to appear on the Broadway stage of 1910 and sing, "Put Your Arms Around Me, Honey."
12. As mentioned before, it is hard to dismiss likenesses between "Maria" from *WSS* as not originating from Blitzstein's opera *Regina* or the one between "To Make Us Proud" from *1600 Pennsylvania Avenue* and Blitzstein's "Bird upon the Tree" in *Juno*.

CHAPTER 4

1. Robert Lowell, from No. 3 of "Three Poems for Kaddish," published in 1979.
2. Letter to Elizabeth Bishop, 24 December 1962.

3. Reported by Ken Keuffel, *Winston-Salem Journal* (24 November 2008).
4. "Reaching for the Note," *Great Performances* on PBS, 1998.
5. See my analysis from *Perspectives of New Music* (1965) in chapter 12.
6. Not to be confused with the concert pianist of the same name; and although Davidovich was Jennie's patronymic, it is not clear that Bella was her given name.
7. Charlotte Haze in Vladimir Nabokov's *Lolita* asks Humbert Humbert, "Do you believe in God?" He replies, "The question is does God believe in me?" There is also an echo of the song "Manchester, England" from the musical *Hair.*

CHAPTER 5

1. For those not familiar with the terminology, a tone row is an arbitrary ordering of all twelve tones without any repetition. The whole composition is based on derivatives of this pitch grouping.
2. He did offer two other Schoenberg works with the New York Philharmonic, but, strangely, never *Transfigured Night*. But then he never presented Gershwin's Piano Concerto in F, either. Jerome Robbins once called me up to ask for LB's recording of the concerto, and was incredulous to learn that he had never programmed it.
3. This row reappears in the curiosity "My Twelve-Tone Melody" LB wrote in 1988 for Irving Berlin's hundredth birthday. It gets mixed in with a distorted version of two Berlin songs "My Russian Lullaby"—remembered nostalgically from LB's youth—and "Always."

CHAPTER 6

1. New Music Recordings, 1940.
2. Phillip L. Berman, ed., *The Courage to Grow Old* (New York: Ballantine Books, 1989), 87.

CHAPTER 7

1. "Colloquy in Boston," *The New York Times* (18 November 1956).

CHAPTER 9

1. From the liner notes that accompanied the LP recording made by the Louisville Orchestra, Robert Whitney, conductor.

CHAPTER 10

1. In fact the music was performed (on tape) by seven members of the New York Pro Musica Antiqua, a group specializing in pre-seventeenth-century music and founded by Noah Greenberg. The countertenor was Russell Oberlin, who had been a soloist in LB's performances of Handel's *Messiah* and Bach's *St. Matthew Passion.*
2. As cited earlier in this book, in 1955 LB wrote to me, "I've just returned from Boston where the 'Lark' had its premiere. . . . It contains the foundation of a short Mass."
3. See his article "The Show That Got Away," *Show Music* (Fall 1992).

CHAPTER 11

1. The telecast took place at the ABC-TV Elysee Theatre on West Fifty-eighth Street, around the corner from the Bernstein residence on Fifty-seventh Street. The Bernsteins, who received one thousand dollars for their participation, were advised to keep it a secret at the risk of forfeiting the fee.
2. San Francisco Symphony Orchestra notes, 13 February 1946.
3. *San Francisco Examiner* (22 July 1945).
4. *Collier's* (13 October 1945).
5. Madeleine Goss, *Modern Music Makers* (New York: Dutton: 1952).
6. New York Symphony Orchestra notes, 1946.
7. *Cosmopolitan* (August 1945).

CHAPTER 12

1. In *Hin und Zuruck*, *Ludus Tonalis*, Horn Concerto and other works.
2. In such works as String Quartets Nos. 4 and 5 and *Music for Percussion, Strings and Celesta.*

3. Including the *Lyric Suite*, *Chamber Concerto* and parts of *Wozzeck*.
4. Isidore Geller was at the organ for the premiere.
5. Such "blasphemy' has a Biblical precedent, of course, in the story of Job, and also has its roots in the folk tradition, as, for example, in the legend of Rabbi Levi Yitzhak of Berditchev. Mr. Bernstein feels strongly the peculiar Jewishness of this man-God relationship: in the whole mythic concept of the Jew's love of God, from Moses to the Hassidic sect. There is a deep personal intimacy that allows things to be said to God that are almost inconceivable in another religion.
6. The row is similar to the one used by Berg in his opera *Lulu*.

CHAPTER 13

1. *The Musical Quarterly* 66, no. 2 (April 1980).
2. "The Age of Anxiety" from the *Collected Longer Poems* (New York: Random House, 1975), 344ff. Used with the kind permission of the publisher.
3. *New York Herald Tribune* (6 March 1966).
4. I believe it was composer Harold Shapero who dared him to write a passage from the top of the piano to the bottom in "The Age of Anxiety." He took on the challenge, and went even one step further, having the winds go in the reverse direction, bottom to top, at the conclusion of "The Seven Ages" section—all of it accomplished with panache.
5. The choice of title may have been based on the James M. Cain eponymous book that LB had seriously entertained as a subject for a stage work in collaboration with Arthur Laurents.

CHAPTER 15

1. Words by James M. Barrie from Act V, Scene 1 of *Peter Pan* (Samuel French edition).
2. A 2005 recording of the fully fleshed-out Bernstein score is found on Koch International, KCH 7596.

SELECTED BIBLIOGRAPHY

Bankhead, Tallulah. *Tallulah: My Autobiography*. New York: Harper & Brothers Publishers, 1952.

Berman, Phillip L., ed. *The Courage to Grow Old*. New York: Ballantine Books, 1989.

Bernstein, Burton, and Barbara Haws. *Leonard Bernstein: An American Original*. New York: HarperCollins, 2008.

Burton, Humphrey. *Leonard Bernstein*. New York: Doubleday, 1994.

Burton, William Westbrook. *Conversations About Bernstein*. New York: Oxford University Press, 1995.

Chapin, Schuyler. *Leonard Bernstein: Notes From a Friend*. New York: Walker & Co., 1992.

Fordin, Hugh. *The Movies' Greatest Musicals*. New York: Frederick Ungar Publishing Co., 1984.

Gottlieb, Jack. *Funny, It Doesn't Sound Jewish: How Yiddish Songs and Synagogue Melodies Influenced Tin Pan Alley, Broadway, and Hollywood*. Albany, NY: SUNY Press, 2004.

Gruen, John. *Callas Kissed Me . . . Lenny Too!: A Critic's Memoir*. powerHouse Books, 2008.

Heinsheimer, Hans W. *Best Regards to Aida*. New York: Alfred A. Knopf, 1968.

Lawrence, Greg. *Dance With Demons: The Life of Jerome Robbins*. New York: G. P. Putnam's Sons, 2001.

Mauceri, John. *Celebrating West Side Story*. Winston-Salem: North Carolina School of the Arts Press, 2007.

Perlis, Vivian, ed. *Copland: 1900 Through 1942*. New York: St. Martin's Press, 1984.

Peyser, Joan. *Bernstein: A Biography*. New York: William Morrow, 1987.

Secrest, Meryle. *Leonard Bernstein: A Life*. New York: Alfred A. Knopf, 1994.

Seldes, Barry. *Leonard Bernstein: The Political Life of an American Musician*. Berkeley and Los Angeles: University of California Press, 2009.

Simeone, Nigel. *Leonard Bernstein: West Side Story*. Burlington, VT: Ashgate Publishing Co., 2009.

Vaill, Amanda. *Somewhere: The Life of Jerome Robbins*. New York: Broadway Books, 2006.

PHOTOGRAPH CREDITS

Unless otherwise specified, all photos are either from the author's personal collection or from undetermined sources. Every reasonable effort has been made to contact copyright holders and secure permission. We offer apologies for any instances in which this was not possible and for any inadvertent omissions.

Page xi: Andrew French. Page 21 (bottom): Roy Stevens. Page 23: Francis C. Fuerst. Page 25: Library of Congress. Page 35: Andrew French. Page 41: Andrew French. Page 45: Bettina Cirone. Page 62 (top and bottom): Courtesy of the New York Philharmonic Archive. Page 78: Courtesy of the New York Philharmonic Archive. Page 93 (top and bottom): Erhardt. Page 98 (top): Private source. Page 98 (bottom): Felici. Page 107: Bettina Cirone. Page 117: Courtesy of Ivan Davis. Page 125: Isaac Berez. Page 126: Isaac Berez. Page 129: Dr. Rolf Zitzlsperger. Page 130: Courtesy of Don Hunstein/SONY Music Entertainment. Page 149: Photograph by Dan Weiner. Courtesy of the New York Philharmonic Archive. Page 171: Bettina Cirone. Page 172: Roy Stevens. Page 185 (top): Courtesy of Dan McCoy/Getty Images. Page 186 (top): Roy Stevens. Page 187 (top): Courtesy of Don Hunstein/SONY Music Entertainment. Page 188: Roy Stevens. Page 247: Courtesy of the Park Avenue Synagogue, New York City. Page 325: Courtesy of Don Hunstein/SONY Music Entertainment.

INDEX